HISTORIES OF AMERICAN CHRISTIANITY

HISTORIES OF AMERICAN CHRISTIANITY
An Introduction

Christopher H. Evans

BAYLOR UNIVERSITY PRESS

Cover Design by Rebecca Lown
Cover Images: (1) Methodist Camp Meeting, engraved by Henry R. Robinson
(fl.1833–1851) 1836 (colour litho), Clay, Edward Williams (1799–1857) (after) /
© Collection of the New York Historical Society, USA / The Bridgeman Art
Library; (2) Anabaptist Ceremony in North America (colour litho), American
School (19th century) / Private Collection / The Stapleton Collection / The
Bridgeman Art Library; (3) J. André Smith, Church-Goers Eatonville, courtesy of
Art & History Museums—Maitland, photograph courtesy of Randall Smith.

Library of Congress Cataloging-in-Publication Data

Evans, Christopher Hodge, 1959–
  Histories of American Christianity : an introduction / Christopher H. Evans.
  415 pages cm
  Includes bibliographical references (pages 373–392) and index.
  ISBN 978-1-60258-545-4 (pbk. : alk. paper)
  1. United States—Church history. I. Title.
  BR515.E935 2013
  277.3—dc23
                        2012043648

Printed in the United States of America on acid-free paper with a minimum of
30% post-consumer waste recycled content.

In memory of Rosemary Skinner Keller

CONTENTS

ACKNOWLEDGMENTS

Many persons deserve recognition for their assistance to me in writing this book. Above all, I am indebted to Carey Newman, Director of Baylor University Press. Carey's encouragement and critique of the manuscript were indispensable. I thank him for his editorial hand and for keeping me focused on the project. Additionally, I am thankful for the assistance of many people at Baylor, including Jenny Hunt, Emily Brower, Jordan Rowan Fannin, and Diane Smith. Randall Balmer and Ted Karpf provided me with valuable feedback on the manuscript, and my apologies to them if I did not incorporate all of their fruitful suggestions. Becky Cecala and Erika Hirsch supplied research assistance at different phases of the project. To my former colleagues at Colgate Rochester Crozer Divinity School and to my current colleagues at Boston University, I give thanks for the ways that you have challenged me to grow as a teacher and scholar. I am grateful to Travis Myers, who as a teaching assistant in one of my courses brought to my attention H. L. Mencken's obituary on J. Gresham Machen quoted in chapter 12. As always, my love and thanks to Robin, Peter, and Andrew for all their support and patience with me.

This book reflects the influence of many scholars whose work has left a permanent imprint on me. One of those persons was the late Rosemary Skinner Keller. As my doctoral advisor many years ago, Rosemary challenged me to strive for excellence as a researcher and writer, and it is to her memory that I dedicate this book.

ABBREVIATIONS

AHMS	American Home Missionary Society
FCC	Federal Council of Churches
GLBT	gay, lesbian, bisexual, transgendered
IWM	Interchurch World Movement
LDS	Church of Jesus Christ of Latter-day Saints
NAE	National Association of Evangelicals
NBC	National Baptist Convention
NCC	National Council of Churches
SBC	Southern Baptist Convention
SPCK	Society for Promoting Christian Knowledge
SPG	Society for the Propagation of the Gospel
SVM	Student Volunteer Movement
WCTU	Woman's Christian Temperance Union
YMCA	Young Men's Christian Association
YWCA	Young Women's Christian Association

INTRODUCTION

For any American living in the early twenty-first century, almost daily exposure to some form of Christianity is inescapable. It comes through a ubiquitous array of televangelists who appear on regional and national radio and television stations. It comes during every drive, short or long, to work, to school, or vacations, when Americans traverse a landscape saturated by churches whose architectural designs often reflect distinctive theological beliefs, historical eras, and regional proclivities. It comes on Saturday evenings and Sunday mornings when millions of Americans, representing communions as diverse as pentecostal and Eastern Orthodox, gather to sing, pray, and worship within thousands of churches, ranging from the inner city to isolated rural hamlets. Even if you have never been inside a church sanctuary, you are reminded of America's Christian influence every time you view a presidential inauguration, attend a variety of civic ceremonies, or look at money and see the words "In God We Trust" staring you in the face.

A generation ago, many scholars in Europe and North America highlighted what they believed was the demise of religion as a driving cultural force in the West. In 1966 John Lennon, member of the rock group the Beatles, was embroiled in a much-heralded controversy by his remarks that the Beatles were "more popular than Jesus." What was forgotten amid the uproar over Lennon's remarks was that he expressed a sentiment already argued by many intellectuals of the period: that Christianity was dying out. It was thought that an era of religious belief, spearheaded largely by numerous institutional forms of Christianity, was being replaced by a new era marked by religious doubt and an increasingly secular worldview (and, keeping with the spirit of Lennon's assertions, a time during which popular culture icons would replace religious figures as the objects of adoration). By the early twenty-first century, proof of this secularism appeared evident in many Western European countries where church membership and church attendance have been in a persistent pattern of decline.

It is significant that Lennon's remarks caused the biggest public outcry in the one Western country where Christianity was the strongest: the United States. In the early years of the twenty-first century, religion in America, particularly Christianity, shows no signs of giving way to any theory of secularization. For decades, pollsters have given frequent attention to the fact that the majority of Americans profess a belief in God or a higher spiritual power. While variances exist in these surveys, two indisputable facts strike us. First, in support of the religious studies scholar Diana Eck's highly publicized arguments, America is by far the most religiously diverse nation in the world.[1] American religion is marked by a lengthy history of pluralism, reflected not only by major world religions such as Judaism, Islam, and Buddhism, but hundreds, if not thousands, of groups that often synergistically combine religious beliefs to suit each group's following.

Second, for all of the country's religious diversity, Christianity was, and still is, the dominant faith tradition in America. I do not make this statement to support the frequently asserted but historically erroneous claim that America is a Christian nation founded upon specific biblical and theological precepts. Rather, to assert that Christianity has played a dominant role in America is to understand the critical role that this diverse and complex faith movement has played in the shaping of American religious *and* secular history. Unlike their counterparts in other Western countries, Americans historically have been attracted to membership in scores of Christian churches and denominations. Membership in the nation's churches has ranged from a low of under 20 percent at the time of the American Revolution in the 1770s and 1780s to over 60 percent by the late twentieth century.[2] Numerous studies have documented the precipitous drop in church attendance that began around 1965, and the ways that increasing numbers of late twentieth-century Americans shunned organized forms of religion. Yet study after study has shown that despite the downswing in attendance within Catholic and several Protestant communions since the mid-1960s, interest in things religious, and specifically in things Christian, remains a powerful factor in motivating the religious and cultural worldview of most Americans. America might very well be made up of a generation of seekers, but many of these seekers still find their way to the potpourri of churches available in the United States. In the early 2000s, surveys estimated that approximately one in four Americans regularly go to church (about 60 million people in a country of approximately 300 million), dwarfing in percentage the number of churchgoers in the nations of Europe that gave birth to historical forms of Catholic, Orthodox, and Protestant Christianities. A 2006 Baylor University survey reported that over 80 percent of Americans identify with some form of Christianity. Perhaps the most striking statistic to come out of this survey was that one-third of the American population, approximately 100 million Americans, identify themselves as evangelical Protestant.[3] The secularization predicted a generation ago may have occurred in many Western countries. Yet American Christianity not only possesses a strong hold on Americans institutionally, but represents amazing adaptability as a series of popular movements in American history.

This book represents an effort to understand Christianity's uniqueness in America, by offering a survey of the significant types of Christianities that have emerged during the history of the United States. While my intent is to provide a text that will be understandable and useful for the student and general reader, in my own way I hope that the book can offer fresh insights into a topic on which there is no shortage of excellent texts. My approach wrestles with two themes that have been at the center of American religious historical writing since the mid-nineteenth century: the unique forms of Christianity that have emerged in American history and the ways in which this religious legacy illustrates the nation's distinctive heritage of religious pluralism.

For most historians, the theme of religious pluralism is *the* central narrative for understanding American religious history. At the same time, scholars have disagreed on how best to fit the story of American Christianity into this pluralistic landscape. For any student of American religious history, a comprehensive study needs to begin with Sydney Ahlstrom's galvanic text, *A Religious History of the American People*. Ahlstrom's account is impressive both for the quality of the writing and the scope of his analysis. Building upon the foundation of an earlier generation of American religious historians, Ahlstrom provided ample attention both to the development of American Christianity and to a variety of non-Christian religious movements, sects, and indigenous folk religions. Since its publication in 1972, Ahlstrom's text has been the standard bearer for all subsequent surveys of American religion. While praised for its undisputed mastery of sources and the scope of his inquiry, the book has been justifiably critiqued both for subjects excluded (especially related to African Americans' and women's religious history) and for some of the author's own biases that favored the nation's Protestant churches.

Since the 1970s, an explosion of historical writing has expanded considerably the parameters of the study of American religious history. We now possess a far greater understanding of the critical roles of women and underrepresented racial-ethnic groups in the shaping of American religion. The scope of historical writing has focused increasingly on what R. Laurence Moore has termed "religious outsiders."[4] In particular, the last twenty years have witnessed an explosion of work on American evangelicalism, fleshing out the theological and historical complexity of this phenomenon. Numerous studies on Roman Catholicism, fundamentalism, and a host of American-born religious movements such as Mormonism and Christian Science reveal how these movements sought to defend and propagate unique faith perspectives that often directly challenged the religious and cultural suppositions of more dominant Protestant groups. We understand far more today about the synergistic nature of American religion. The presence of folk theologies and their impact on institutional forms of religious belief has shaped a growing awareness of what many scholars term "popular" (or "lived") religion in American culture. While Ahlstrom represented the culmination of a long-standing historical tradition that strongly believed in the existence of a largely Protestant religious center, successive generations of scholars have raised questions about the exact nature of that center, indeed calling into question whether or not that center ever existed.[5]

Not only has America been characterized by an array of innovative religious movements, but the vast proliferation of new movements makes it difficult to draw concise institutional parameters around many religious groupings. Even nineteenth-century chroniclers of American religion could not help but notice that the nation was home to a range of religious groups that made the United States different from any other Western nation.

And yet, for all the emphasis that historians have placed on American religious pluralism, especially for non-Christian religions, most, if not all, of the major surveys on American religious history written since Ahlstrom still place the story of American Christianity (and American Protestantism, in particular) center stage in their narratives. For all the innovative ways in which American religion has been studied, historians understand that to ignore the role of Christianity in American religious history is analogous to studying the sixteenth-century Protestant

Reformation without mentioning Martin Luther. No matter how scholars may expand the field of inquiry into American religious history, an engagement with the American Christian past, and in particular its evangelical Protestant heritage, is essential to understand the uniqueness of the American religious experience generally, and to see how Christianity continues to play a central role in shaping the religious and cultural identity of Americans in the twenty-first century.

Robert Baird's *Religion in America*, originally published in 1844, is often considered the first comprehensive treatment of American religious history. While in many respects Baird's book reads like a time capsule from the mid-nineteenth century, he echoes themes with which every subsequent historian has had to wrestle, particularly the question of how America's religious heritage casts light on what it means to be an American. Christian leaders throughout America's history have frequently appealed to visions of a common American identity. Yet inescapably, the story of American Christianity is marked not only by divisions in theology, but by larger issues that have divided Americans along the lines of race, gender, ethnicity, class, region, and politics.

American Christianity produced many articulate spokespersons who strove to highlight a shared purpose for God's people in America, in language and meaning that transcended their eras and left an indelible imprint on the American historical imagination. Yet the call toward a specific purpose and mission has often led Americans to adapt Christianity in ways that have often been highly individualistic, if not self-serving. Christianity in America has at times reflected unique examples of how individuals and groups sought ways to stand out from everyday American life. But it has also served as a means for disparate groups to find their niche within the American cultural landscape. Quite simply, a study of American Christianity points not only to what is extraordinary about the American experience but also—and just as importantly—to what is ordinary.

THEMATIC DIRECTIONS IN THE HISTORIES OF AMERICAN CHRISTIANITY

For two thousand years, Christianity has been contested by a disparate range of individuals, churches, sects, and theologies. While American Christianity is arguably a small component of the larger Christian narrative, it is a story anchored in a wide range of characters, movements, and interpretations.[6] I chose the title *Histories of American Christianity* for this book not only to draw the reader's attention to the proverbial question "what happened?" but also to encourage readers to reflect upon the choices historians made—in terms of both what they felt was important to cover and, as will be pointed out repeatedly in this narrative, what they left out.

Like every historian who has come before me, I recognize that this book reflects similar patterns of inclusion and exclusion. There is the immediate challenge of deciding which individuals, churches, and movements to include in the narrative (indeed, given the way in which many religious movements in the U.S. mixed together Christian and non-Christian beliefs makes it difficult even to address the question of who counts as part of the American Christian tradition). While the narrative of the book by and large takes a chronological format, the volume is oriented around three major themes that help define and clarify how American Christianity has been chronicled by historians.

CHRISTIANITY AND THE INTELLECTUAL MIND

The first theme that this volume explores is the most widely traveled road of religious historians: Christianity's impact upon American intellectual history. This particular pathway has argued that American Christianity, while in some respects derived from European sources, nevertheless represented a creative theological synthesis that had a major impact upon the larger terrain of American intellectual history. It is this pathway that has largely focused almost exclusively on the legacy of American Protestantism, especially leaders and churches that have spawned from the heritage of New England Puritanism. While the Puritan legacy has been justifiably critiqued on a number of levels, few would doubt the ways in which this legacy has captivated, and continues to captivate, the American imagination. Although this book will argue, as have other histories, that the Puritan influence was never as sweeping or theologically oppressive as some might claim, the impact of Puritanism upon shaping a distinctive American intellectual tradition cannot be glossed over. Jonathan Edwards in the eighteenth century, Horace Bushnell in the nineteenth century, and Reinhold Niebuhr in the twentieth century represent vastly different historical eras, and each articulated unique theological interests. However, each in his own way expanded upon, either consciously or unconsciously, the theological heritage articulated by John Calvin in the sixteenth century. This heritage was concerned not only with how individuals needed to order their lives before the judgment seat of a righteous God, but also how God's grace had the potential to bring order and unity to the whole of society.

More than the longevity of the movement, Puritanism still resides at the psychological center of the American Christian story. The fact that New England Puritanism was predated in the Americas by other English-speaking Protestants and that all Protestant churches in America were predated by more than a hundred years by a variety of Spanish and French Catholic missions misses the point. What Puritanism gave America was a faith language that spoke of the inherent connection between a Calvinist view of God's power over history and how that divine power drove people to build a just society within history. That theme has played a significant role within Christian churches that never heard of Calvin, and it expresses a common theme propagated by many church leaders in American history: the power of Christianity to make America a just and righteous society. Today those who look with alarm to the political weight of the so-called "Religious Right" need to be reminded that the goal of "Christianizing America" has never been the sole domain of one theological tradition. Whenever church/denominational assemblies have taken a stand on a political issue or a larger issue that occupies the public's imagination, either through words or actions, they have demonstrated something that American Christians have long believed about their faith—that a Christian worldview is indispensable to the building and sustaining of a just society. This basic belief has led numerous Christian traditions to argue that their particular brand of Christianity is vital (if not critical) toward the construction of an authentic Christian experience.

Beyond New England, signs of Christianity's influence as intellectual leaven in America are omnipresent. That legacy can be found throughout the theological battles that pitted revivalists versus traditionalists and that have been waged in America in one form or another since the colonial era. The legacy can be seen in the contributions of numerous "outsider" movements in American Christianity, whether one discusses the nineteenth-century American Catholicism envisioned by Orestes Brownson, or the mid-twentieth-century vision of Christianity embraced by Martin Luther King Jr. What becomes evident from the history of American Christianity is how a variety of Christian spokespersons often have made distinctive and persuasive arguments for how specific theological worldviews offer Americans a more meaningful life, both individually and communally. What is painfully ironic, however, is that for all the intellectual acumen evident in the history of American Christianity, the nation's churches often failed to come to any consensus on the pressing social, political, and theological issues of the day (accentuated in particular by the failure of Christian movements to engage in one voice against the evils of slavery during the first half of the nineteenth century). Many historians such as Sydney Ahlstrom were convinced that the intellectual heritage of American Christianity (especially of its Puritan persuasion) was the essence of America's intellectual greatness because it promoted shared values of justice and social transformation. Some of the chief historical characters in this volume reflect this larger prophetic vision. However, for every prophet whose voice transcended the historical parameters of his or her lifetime, there are scores of others whose voices reflect the predominant biases of their times. Both perspectives are important to this text.

CHRISTIANITY AND SECTARIANISM

Despite the best efforts of Christian leaders to promote intellectual and theological consensus, perhaps the most striking aspect of American Christian history has been the tendency to reject any consensus. Throughout much of American history, there has been a repeated pattern of religious sectarianism that serves as the second major motif of this study. Religious sectarianism is hardly an American ideal; in fact, understanding the nature of sectarian movements is essential to understanding Christianity's historical development as a global religion. And yet America, perhaps more than any other nation, embodies the essence of the sectarian impulse. Put simply, in America, if one is dissatisfied with a particular church, nothing is stopping one from setting up a new one more to one's liking.

Contemporary views of religious sectarianism owe a great deal to the pioneering work of Ernst Troeltsch and H. Richard Niebuhr in the early twentieth century. Troeltsch postulated the argument that Christian history in the West was characterized by a sect-church dichotomy, whereby religious movements (sects) were born out of struggle with dominant but often theologically stagnant traditions. Troeltsch envisioned church history as a perpetual process of continuous conflict and change whereby sectarian movements were born and conveyed a dynamic and exclusive theological message that galvanized followers to commit themselves fully to living out that message in the world (often at tremendous personal cost). Over time these sects either disappeared or morphed into institutional forms of Christianity (churches), which were more concerned with worldly status, institutional preservation, and missional cooperation with the state. In juxtaposition to the fluid and dynamic character of faith present within the sect, churches were intent on preserving and enforcing strict standards of ecclesiastical order and discipline, ultimately giving shape to the rise of denominations in the West. The implications of Troeltsch's arguments for American Christianity were developed brilliantly by Niebuhr in his 1929 book *The Social Sources of Denominationalism*. At a moment when many leaders in American Protestantism were waxing poetically about the future prospects for Christian unity, Niebuhr argued that the sectarian historical pattern of American Christianity made ecumenical unity an elusive goal.

Niebuhr's analysis is significant because it paints a largely accurate portrait of American Christianity as a competitive, not cooperative, enterprise. Many scholars have argued that the First Amendment of the Bill of Rights, guaranteeing freedom of worship and the disestablishment of religion (i.e., abolishing the model borrowed from Western Europe of one government-supported church), has stoked the fires of religious sectarianism in the United States. The freedom to choose how one practices religion must be seen as a contributing factor to sectarianism. Yet many of the sectarian movements explored in this book shared common suppositions that transcended differences in theology. Niebuhr was atypical of many historians of his generation by seeing the sectarian impulse as a source for Christian renewal. At the same time, his conception of a relevant Christianity, like scholars who came before and after him, was predicated upon building up deeply rooted historical churches (mostly Protestant). In fact, the vast majority of historians of American Christianity, including Ahlstrom, tended to view sectarian groups with a certain amount of embarrassment, in juxtaposition to more intellectually rigorous churches rooted squarely in many of the Protestant churches that came out of the sixteenth-century Reformation. Yet I believe that sectarianism in America has been one of the major signs of Christianity's strength, vitality, and intellectual creativity, because it points to the ways in which Christianity dynamically shapes religious and secular meanings in American history. While meant as a polemical assertion, one nineteenth-century Catholic leader reflected a wider truth when he noted that the heritage of American religious liberty owed as much to Joseph Smith (founder of the Church of Jesus Christ of Latter-day Saints) as it did to any of the nation's founding fathers. For many American Catholics, Smith represented the sins of American Protestantism epitomized by individualism and sectarian schism. Yet historically, this sectarian impulse has been manifested by a diverse array of religious movements who believed they were establishing a true fellowship of believers, amid a world of unbelief or false belief. Such a reality is disheartening for those who see the theological goal of

Christianity to be religious unity. Yet a study of Christian sectarianism is indispensable for historians interested in understanding American religious diversity.

It is important to note that sectarian movements are not necessarily small bodies. In this study, I argue that the success of two very large Christian traditions, Catholicism and pentecostalism, relate to how each movement has used sectarian language in ways that differentiate them from more culturally dominant forms of Christianity. Since the 1870s, the Roman Catholic Church has been the single largest faith tradition in the United States. However, much of its history in America has been defined by a sectarian impulse. On one hand, many Catholic leaders stressed the importance of being good Catholics and Americans through processes of assimilation with their Protestant neighbors. Yet other segments of the Catholic Church fought tooth and nail against assimilation. These Catholics preserved strong ethnic identities, whereby Catholicism was central to keeping one's ethnic identity intact. This posture caused much tension among many Protestant churches that increasingly attacked the Catholic Church for its fostering of an un-American spirit (a tension manifested especially in a long-standing belief that American Catholics had no use for American democracy). Yet Catholic separatism fostered not only a spirit of solidarity and purpose among American Catholics, but also a tapestry of theological, liturgical, and cultural expressions that define the rich diversity of the American Catholic experience to this day.

Theologically, pentecostalism is a world removed from the contours of Catholic tradition. Yet pentecostalism's emphasis on religious experience (if not outright ecstasy), its egalitarian stress on the ministry of the baptized, and its belief that the movement was engendering a model of Christianity that harkened back to the church of New Testament times bespeaks a characteristic of Christian sectarianism in America: the belief that such movements represent authentic Christian truth claims in a nation filled with apostate groups. Catholicism and pentecostalism represent the largest but not the only movements that have manifested this strain of sectarian Christianity. Engaging the phenomenon of religious sectarianism in America not only provides a window for viewing the free-market qualities of American religion but also allows us to see how this impulse led to the creation of many unique forms of Christianity. Today when one looks at the growth of Christianity outside of the United States, one can point to several sectarian movements that were birthed within the unique historical environment of the United States.

CHRISTIANITY AND POPULAR RELIGION

Finally, this study seeks to examine Christianity in terms of what has been called popular religion. The phrase "popular religion" in its own right is elusive. Several scholars see the term in relationship to any religious impulses and rituals that emerge outside the parameters of an institutional form of religion (what has come to be known in the West as a denomination). Others have used the phrase popular religion as a pejorative designation to define movements that are perceived as anti-intellectual or encompassing traditions and belief patterns not normally part of more formal religious structures. Jon Butler has argued that popular religion is nothing more than the specific beliefs of laypeople within a given historical time period.[7] Butler's definition is helpful because it reminds us that what is defined as popular religion is not necessarily confined to the world of the religiously exotic. In fact, one could make the case that the study of popular religion in American Christianity exposes us to what is actually part of the ordinary and everyday, as much a part of our existence as the air we breathe. Few Americans who visit secular bookstores and purchase books such as Rick Warren's *The Purpose Driven Life*, Tim LaHaye and Jerry Jenkins' *Left Behind*, or William Young's *The Shack* reflect on the ways in which these works embody deep-seated historical currents in American Christianity. Yet each work accentuates the ubiquity of Christianity in American culture in ways that transcend the numbers and influence of individual churches and denominations. American churchgoers may know little or nothing of the legacy of American Christianity's great theological intellectuals or prominent church leaders of major denominations. Yet the chances are good that they would recognize the names LaHaye and Warren, even if they are ignorant about the historical movements these men represent in American Christianity. LaHaye and Jenkins' apocalyptic fiction is a direct outgrowth of dispensationalism, a movement that spawned both intellectual proponents and popularizers, while Warren's career is an offshoot of numerous prosperity gospel movements to emerge out of American Christianity since the late nineteenth century. While not meant to cheapen the theological power of Christianity in America, it needs to be said that in the past as well as the present, Christianity has been a highly malleable and marketable commodity with an authority and power that frequently have transcended the control of institutional churches. This reminds us of the ways in which Christianity has spoken to millions of Americans with messages that are persuasive and compelling, even if not intellectually robust.

Reflecting on the role of Christianity as popular religion is an opportunity for us to take a look at mainstream American life. Years ago, in a small-town, middle-America church pastored by my spouse, a parishioner said to her in a matter-of-fact fashion, "as the Bible says, 'to thine own self be true.'" It would be easy to ridicule this person for confusing William Shakespeare with the Word of God. But to view this conversation merely as a matter of biblical illiteracy or all-American parochialism misses an important point. The real question to ask here is what would cause a person who loved to quote chapter and verse from the Bible to confuse an assertion of individualism with the Word of God. While it is true that there is a strong relationship between popular religion and religious sectarianism, the two need to be seen as distinct phenomena. The discussion of popular religion generally, and popular forms of Christianity specifically, often concerns a patchwork quilt of beliefs that may not stand up to intellectual scrutiny. However, those who chronicle the story of American Christianity need to view these beliefs with a sympathetic as well as critical eye. An investigation of popular religion in American Christianity will not necessarily lead to a discovery of clearly delineated belief patterns, but it can tell us a great deal about beliefs that for many Americans lie close to the surface.

SEEING THE BIG PICTURE
From Protestant Desire to Pluralistic Cacophony

My effort to tell what to many might be a very old (and familiar) story comes down to a desire for the reader to see the big picture of Christianity's historical development in the United States. As a means of highlighting the three themes I've outlined above, I have chosen to frame each of the five sections of this book in the form of a dialogue with some of the most significant surveys of American religious history written between the mid-nineteenth century and the mid-twentieth century. Beginning with Robert Baird's groundbreaking 1844 history and concluding with Sydney Ahlstrom's 1972 study, the reader can see the evolving contours of how a particular heritage of American Protestantism laid claim to a segment of the American intellectual imagination. R. Laurence Moore is accurate in terms of describing the general pattern of historical writing between Baird and Ahlstrom as a "historiography of a desire," in that these scholars embraced a hope that America's religious history was essentially a story of the triumph of an intellectually rigorous, ecumenically oriented Protestant Christianity (and, in particular, a genre of Christianity closely allied with the legacy growing out of New England Puritanism).[8] Yet in exploring these authors carefully, it is apparent that all of them, metaphorically speaking, saw the barbarians at the gate. Nineteenth-century historians by and large were Protestant, and the religious vision they championed, not surprisingly, looked a lot like their own particular faith commitments. Yet these men were not blind. They saw threats to their beloved visions of a Protestant country. They were clearly worried about sectarian movements such as those practiced by the Mormons, Adventists, New Thought adherents, free thinkers, and, most especially, Roman Catholics. Even as immigration, urbanization, and industrialization transformed the shape of America by the early twentieth century, historians still saw the religious core of the nation defined in one form or another by a vision of Protestant providence that stood ready to face down the challenges of false religion.

Yet one thing needs to be said about these earlier histories: for better or worse they crafted a narrative of American religion that has been remarkably resilient. For all the ways they attempted to use data and statistics to support their claims of Protestant dominance, nineteenth-century historians clearly saw and recognized the ways that diverse social and religious forces were encroaching upon their Protestant paradise. While it is true that the tone of argument against outsider groups such as the Mormons was often cavalier, these Protestant spokespersons worried that their vision of America as a Protestant nation was in some way being threatened. By the twentieth century, new threats to the earlier Protestant vision emerged. Yet even as the traditions that represented the Protestant insiders splintered in the twentieth century, historians still held out hope that the older vision had survived, even as the nineteenth-century language of providence disappeared. While Ahlstrom is largely seen as part of a progression of historians upholding the sanctity of an intellectualized Protestant theological vision, he wondered if this vision was going to have much of a future in America. Indeed, one could argue from his chapter headings that Ahlstrom was writing the story of New England Calvinism's rise and twilight. In some respects, his book serves as a fitting capstone for over one hundred years of historical writing and sets the stage for the type of historical scholarship since Ahlstrom's era.

And yet, all of these historians identified important themes. As they chronicled events of the past, they also recognized the fact that the intellectual traditions of Protestant Christianity that they inherited served as a central melody around which the story of American religious history could be sung. Part of the task of this book is to remind the reader that these traditions are still around even though their melodies do not resonate with Americans in quite the same way as they did in the past. Yet even as we recognize the power and adaptability of this tradition of American Protestantism (as did many historians leading up to Ahlstrom), we must also understand the musical counterpoints sounded by religious and Christian traditions that dissented from this dominant tune.

The narrative that follows is predicated on the belief that the best way for readers to discern larger historical themes essential toward understanding Christianity in America does not come primarily through a recitation of denominational statistics. Rather, the best way is implanted by telling the significant stories of religious groups and, in particular, the stories of individuals who were most responsible for making history. I want readers to be reminded that discerning any set of larger historical themes relates to the task of telling an intriguing set of stories. I have made an effort in the narrative that follows to select a cross section of characters representing a mix of familiar and not-so-familiar figures. The intent of each chapter is not to offer concise biographical narratives of individuals, but rather to show how individuals make and define the history we read. It is my hope that each chapter that follows will offer the reader a glimpse into the worldview of each major character and flesh out the larger themes related to the study of Christianity in America that I have outlined in this introduction.

One aspect important to state at the outset is that I place a tremendous emphasis in this narrative upon the nineteenth century and the early twentieth century. These periods are significant not only for how they illustrate the sectarian and popular themes within American Christianity, but for how they highlight the resiliency of an earlier Puritan ethos. I would argue that one of the critical themes within American Christianity (and American religion) is how the ideals of Puritanism—its stress on individual virtue and on the theme of God's unique covenant with the nation—continue to find new expression in America, even as many pundits have pronounced the tradition dead.

While the narrative takes pains to assess the impact of particular movements and themes in the history of American Christianity, its conclusions about the larger impact of Christianity in America reflect a story marked at most turns by ambiguity. At times, American Christianity has been represented by persons of transcendent vision who offered people visions of justice and social transformation that pushed the nation to rethink its mission and purpose along truly prophetic lines. At other times, the story of American Christianity only accentuates the gaps that have existed throughout American history between rich and poor, white and non-white, male and female, Christian and non-Christian, and, most especially, Christian and Christian. Yet the enduring legacy one encounters in this narrative is not only one of continuous change, but one in which the dividing line between who is labeled a saint and who is labeled a sinner is often unclear. In the narrative that follows, it is largely the responsibility of readers to decide which individuals fall under which category.

PART I

Constructing a Protestant Worldview, 1600–1800

In 1844 a Presbyterian minister named Robert Baird made one of the first efforts to write a detailed narrative of America's religious history. Even though America's historical legacy was minute compared to centuries of European history, Baird recognized that telling the story of American religion would not be easy. For one thing, he was confronted with a religious model unlike anything operational in other European countries at the time. Europe followed the pattern established by Roman emperor Constantine in the fourth century whereby Christianity was provided with political support from the state. Even at a point in time 1,200 years later in the Reformation when Europe was splintered between Catholic and (numerous) Protestant churches, few questioned the idea that government needed to serve as the protector and supporter of one particular brand of Christianity. In the nineteenth century, most Europeans took for granted that the best way for the state to promote religion was to ensure that one form of Christianity, whether Catholic, Lutheran, or some other type of Protestantism, would receive government sanction (including the taken-for-granted assumption that taxes would be collected in support of the church). By the mid-nineteenth century, most European countries supported toleration of minority religious groups, but the idea of the government supporting one religious establishment was seen as a necessary means to promote civil and ecclesiastical order, saving Europeans from the specter of unbelief on one hand and radical religious and political ideologies on the other. But America did not work that way. For starters, Baird sought to clarify for his readers a principle that for many Europeans

17

was the most bizarre aspect of American religion: its voluntarism. Going against hundreds of years of historical precedent, American churches and religious institutions received no support from the government other than a legal guarantee that the country's citizens were free to worship in any matter they chose. In short, there were no state-sponsored religious establishments in the United States, and Robert Baird was concerned among other things with explaining to a European audience why the American model of religion was so effective. Yet Baird's explanation of what he called the American "voluntary principle" was not confined to a discussion of the simple mechanics of religious disestablishment. Like many white Americans of the nineteenth century, Baird believed that there was something inherently unique about the American people that made the American religious voluntary system work. This uniqueness is evident in the opening of his book in which he describes America as an idyllic land, awaiting the hand of its European settlers to build up a great civilization.

> A profound and solemn silence reigned everywhere, save when interrupted by the songs of the birds which sported amid the trees, the natural cries of the beasts which roamed beneath, the articulate sounds of the savage tribes around their wigwams, or their shouts in the chase or in the battle. . . . Two hundred years more pass away, and how widely different is the scene! . . . The forests are giving way to cultivated fields, or verdant meadows. Savage life, with its wigwams, its blanketcovering, its poverty and its misery, yields on every side to the arts, the comforts, and even the luxuries of civilization.[1]

Baird's central task was not just to tell the story of American religious history, but to help his European and American readership understand a theme that dominated most accounts of American religious history throughout the nineteenth century: a belief that God's divine providence was guiding the nation's mission and destiny. "Upon what, then, must Religion rely? Only, under God, upon the efforts of its friends, acting from their own free will, influenced by that variety of considerations which is ordinarily comprehended under the title of a desire to do good. This, in America, is the grand and only alternative."[2] As Baird wrote and later revised his text, he went to great lengths to outline the diversity of religious movements that had emerged in America since the adoption of the U.S. Constitution in 1789, citing an array of statistics related to the growth of a variety of different Christian traditions. But even as he discussed these movements, he struck a confident and reassuring tone that despite all the unusual species of religious movements that had been spawned in America, the core identity of the nation rested securely within a heritage of evangelical Protestantism. These core traditions were moving America into the position of being the most God-fearing nation on earth. For Baird and for other historians after him, it was a religious and cultural vision rooted within the great Christian traditions birthed by the Protestant Reformation in the sixteenth century. But it was also a type of Protestantism that spoke with a distinctive American accent.

Baird's sense of God's providential hand at work in America was echoed by an array of American historians throughout the nineteenth century. Among them was a contemporary of Baird's, a Swiss-born historian, Philip Schaff. Schaff also saw God's hand actively guiding America to a destiny distinct from other nations. Immigrating to the United States in the mid-1840s, he became one of the pioneers in American religious historical writing in the nineteenth century and, like Baird, a believer that America possessed a uniquely divine purpose in the world. As Schaff noted in 1855, "providence has evidently prepared this country and nation for the greatest work, and no power on earth can arrest its progress and prosperity, if we are true to our calling, if we fear God and love righteousness, mindful of the maxim—'No liberty without virtue; no virtue without religion; no religion without Christianity; Christianity, the safeguard of our republic and hope of the world.'"[3] For Robert Baird and Philip Schaff, the uniqueness of American Christianity was equivalent to the uniqueness of the United States. This sentiment represents a recurrent theme throughout future interpretations of American Christianity, and to understand where this belief originated, one needs to travel back to the psychological center of American Christianity: colonial New England.

≪ 1 ≫

AMERICAN PURITANISM REVISITED

In June 1630 John Winthrop, the founding governor of the Massachusetts Bay Colony, gave one of the most famous and misunderstood orations in American history. As he and his party prepared to disembark from their flagship, the *Arbella*, Winthrop summed up the mission that faced the new arrivals to the colony: "We shall find that the God of Israel is among us, when ten of us shall be able to resist a thousand of our enemies; when he shall make us a praise and glory that men shall say of succeeding planta- tions, 'the Lord make it like that of New England.' For we must consider that we shall be a city upon a hill." Winthrop's words would be interpreted by later generations as a sign of America's preferential status in the eyes of God, used later on to support claims of an American "manifest destiny" in the world. Yet as Winthrop continued his oration, a more nuanced per- spective on his words emerges. "The eyes of all people are upon us, so that if we shall deal falsely with our God in this work we have undertaken, and so cause him to withdraw his present help from us, we shall be made a story and a byword through the world. . . . We shall shame the faces of many of God's worthy servants, and cause their prayers to be turned into curses upon us till we be consumed out of the good land whither we are agoing."[1]

This pivotal moment in American religious history revolved around two themes that are recurring in the early twenty-first century, in effect, providing a psychological center for understanding the historical devel- opment of American Christianity. First, the group of New England colo- nists known as Puritans carried an obsession with the Old Testament concept of covenant. While Winthrop and his Puritan colleagues did believe that they had received a special blessing from God, this blessing required a unique obligation from the colonists to build a just society. Contrary to popular mythology, the Puritan colonists had no desire to create a theocratic kingdom in which the government would be ruled by God through the ministrations of the church. Rather, the Puritans believed that God expected the converted to behave justly and that the actions and decisions of secular leaders (such as Winthrop) would be in accord with the teachings of Scripture, and that a righteous society would emerge as a result.

Second, Puritans such as Winthrop believed profoundly in the reality of human sin. Like many Protestants influenced by the theology of the sixteenth-century reformer John Calvin, they believed human beings were corrupted by sin from birth and consequently could do nothing of value outside of God's saving grace. Paradoxically, the Puritans believed that the chief way that persons lived out their faith was through an engagement with the world. It was Christianity that gave to men and women the possibilities of a good life as well as the ability to persevere during times of doubt and despair. It was Christianity that served as the primary means to make sense of the world in all of its complex ambiguities, calling upon individuals to use Scripture as a way to interpret the natural and human world. It was Christianity that proved the means to constrain the sins and evils of an immoral humanity, and it was Christianity that offered hope of life beyond this world. These critical themes would be carried forth within American Christianity by a diverse array of religious movements far removed from the shores of seventeenth-century Massachusetts Puritanism. In microcosm, this theological tradition represented the best and worst of the American Christian tradition.

POST-REFORMATION CHRISTIANITIES AND NORTH AMERICAN COLONIZATION BY EUROPEANS

The first permanent European settlements in North America that occurred over an approximately 100-year period between 1530 and 1630 were dominated by churches wrestling with the religious and political fallout of post-Reformation Europe. Protestant traditions that emerged in the sixteenth century believed they were championing biblical views of scriptural interpretation and structures of ecclesiastical organization that were in accord with apostolic principles of the early church. However, the majority of Protestant churches born in the years of reform between 1517 and 1550 shared something in common with their Catholic counterparts: a belief that secular governments had a mandate to support only one true church. Religious toleration was still a largely unknown concept in post-Reformation Europe, and with the exception of certain Anabaptist groups (traditions that emphasized adult baptism and withdrew from active participation in the state), Catholics and Protestants saw success largely in terms of whether they could make secular rulers embrace and support their religious ambitions.

For all the successes of Protestant church leaders such as Martin Luther and John Calvin, by 1600 the majority of Europe was still predominantly Roman Catholic. In fact, outside of Switzerland, the Netherlands, Scotland, and England, Protestants were in a precarious position, theologically and politically. In Germany, the heart of Luther's reformation, principalities often swung back and forth between Catholic and Lutheran control. The 1550s had brought an uneasy alliance among the German nobility that left matters of religious affiliation in the hands of local princes. The instability of this religious settlement served as one of the catalysts that would engulf much of Central and Northern Europe in the Thirty Years' War between 1619 and 1649. The end result of this religious and political warfare was that Lutheran growth was largely limited to regions of Germany and Scandinavia where its status was protected legally by established monarchies. Yet as the seventeenth century progressed, Protestant fortunes began to turn. The successes achieved by Protestant churches were partly a reflection of the political and military gains achieved by countries such as the Netherlands, Sweden, and most especially England. The patterns of North American colonization that occurred in the late sixteenth and early seventeenth centuries not only carried on the political battles of Europe, but the religious and theological battles as well. In many ways, the colonial settlement of what became known as the United States embodied the European religious struggles of that era.

ROMAN CATHOLICISM

The so-called Catholic Counter Reformation in mid-sixteenth-century Europe was both a theological response to the growth of Protestantism and an effort to solidify Catholic doctrine and create uniform standards of faith among European Catholics. The Council of Trent from 1545 to 1563 reaffirmed numerous aspects of the Catholic Church's late medieval theological heritage. With its reaffirmation of church doctrines related to the centrality of the church and its sacraments, as well as its rejection of Protestant assertions related to salvation through faith alone, European Catholicism was poised to embark on a new era of growth and expansion. Central to this vision was the role of the Society of Jesus (the Jesuits), an order that was established in 1540 by Ignatius Loyola and created for the purpose of teaching and defending Catholic doctrine. Within a generation of its founding, Jesuit missionaries had spread throughout Europe and into fledgling Spanish colonial settlements in the Caribbean islands and the Americas, including lands that would become part of the future United States. The Jesuits were not the only religious order critical to the spread of Catholicism in the sixteenth century. As Spain engaged in military and colonial expansion in South, Central, and North America, Franciscans, Dominicans, and Augustinian missionaries followed. As would be the case with future Protestant mission efforts, many early Catholic missionaries carried a paternalistic, if not hostile, view toward the indigenous peoples that they encountered. Some sixteenth-century missionaries, such as Antonio de Montesinos and Bartolomé de las Casas, challenged practices of forced conversion and the enslavement of native peoples imposed by Spanish military leaders (although de las Casas was one of the first Europeans to propose African slavery as a substitute for the enslavement of indigenous peoples). While there were other missionaries who shared the views of these early missionaries toward indigenous "New World" peoples, both Catholic and Protestant missions over the next several centuries would often be characterized by a spirit of paternalism.

The first permanent European colonial settlement in present-day America was established by the Spanish in St. Augustine (present-day Florida) in 1565 (in part to stave off the threats of a permanent French Protestant settlement in that region). This settlement was followed by other Spanish colonies in what is now the southwestern United States, leading to the establishment of numerous, yet often isolated, mission communities. These early Catholic missions in what became the future states of Arizona, New Mexico, and California helped preserve a distinctive religious and cultural worldview that would not be challenged for centuries. This legacy of Spanish Catholicism served as important counterpoints to the type of religious culture shaped by the English and predominantly Protestant colonies established in New England, the Mid-Atlantic, and Virginia in the seventeenth century.

Despite these early Spanish successes in establishing colonies in what would become the United States, their successes were short-lived. The defeat of the Spanish Armada in 1588 by England marked the gradual decline of Spain's dominant role in European politics and the beginning ascent of England and France as the two major political and military powers of Europe. Spanish colonies would flourish in Central and South America over the next two centuries, but their claims on parts of North

America would grow increasingly precarious as the French and English accelerated their colonization.

French colonization in North American began in earnest by the early 1600s, and was marked by the establishment of Catholic mission outposts in present-day Canada (Quebec) and throughout the Great Lakes region in present-day Michigan and upstate New York. The repeated pressure of French colonization in North America ultimately stoked persistent military tensions that would erupt in warfare with English colonies to the south during the 1750s and 1760s in the so-called French and Indian Wars. At the center of the conflict were not only issues of which nationality would control North America, but whether the continent would be Catholic or Protestant. French Catholic colonization in North America would be felt mostly in Canada, whereby Catholicism played a major role in shaping the religious and political orientation of Canadians in the province of Quebec.

The significance of these early Catholic missions reflected an aspect of America's diverse religious heritage not readily embraced by future generations of American Protestantism. However, the story of these early Spanish and French missions would epitomize the country's later history of religious diversity, despite the tendency of some future commentators to see America solely as a Protestant nation.

European Reformed Protestantism

The Reformed Protestant tradition is most frequently associated with the reformation in Geneva, Switzerland, which was spearheaded by John Calvin between 1541 and 1564. While the Swiss reformer Ulrich Zwingli initiated the movement in Zurich that would mark this wing of Protestantism, it was Calvin who provided the movement with its main theological underpinnings. Like Zwingli's, Calvin's theology stressed the intellectual resources of late medieval humanism. This movement exploded into numerous European universities in the early 1500s and placed its emphasis on the methods used in pursuit of knowledge. In the realm of theology, this translated into a concern for understanding the nature of early Christianity and led many humanist reformers to encourage study of scripture in its original Hebrew and Greek sources. Most especially for reformers such as Zwingli and Calvin, humanist influences challenged them to think critically about the nature and role of the church in society. Calvin and his followers certainly shared many of Martin Luther's concerns for the recovery of Pauline doctrines in Christian theology, especially the Pauline emphasis on justification, in which an individual is saved by faith alone. However, more so than Luther or Zwingli,

John Calvin was interested in developing a systematic theology that placed stress on two themes: the divine attributes of God and the appropriate response of Christian faith communities in light of these divine attributes.

Discussions of Calvin's theology inevitably turn to his beliefs on predestination, the idea that from birth certain individuals are predestined for salvation. Yet Calvin's interest in this doctrine needs to be viewed with caution. For one thing, the vast majority of Christian theologians, whether Catholic and Protestant, during the Reformation era believed in some form of predestination. Indeed, predestination was a major doctrine of early Christian communities, including the theology of the most important theologian for most Protestant reformers: Augustine. Like Augustine before him, Calvin's concern was not to draw attention to a God who was arbitrary or cruel. Rather, for Calvin, the main issue was God's graciousness, the ability of God to save sinners. Like many who would follow in his wake, Calvin stressed, indeed marveled in, God's sovereignty and took delight that amid the great chasm that separated human beings from knowing God, it was still possible for us to receive God's gracious and unconditional gift of salvation.

Part of Calvin's dilemma, indeed a question that plagued many Catholic and Protestant reformers in the sixteenth and seventeenth centuries, was how one distinguished between those who were saved and those who were not. While the choice of salvation rested with God, Calvin and his theological successors did not see the church as a passive community. Although Reformed theology never confused good works with salvation, Calvin and his heirs saw works as a potential sign of conversion. Far from making individuals complacent, the church for Calvin, while made up of both the saved and damned, always called forth the best efforts of the converted to live out their faith within the larger society. Throughout his years in Geneva from 1541 until his death in 1564, Calvin called upon Christian communities to engage the social-political issues that plagued the city. In particular, he preached frequently against the evils of usury (the charging of exorbitant interest rates), and engaged churches to reach out to serve the needs of the city's poor. Paradoxically, while Calvin stressed God's complete separateness from humanity, the redeeming grace of God placed Christians under obligation to make society a better place for all of its citizens to live. This basic orientation of Calvin's thought would not only be critical to Calvin's successors, but this orientation of the church toward society (what the theologian H. Richard Niebuhr referred to in the 1950s as "Christ transforming culture")[2] was foundational to how many future

American churches would orient their mission toward American social and political institutions.

Unlike the Lutheran reformation, the Geneva reformation proved remarkably adaptable in its spread. Following the teachings of Martin Luther, Lutheranism relied on secular monarchs to uphold and sanction the church's role in society. Using Calvin's Geneva as a model, generations of Reformed churches in the latter half of the sixteenth century proved adept in establishing congregations throughout Europe, including in countries like France and England where the Reformed faith was not the established church. Eventually, this movement led to the growth of a polity made up of ministerial synods and presbyters, whereby churches were held together increasingly by allegiance to specific confessions of faith. Additionally, the main theological tenets of Calvinism had a major impact on the development of the Anglican Church in the late sixteenth century and the first English Baptists churches formed in the early seventeenth century.

Baptist origins have been hotly debated by scholars. The early seventeenth-century Baptist communities emerged as dissenting groups in the Netherlands and England, affirming the idea of "believer's baptism." That is, only those persons who professed faith in Christ could be baptized. This position often prompted critics to refer to these groups as "Anabaptists," referring to a variety of radical reformation movements that stressed adult baptism and withdrawal from society. On the other hand, many of these early Baptist communities affirmed a strong fidelity to several theological tenets associated with Calvinism.

Yet some of these Baptist communities did not follow Calvinist teaching and reflected a wider questioning among some Protestants of the doctrine of predestination. By the early 1600s, Jacobus Arminius, a Dutch theologian, attempted to modify Calvin's theology in ways he hoped would lead to a more practical theology of predestination. While believing that God knew whether a person was to be saved, Arminius argued that it was possible for individuals to respond in some measure to the invitation of God's grace. Such theological wiggle room was unacceptable to orthodox Calvinists who condemned Arminius' teaching at the Synod of Dort in 1619. For the synod, Arminius' teachings sounded too much like the fifth-century British monk Pelagius who argued that individuals had a very real role to play in their salvation (especially through works). While Arminius had no intention of embracing this tradition (and was already dead by the time the Dort synod met), his name was already becoming attached to a movement that would sweep through many Protestant traditions over the next century. By the end of the seventeenth century, the term "Arminian" was used to describe anyone who felt that one's salvation was, at least in part, dependent upon an individual's free will to respond to God's gift of grace.

Partly as a response to Arminius, but also emerging out of a desire to go further than Calvin, Reformed Christianity produced many church leaders who argued that Christians needed to find some assurance that God was going to save them. In England in the early seventeenth century, theologians such as John Preston and William Ames were arguing that the manner of one's election, that is, one's salvation, could be revealed by the righteous activities of the saved. While Calvin himself would have shunned the idea that good works on their own were a mark of salvation, for many Calvinists these works were nothing short of a sign that God was upholding his part of a sacred covenant between God and humanity. In words steeped in Old Testament language (especially recalling God's covenant with Abraham in Genesis 17), Calvinists strove not only for signs of their election, but also to instill in their followers the faith that their churches were made up of fellowships of saintly people that would serve as Christ's true church on earth.

Later generations of Protestant evangelicals would often relate Christian conversion to a specific experience or event that changed and reoriented the believer to a life of devotion to God. Reformed Protestantism certainly did not dismiss the importance of what was in a person's heart. However, for seventeenth-century Calvinists, conversion was not simply to speak of a singular experience but an ongoing commitment to a lifestyle whereby an individual's devotion to God was measured by a passion to serve the church *and* the world. It is also important to note that while Calvinist churches rejected the Catholic sacramental view of the church (in which the seven sacraments were seen as essential to one's salvation), this theological heritage hung onto aspects of Catholic theology that saw participation in the church as vital to the Christian life. However, while Puritans placed a high premium on church membership and conceded that humans had some "rational comprehension" to discern God's will, the question of how conversions occurred was entirely under God's control. In the words of one Calvinist divine, "the Conversion of a Sinner does not depend so much on the outward Means of Grace, as on the good pleasure, and Will of God."[3] Seventeenth-century Calvinist leaders agreed wholeheartedly on the fact that the church needed to be made up of godly men and women. However, they soon disagreed on the question of who was godly.

It was this idea that sinful human beings could nevertheless find a degree of godly perfection through the fellowship of the church that gave rise in England to the Puritan movement. While often associated with a number of emerging English churches, including Presbyterians, Congregationalists, and Baptists, the movement's origins centered on the one branch of the Reformation that attempted to preserve aspects of Catholic ecclesiastical tradition: the Church of England.

THE CHURCH OF ENGLAND AND THE
EMERGENCE OF PURITANISM

In the 1530s, a small number of Huguenots, the dissenting Reformed Calvinists from France, in an effort to escape persecution, briefly established a colony in present-day Florida. These Reformed Protestants would be followed almost a century later by Dutch Calvinist settlements around present-day New York City. However, the major impact of the Reformed Reformation in North America came from English Calvinists, in particular dissenters within the Church of England.

Despite the fact that the Anglican theological heritage stresses its mediating role between Catholicism and Protestantism, its history by the end of the sixteenth century left little doubt that its chief tenets lay with the Protestant reformers, especially those emerging from Geneva. The major figure in shaping the theological contours of Anglicanism was Thomas Cranmer. As archbishop of Canterbury under King Henry VIII and Henry's son, Edward VI (reigned 1547–1553), Cranmer moved the English church toward a fuller embrace of Protestant theological practices. During Edward's reign, Cranmer was instrumental in influencing the Church of England to adapt the *Book of Common Prayer* and Articles of Religion (42 in number) that showed the Church moving closer to the theological commitments of Geneva. Cranmer's own theology was a mix of Lutheran, Zwinglian, and Calvinist influences, and while Anglicanism still maintained liturgical practices associated with the Catholic tradition, the 42 Articles left little doubt of that church's Protestant sympathies (for example, embracing Protestant perspectives on two sacraments rather than seven and several articles marked by strong Calvinist sentiments on matters such as predestination).

The circumstances for the Church of England changed drastically during the reign of Mary I (1553–1558). In addition to her foreign policy, which attempted to bring about an alliance between England and Spain through Mary's unpopular marriage to the Spanish king, Philip II, Mary sought to reinstate Catholic control of the English church (events that would lead to the execution of several prominent Anglican clerics, including Archbishop Cranmer). It was during this period of uncertainty, however, that several leading Anglicans sought refuge from Mary's crackdown by fleeing to the European continent with several individuals ending up in Geneva. When these exiled church leaders returned home after Mary's death, they were ready to push Anglicanism closer to a Reformed theology and polity.

Queen Elizabeth's reign (1558–1603) provided much of the theological and liturgical direction that would shape the Anglican Church for the next two centuries. Reaffirming Cranmer's articles of religion (now reduced to 39), and reestablishing the primacy of the *Book of Common Prayer* in matters of ecclesiastical governance, the so-called Elizabethan Settlement appeared to bring stability to the church. Setting the current for many Anglicans in the late sixteenth century were the writings of Richard Hooker, whose emphasis on a threefold model of scripture, tradition, and reason attempted to provide a mediating influence in the English church between those who favored a return to Catholicism and those who insisted that the church needed to move toward a fuller embrace of Reformed Protestantism. What tied many Anglicans together was the idea that the English monarch and not the pope was the supreme head of the church. In the latter years of the sixteenth century, this idea tended to provide a common ground for many Anglicans to find agreement amid considerable theological differences.

However, toward the end of Elizabeth's reign and in the years of her successor James I's reign, the Church of England was pulled at all sides by a variety of theological currents, with some members who advocated a position that became associated with a "free grace" theology of Jacob Arminius, and others who identified with Puritanism. The term "Puritan" in its original inception referred primarily to members of the Church of England who believed that Anglicanism had not gone far enough in its embrace of Geneva's Reformed theological legacy (and not surprisingly, many of the first English Puritans had lived in Geneva turning the reign of Mary I). Indeed, what later united many Puritans, whether they were Anglican or non-Anglican, was the desire to construct churches made up of godly and God-fearing men and women. In effect, the goal of Puritanism was nothing short of constructing a truly reformed church that was faithful to the theological and ecclesiastical precepts of the early church.

THE PURITAN SPIRIT COMES TO AMERICA

The first permanent English Protestant settlement in the present-day United States was established in Jamestown, Virginia, in 1607. While these colonists were theoretically Anglican, religion was not a major motivation for colonization. The original inhabitants of Jamestown had one priest (who soon died), and the colony's ethos was driven mostly by economics, not theology (it was not until 1626 that Virginia established the Church of England as the colony's official church). It was within the matrix of two colonies located in Massachusetts that the full force of Protestant Christianity was imported to North America.

Historians and popular writers have long been attracted to the theological motivation of the Puritans, seeing in their cause either what is noble or fanatical in the American religious imagination. The first thing that one needs to remember in discussing the New England Puritans is that their religious, political, and economic goals were directly tied to what one of their early leaders called an "errand into the wilderness." The original settlers of New England held to the fact that they were citizens of England who had received a distinctive call to be part of the New England colony. Many of the theological ideals of the Puritans, in particular their idea of sharing a unique covenant with God, would emerge in later generations as part of an American ideology that mixed religious rhetoric with the belief that America had a providential mission to the world. Yet the first generation of New England Puritans was largely concerned about how their peers in England would judge their mission, as opposed to how future generations of Americans would evaluate their successes or failures. Like other North American colonies established in the seventeenth and eighteenth centuries, New England was settled by men and women in search of economic opportunity. Yet more than most colonial settlements before the American Revolutionary War, the early wave of immigrants who came to New England was galvanized by powerful religious motivations.

By 1620 many Puritans had to make a choice of whether to stay loyal to the established Church of England. While James I initially showed signs of support for the principles of Reformed Protestantism (and attached his name in 1611 to the most popular and widely used English Bible in the world, the King James Bible), it became evident by the 1610s that James was lukewarm, if not hostile, to church reform. Ultimately, some of the Puritans became separatists, leaving the Church of England behind and levitating toward the model of establishing church authority predicated on the autonomy of each individual congregation. This was the path chosen by the fledgling Baptist and Congregational sects who fled England to settle in Holland in the early 1600s (being one of the few European countries at the time with a high level of religious toleration). Under the leadership of William Bradford, the most famous of these separatist communities, a group of English exiles, was led from the Netherlands to America. In November 1620, after their ship went off course, the colonists disembarked near present-day Cape Cod, Massachusetts, leading to the establishment of the Plymouth Colony.

American popular mythology tends to confuse the "Pilgrims" of the Plymouth Colony with the later Puritan settlement of Massachusetts Bay. Although the two colonies eventually did merge (in 1691), they initially represented two distinctive brands of Puritanism. Unlike the later Massachusetts Bay Colony of John Winthrop, the Plymouth Colony believed that the official English church was corrupted to the point of being beyond reform. Despite the image of the Pilgrims' first winter in the Americas, replete with comforting images of later American Thanksgiving rituals, the Pilgrims were beset by personal and economic hardships. While Bradford gave glowing accounts of the colony's early years in New England, the population suffered slow growth, high death rates, and economic and political isolation.

What is often forgotten about the earliest American colonies, whether one is discussing the Virginia colony or the various New England settlements, is that their future was predicated on economic survival, not merely a desire for religious freedom. While Virginia witnessed the emergence of strong agricultural communities by the late seventeenth century, many of the New England colonies were beset by poor economic outputs, frequent defection of colonists who returned to England, and, like their neighbors in Virginia, constant tension, if not open warfare, with Native American tribes.

Yet, far more than was the case in Virginia, the Puritan appeal to create a godly church served as a tool to bring English immigrants to New England. Theologically, what united the Plymouth Colony with the later Puritan colonies chartered in New England was a deeply felt impulse to seek out in their fellowship the spirit of the early church. Initially, however, the Puritan impulse in Massachusetts was not toward separation. Governor Winthrop's "city upon a hill" oration was meant to be a call to New Englanders to build a church that would not abandon the national Church of England, but complete the process of reform that would make their church's ecclesiastical and theological precepts a model that other churches could emulate.

While the Massachusetts Bay Colony was chartered by Christians who were theoretically Anglicans, they developed practices that modeled many of the separatist practices established earlier at Plymouth in that they insisted upon a congregational polity of local church governance. Echoing the themes of the Geneva reformers, they embraced a church government revolving around the authority of local churches (especially the authority of the clergy within these churches). They soon assembled the colony's clergy into synods that would, in theory, carry responsibility for overseeing the religious affairs of the colonies. Like their European counterparts, the New England Puritans (regardless of the particular colony) believed fervently in the idea that converted Christians would be able to build a godly community ruled by God's commandments. However, the original colony established in Massachusetts Bay was not the theocracy that many later envisioned. While the Massachusetts Bay Colony saw its religious values unifying the colony, in reality the colonists drew a sharp distinction between civic and religious authority. New England colonial ministers were not allowed to hold public office, and magistrates such as Winthrop were to leave matters of ecclesiastical polity in the hands of the colony's clergy.

Despite the fact that church attendance was mandatory, accounts of the early New England settlements indicate that many members remained aloof from religion, despite the constant threat of punitive measures. In part, the barrier to church attendance was likely predicated on the high membership standards that the leaders of these colonies placed on the population. While Puritan theology emphasized the belief that factors such as works were a manifestation of the covenant that one had with God (and a sign of one's salvation), church membership was reserved solely for those who could attest to some type of a conversion experience. Yet at the same time, Puritans wrestled with an issue that would plague the theological tradition over the next hundred years: what about those in the church who were not converted?

The early New England Puritan colonies carried the hope that Christian believers would be able to build righteous communities on earth. However, Winthrop's "city upon a hill" was not envisioned as a heavenly utopia. As Edmund Morgan notes, the Puritan worldview contained a paradox. On one hand, the Puritans emphasized the sinfulness of humanity, a mark of humanity's fall as depicted in Genesis 3. However, human beings through divine grace were capable of making the church and, by extension, the society more godly in its behaviors and morals.[4] Unlike Calvin, who saw the church as a mixed assembly of saints and sinners, the Puritans saw the true church as an assembly of the elect, who by extension would use their faith to influence the larger political and economic fabric of society. While the blueprint for such a model of the church rested with Calvin, the Puritan mindset placed even greater emphasis on the role of the church as an assembly of converted sinners. Behind the New England Puritan vision was the hope that the righteous could stave off the power of human sin in the colonies, and it was hoped that this righteousness would be carried into the larger culture by every converted man, woman, and child.

Yet another vital theme within the theology of New England Puritanism was a strong current of what has been called millennialism. One of the central ideas of the early church, especially evident in the teachings of the Apostle Paul, was a belief that human history would soon end, marked by a second appearance of Christ upon the earth. Although belief in the second coming of Christ became muted with the passage of time, faith rooted in the belief that God would divinely intervene in history and cause a sudden, perhaps even a violent, end to human history never disappeared from Christian history. With the coming of the Reformation, based on the idea of the centrality of Scripture, belief that the world was perhaps in its final days was given new credence. With particular focus on the Book of Revelation (the final book of the New Testament), many Christians looked for clues that they were perhaps living amid the last days of earth. Central to this reading were verses in Revelation 20 and 21 that foretold of a 1,000-year period in which converted Christians stood poised to witness dramatic events that would mark the final return of Christ. As we shall see, these themes of God's millennial reign on earth would extend beyond New England Puritanism and affect a wide range of religious movements throughout American history.

Most historians note that the zeal of the Massachusetts Bay Colony went into decline by the mid-seventeenth century. Even during the lifetime of John Winthrop, however, the colony was struggling with its religious identity. In addition to disillusioned colonists who returned to England, the reality of religious and political instability in England, which ultimately led to civil war in the 1640s, made the religious experiment in New England less important to the affairs of political leaders back in England. By the time of the English Civil War, the colony had already experienced dissent among Puritan enthusiasts who shared different visions of God's plan in the New World. At the center of this dissent were two individuals who seemed to be perfect embodiments of the American Puritan ethos: Anne Hutchinson and Roger Williams.

THE COMING OF ANNE HUTCHINSON

Anne Hutchinson entered the Massachusetts Bay Colony at a critical moment in the colony's history. Born in 1591, Hutchinson grew up in England toward the end of Queen Elizabeth's long reign. Her father, an Anglican minister, carried overt Puritan sympathies and apparently castigated clergy whom he perceived did not show the attributes of a converted Christian life—a theme that would be given powerful expression by his daughter in later years. After her marriage in 1612, Hutchinson settled into the role of raising an increasingly large family, but she was drawn to the prospect of the religious life offered by the various adherents of the Puritan movement. Arriving in Massachusetts with her husband, William, and her family in 1634, she followed her beloved minister, John Cotton (1585–1652), to the colony. Cotton was an orthodox Puritan who held steadfastly to the idea that a truly biblical church needed to be marked by a fellowship of the converted. As will be discussed in the next chapter, Cotton's descendants would produce one of the most prominent clergy families in New England. Yet his emphasis on the necessity of conversion as mandatory for church membership opened up an issue critical for future generations of American Protestants: how does one judge the authenticity of an individual's conversion? Anne Hutchinson, in her short but memorable career, not only had a distinctive answer to this question, but she provided a recurring blueprint that would be used by successive generations of American religious leaders.

The year 1636 was a watershed period for the Massachusetts Bay Colony. The previous year, Roger Williams, a minister in the town of Salem, engaged in repeated attacks against many of the colonial leaders for what he saw as their corrupting influences upon the larger church in the colony. Leaning toward a separatist theology such as that of Plymouth, and a belief that baptism should be offered only to those who could publically profess Christ, Williams and a group of followers left to establish an independent colony in Rhode Island. Now disturbing reports began to circulate in and around Boston that Hutchinson was providing religious instruction in her home. This fact alone probably would not have gotten her expelled from the colony, as precedents (though unpopular) did exist within European Protestant communities of individual women offering faith instruction in their homes. What got Hutchinson into trouble was the nature of her teachings. Hutchinson was nothing but an excellent Puritan in that she stressed the necessity of a converted church led by a converted ministry. However, her insistence that the outward appearances of godly behavior did not necessarily prove a mark of conversion angered colonial authorities. The heart of her teaching was that most of the colony's clergy were not truly converted. Hutchinson's challenge was radical not only because she was a woman, but because the support she received from her fellow congregants threatened to undercut the clearly defined religious and secular lines of authority envisioned by the colony. What also made Hutchinson's assertions so egregious was that she claimed to receive direct inspiration from the Holy Spirit. As Edmund Morgan noted, Hutchinson asserted beliefs that "threatened the fundamental conviction on which the Puritans built their state, their churches, and their daily lives, namely that God's will could be discovered only through the Bible."[5] The charge leveled against Hutchinson was that she was an "antinomian," a term used to designate individuals who did not believe in the law and teachings of Scripture, but emphasized their own interpretation of religious truths.

Initially, Puritan leaders attempted to dissuade Hutchinson not by threats of sanction, but by rational persuasion. While Hutchinson's pastor, John Cotton, initially supported her, he too worried that her insistence on direct revelation of the Holy Spirit would bring instability to the colony. The concern of colonial leaders was that by directly appealing to the Holy Spirit, colonial religious and secular authority was being undermined. Finally, after two trials, one before a colonial court and one in her church, Hutchinson was censured and ordered to leave the colony. The nature of Hutchinson's threat to the religious and political authority of the colony was captured at her first trial by these words from one of her chief critics. "You have stept out of your place, you have rather bine a Husband than a Wife and a preacher than a Hearer; and a Magistrate than a Subject."[6] On one hand, this statement clearly indicates the ways in which Hutchinson violated the gender roles of her era. In a period during which Puritan theology viewed human beings as permanently corrupted by original sin, women were seen as especially sinful and prone to evil. Hutchinson had helped support her family as a midwife; this profession contained a long history in Europe for its association in the eyes of men with witchcraft and various occult practices. Yet the fervor over Hutchinson also reflects upon a larger tension that would be an issue in American Christianity long after the demise of the New England Puritan experiment: who has a right to exercise religious authority? By directly appealing to the power of the Holy Spirit, Hutchinson bypassed the authority of ordained clergy and asserted that she had discerned the will of God for the people of New England. Hutchinson was one of the first persons in American history to make this bold claim, but she was by no means the last.

ROGER WILLIAMS AND THE LEGACY
OF RELIGIOUS LIBERTY

Roger Williams' name is rightly connected to a larger American heritage of religious liberty. Yet like Anne Hutchinson, Williams was an individual who saw himself first and foremost as a good Puritan. Educated at Cambridge University, Williams arrived at the Massachusetts colony in 1631. While colonists such as John Winthrop appreciated his steadfast beliefs and commitment to the colony, signs of things to come occurred early in Williams' tenure in Massachusetts when he declined an invitation to become pastor of a church in Boston. To Williams, this church and other churches in the colony were too tied to the idea of reforming the Anglican Church, and his refusal prefigured events that would later get him expelled from the colony. After preaching at the church in Salem for a time, Williams moved to the Plymouth Colony, yet even that colony's leaders found aspects of Williams' faith unsettling. William Bradford noted that Williams was "a man godly and zealous, having many precious parts, but very unsettled in judgmente."[7] When Williams returned to Massachusetts Bay and to the Salem church in 1634, he soon found himself drawing the ire of the colony's leadership. What was most at issue for Williams was not only concern that the New England churches were too tied to the tradition of Anglicanism, but the fact that the biblical teachings and fellowship of the churches were too entangled with the state.

Both Hutchinson and Williams displayed theological tendencies that echoed themes within the movement of sixteenth-century Protestantism often referred to as the Radical Reformation. This tradition, which included a number of Anabaptist groups, increasingly saw entanglement with government as corrupting the spiritual power of the church's mission. Unlike Hutchinson, however, who emphasized that the Holy Spirit provided the justification for her ministry, the solution for Williams rested entirely in the words of Scripture, and it was Scripture that pointed Williams to one conclusion: New Englanders needed to strive to recapture the true spirit and intent of the early church. This spirit of "primitive Christianity" was central to the ways that various Puritan colonists understood their mission in America. Initially, this impulse was reflected in the movement of Puritans to disassociate themselves from Anglican ecclesiology (such as abandoning the use of bishops in favor of congregationally based governance). However, the impulse soon galvanized other disputes over doctrine that caused other schisms within New England churches. At the same time that tensions over Anne Hutchinson were rising, Thomas

Hooker, who had arrived in Massachusetts a few years after Williams, left the colony and was responsible for establishing a Puritan colony in Hartford, Connecticut. Yet Williams was perhaps the first example of a tradition of Christian restorationism that became a feature of American religious life in subsequent centuries. This restorationalist tradition deemphasized the role of creeds and ecclesiastical structures in favor of using the Bible to discern the true nature of the church.

Yet Williams also reflected a strong Puritan trait that believed the power of sin might corrupt all human efforts to build a righteous church or society. Specifically, he wrestled with a question foundational to later generations of Americans: what is the proper relationship between religion and government? While united in their idea of reforming the church, New England politicians such as John Winthrop and influential clergy such as John Cotton worried about the consequences of how sin might corrupt both the church and civil society. "It is necessary, therefore, that all power that is on earth be limited, Church power or other," noted Cotton. "It is therefore fit for every man to be studious of the bounds which the Lord hath set; and for the People, in whom fundamentally all power lyes, to give as much power as God in his word gives to men: And it is meet that Magistrates in the Commonwealth, and so offices in the Churches, should desire to know the utmost bounds of their own power."[8] For Williams, part of the corrupting influence of human sin occurred when the affairs of the church and of government became too entangled. It was not enough that clergy could not hold public offices; what was needed was a complete separation of the church from the legal affairs of state—including the long-accepted idea of the government establishment of particular churches. As Williams liked to point out, to try to plant the foundation of a true church on the mantles of secular government was "to raise the form of a square house upon the Keel of a Ship."[9] While he agreed with Anne Hutchinson that the church needed to seek out converted men and women, it also needed to be built upon a foundation that avoided entanglement with secular government. Drawing upon Scriptures (and also reflecting on the unsettled political nature of seventeenth-century Europe), Williams argued that the example of ancient Israel revealed what can happen to a people who confuse religious zeal with national loyalty.

> 'Tis true, the people of Israel, brought into covenant with God in Abraham and so successively born in covenant with God, might (in that state of a national church) solemnly covenant and swear that whosoever would not seek Jehovah, the God of Israel, should be put to death, whether small or great, whether man or woman.

> But may whole nations of kingdoms now . . . follow that pattern of
> Israel and put to death all, both men and women, great and small, that
> according to the rules of the Gospel are not born again, penitent, hum-
> ble, heavenly patient? What a world of hypocrisy from hence is practiced
> by thousands that for fear will stoop to give that God their bodies in a
> form whom yet in truth their hearts affect not?[10]

Williams did not disavow the ideal that secular government should be
made up of virtuous Christians. His issue was that the Bible and church
history pointed to the fact that secular governments would inevitably corrupt the moral power of the church *and* use religion to sanction all sorts
of evils.

In the fall of 1635, he was expelled from the Massachusetts Bay Colony,
and after several weeks of travel with a group of followers, established the
Rhode Island colony with its center in the newly christened capital of
Providence. Like many who followed him to Rhode Island, Williams not
only carried what could be called an Anabaptist view of the church in relationship to the government, but came to embrace the view that only those
who could profess a conversion experience should be baptized. Under
Williams' leadership, the first recognized Baptist congregation in North
America was established in Providence, Rhode Island, in 1638.

With justification, Roger Williams has been identified as the founder
of the Baptist tradition in America. However, in many ways, the rise of the
Baptist tradition in America owes more to Williams' colleagues in Rhode
Island. Two of these early Rhode Island Baptists, John Clark, a pastor in
Newport, Rhode Island, and Obadiah Holmes represented the foundation
for many fledgling American Baptists who came after them. In the 1650s,
Holmes carried his beliefs north to Massachusetts to evangelize, where for
many years "Anabaptist" groups were outlawed (and where Holmes found
himself for a time imprisoned by Massachusetts authorities). Yet the cause
of religious freedom proved more pressing for Williams than the particu-
larities of doctrine. By the mid-1640s, Williams had left the Baptists and
worried that the obsession of some of his colleagues over the precise nature
of baptism succumbed to the human tendency to confuse specific doctrines with the will of God. Yet Williams continued to defend the rights
of Baptists and, as will be discussed in the next chapter, other religious
minorities who found their way to New England.

Williams spent the majority of his long life until his death in 1683
not only arguing on behalf of religious liberty, but also seeking to defend
the rights of Native Americans to their land. He was one of the few
European settlers who took time to learn Native American languages,

and frequently defended Native American rights to their property against colonial encroachment. More than any other religious leader in the seventeenth century, Williams helped craft a distinctive model of religious liberty that became one of the major blueprints over a century later when the U.S. Constitution legally embraced a nation predicated on religious disestablishment.

For all his devotion to religious liberty, Williams was far from a freethinker. While Rhode Island increasingly served as a point for new religious groups to settle, by the mid-seventeenth century, Williams expressed a degree of disdain toward "antinomian" groups such as the Quakers who from his perspective were denying the authority of Scripture. Also, Williams played a secondary but important part in one of the first New England colonial wars against the Pequot Native American tribe in 1637. Williams warned John Winthrop of an imminent attack from the Native Americans, and the resulting conflict nearly led to the slaughter of the tribe. This conflict reflected one of the first events in English North American history whereby Christian ideology was used to defend the violent displacement of Native American tribes. While Winthrop had initially taken a perspective that there was plenty of land to be shared among Native American and European settlers, the Pequot War helped shape a growing American ideology that Native Americans were agents of Satan who, if they could not be converted to Christianity, needed to be killed.

This view prefigured the much larger conflict that erupted between the New England colonists and Native Americans in 1675–1676, the so-called King Philip's War. King Philip (the name settlers gave to the Wampanoag chief associated with uprising) reflected tensions that would plague relationships between white settlers and Native Americans for centuries to come: encroachment on Native American lands and an inability of white missionaries to appreciate and adapt Christianity to the cultural context of Native Americans. While some colonists engaged in active missionary work with these indigenous tribes, conversions were slow and by and large interest in adapting native cultures to the theological worldviews of European Christianity was not tolerated. One of the ironies of the war was that Roger Williams' home was looted and burned by Native Americans, representing an unfortunate culmination to the life of a man who devoted many of his efforts to promoting peace and harmony among all the inhabitants of New England.

PLANTING SEEDS OF RELIGIOUS DISSENT
AND DIVERSITY

Roger Williams and Anne Hutchinson were more than religious dissent-ers. They were prototypes of many themes that would resurface in the sub-sequent history of American Christianity. Their fidelity to Puritan ideals of personal and community righteousness, their insistence on personal conversion, and, in the case of Williams, a belief that the church and state needed to become disentangled from one another represented ongoing themes in American religious history.

In the short run, the challenges presented to the Puritan experiment in Massachusetts appeared to fail, and for Anne Hutchinson that failure had tragic consequences. After residing for a time in Rhode Island she moved to a region along the Long Island Sound where tragically she and several of her children were murdered by Native Americans in 1643 (an act that was seen by some in Massachusetts as a providential and just sign of God punishing a wicked sinner). Yet over the long-term history of American Christianity, Hutchinson's shadow would loom large. As the Massachusetts Bay Colony staved off her challenge, ultimately it proved unable to regulate the beliefs of the colonists or control emerging histori-cal factors that would quickly turn the larger North American landscape into a sea of religious diversity. At the same time that Hutchinson was mounting a challenge to colonial authority, other leaders were expressing dissatisfaction with the lack of religious rigor in the colony. In addition to Williams' exodus to Rhode Island, other Puritan dissidents established two separate colonies along the Connecticut River Valley. By the time of Hutchinson's death, four colonies existed in New England that attempted to implement their own version of a righteous Puritanism. By Roger Williams' death forty years later, the situation in New England already reflected an environment far different from John Winthrop's city upon a hill. The English Civil War of the 1640s left a legacy in England that looked upon the religious practices of the Puritans with growing sus-picion. The restoration of the monarchy in 1660 returned the Anglican Church to a place of civic prominence and ended in the minds of many New Englanders the hope that their movement could reform the English national church.

By the late seventeenth century, New England was surrounded by colonies to the south that from their perspective did not share the zeal for creating a Christian commonwealth. In the South, the Virginia colony existed with a weak Anglican establishment and already was cultivating an economic model of plantation farming, centered upon a slave economy that shaped a distinctive religious and political heritage far different from that developing in New England. While the Dutch colony of New Amsterdam and a Swedish colony in Delaware were short-lived, English colonization in midcentury saw the rise of new colonies that seemed to many New England minds to be predicated on false religious principles. In particular, the Pennsylvania colony not only was founded by Quakers, but it gave religious refuge to a variety of dissenting religious traditions from the European continent. It is no wonder that this proliferation of religious diversity made some New England stalwarts view other sections of the North American colonies as cesspools, filled with dangerous religious radicals. As the colonial landscape took shape in the seventeenth century, the New England heirs to John Winthrop, John Cotton, Anne Hutchinson, and Roger Williams found that they were not able to maintain the zeal of their forefathers and foremothers.

Yet these early seventeenth-century theological incarnations coming out of New England reflected another theme often overlook by many studies of colonial religion. For all the dissent caused by figures such as Hutchinson and Williams, they shared with other Puritans a sense that they were living at a time when life on earth stood in the balance between Heaven and Hell. History might very well be coming to an end, replaced by the realization of Christ's second coming upon the earth. With the onset of the Reformation, this apocalyptic theology became a critical feature of many nascent Protestant churches. It remains a persistent theme within a wide range of popular theologies to this day.

In microcosm, seventeenth-century New England Puritanism represented a central theme in the future development of American Christianity. The early Puritan effort to recast the relationship between God and humanity, to maintain doctrinal commitment, to define the parameters of ministerial authority and, in particular, to focus upon the centrality of Scripture were central to how these traditions sought to reform the church—and the wider society. Yet the struggles of Anne Hutchinson, Roger Williams, and other seventeenth-century New Englanders also reveal an ongoing tension in the history of American Christianity whereby the desire to create religious uniformity was often exceeded by the creation of a wide range of religious dissenters.

This tension would be a recurring theme throughout American religious history.

« 2 »

UNINTENDED DIVERSITY
THE GROWTH OF COLONIAL CHRISTIANITY

In 1709 Cotton Mather, one of the most prominent New England clergymen of his time, delivered a sermon to the Massachusetts General Assembly in which he gave expression to what became a timeless theme in American Christianity. This "Golden Street of the Holy City" address shows how aspects of an earlier Puritan zeal had not dampened since the founding of the Massachusetts Bay Colony. "There are many Arguments to perswade us, That our Glorious LORD, will have an Holy City in AMERICA, a CITY; the Streets whereof will be *Pure Gold.*" Mather saw New England as the gateway to usher in the return of Christ. Yet, the promise of the second coming was that it would include all righteous people identified in America. "The kingdom here will be the Lord's," he proclaimed, "and the Lord will be Governor among the nations. . . . O NEW ENGLAND, There is room to hope, That thou also shalt belong to the City. Thou hast already made a *Seisin* [a fiefdom] *of America*, on behalf of thy GLORIOUS LORD."[1]

While Mather's sermon reflected upon a past heritage of New England Puritanism, it also anticipated later developments in the eighteenth century. Like his Puritan forebears, Mather saw New England's destiny in terms of how the godly would overcome the forces of evil (one example of these evil forces for Mather and his contemporaries was the threat to New England from French colonies to the north in Canada). Yet Mather's address, while stressing familiar Puritan themes of the unique place in God's kingdom for New England, also reflected a burgeoning

43

eighteenth-century theme that God's righteous kingdom would not simply be confined to New England.

During Mather's lifetime, the legacy of the Puritans, while still powerful in New England, was far removed from the theological goals espoused by John Winthrop. As the seventeenth century progressed and the political fortunes of England ultimately solidified the official status of the Church of England, later Puritans no longer were motivated by the goal of reforming the Anglican Church. Yet successive generations of New Englanders took seriously the idea that New England was a land of special blessing and at the center of God's divine plans.

By the 1720s Cotton Mather, heir to one of the most famous (or depending on one's perspective, notorious) clergy families in New England, reflected on the future of the noble experiment of his Puritan ancestors from a century earlier. In a series of missives written not long before his death in 1728, Mather described the ways that many New Englanders had forsaken religion to take on various worldly vices and observed that Europeans who came to the New World "will not find New-England a New Jerusalem." Mather continued to hope, as his grandfathers and father had done before him, that New England would be at the center of God's millennial kingdom. However, unlike his ancestors, Mather did not identify his ministry with the earlier Puritan mission of converting persons in his ancestral home, England. He was part of a generation that more and more identified itself as American. As one of Mather's biographers noted, "no other person born in America between the time of Columbus and of Franklin strove to make himself so conspicuous—strove, more accurately, to become conspicuous as an American."[2]

Mather's birth in 1663 came at a moment when the New England colonies were in the process of reassessing the extent to which they needed to open their doors to the unconverted. Before Mather's birth, Massachusetts Congregational clergy affirmed what came to be known as "the Half-Way Covenant" in 1662, whereby the children of church members who had not professed a conversion experience akin to their parents were eligible to have their children baptized. This seemingly modest measure represented not just an issue that would be fought within the churches of Puritan New England, but a larger struggle, faced by successive generations of American churches, of maintaining religious commitments amid changing historical and cultural circumstances.

While Mather mostly addressed his comments to the theological and moral state of New Englanders, he also reflected a larger anxiety about how the American colonies were being reshaped politically and socially from the mid-seventeenth century to the early eighteenth century. By 1700 what began as a series of disparate settlements in the early 1600s had emerged into distinctive colonies under British royal authority. Although this development did not overturn the Congregational Church establishments in places such as Massachusetts and Connecticut (or the tradition of religious liberty in Rhode Island), later colonial charters, in particular in the southern colonies of the Carolinas and Georgia, followed Virginia's lead by granting legal status to the Church of England. In many of the middle colonies, such as Maryland and Pennsylvania, colonial charters allowed a great deal of religious diversity. In some ways, Mather was the embodiment of the zealous New England Puritan. He was dedicated to his faith and also continued to see his beloved New England as the model for God's coming kingdom. Increasingly, however, Mather recognized that the religious situation he faced was far different from that confronted by his grandparents, who were first-generation clergy in the Massachusetts colony. What Mather had to wrestle over would become a fundamental question for future religious leaders in America: how does one proclaim a vision of a common American religious unity amid so many diverse voices?

NEW ENGLAND TRANSFORMED

Cotton Mather's grandfathers, John Cotton and Richard Mather (1596–1669), and his father, Increase Mather (1639–1723), labored to reinforce the grand vision of Massachusetts as a holy colony of God. As was discussed in the previous chapter, John Cotton (as well as serving as Anne Hutchinson's minister) was probably the primary theological voice in the Massachusetts Bay Colony's first generation, but Richard Mather certainly left his own legacy. Mather arrived in Massachusetts in 1635 and served for many years as pastor of a church in Dorchester, Massachusetts. His theology reflected the classic New England themes of divine covenant and a discernable millennialism that saw the second coming of Christ as imminent. These themes were passed on to Richard's son, Increase, and his grandson, Cotton.

Increase Mather became one of the most significant leaders of the Massachusetts colony in its second generation. While he initially opposed what became known as the Half-Way Covenant, he later reconciled himself to the practical necessities of this doctrine. Also, his sermons reflected the mainstay of many Puritan sermons, combining the importance of a moral life with the expectancy in the second coming. Part of what characterized the New England preaching of the Mathers was the jeremiad, a method of sermonizing that stressed the moral imperative that the converted needed to strive for righteousness in all aspects of their living. After becoming pastor of the Second Church, Boston (or Old North Church—not to be confused with the church of Paul Revere fame), Increase Mather's sermons reflected classic remonstrates to his congregation to live moral lives and to be watchful for the full manifestations of God's power and glory in New England. "Without doubt the Lord Jesus hath a peculiar respect unto this place, and for this people," he asserted in 1674. "This is Immanuel's land. Christ by a wonderful providence hath dispossessed Satan, who reigned securely in these ends of the earth, for ages the Lord knoweth how many, and here the Lord hath caused as it were New Jerusalem to come down from heaven; he dwells in this place: therefore we may conclude that he will scourge us for our backslidings."[3]

Increase Mather's preaching embodied a theological tradition commonly referred to as *postmillennialism*. Relying heavily on themes within the Book of Revelation (in particular, Revelation 20:1-6) Mather and other Puritan divines believed that Christ's second coming would occur *after* Christians succeeded in building a truly righteous society upon the earth. For centuries, Christians from numerous theological contexts had speculated that they might be living at the end of the thousand-year period of peace foretold in Revelation and the Puritan spirit held in tension the themes of righteous living with the hope that they might witness Christ's second coming. By the time that Increase Mather's son, Cotton, was born, the intensity of this millennialism, though muted, was still a feature of many aspects of Puritan theology.

Cotton Mather picked up where his father and grandparents left off. After graduating from Harvard College, he became co-pastor with his father at Old North, assuming primary pastoral responsibilities in 1685. Part of the negativity surrounding the Mather family's historical legacy is that both Cotton and Increase Mather became associated with the infamous Salem Witch Trials of 1692. Long associated with a religious heritage of intolerance and superstition (especially as the trial has been reinterpreted through a tradition of mid-nineteenth-century literary romanticism), both of the Mathers were typical of most seventeenth-century Europeans who sought to reconcile the natural-scientific world with the supernatural. It is important to remember that the Salem trials in some ways represented one of the final occurrences in the West of persons being put to death for alleged sorcery. Witch trials had been commonplace throughout the late medieval period, but had begun to decline in Europe by the end of the seventeenth century. However, accusations of witchcraft were frequent in Cotton Mather's New England, and Increase Mather went as far to publish a work on the "spectral evidence" of witchcraft, even as he and his son called for restraint in the persecution of alleged witches.

More than the superstitious and narrow-minded figure caricatured in popular culture, Cotton Mather possessed a lifelong fascination with study and learning, especially of the natural sciences. Amid his numerous publications, he wrote extensively on scientific topics and was a member of London's prestigious Royal Society. Most especially, Mather was ahead of his time in arguing for measures of disease prevention, including being an early advocate for immunizations against smallpox, a stance that at times put him at odds with members of his congregation and fellow clergy.

Yet Mather's primary identity was as a working minister who preached, taught, and offered pastoral care to his Boston congregation. For all of his renown in the American colonies and in England, he never ventured outside of New England and it is probably accurate to say that Mather followed the lead of many Puritan ministers who came before him by literally working himself to death. However, while he clearly reflected the continuation of the Puritan legacy from the first generation, Cotton Mather's life saw drastic changes in the colonial context, from a series of isolated colonial settlements established by a disparate range of European settlers, to a growing number of British colonies that identified as American. Even at the beginning of his ministry at North Church in 1685, the makeup of the American colonies looked far different than it had in the 1630s.

THE COMING OF THE QUAKERS

Roger Williams might have been seen by some devoted Puritans as a radical freethinker, but his experiment of religious freedom in Rhode Island opened the floodgates for other religious refugees to make their way to that colony in the middle and latter years of the seventeenth century. By far, the religious group that most challenged the limits of colonial religious toleration was the arrival in Rhode Island of small numbers of English colonists in the early 1650s who went by the designation "Friends." The Society of Friends, who became more popularly known as the Quakers, were associated with the teachings of the English cobbler George Fox. Fox suffered numerous religious stirrings in the 1640s and reached a point at which he became convinced that other churches were missing the clear message of Jesus' teachings. Fox stressed the importance of the "inner light," the truth of Christ that could not come to someone by virtue of the preacher's sermons or the church's sacraments or even the Bible, but only by waiting in silence for God's blessing to befall the sinner. In the context of a time during which England and much of Europe were divided over wars of religion, Fox's message and his tactics, which included interrupting worship services by calling upon persons to disassociate from the teachings of these apostate churches, led to his imprisonment on numerous occasions. More odiously, Fox and his followers refused to take loyalty oaths or pledges to civil authorities, arguing that such oaths could only be made to God, not to governments constructed by humans.

What also characterized Fox's followers in their early years was a strident belief in an apocalyptic end to history. As we have seen, the sixteenth-century Reformation gave rise to heightened speculation about the end of the world. Many Anabaptist groups went further than other Protestant churches by increasingly seeing events of their own days through this apocalyptic lens. As time passed, the Quakers' stress on apocalyptic thought would fade, but other groups would pick up the mantle of apocalyptic speculation.

An unusual characteristic of the Friends was not only the ways in which they shunned worldly excesses, but how their meetings stressed the equality of men and women, with the testimony of both genders recognized as emanating from the spirit of God. As opposed to preaching or liturgical services, Friends gatherings reflected services of prolonged silences punctuated by people giving testimony to the grace of God in their lives; it was these spirited testimonies that led to the popularization of the name Quakers to refer to Friends.

Quakers were received with equal levels of enmity throughout the colonies. Even in Rhode Island, a colony seen by many Puritans as the religious cesspool of New England, Quaker toleration was seen by some as offensive. Although Roger Williams welcomed the group to Rhode Island, he viewed the Quakers as a body of unsound doctrine and faith practices. Yet Quakers found refuge from persecution in Rhode Island, a benefit they did not enjoy to the north in Massachusetts. Even as Massachusetts officially barred Quakers from entering the colony, by the late 1650s, Quakers came to Massachusetts and openly proselytized. Finally, several Quakers were arrested for violating the colony's ban on the group, and in 1660, a small group was executed on the Boston Common; these were the first persons to be put to death in American history because of their religious convictions. One of the first persons to be executed was a former supporter of Anne

Hutchinson, Mary Dyer. Dyer and her husband had followed Hutchinson to Rhode Island, but after returning to England in the 1650s, Dyer was drawn to the teachings of the Friends and chose to return to Boston to bear witness to her new convictions. Refusing to take sanctuary in either Rhode Island or the Dutch colony of New Amsterdam (later New York), Dyer stood firm in her convictions and defied Massachusetts law, which barred Quakers from the colony. As she stood in judgment before the General Court of Massachusetts after her death sentence was passed, she castigated the officials for their religious hypocrisy:

> Was ever the like Laws heard of, among a People that profess Christ come in the Flesh? And have such no other Weapons, but such Laws, to fight against Spiritual Wickedness withal, as you call it, Wo is me for you! Of whom take you Counsel? Search with the Light if Christ in ye, and it will shew you of whom, as it hath done me and many more, who have been disobedient and deceived, as now you are; which Light, as you come into, and obeying what is made manifest to you therein, you will not Repent, that you were kept from shedding Blood, tho' it were from a woman.[4]

Mary Dyer's death underscored the fact that despite the gradual weakening of Puritanism's initial fervor in Massachusetts, religious toleration was still an ideal years away from being realized in that colony. Additionally, Quakers found similar hardships in other colonies during the seventeenth and eighteenth centuries. Yet the experiment of religious toleration in Rhode Island represented, in microcosm, a model for later colonial development. By the early 1700s, Rhode Island was characterized not only by a high level of diversity among various Christian groups, including Baptist, Congregational, Anglican, Catholic, and Quaker, but also a fledgling Jewish population. In 1763 the oldest synagogue in America was dedicated in Newport, Rhode Island.

THE PENNSYLVANIA COLONY AND
RELIGIOUS SECTARIANISM

By 1700 the American colonies resembled a patchwork of groups that were often tied together by economic opportunism as opposed to anything resembling a unified national identity. The same type of patchwork character was reflected in the increasing variety of Christian groups that were starting to settle in North America. In some respects, part of the changes dealt with the situation in England. After years of political unrest, the nation moved toward greater political stability. In 1689 the English Parliament passed an Act of Toleration that recognized the authority of the Church of England as the national church and allowed certain religious groups the freedom to register with the government as dissenting churches (the one major exception being the Roman Catholic Church, which was seen as an enemy of the state in part because of its connection to the discarded Stuart monarchy). Even though British political administration became a feature of all the colonies in what would become the United States, the evolving political situation in England allowed for greater religious diversity within the various English North American colonies.

Outside of New England, the colonies of New York and New Jersey possessed a significant number of churches, especially coming out of the Reformed tradition of Geneva. New York began as a Dutch colony, but when the British occupied the colony's port city of New Amsterdam (soon to be renamed New York) in 1664, the colony was claimed for the British crown. Nevertheless, New York (as well as neighboring New Jersey) continued to have a significant Dutch immigrant population, and several Dutch Reformed as well as English Presbyterian churches flourished. Maryland was originally established as a Catholic colony in 1632 under the auspices of George Calvert. In 1625 Calvert, a former secretary to King James I, received the title Lord Baltimore from the king for his patronage to the monarchy. Calvert converted to Catholicism later in life, yet held a belief that one's Catholicism should stay a private matter (in large part not to alienate potential Protestant patrons). Although Maryland was technically chartered as a Catholic colony, Catholicism's impact upon that colony was marginal. The first governor of Maryland, Calvert's son Cecil, oversaw the colony's charter that guaranteed freedom of worship, regardless of whether one was Catholic or Protestant. However, the Glorious Revolution in England in 1688 brought a Protestant monarch, William of Orange, to the English throne, and led to the formal establishment of the Anglican Church in the Maryland colony. By 1700 the Catholic presence in Maryland was as a small, often persecuted religious minority.

Another colony that reflected a blending of religious (and national influences) was Delaware. Initially claimed by Sweden in 1638 (which dubbed the colony "New Sweden"), the colony was contested for many years between Sweden, the Netherlands, and England. The eventual ousting of the Swedish and then, ultimately, the Dutch by the English left the colony with a number of different churches, including Dutch Reformed, Swedish Lutheran, and English Presbyterians. The Presbyterian churches that were established in colonies such as Delaware and New Jersey shared with the New England Congregationalists a strong fidelity to Puritan theological themes. The chief difference from the Congregationalists, however, was that the Presbyterians vested greater governing authority in regional clergy synods and ultimately national assemblies. By the early seventeenth century, Presbyterian churches were a growing part of the colonial landscape in several of the Mid-Atlantic colonies.

Outside of Rhode Island, New Jersey, and Delaware, one of the most religiously diverse colonies was Pennsylvania. What made the Pennsylvania colony contentious in the eyes of many Puritans was that its principal founder was a Quaker. Established by William Penn in 1681, the colony reflected Penn's strong belief that the colony was not meant just for Quakers seeking refuge from persecution, but that it was open to persons of all religious backgrounds. On one hand, Penn's religious convictions profoundly set a tone of religious diversity unprecedented for its time. On the other hand, Penn was a shrewd leader and recognized that there was no contradiction from making Pennsylvania economically profitable and religiously tolerant. Coming from a prosperous upper-class background, Penn had studied at Oxford before his conversion to the Friends. With Penn as Pennsylvania's founding governor, the colony prospered, yet after his return to England in 1701, the colony's Quaker administration was soon absorbed by increasing numbers of non-Quakers. Penn's shadow would remain strong in America's future, not only in terms of his model of religious toleration, but for the fact that he was one of the first figures in the American colonies to argue the case for a united model of British colonies that could make shared economic and political decisions. After Penn's death in 1718, Pennsylvania became a British royal colony, although throughout the eighteenth century Pennsylvania was one of the most diverse colonies, religiously and ethnically.

THE PIETIST SPIRIT IN EUROPE AND AMERICA

A striking aspect about Pennsylvania was the fact that many of its residents came not from Great Britain but from Germany. During the mid-1600s, much of central Europe was in the midst of the Thirty Years' War, a series of conflicts that not only centered on questions of political control, but ultimately pitted Catholic and Protestant rulers against one another. Many of the Germans who ended up in Pennsylvania represented an assortment of groups associated with the Anabaptists. These early German immigrants (who erroneously would be referred to by English settlers as "Pennsylvania Dutch") shared strong pacifist beliefs, and some of these German immigrants had a strong fidelity with a tradition known as "pietism." In the century after Martin Luther's reformation, many German Lutherans became worried that their faith was becoming too creedal and was neglecting the rudiments of the spiritual life. By the late 1600s, Lutheran clergy such as Philipp Spener were emphasizing the need for Christians to garner authentic religious experiences by gathering in small groups for the purpose of prayer and Bible study.

Spener was part of a wider movement that would carry well beyond Lutheranism and influence many disparate Protestant groups over the course of the eighteenth and nineteenth centuries. In Pennsylvania these German pietists were small, and in that colony, and other colonies where they eventually settled, their impact was negligible. Some of these German immigrants, notably the Mennonites and Amish, established Anabaptist communities under the principle of absolute separation from civil authority—a practice that caused them to be persecuted in Europe. These Pennsylvania Anabaptists maintained strict fidelity to sectarian separation from the rest of society. Yet other German immigrants associated with a number of other traditions found their way over time to the Pennsylvania colony in the eighteenth century, including German Reformed, Lutheran, and the Moravians. Some of these pietist streams produced a foundation of popular evangelicalism that would sweep through America in the years leading up to the American Revolution, and that continues to be an ongoing feature of American religious life. The question of how conversion touches the heart has been a key feature of popular Christianity in American history. In the years leading up to the American Revolution, this theme would take on new meaning through numerous waves of revivalism that serve as a central narrative for the next chapter.

ANGLICANISM IN THE SOUTH AND NORTH

For much of the seventeenth century, American Anglican parishes were mostly confined to the eastern seaboard of Virginia and Maryland, with underfunded parishes and ministerial morale often low. Despite difficulties incurred by Anglican churches in many colonies, they did become a dominant movement in the South. Yet the sense of divine providence that characterized the founding of the various New England colonies was often missing from Anglicanism in the South. In many ways, the plight of the Virginia colony's Anglican clergy appeared to corroborate the view of the Puritans that a congregational-based policy was the most biblical and practical model for God's people. Lacking any American bishops to ordain them, Anglican clergy needed to be recruited from England and they often found themselves serving remote rural parishes. Many seventeenth-century Anglican priests in colonial Virginia not only lamented the religious indifference of their flocks, but also the relative isolation they experienced in that colony.

By the end of the seventeenth century, Anglican missions in America received a boost through the founding of two groups, the Society for Promoting Christian Knowledge (SPCK) and the Society for the Propagation of the Gospel in Foreign Parts (SPG). These organizations played a critical role in reviving Anglican missions in America, ultimately playing a critical role in the establishment of the Georgia colony in 1733 while also helping to establish churches in the New England colonies of Connecticut and Massachusetts.

Many of Georgia's early settlers were sent to the colony as an alternative to England's notorious debtor's prisons. Its founding governor, James Oglethorpe, established Georgia not only with the hope that the Anglican church would provide a backbone of civic order, but that the colony would be free from the bane of an institution that in the early 1700s was a presence in most of the British colonies: African slavery. Sadly, Georgia soon embraced this social evil, with many of its clergy following a pattern employed by other colonial clergy who justified slavery as an economic necessity that would at least expose African slaves to the benefits of European civilization, including its religion. One of the earliest Anglican ministers to come to Georgia, who early on questioned these rationalizations in support of slavery, was John Wesley; his story, and the movement he helped found, will be described later.

Ironically, one of the places where the Anglican Church fared best was New England. While Anglicans never could compete on the same scale as the Congregationalists, by the early eighteenth century, the efforts of the SPG and the SPCK helped plant a number of churches in Massachusetts and Connecticut. In 1722 the Anglican Church pulled off a symbolic coup when Timothy Cutler, the rector of Yale College, converted to Anglicanism (despite long-standing efforts by New England Congregational synods to keep Anglican churches at bay).

By the early 1700s, colonial Anglican churches enjoyed their biggest successes in several urban areas. Although Anglicanism was often seen by many Puritan-oriented church leaders as an apostate movement hanging onto the ceremonialism of the Catholic Church, the tradition found success, especially in the South and in major cities along the eastern seaboard. Despite persistent problems with finding English clergy willing to immigrate to America, Anglicanism would continue to grow steadily up to the time of American independence. By the mid-eighteenth century, Anglican parishes were a presence in every American colony including, much to the consternation of several Massachusetts Congregationalists, several parishes in and around Boston.

By the early 1700s, colonial religious affiliation embodied the diversity that would become even more complex after American independence. In the New England colonies, outside of Rhode Island, the Congregational churches held a dominant role, although they would be challenged to a small degree by Anglican encroachment. While containing great diversity, the middle colonies (New York, New Jersey, Pennsylvania, Delaware, and Maryland) were largely dominated by Anglicans and a variety of Reformed Protestant churches, particularly Presbyterians. In the South, Anglicans, while firmly rooted in colonial religious establishments in colonies such as Virginia, the Carolinas, and Georgia, were dealing with competition, not just from groups such as the Presbyterians, but by coteries of Huguenots (Reformed Calvinist exiles from France) and, as the century progressed, by a range of Baptists.

Even though Baptists agreed on the need for persons to profess their faith before baptism, the developing patterns of American Baptist identity revealed divergent theological and cultural outlooks. Subsequent generations of Baptist leaders in Rhode Island, other New England colonies, and the rest of the colonies outside of New England often differed extensively on matters of doctrine, theology, and practice. As the first chapter indicated, many Baptists were firmly rooted in Calvinist theology and held to many of the same creedal convictions as their Reformed Protestant colleagues. This group became known as Particular Baptists because they believed in Calvinist ideas of limited atonement (i.e., the belief that Christ died only for the elect). At the same time, several Baptists came under the sway of Arminian notions of free grace, believing that God's grace was available to all penitent sinners, a position that identified this group as General Baptists. In the seventeenth century, Baptist communities were primarily confined to Rhode Island, and scattered parts of New England and Pennsylvania. By the early 1700s, however, the Baptist presence in America would become increasingly ubiquitous throughout the colonies and these churches played a critical part in a larger conversation about the role of religion in the newly founded United States.

Besides the Friends, the group that dealt with the greatest prejudice in the English American colonies was the Catholics. Before the nineteenth century, British Catholic communities were small and often made up of persons who had been connected with the aristocracy in England (such as the various Lords Baltimore associated with the founding of the Maryland colony). Outside of Maryland, Catholic churches were confined to a few cities along the eastern seaboard, and the dominant perspective of these churches was one predicated on cooperation and conciliation with their Protestant neighbors. The question of why these English Catholics took the road of what came to be known as Americanization was in part predicated by the constant fear of the French for much of the seventeenth and eighteenth centuries. In the sixteenth and seventeenth centuries, France, the birthplace of John Calvin, was engaged in what amounted to a civil war over religion, pitting for decades Protestant Huguenots against Catholics in a contest for control of that nation's monarchy. The fact that the Catholics ultimately won control of the monarchy helped contribute to the long-standing political and military tensions that had existed between France and Great Britain. In addition to possessing colonies in what would become Canada (within present-day Quebec and Ontario), the French had outposts throughout the Great Lakes and were encroaching on British colonies from New England to Pennsylvania. Part of the eventual military conflict that erupted between Britain and France in the 1750s and 1760s not only had political ramifications in the American colonies, but theological ones, as Catholic France became associated with a false form of Christianity and with the devil himself.

NATIVE AMERICAN AND SLAVE MISSIONS

There are two extreme historical perspectives on Native American missions. One view sees missionaries providing the basic tenets of Christianity to a population eager to receive the good news of the gospel. Another perspective sees Native American missions as a tragic portrait of how economically greedy Europeans destroyed the idyllic pre-European civilizations of various Native American tribes. The truth lies somewhere in the middle. Clearly, mission efforts to Native Americans were often characterized not only by a high level of cultural paternalism, but at times a desire to connect the cause of religion with the national destiny of a particular political power (as was often the case with many examples of Spanish missionary efforts in the sixteenth and seventeenth centuries). Yet some seventeenth-century religious leaders showed a tremendous sensitivity to the cultures and traditions of Native Americans, perhaps no one more than Roger Williams.

Williams' first extended encounters with Native Americans occurred between 1631 and 1633 when he lived in the Plymouth Colony. Part of what made Williams unique from other Europeans is that he took time to learn the languages of various Native American tribes (he also published a guidebook on native languages for future colonists to New England). What also made Williams unique was his advocacy for Native American rights, especially denying that European settlers had a natural claim to Native American lands. For all of Williams' elusive life quest to achieve the theological realization of his ideals in a worldly church, he became a harsh critic of many missionary efforts toward indigenous Americans, even going as far at times to suggest that there was nothing inherently wrong with Native American culture or religious orientations. As he noted in a poetic verse,

> Boast not proud English, of thy birth & blood,
> Thy brother Indian is by birth a Good.
> Of one blood God made Him, and Thee, & All,
> As wise, as fair, as strong, as personall.[5]

Yet Williams' toleration and respect toward indigenous Americans that was shared by some first-generation New England Puritans increasingly gave way to a perspective in which Native Americans, even those who converted to Christianity, were viewed with suspicion. In 1675–1676 New England was engulfed in what was known as King Philip's War. In the context of this conflict, Mary Rowlandson, the wife of a Massachusetts minister, and her children were taken captive by Native Americans and held as prisoners for several months. After their release, Rowlandson wrote an account of her ordeal that helped pioneer the American literary genre of what became known as "captivity narratives." Beyond providing readers a clear account of her ordeal, Rowlandson gave classic expression to her faith, seeing the hand of God in her family's release and the triumph of good over evil.

> Now have I seen that scripture also fulfilled, Deut. 30:4-7, *If any of thine be driven out to the outmost parts of heaven, from thence will the Lord thy God gather thee, and from thence will he fetch thee. And the Lord thy God will put all these curses upon thine enemies, and on them which hate thee, which persecuted thee.* Thus hath the Lord brought me and mine out of that horrible pit, and hath set us in the midst of tender-hearted and

compassionate Christians. 'Tis the desire of my soul that we may walk worthy of the mercies received, and which we are receiving.[6]

Rowlandson's contrast between good and evil, Christian and heathen, would categorize many later accounts written by European settlers held captive by Native tribes during the eighteenth century. These captivity themes used by Rowlandson would be adopted in the early nineteenth century by women who wrote about their "escapes" from the evil clutches of an institution that came to symbolize for many Protestants the greatest danger to America's democratic heritage: the Roman Catholic Church.

In the first generation of colonial life in colonies such as Plymouth and Massachusetts Bay, settlers relied on Native American tribes for trade and protection. For all the ways that these New England settlers were driven by a desire to preserve the truth of their religious and cultural worldviews, they often showed a remarkable level of acceptance and friendship with indigenous Americans. However, as these colonies grew in size and economic stature, patterns began to shift, and in the case of Native Americans, initial motivations for understanding gave way to paternalism and abuse.

If records of evangelism toward indigenous Americans reflect a mixed legacy, the record of missions to the American colonies' growing number of African slaves was even more abysmal. Northern Africa was the site of one of the major centers of Christian expansion during the religion's first three centuries of existence, and some slaves came to America already as practicing Christians (as well as those who were Muslim). Yet the realities of African slavery created a historical context that still leaves scholars to speculate on how much Africa's religious heritage (including African Christianities) survived the slave-ship passage to America. The origins of American slavery can be traced to the Portuguese and Spanish explorations of the early sixteenth century. By the early seventeenth century, English explorers often captured Native Americans and frequently sold them as slaves (especially to Spanish colonies in the Caribbean islands), and in some cases used captured Indians as slaves in the colonies. Yet just as African slavery represented a profitable enterprise for the Spanish and Portuguese, the English adopted and expanded African slavery into North America. By 1700 African slavery was legal in every American colony, even in Quaker Pennsylvania.

Missionary efforts to African Americans were sporadic in the seventeenth century and little better in the early eighteenth century. When the English monarchy was restored in 1660 in the aftermath of England's civil war, King Charles II encouraged the promotion of evangelism among Native Americans and African slaves. The struggles of church planting in colonies such as Virginia, however, made these missions a low priority, and several clergy within various church traditions drew attention to the resistance to evangelism that often came from slave owners. Many colonial leaders viewed African slaves as no more than beasts and saw little practical use for converting them to Christianity (it was even debated whether or not Africans had souls).

Yet many slave owners feared the consequences of exposing their slaves to Christian teachings. One Anglican bishop summed up the situation well when he noted that some slave owners "it may be feared, have been averse to their slaves becoming Christians, because, after that, no Pretence will remain for not treating them like Men."[7] This remark suggests an early quandary for several colonial leaders and clergy. If one truly acknowledged the equality that comes through Christianity, does that fact on its own necessitate the abolition of slavery? By the early 1700s, several colonies passed statutes that said no to this question, affirming that Christian baptism did not alter a slave's status "as to his bondage and freedome." Cotton Mather was a typical clergy member of his era not only in the fact that he owned slaves, but that he tended to view Africans as being inferior. Yet he challenged the perspective that Africans lacked a soul, arguing for rigorous evangelization among the slaves. "One Table of the Ten Commandments, has this for the Sum of it; *Thou Shalt Love thy Neighbour as thy Self.* Man, Thy Nefor is thy Neighbour. . . . Yea, if thou dost grant *That God hath made of one Blood, all Nations of men*; he is thy Brother, too."[8] However, Mather stopped short of arguing for the emancipation of slaves, and struck a middle ground that would become the de facto rule for many American churches for the next century and a half— equality in Christ was spiritual, not social. Pauline texts from books such as Ephesians that spoke of slaves obeying masters could be used to preach slave passivity, yet as later developments in African American Christianity reveal, this tactic would ultimately fail. Significant inroads to converting African slaves would not become evident until the colonial era's Great Awakening.

THE MORAVIAN SPIRIT

Although associated with religious developments of the seventeenth century, many pietist leaders looked back through the history of Christianity for keys to understanding their heritage. Among these groups was the

Moravian Brethren, a tradition that traced its origins to the fifteenth-century reformer Jan Hus (who stressed reformation ideals of the centrality of Scripture and the fallibility of the papacy). Like the Quakers, the Moravians insisted on the necessity of a conversion experience that was both deeply personal and warranted some form of public testimony. While initially concentrated in Germany, by the 1730s Moravian communities were migrating outside of Europe with many settling in the American colonies, and eastern Pennsylvania became a major point of settlement for the group (forever immortalized in the name of one of their early communities and future center of the American steel industry, Bethlehem, Pennsylvania). While perceived by more dominant religious groups as part of the Anabaptist influx from Germany, Moravians were not Anabaptist, per se, and many of their converts and leaders were pulled from the ranks of German Lutheranism. Yet they mingled easily with many diverse religious groups who found a home in Pennsylvania, including movements to grow out of the Anabaptists, including the Mennonites, Church of the Brethren (or, as they were commonly called, "The Dunkers"), as well as the state's growing population of Lutherans.

For all the ways that Moravians were often associated with the Anabaptists, its leaders worked hard not to associate themselves with any particular church. Rather, the Moravians saw themselves as a movement to effect renewal within all churches. However, many early pietists, whether Moravians or not, were clearly reacting against what they perceived to be the stale religion of seventeenth-century Protestant confessionalism. The reaction that set in against this sort of creedal faith was in part led by German ministers such as Philipp Spener and many of his successors who planted the seeds of pietism within numerous Christian traditions. By the early eighteenth century, pietism was becoming part of the institutional fabric of German Protestantism. August Francke, a disciple of Spener's, was responsible for founding a pietist university in the German city Halle in 1694. The University of Halle would represent one of the primary institutions responsible for training clergy within Lutheranism and the German Reformed Church that had a widespread impact on the future of Western Christianity. One young Lutheran who received his formative education at Halle, Nicholas von Zinzendorf, eventually became the leader of the Moravian Brethren.

Coming from an upper-class background, Zinzendorf had been a pupil of Francke. While brought up as a Lutheran, Zinzendorf spent much of his adult life cultivating a relationship with Christians who shared his passion for the stress on personal conversion. By 1722 Zinzendorf was using his German estate at Hernnhut (meaning "the Lord's Protection") as a refuge for many Moravians. It was through this base that many Moravians extended their mission efforts, first to Europe and then ultimately to North America. It would be several years before the Moravians would constitute themselves as what we would call today a denomination. While functioning with a clear theological identity and mission, the Moravians viewed themselves as ecumenical in the sense that their mission was not so much to supplant other churches, but to aid in their renewal. By the 1730s Zinzendorf's Moravians were not only establishing settlements in Pennsylvania, but were also making inroads in the new colony in Georgia. In this context, the Moravians would influence the future history of one of American Christianity's most influential traditions: Methodism.

THE WESLEY BROTHERS AND POPULAR PIETISM

The mid-eighteenth-century rise of Methodism has been seen by some scholars as the culmination of the theological innovations in Protestantism that began with the sixteenth-century Reformation. Born in 1703 and 1708 respectively, John and Charles Wesley were children of Samuel and Susanna Wesley, two individuals from dissenting English Puritan backgrounds who nevertheless joined the Church of England as young adults.

The Wesley brothers drank deeply from the reservoirs of seventeenth-century Anglicanism that sought to incorporate Protestant theological practices with traditions coming out of the early church period. As a student at Oxford University, John Wesley was influenced by Thomas à Kempis' late medieval classic, *The Imitation of Christ*, and Jeremy Taylor's *Exercises in Holy Living and Holy Dying*. Taylor, a seventeenth-century Anglican bishop, emphasized the importance of the personal devotional life and the quest for the Christian to live a holy life in word and deed. Coming out of this Anglican tradition that stressed the interplay between faith and works, John Wesley was deeply drawn to the doctrine of sanctification. For many first-generation Protestant reformers, the chief importance of conversion was the Pauline stress on justification by faith, bespeaking how the grace of God saved persons from the power of sin. However, many sixteenth-century reformers, such as Calvin, also stressed the doctrine of sanctification that emphasized the ways God's love worked within individuals to make them holy in thought, word, and deed. While subsequent developments in Calvinism often submerged this doctrine, the Anglican Church by the end of the seventeenth century gave increasing voice to the doctrine of sanctification, as well as to the growing movement of Arminianism within that tradition.

By the early eighteenth century, the theological perspective of Arminianism was not only used as a term to categorize persons who denied the doctrine of predestination, but was used to describe people who rejected the doctrine of limited atonement (that Christ died only for the elect). Instead, Arminianism, as it developed in several churches, affirmed a belief in universal atonement, that is, that all people in theory had the choice of accepting or rejecting God's gift of divine grace. Throughout the seventeenth century, a variety of Protestant churches that came out of Reformed traditions simultaneously condemned Arminian theology and affirmed an array of confessional statements strengthening their fidelity to Calvinism. At the same time, Arminian themes of free grace found supporters both within fledgling Baptist communities and among many Anglicans—including the Wesley brothers. While both brothers studied at Oxford in the 1720s and 1730s, they employed a wide range of resources in their pursuit of a holy life. By the end of the 1720s, a small group of Oxford students congregated around John in their desire to promote personal piety in a fellowship that become known as "the Holy Club." Embodying the precepts of ancient and contemporary spiritual resources, as well as providing spiritual comfort to prisoners in the city of Oxford, the Wesley brothers not only sought to nurture personal piety, but fueled the group's desire to cultivate actions that promoted Christian holiness, or sanctification—the belief that Christians could in some way approximate a sinless life.

In 1735, at a critical junction in their ministries, the Wesley brothers volunteered for mission service in the Georgia colony under the sponsorship of the SPG and SPCK. Charles served as an assistant to the colony's governor, James Oglethorpe, and John, while initially hoping to become a chaplain to the colony's Native Americans, became the priest to the Anglican parish in Savannah, Georgia. Accompanying both brothers on their journey to America was a group of German Moravians. Amid their voyage to America, the ship was overtaken by a violent storm. In the grip of the terror felt by John Wesley and his companions, he remembered the calm of the Moravians, their ability to reflect an assurance of their own salvation even amid the possibility that their ship might founder.

Both brothers had disastrous experiences in Georgia. While Charles soon returned to England, John labored for two and a half years, serving as parish priest in Savannah and finding it impossible to engage in any effective outreach to Georgia's Native Americans (in addition to a failed romance). Faced with an uncertain future, John Wesley returned to England in early 1738 musing in his journal that he came to America to convert the heathen, "but who will convert me?" Disillusioned by his experience in the Georgia colony, John Wesley sought counsel from a German Moravian community in London that stressed to him the need to wait upon the Lord for the gift of what was often referred to as "the New Birth." At that time, the Moravians had established numerous religious societies in many English cities to encourage the piety that could bring about conversion.

In May 1738 John Wesley attended one such society meeting at Aldersgate Street in London where, as he later recorded in his journal, after hearing someone read from Martin Luther's commentary on the epistle to the Romans, he felt his heart "strangely warmed." In the aftermath of this so-called "Aldersgate experience," Wesley found new purpose as a religious leader and soon began the process of forming the Methodists, one of the most significant religious movements of the modern era. During the course of his long life and career, John Wesley spent only about two and a half years in America. Yet the influence of his failed Georgia ministry helped set the stage for a popular revolution within evangelical Protestantism. One hundred years after he left Georgia that legacy had dramatically altered the American religious landscape. While Wesley and many other emerging evangelicals of their generation would honor the theological traditions of their birth, they increasingly came to believe that one of the central marks of faith was not whether one was an Anglican, Presbyterian, Congregational, or Baptist, but whether one could testify to some sort of experience of "New Birth" that came to the sinner not by the intellect but from the heart. This belief in the doctrine of assurance, in which one could give direct testimony that they had been saved by God's grace, set the context for a coming revolution in American theology

For many Puritans and other Calvinist groups during the colonial era, the idea of one having a personal conversion experience was central to a person's understanding of faith. Yet part of the Calvinist paradox was often that persons could never be sure if they were one of the elect. As Puritans in the lineage of the Mathers called for conversion, these New England Calvinists did so believing that fidelity to Scripture, especially ascent to the promises of Scripture, as well as showing marks of a Christian life (such as service to one's community) were clear signs of one's salvation. The flip side was that understanding conversion in the Puritan context often took years of personal discernment on the part of the penitent sinner. Pietism gave expression to a wider evangelical stress on conversion as a distinctive experience or event. As the eighteenth century progressed, what became increasingly important to many Christians in America was not simply if one was a Presbyterian or Anglican, a Calvinist or Arminian, but if one could identify the moment in one's life when one experienced the New Birth manifested by God's forgiveness of sins.

COTTON MATHER'S AMERICA

Throughout his life, Cotton Mather earned a reputation not only as a major theologian, but also as someone who, despite his defense of the New England heritage, had a theological outlook that extended beyond his inherited tradition. Toward the end of his life, Mather could see God's hand at work in a number of different Christian traditions. At one point, he participated in the ordination of a Baptist clergyman and even could see the hand of God at work in groups such as the Quakers. At times in his ministry, he shared his grandparents' optimism about the holy experiment of New England, emphasizing in his sermons and writings that New England represented the staging area for Christ's second coming. Yet Mather increasingly saw the hand of God in a number of different churches, including the Anglican, Baptist, Quaker, and even Catholic churches. Although Mather could still speak about the privileged position of New England churches, his view of that status was increasingly a consequence of affirming ideals of Christian unity, as opposed to simply identifying theological truth with one tradition. "A Charitable Consideration of nothing but PIETY in admitting to Evangelical Privileges, is a Glory that the Churches of *New -England*, would lay claim unto. . . . Every *particular Church* is to consider itself as part of the *Catholic*, and owes a Duty to the *whole Visible Church* of our Lord in the World."[9] Few of Mather's Congregational colleagues in New England could accept such a "liberal" ecumenical view.

By the same token, in his final years Mather developed an evolving understanding of the end times. While he still fervently believed in the return of Christ, his language grew less allegorical, more literal, and, in some ways, more wrathful. The end was not about building a city of gold-plated streets, but how God's judgment, indeed wrath, would be felt.

> It may NOW, most awfully be said, His wrath will QUICKLY flame!—
> we NOW know of nothing that remains to go before the Fulfillment of
> that Word, *The Son of Man shall come in the Clouds of Heaven*: At which

there comes a tremendous CONFLAGRATION on a World horribly *Ripened* for it: and as *Thoughtless* of it![10]

Mather's life reflects upon some of the historical and theological tensions that would be felt in Christianity's future in America. On one hand, Mather emphasized an optimistic millennial vision of hope in the future characterized by a concern for the personal and collective welfare of individuals, where diverse Christian communities could find ways to unite under the banner of a shared spirit. On the other hand, however, Mather saw the end times as apocalyptic judgment, whereby true believers would be saved and others must face the consequences for their lack of saving faith.

For all the ways that Mather struggled with the nature of his New England legacy and God's relationship to the American colonies, he constantly hoped that the movement of which he was a part would lead to a wider convergence of evangelical forces, in which the Congregational churches of New England represented one vital component. At the very moment of his death in 1728, this larger evangelical "revolution" was being felt in other colonies. In New Jersey, a Dutch Reformed minister, Theodorus Frelinghuysen, was conducting a series of revivals that were stirring new passion for a heart-felt pietism that led to several conversions. A decade later, these pietistic themes would be recast by a wide range of theological voices and became integral to the wider colonial landscape. Included in this new theological synthesis would be a new generation of ministers, such as William and Gilbert Tennent, George Whitefield, and New England's Jonathan Edwards.

Mather did not live to see the fulfillment of the millennial vision for which he hoped and prayed. However, the heirs of many of his theological perspectives can be seen in a wide-ranging legacy of American Christianity. Echoes of Mather's hopes can be heard not only through the heirs of American Calvinism, but other traditions of American Christianity that have struggled with concerns over personal conversion, social holiness, and ecumenical witness. As the American colonies moved through the eighteenth century, the many facets of Cotton Mather's life would help create their own unique alchemy in terms of shaping the legacy of American Christianity. A major aspect of that legacy is how some of the persistent theological themes coming from the Puritan ethos increasingly spoke to many Americans outside of New England.

≪ 3 ≫

THE GREAT AWAKENING

As we have seen, the realities of colonial religious establishment left many of its leaders constantly on guard against religious dissenters and seeking ways to stoke the fires of faith within their own traditions. Cotton Mather's growing frustration with the low state of colonial moral scruples was a reflection that by the early 1700s, the American colonies were a far cry from achieving any sort of vision of a New Jerusalem envisioned by the Puritans. Religious adherent rates were generally low throughout the colonies and, with exception of the Congregational churches in New England, there was no one segment of Christianity that was numerically dominant. By the mid-1700s that landscape became even more complicated in the aftermath of an event that historians commonly label the "Great Awakening."

Between approximately the late 1730s through the late 1740s, the eastern seaboard and parts of New England experienced a series of events that signaled the beginning of an evangelical revivalist tradition that has been a constant feature of American religious history ever since. These revivals eventually would carry throughout most of the colonies and served as a template for a new chapter in American Christianity that would begin soon after the American Revolution. The series of events and major personalities that made up this initial awakening reflected the interplay among a variety of theological currents that had been simmering in Europe for almost a century. Even as the initial wave of revivalism died down by the end of the 1740s in New England and the Mid-Atlantic colonies, it had a prescient effect on the southern colonies that extended to the eve of the American Revolution. For all the ways that the Great Awakening would transform the religious character of America, ultimately the legacy of this tradition would be embodied through the careers of two individuals: George Whitefield and Jonathan Edwards.

NEW ENGLAND STIRRINGS

Over a period of several months in 1734 and 1735, many clergy and laity within parts of Massachusetts became aware of an unusually large outbreak of religious enthusiasm. This outpouring of religion was centered in the western Massachusetts town of Northampton. On one hand, Northampton was far removed from the religious and cultural hub of the Massachusetts colony that revolved around Boston. Yet Northampton possessed one of the colony's most stalwart Congregational churches that had been for decades pastored by one of New England's most venerable pastors, Solomon Stoddard (1643–1729). Stoddard served as pastor of the Northampton church for close to fifty years and earned the nickname as "the Pope of the Connecticut Valley." Like other clergy in New England's congregational establishments, Stoddard was a staunch Calvinist, yet consistent with the Half-Way Covenant from the 1660s, he supported measures in his congregation to lessen membership barriers, especially allowing those who could not profess a conversion experience to receive communion. Beginning in the 1680s, Stoddard noted periodic occurrences where his church experienced outbreaks of religious enthusiasm. However, it would be Stoddard's grandson, Jonathan Edwards, who would be the full beneficiary of this revivalist legacy.

Born in 1703, Edwards studied at Yale College in New Haven, Connecticut while still in his teens. After spending time at Yale as a tutor and a brief pastorate at a New York City Presbyterian church, he returned to Northampton to serve as his grandfather's assistant minister and then, upon his grandfather's death, the congregation's minister. Although Edwards shared many aspects of Solomon Stoddard's theology, eventually he went against his grandfather's accommodation to allow congregants who did not have a conversion experience to receive communion (and Edwards' decision to rescind his grandfather's more lenient practice led to his dismissal from Northampton in 1749). Yet he shared his grandfather's desire to promote religious piety, and when a fresh season of revivalism broke out in 1734 and 1735, Edwards' congregation was not only at the center of this outbreak, but Edwards himself became its primary chronicler.

In his published account of these revivals, Edwards made clear that prior to the outbreak of these renewals, Northampton and other neighboring communities were beset with a temper of irreligion and a lack of public morals—especially among the youth. ". . . they were many of them very much addicted to night walking, and frequenting the tavern, and lewd practices, wherein some by their example exceedingly corrupted others." However, the death of a youth in the community opened the hearts of some young people to be convinced of their sinfulness and, aided by Edwards' preaching, to repent of their sin. For Edwards, these conversions were a clear sign of new vitality for New England's Congregational churches. As more persons converted to Christ, more people would find their way to church. As he reflected on the state of affairs in Northampton at the height of these revivals, "the town seemed to be full of the presence of God: it never was so full of love, nor so full of joy. . . . Our public assemblies were then beautiful; the congregation was alive in God's service, every one earnestly intent on the public worship, every hearer eager to drink in the words of the minister as they came from his mouth."[1]

These stirrings of religious revival marked what some historians have seen as the origins of the Great Awakening (or what is sometimes called the First Great Awakening). In American religious history, the concept of "great awakening" represented an often used and, to a degree, contested historical concept that refers to periods of religious outbreak often accompanied by numerical growth and, in some cases, major religious realignments. Most of the contemporaries caught up in the Great Awakening, and in subsequent religious revivals in American history saw these events in providential terms, believing that God was doing something new and unique among a particular group of people. However, even amid seventeenth-century concerns that religious commitment was waning in New England and other colonies, there were periodic reports of religious outbreaks that for a time appeared to stir the religious affections of many. The difference between what Edwards was describing in the 1730s and earlier outbreaks of seventeenth-century religious enthusiasm was not so much the events themselves, but the way that these new patterns of revivalism became institutionalized within a number of American churches and denominations.

Part of the significance of what occurred in Northampton is that the tempers of revivalism that flared for a time were embraced by a network of influential ministers in North America *and* Great Britain—even as Edwards and other New England ministers worried that the religious fervor of the mid-1730s would die out. In fact, Edwards' chronicle of the religious stirrings in Northampton was only the beginning of a far-reaching movement of transatlantic revivalism that struck New England and the rest of the American colonies in full force by the end of the decade. The principal figure behind these religious awakenings would come from an Anglican clergyman who, before his conversion, had dreamed of a career in the theater.

GEORGE WHITEFIELD: AN "AMERICAN" ORIGINAL

It is not an overstatement to suggest that every revivalist in American history owes a debt to George Whitefield. In microcosm, his life accentuates three critical themes that would became touchtone features for later traditions of Protestant evangelicalism: (1) a heightened emphasis on personal conversion; (2) the centrality of charismatic revivalists (specifically, compelling oratorical skills); and ultimately (3) the undercutting of established patterns of church-denominational authority. This final theme became a major aspect of the success of a number of evangelical Protestant movements that would emerge in America in the aftermath of the American Revolution.

Whitefield was born in Gloucester, England, in 1714 to a family of innkeepers. As a youth, he dreamed of a career as an actor, a pursuit that was considered uncouth by his family (and by respectable society at large). While never a particularly diligent student, he secured a place at Oxford University in 1732. It was there that he became a friend and, for a time, a close associate of the future founder of the Methodist movement, John Wesley.

John Wesley's theology was deeply influenced by various movements of continental pietism, especially coming from the Moravians. Not only did this tradition place a tremendous emphasis on a belief in the New Birth that comes to the believer, but the ways that conversion led the convicted sinner on the road to holiness (sanctification). For centuries, the doctrine of sanctification played a major role in the thought of many Catholic Church leaders, who emphasized that Christian conversion was not just an event. It represented a commitment to a life of holiness manifested in service to the church and to the world. While many sixteenth-century Protestant reformers tended to put this doctrine in a subservient position to that of justification (although parts of the Calvinist legacy emphasized the importance of the holy life), eighteenth-century Anglicans such as John Wesley saw the pursuit of Christian holiness as central to the process of conversion. Although Whitefield shared this passion to work for holiness in his life, there was one important difference between his theology and the Wesley brothers. Both John and Charles were Arminian in orientation, emphasizing the availability of grace to all sinners. Throughout his life, Whitefield was a proponent of Calvinism (although as he later confessed, he never actually read Calvin). While this difference eventually caused a rift between himself and Wesley's Methodist followers, Whitefield left a permanent imprint on the development of this fledgling movement. Although ordained an Anglican priest in 1736, Whitefield never served a parish. Instead, he set out on a career as an itinerant revivalist who helped establish an important pattern of transatlantic revivalism between North America and Great Britain that would impact the development of American Christianity well into the nineteenth century.

Like the Wesley brothers, Whitefield also originally came to Georgia under the auspices of the Society for the Propagation of the Gospel and did not stay long in America. However, unlike the Wesleys, who never returned to America, Whitefield made six more trips to the colonies. Over the next thirty years, his revivals helped cement his legacy as one of the most innovative preachers in America history.

One of Whitefield's major contributions to the history of revivalism was his success as a "field preacher." In the 1730s English clergy were expected only to conduct services within the consecrated grounds of their own parish churches. By 1739 Whitefield was conducting several services in open fields around the coal fields and town squares of Bristol, England, and his success had tremendous impact on his friend, John Wesley, who soon afterward embraced the practice for his new Methodist movement. Both Wesley and Whitefield were at the center of a popular religious revolution in Great Britain and North America. Although previous generations of revivalists emphasized beliefs in pietism and the accompanying doctrine of assurance whereby the penitent sinner knows in his or her heart that they have been saved by God's grace, these men spearheaded movements that largely drew audiences from outside the religious establishments of their respective contexts. Their evangelicalism helped spearhead a movement of popular Christianity that represents one of the enduring legacies of evangelicalism in the West.

Whitefield's second visit to America became a popular culture phenomenon. Between mid-1739 and late 1740, Whitefield conducted a series of revivals that ran from the Carolina colonies up through New England. While signs of a religious awakening had been brewing for years, as is reflected in Edwards' earlier Northampton chronicle, Whitefield's impact was central to the permanent importance of the awakening to the future of American Christianity. Part of Whitefield's appeal was his appearance. Still in his twenties, he struck many by his youthfulness (to the point that some described him as angelic). Further, he was cross-eyed, which from the perspective of those who heard him preach probably enhanced his charisma (one can only speculate about how his appearance would be received in a modern media age). As a preacher, Whitefield put his earlier desire to be an actor to good use. He learned how to use his voice in ways that could project to large crowds and, most especially, he preached without notes, introducing a tradition of extemporaneous preaching that served as a cornerstone for many future American revivalists. More than anything else, however, Whitefield was a master communicator. In juxtaposition to the learned sermons written out by most American clergy who were Congregational, Anglican, or Presbyterian (and even within some Baptist pulpits), Whitefield had the gift of making complex theological questions understandable and accessible to a typical colonist of that era (who largely lacked understanding of the fine points of theology). While his critics saw him as self-serving and as the promoter of vulgar methods of revivalism, Whitefield's success was ensured in large part because of his ability to create an organizational structure that supported his campaigns financially and practically.

Whitefield has been credited as one of the first modern revivalists to use publicity to promote his campaigns. Weeks before he would arrive in a city, town, or village, bulletins would be posted announcing the revivalist's impending visit, and the growing number of colonial newspapers eagerly followed his exploits. Additionally, Whitefield built a judicious network of supporters that further scandalized him because he freely crossed denominational boundaries. His base of support came from segments coming out of Congregationalist, Presbyterian, Baptist, and even some Anglican groups, setting the pattern that would characterize future generations of interdenominational revivalists (the most notable of these during the twentieth century was Billy Graham). In the process of his first and subsequent tours of the colonies, he succeeded in garnering the patronage of many prominent colonists, including, most notably, Benjamin Franklin. While Franklin tended to be a religious skeptic (although he believed in the importance of religion to the general welfare of society), he developed a friendship with the revivalist, in addition to providing favorable appraisals of Whitefield in his Philadelphia newspaper (including one famous account by Franklin who, upon hearing Whitefield preach, felt compelled to give all of his money to the revivalist, in support of an orphanage that Whitefield sponsored).

While all of these factors were important to Whitefield's success, such support could not have been sustained unless he produced results. In many respects, Whitefield's reception within the cities and towns he preached was not unlike the adulation experienced by media personalities of later eras. One account of a Whitefield revival in October 1740 reflects upon the excitement that his personage generated.

> When I saw Mr. Whitfield [*sic*] come upon the Scaffold he Lookt almost angelical; a young, Slim, slender, youth before some thousands of people with a bold undaunted Countenance, and my hearing how God was with him every where as he came along it Solemnized my mind, and put me into a trembling fear before he began to preach; for he looked as if he was Cloathed with authority from the Great God. . . . And my hearing him preach, gave me a heart wound; By Gods blessing: my old Foundation was broken up, and I saw that my righteousness would not save me.[2]

Although some accounts of the total number of persons attending his revivals probably at times were exaggerated, it is likely that thousands heard Whitefield preach on any given occasion. By some estimates, he preached over 30,000 times in North America and Great Britain in the course of his lifetime. Many who heard Whitefield reacted with an outpouring of emotion, and some listeners even fainted. This emotionalism, what contemporaries referred to as "religious enthusiasm," became another cornerstone for many later traditions of American revivalism.

The other dimension that probably contributed to Whitefield's success was the fact that opposition to his means (and to his message) was as intense as those who praised him. The divisions were especially evident in Congregational New England, where many clergy were split on the desirability of using the methods embraced by Whitefield. Those who rejected the tenets of revivalism and remained steadfast to the doctrinal standards laid out by earlier Calvinist confessions, are usually referred to as "Old Lights." Other clergy, often dubbed by historians as "New Lights," saw much to be admired in Whitefield's tactics and message, and committed themselves to promoting revivals in their own churches and the larger community. The major colonial figure to provide a sustained theology for this "New Light" posture was Jonathan Edwards, whose writings on religion and revivalism contributed to his legacy as one of America's most significant theologians.

THE LEGACIES OF EDWARDS AND WHITEFIELD

Historical and theological interpretations of Edwards' work are in abundance. However, one aspect of Edwards' life that is sometimes overlooked is that he spent the majority of his career as a working minister, and the full impact of his writing was not felt until after his death in 1758. After Edwards was forced to leave Northampton, he moved farther into the western wilderness to West Stockbridge, Massachusetts, where he served as the minister to a Native American settlement. In 1757 he became president of the fledgling College of New Jersey (which later became Princeton University). Sharing Cotton Mather's positive view toward science and medicine, Edwards agreed to have his family inoculated against small pox. While the primitive vaccine worked for his family, Edwards developed a fatal reaction to the inoculation and died.

On the surface, there was much to Edwards' life that stood in continuity with an earlier heritage of New England Puritanism. His unpopular support of a closed communion, whereby the church would only admit to the Lord's Supper those who could profess conversion harkened back to the first generation of New England Puritan settlers. Yet Edwards' outlook reflected a distinctive blend of his Calvinist heritage with an emerging awareness of Enlightenment philosophical traditions that influenced a range of eighteenth-century evangelicals in Europe and North America. Edwards had a deep (though not uncritical) fondness for the British philosopher John Locke, who, while affirming the primacy for rational thought, made room for the place of divine revelation in his epistemology. Edwards is probably best known for his sermon with the hard-to-forget title, "Sinners in the Hands of an Angry God." The sermon hit home on two central themes that had long been part of Reformed Calvinism: God's sovereignty and sinful humanity's dependence upon God's grace for salvation. Yet Edwards' enduring legacy in Western theology was the way he wrestled with the question of how humans came to a saving knowledge of God. While affirming the doctrine of divine sovereignty and the doctrine of predestination (as a consequence of believing in God's sovereign power over creation), Edwards affirmed and celebrated the way that humans came to an awareness of God through their senses, or what many evangelists of that era called "affections." In many of his works, Edwards affirmed the beauty of nature and the ways that the natural world revealed and gave hints to the wonders of God. In his 1746 book *A Treatise Concerning Religious Affections*, Edwards made the following observations.

> Hence therefore the religion of heaven, consisting chiefly in holy love
> and joy, consists very much in affection: and therefore undoubtedly,
> true religion consists very much in affection. The way to learn the true
> nature of anything, is to go where that thing is to be found in its purity
> and perfection. If we would know the nature of true gold, we must view
> it, not in the ore, but when it is refined. If we would learn what true
> religion is, we must go where there is true religion, and nothing but true
> religion, and in its highest perfection, without any defect or mixture.[3]

Edwards became well known within many theological circles in North
America and Europe during his lifetime (even though he spent the bulk of
his life in New England). In the years after his death, his theology would
be the standard by which later generations of American Reformed theologians measured their work. Edwards' perspectives on the "affections"
would not only resonate within a revivalist tradition of Calvinism, but
would become a mainstay for numerous traditions of evangelical theology in years to come (John Wesley, while a staunch anti-Calvinist, nevertheless recommended that his followers read Edwards' account of the
Northampton awakening).

However, Edwards' future reputation may not have been as enduring
had it not been for the success of revivalists such as George Whitefield.
Whitefield lacked the philosophical and theological sophistication of
Edwards, and while the two figures did meet during Whitefield's 1740 tour
of New England, they never developed a close relationship. Yet Whitefield
powerfully demonstrated that religious truth was not simply an ascent
to doctrine, but needed to contain a lived experience of conversion.
Although Whitefield identified himself as part of the growing network
of Calvinists who promoted revivalism, his ability to connect preaching
to the conversion of sinners would ultimately emerge as the dominant
theme in American revivalism, as opposed to whether persons identified
themselves with a particular church tradition. By the same token, in the
course of his subsequent visits to America over the next three decades,
Whitefield left a legacy not only as a spellbinding preacher, but as someone
who, despite being an English citizen, was quintessentially American.

SPREADING REVIVALISM

In the wake of Whitefield's colonial success, a number of revivalists
appeared in the colonies during the 1740s and 1750s and achieved success in a style and fashion similar to Whitefield. David Brainerd, a young
Congregational minister engaged in a brief but well-publicized career that

led him to missionary work among Native Americans until he died of tuberculosis in 1747 (and his posthumous fame owes a great deal to Jonathan Edwards, who published Brainerd's diary). Although Brainerd's success in that ministry met with limited success, the popular image of Brainerd's life, marked by frequent travels, personal sacrifice, and death at an early age, became a sort of prototype for future generations of evangelical revivalists who would emerge in America in the aftermath of the American Revolution.

Although most of the attention on the Great Awakening focuses on New England, the movement also had a major impact throughout the other American colonies. Henry Muhlenberg, a German Lutheran minister and disciple of the pietist teachings of August Francke, immigrated to the Pennsylvania colony in the 1740s and became the chief figure in the establishment of the first Lutheran denomination in the United States. Muhlenberg practiced many of the same principles as other pietists, seeing the fruits of his ministry in terms of the New Birth, that is, those who came to have a relationship with Christ as opposed to with the formal church or denomination to which a person belonged.

Two Presbyterian ministers, Gilbert Tennent in Pennsylvania and New Jersey and Samuel Davies who preached in Virginia, became strong advocates of revivalism in the Mid-Atlantic and South, respectively. Tennent's background reflects upon how predominant evangelical currents in Europe found their way to North America throughout the eighteenth century. Tennent's father, William, had been a licensed Presbyterian minister in Scotland before moving to Ireland. After the family's emigration to Pennsylvania in 1718, William joined the Presbyterian Church and, while committed to Calvinist doctrines of predestination, emphasized pietist themes that Christianity was not just about embracing intellectual doctrines, but about the ways the experience of conversion led one to live righteously. In 1726 William Tennent established what is considered the first Presbyterian theological seminary in America, named simply "the Log College." For the next twenty years until William's death in 1746, this cabin in Warminster, Pennsylvania, trained a small number of persons in a Calvinist theology much similar in spirit to the theological themes of Jonathan Edwards. After 1746 many students at the Log College ended up transferring to the recently established College of New Jersey (Princeton).

Outside of George Whitefield, William's son, Gilbert Tennent, might very well have been the most well-known revivalist of the Great Awakening era. After his graduation from Yale College, Tennent was highly influenced by the pietism of the Dutch Reformed preacher, Theodorus Frelinghuysen, who led several revivals in New Jersey during the 1720s and 1730s. From his base at the First Presbyterian Church in New Brunswick, New Jersey, Tennent earned the reputation as a passionate preacher and a staunch defender of revivalism. Yet Tennent resurrected earlier themes in American Puritanism that echoed the dissenting tradition of Anne Hutchinson a hundred years earlier. His 1739 sermon "the Dangers of an Unconverted Ministry" sparked a major controversy within the Presbyterian Church over the place of revivalism. While Whitefield largely took an irenic posture toward his critics, Tennent harshly condemned many colonial clergy for lacking the substance of a converted life, viewing them as hypocrites.

> The old Pharisees were very proud and conceity; they loved the upper-most Seats in the Synagogues, and to be called Rabbi, Rabbi; they were masterly and positive in their Assertions, as if forsooth Knowledge must die with them; they look'd upon others that differed from them, and the common People with an Air of Disdain; and especially any who had a Respect for JESUS and his Doctrine, and dislik'd them; they judged such accursed.[4]

By the 1740s Presbyterians were facing a series of divisions over revivalism similar to the divisions occurring within New England Congregationalism. Presbyterians were split between revivalists such as Tennent (called "New Sides") and those who adhered to a strict interpretation of seventeenth-century orthodox Calvinism (called "Old Sides"). This division would serve as a major point of contention within the Presbyterian Church for decades to come, and became a focal point for numerous debates about the place of revivalism within that tradition that would extend into the nineteenth and twentieth centuries.

Davies was a Presbyterian minister who spent a good part of his career pastoring congregations in Virginia. An effective itinerant preacher, Davies became an early voice challenging the legal prerogative of the colony's Anglican establishment. In 1759 Davies succeeded Jonathan Edwards as President of the College of New Jersey, however, like Edwards, his tenure was short-lived because Davies died in 1761. Davies was not only an important figure in the spreading of a revivalist ethos in the South, but he also helped shape a distinctive American religious legacy that welded together Christian theology and American political destiny.

By the time of Davies' death, many of the earlier currents of revivalism had waned, but the ethos of revivalism had hardly ended. Of all the regions of the colonies affected by the Great Awakening, the South was the last to experience the theological fallout. In southern colonies such as Maryland, Virginia, North Carolina, and Georgia, Anglican establishments amid all their weaknesses were firmly entrenched within important centers of commerce, especially in settlements along the Atlantic coast. By the same token, events in these colonies in the 1750s and 1760s provided early signs of religious changes that would become more apparent by the early nineteenth century.

In many ways, one of the most overlooked developments associated with the Great Awakening was how it helped spread the influence of the Baptists. Prior to 1750, Baptist congregations were mostly concentrated in New England, New Jersey, and Pennsylvania, with isolated congregations sparsely scattered throughout the remaining colonies. By 1775, however, Baptists were making significant inroads in many colonies, especially in Anglican Virginia, where several Baptist communities sprouted in rural sections in the western and central parts of that colony. Reflecting the theological divisions that had impacted Baptist churches in the seventeenth century, colonial Baptists divided between General Baptists who held more to an Arminian theology of free grace and Particular Baptists who adhered to a more rigid Calvinist theology of predestination. What united all Baptists, however, was not only the belief in the authority of the local congregation, but the precedent of "soul liberty," expressing the ethos of seventeenth-century pioneers such as Roger Williams that faith in Christ was a personal matter that could not come about through outside coercion, including by civil authorities. By the end of the American War of Independence, Virginia Baptists would serve as one of the key groups that helped pass a state law in 1786 disestablishing religion and setting the stage for a larger national debate on religious liberty.

CONSEQUENCES

Scholars have long speculated about what factors helped fan the fires of revivalism associated with the Great Awakening of the 1730s and 1740s. The ethos of New England Reformed theology had always carried a strong current of millennial speculation, and certainly the heightened sense that the world might end soon could have driven colonists to embrace Christianity more readily. Some point to a rise of apocalyptic speculation just prior to the Great Awakening, in part stoked by the occurrence of natural disasters including a major earthquake in Massachusetts in 1727, that heightened speculation about the end times. These events helped foster a general belief among some people that they stood on the brink of the last days of history before the second coming of Christ. However, other scholars point to the sheer difficulty of life in the colonies, economically and politically, especially noting the precarious political situation with France that left many in New England ill at ease about the prospect of French encroachment within their colonies (a factor that had religious as well as political consequences, as France was associated as propagating the false teachings of the Catholic Church). While circumstances were different in the South, many southern colonies, such as Virginia, were characterized by a growing division between a wealthy gentry class along the eastern seaboard, with increasingly poorer communities in the colony's interior. As we will see in subsequent chapters, part of the fundamental message of the Great Awakening was that all persons, regardless of their class status, stood under divine judgment and could receive the converting grace of Christ.

Although there were certainly numerous political, cultural, and theological factors at work, another point to remember is that the so-called Great Awakening was part of a larger transatlantic movement of revivalism, bringing to the forefront a number of evangelical figures in Great Britain and North America who preached comparable messages of New Birth and salvation through faith in Jesus Christ. Although figures such as John Wesley and Jonathan Edwards shared different theological orientations on matters of predestination, the linking point for the two men (as well as other revivalists) was the shared emphasis on heart religion.

However, it is important to remember that by and large the leaders of these transatlantic awakenings were not seeking to overturn doctrine or consciously working to undermine tradition. Unlike later movements of American revivalists, Great Awakening leaders believed strongly in the theological tenets of their traditions, and often went to great lengths to defend the integrity of their particular church's doctrines. At the same time, they continued to lift up the question that would be vital for future revivalists in American history, mainly, who has the right to speak on behalf of God?

Gilbert Tennent, like many colonial clergy, proposed the prickly question that had been posed by Anne Hutchinson one hundred years earlier: can one assume that just because a person is ordained that they are truly converted? This question created a difficult dilemma for many colonial ministers and their congregations who struggled not simply with following doctrinal teachings, but sought to define the exact meaning of conversion. For many Calvinists, to speak of conversion was not necessarily to speak of Christian experience in a subjective idiom, but to give public ascent to the truths of scripture as taught through a particular confession or catechism. Many New Light and New Side revivalists certainly would have affirmed the importance of tradition in their teaching and preaching, but they also challenged believers to take their faith a step further by speaking of the New Birth that comes through faith in Jesus. Without intending to do so, Whitefield and his colleagues set the stage where conversion was not measured so much by one's allegiance to a particular church or confession of faith, but an individual's fidelity to one's God.

This theme led to another lasting consequence of the Great Awakening—the role of the charismatic revivalist in American religion. Since the time of the early church, the history of Christianity has been filled with charismatic preachers and teachers. Yet Whitefield and those who followed his path used revivalism as a means that intentionally and unintentionally undercut the authority of colonial church establishments. While Anglican establishments were relatively stable in the South, and Congregational establishments even stronger in the North, the impact on both regions of the country was similar. Mainly, these waves of revivals signaled the eventual appearance of emerging evangelical movements that often built their followings at the expense of colonial establishments. Many colonial critics of revivalism recognized this and increasingly leveled attacks against preachers like Whitefield that were predicated not only on their theology, but their lack of respect for traditional colonial religious boundaries.

By far the most well-known colonial critic of revivalism was the Congregationalist minister Charles Chauncy (1705–1787). For all the ways that Chauncy can be viewed as fighting a losing battle against the torrent of colonial revivalism, his perspectives would live on in later iterations of American theology, in particular the rise of both New England Unitarianism and theological liberalism. Chauncy was one of the most influential New England ministers of his time and had a family pedigree to back it up. His great grandfather had served as the second president of Harvard College, and from the time of his ordination in 1727 until his death in 1787, he served as the pastor of the First Congregational Church in Boston.

Chauncy has been frequently dubbed by historians as part of the New England Old Light faction that opposed revivalism. Although that is part of his claim to fame, Chauncy's theology also reflected another division that would become more pronounced in New England Calvinism later in the eighteenth century. As we have seen, many American clergy in the early eighteenth century were eager to engage new scientific and philosophical points of view. Likewise, European and North American evangelicals such as Wesley and Edwards sought ways to incorporate aspects of the Enlightenment rationalism of persons such as John Locke. However, while Edwards and Wesley engaged figures such as Locke as a way to show the compatibility between experience and reason, Chauncy argued that when it came to religion, reason trumped the experiential.

There is no doubt that Chauncy found the emotionalism of revivalism socially distasteful and theologically uncouth. He was appalled by what he saw as the unnatural behavior of those affected by the revivalist ethos and commented on the "strange Effects upon the Body such as a swooning away . . . Shriekings and Screamings; convulsion-like Tremblings and Agitations, Strugglings and Tumblings, which in some Instances have been attended with Indecencies I shan't mention." Yet these external manifestations of revivalism were only half the problem. For Chauncy, these passions went against the heart of true religion's purpose to cultivate the mind. Revivalists "place their Religion so much in the Heat and Fervour of their Passions, that they too much neglect their Reason and Judgment."[5] While it would be easy to identify persons like Chauncy as being on the wrong end of history, their challenges to the perceived excesses of revivalism have also been a constant within American religious history. What is often forgotten about figures such as Chauncy is that he was far from a dogmatic Old Light Calvinist, but represented the stirrings of a movement within New England Congregationalism that began to question many of the suppositions of Calvinism's views on human depravity.

When Chauncy first published his reflections on revivalism in the early 1740s, he stood within Massachusetts' Calvinist heritage. Over the next several decades, however, Chauncy's thought diverged in a number of directions. By the 1760s he not only became identified with Arminianism (believing that the Calvinist doctrine of limited atonement was a fallacy), but increasingly with the heterodox belief that Christ's death offered universal salvation, that is, the belief that all of humankind would be saved. As he noted in the last years of his life, "In as much as the Saviour of the world has atoned for the sins of every creature, and God earnestly desires the salvation of all, it is inconceivable that any should perish everlastingly. His infinite power, wisdom and goodness forbid such a dishonourable supposition."[6] Chauncy had come to embrace a theological position that had been an undercurrent within Christian theology within previous periods of church history (in particular, associated with sixteenth-century Protestant developments called Socinianism). He helped to ignite an ongoing controversy within New England Congregationalism that would ultimately lead to a separation between Congregational churches that favored traditional Calvinist teachings on human depravity and limited atonement, with those churches that took a more positive Enlightenment-orientated view toward human goodness. These developments became associated with the early nineteenth-century rise of Unitarianism and, ultimately, theological liberalism.

Beyond how critiques of the Great Awakening offended rationalists such as Chauncy and a number of Old Light/Old Side Calvinists, the revivals largely failed in their efforts to evangelize to Native Americans. Throughout the eighteenth century, numerous churches sponsored mission efforts to Native Americans throughout the colonies (such as John Wesley's ill-fated Georgia mission). Some, such as the Quaker leader John Woolman, followed the earlier example of Roger Williams by seeking to engage Native American languages and cultures. However, others continued a long-standing paternalism toward potential converts. Even David Brainerd, an individual who became a model for future generations of Christian missionaries to Native Americans, was largely unsuccessful in his evangelistic efforts toward native peoples. There is no doubt that many Protestant missionaries in this period approached their work with altruistic intensions. Yet what often emerged were missionaries who showed great insensitivity to the cultural worldviews of the persons they were trying to convert. Brainerd frequently noted in his journal that the Indians with whom he worked were often "brutishly stupid and ignorant of divine things."[7] It is easy to castigate the prejudices of Brainerd, yet, as was discussed in the previous chapter, Brainerd reflected the dominant worldview of the majority of Anglo-Americans toward Native Americans and African slaves.

Outwardly, the Great Awakening changed little for the growing numbers of African slaves. Slave owners from both the North and South continued to express a dominant worldview that slavery could serve as a benign form of bringing Christianity to Africans, a rationale supported by both Jonathan Edwards (a slave owner) and George Whitefield. With the exception of smaller religious groups such as the Quakers (although some wealthy Quakers did own slaves), slavery was often sanctioned on religious grounds for the ways it could provide means to facilitate African American exposure to Christianity. Although revivalists such as Whitefield advocated for the humane treatment of slaves and encour-aged the education of African slaves, he embodied the perspective of most revivalists that spiritual equality did not equal social equality. Also, the Great Awakening did little to transform the reluctance of many slave own-ers to offer religious instruction to their slaves.

And yet, the egalitarianism of the Great Awakening did plant seeds. While American Great Awakening revivalists preached a Calvinist mes-sage of divine election, they stressed that wealth, status, or political power was no guarantee of gaining entry into heaven. One of the foundational messages of conversion was that God did not judge people on the basis of whether they were rich or poor, slave or free. The appeal of this message planted seeds both among the small numbers of free blacks living in the North and among several slaves living in the South. By the end of the eighteenth century, the theological themes of the Great Awakening would increasingly find expression among African Americans, setting the stage for the rise of distinctive traditions of African American Christianity in the nineteenth century.

The colonial awakenings exposed patterns that would lead to an explo-sion of popular religion that later swept over North America. However, there were still theological parameters that the majority of American revivalists wouldn't cross. For starters, all of the major North American revivalists of the Great Awakening were Calvinists who most directly influenced developments within the Congregational, Presbyterian, and Baptist churches of the Mid-Atlantic and New England colonies. They were also mostly ordained clergymen who by and large operated within the auspices of specific churches and denominations. Yet their emphasis on the believer's responsibility in hearing and receiving the message of Christ would become a major theme in the subsequent history of reviv-alism. Even as these debates raged in America, new developments in Great Britain were already writing an important chapter for the future of American Christianity.

As public enthusiasm over the Great Awakening started to die down by the end of 1740s (or later depending on the particular region of the colony one resided), on the surface, colonial religious establishments were alive and well. In the decades leading up to the American War of Independence, the Congregational establishment in New England main-tained a near hegemonic dominance in Massachusetts, New Hampshire, and Connecticut. In 1775 Massachusetts had approximately two hundred fifty Congregational churches; the second largest group, the Baptists, had fifty-one. In the Mid-Atlantic and the South, despite divisions over revivalism, Presbyterians continued to secure their position as one of the major denominations, even in colonies where they were officially a religious minority. Although the majority of Anglicans resisted the message of New Birth preached by the likes of Whitefield, Anglican Church establishments in colonies such as Virginia remained secure (although, as noted, their major strength was in the eastern part of the colony).

Yet the various colonial awakenings that extended in some areas into the 1760s were laying the seeds for seismic changes. Baptist growth in the Virginia colony rapidly rose in the decade preceding American independence, and they were soon joined by a tiny number of Methodists. Unlike revivalists such as Whitefield, Wesley and the Methodists carried an increasingly strong antislavery theology that would prove beneficial to the movement's appeal by the end of the eighteenth century among many African Americans in both the North and the South.

Methodism would not constitute itself as a formal denomination until 1784. However, by 1770 small numbers of Methodists were present in the colonies, at that point mostly residing in coastal cities along the eastern seaboard. While barely a presence on the colonial religious radar, they were a movement that already was laying a foundation for the transformation of American Christianity. Central to the ethos of Methodism was not only the Arminian-based pietism of the Wesleys, but also that much of the movement's power emerged from the innovative leadership of laity.

THE GREAT AWAKENING AND LAY RELIGION

Overwhelmingly, the major shapers of the colonial Great Awakening were Calvinist clergy who came out of the historical Protestant churches associated with the sixteenth-century reformations. By the same token, the ethos of the Great Awakening left a profound imprint upon future iterations of popular theology, especially among laity. Thousands of miles away from the American colonies, John Wesley was building the foundations of a religious movement that would eventually have transformative consequences upon American religious history. While lacking the same charismatic appeal of Whitefield, Wesley was far more concerned with building a religious movement that could transcend the charisma of individual preachers. Whitefield was content to leave matters of grassroots organization to area clergy once he had passed through a community. Wesley, on the other hand, was concerned with building a movement that could provide the basis of a permanent religious organization. Embracing models of organization that he learned from the Moravians and continuing to emphasize small groups as the primary means to promote individual acts of holiness, the Methodists became by 1750 a noticeable feature of English life.

While Wesley saw the Methodists as a renewal movement within the Church of England, many people attracted to Methodism were nominally connected to Anglicanism and were drawn to the movement from a variety of dissenting Protestant traditions or were not actively involved in any church. Wesley set a pattern for future Methodist leadership in America, by stressing an unquestioned authority over every aspect of the movement (including instituting means to hold in check many Methodists who desired to formally break from the Church of England). At the same time, one of the reasons why Methodism spread first in Great Britain and later on in North America was that the movement centered on lay leadership. Methodists were divided up into an array of groupings in which Wesley took the Moravian idea of a religious society (as opposed to a church or congregation to underscore that he was not trying to separate formally from the Church of England), dividing it up into groupings of classes (approximately twelve members) and bands (approximately six members). Each level of organization was overseen by lay leadership. Most scandalous is that Wesley by the mid-1740s actively promoted lay preaching as a means to carry forth the Methodist theological message of free grace and works of charity and mercy among the poor. The embrace of lay preaching went beyond the parameters of lay enthusiasm that were tolerated by clergy establishments in North America during the Great Awakening. As he grew older, Wesley went even further in his encouragement of lay preaching when by the 1770s he allowed certain women to become Methodist lay preachers.

These developments in England foreshadowed the changes that would sweep American society in the early nineteenth century. Yet colonial events in America during the Great Awakening gave glimpses of larger changes that would affect women in American religion. Sixteenth-century Protestantism introduced a new religious vocation for women: the minister's wife. Since the time of Martin Luther and his wife Katie in the era of the Reformation, women married to ministers had acted in traditional roles as "helpmeet" to their spouses. Many spouses of prominent eighteenth-century clergy, such as Sarah Edwards, the wife of Jonathan Edwards, carried on a tradition of "pious women" who not only supported their husband's work by caring for their families (and in Sarah Edwards' case, this meant taking care of eleven children), but also exhibiting a model of faith that other women should emulate.

Earlier Puritan stress on the doctrine of original sin tended to see women as being more vile and sinful than men (epitomized by the fact that it was Eve who tempted Adam in the Garden of Eden). Later in the eighteenth century, however, this perspective on the natural wickedness of women was being reshaped by an emerging worldview that women were more naturally predisposed to faith than men. This view would have a major impact on developing understandings of gender by the early nineteenth century, but even in the eighteenth century it allowed certain women to assume roles of religious leadership.

The example of Sarah Osborn is indicative of the larger role that women would come to play in the larger history of American Christianity. A native of Newport, Rhode Island, Osborn professed a conversion experience largely attributed to the influence of the revival preaching of Whitefield and Tennent. As a young woman, Osborn periodically had to support her family through teaching, but through her pastor's encouragement she began a women's religious society that she held in her home for several decades. Within this context, Osborn encouraged her audiences, including both white and African American women, to use their gifts to serve God and society. Although some opposed her work, Osborn frequently used an argument that would be picked up by many women in the nineteenth century: if men wouldn't do the work of ministry, then who would?

> I am rather as a Servant that Has a Great work assigned him . . . and However ardently He may wish it was in Superior Hands, or that His Master would at Least Help Him, yet if He declines He dares not tell Him, well if you don't do it your self it shall go undone for I will not, but rather trys to do what He can till God in his providence point out a way for it to be better done.[8]

Osborn's work to create a female religious society reflected a theme that would increasingly become part of an American secular and religious ideology in the nineteenth century: the role of women as the moral caretakers of society. While seventeenth-century Puritanism had carried forth on a centuries-old worldview that women were inherently sinful, the end of the eighteenth century began to witness a shift away from this view. Increasingly, women were seen as natural caretakers by virtue of their feminine traits of nurturing that came through the roles of being wives and mothers. This gender ideology reflected what some scholars have called "the cult of true womanhood," a belief that women's nature was more predisposed to nurturing goodness, including religiosity. In its own way, this conservative ideology would be used effectively by a cross section of American women well into the nineteenth and twentieth centuries as a means for women to find public voice and lead to the creation of innovative religious movements. While still in embryonic form, the Great Awakening helped stir the seeds that would not only lead eventually to a larger public role for women, but would help lay the foundation for one of the dominant motifs for understanding religion in American history: its tradition of volunteerism.

ON THE EVE OF SECULAR AND RELIGIOUS REVOLUTIONS

By 1770 political events in the colonies might have circumvented the attention of many colonists from matters of religion as the relationship between Great Britain and its American colonies rapidly deteriorated. Yet as the colonies moved closer to an open rebellion against British colonial authority, the religious themes that had been unearthed during the Great Awakening era bubbled to the surface. The greatest of the era's revivalists, George Whitefield, in the midst of his final visit to North America, died in Newburyport, Massachusetts, in September 1770 (and in accordance with his dying wishes was buried beneath the altar of Old South Presbyterian Church in that city). Phillis Wheatley, a free African American woman living in Boston, wrote a poem memorizing Whitefield's impact, echoing Whitefield's insistence that Christ died not just for whites, but for African Americans.

> Take him, ye *Africans*, he longs for you,
> *Impartial Saviour* is his title due:
> Wash'd in the fountain of his redeeming blood,
> You shall be sons, kings, and Priests of God.[9]

Wheatley's poetic voice would be used to memorize numerous personages during the era of American independence from Great Britain (including George Washington). Yet her words here are prophetic, not only in terms of their impact upon African Americans, but as a weathervane for America's religious future.

From the time of Whitefield's death in September 1770 to the death of America's first president, George Washington, in December 1799, the American colonies fought a war for independence and established (although at times precariously) a union of these former colonies into a federal government. In this same time, the earlier seeds of Great Awakening revivalism were already in the process of creating a series of popular religious outpourings that forever changed the American religious landscape. Even though the majority of the leaders of the Great Awakening were clergy within networks of established denominations, the overwhelming tenor of their theology stressed that the most important quality of the Christian life was whether one had a personal relationship with Jesus Christ. This relationship with God was available (potentially) to all people regardless of race, class, or gender. By the end of the eighteenth century, this theme would become critical to a new generation of popular revivalists who, in a short amount of time, would radically alter the religious demographics of the United States.

This spirit of revivalism would foreshadow future developments in American Protestant theology that eventually witnessed the decline (but not the disappearance) of an older Calvinist theology. Yet Calvinism would continue to influence the theological contours of American theology, even as the tradition relived earlier struggles regarding how far one could incorporate revivalist themes within a Calvinist theological framework. In the years following the deaths of Jonathan Edwards, Gilbert Tennent, and Samuel Davies, Calvinists within the New Light/New Sides tradition had to wrestle with the problem posed by revivalists such as Edwards and Whitefield: how does one reconcile belief in traditional Reformed doctrines (such as God's sovereignty and predestination) with the necessity of New Birth conversion? This tension synthesized one of the major intellectual traditions in American Protestant history, what many historians refer to as "New Divinity" theology. In the shadow of Jonathan Edwards, this legacy raised significant questions not only concerning the relationship of God's grace upon the individual, but in the 1760s and 1770s, how this grace bestowed a special blessing upon Americans within its thirteen colonies. The stage was set for distinctive strands of this Calvinist theology to take on new meaning in the face of changing political circumstances, particularly themes related to America being at the center of God's millennial kingdom.

Even as many aspects of the Great Awakening were rooted within distinctive heritages of Calvinism, the subsequent history of American revivalism would largely be written by movements outside of formal Calvinist networks. Yet American Calvinism would cast a powerful historical legacy upon America, not primarily because of what the tradition said about divine sovereignty or predestination. Rather, a major component of Calvinism's legacy in American Christianity rests with how it helped support arguments for a new model of republican government.

<< 4 >>

The Revolutionary War and Religious Disestablishment

The relationship between religion and the American Revolution remains hotly debated. Throughout American history, a variety of religious and political leaders have appealed to the widely employed claim that America was founded as a Christian nation. However, most aspects of American independence revolved around secular issues, and it is clear that the two major documents produced by this political struggle, the Declaration of Independence and the U.S. Constitution, say nothing about American roots in Christianity. By the same token, it is evident that a full understanding of the American Revolution cannot be grasped without examining the ways religion played into the development of a distinctive American ideology. This ideology grew in significance in the years preceding American independence as the thirteen American colonies, echoing earlier Puritan themes, saw their religious past as key to understanding America's political future. Developments during the French and Indian War from 1756 to 1763 and the American Revolution from 1775 to 1781 reveal how earlier Puritan traditions contributed to distinctive changes in the way that Americans understood the nation's providential mission. These changes can be assessed by examining two critical themes: first, the way that earlier understandings of personal morality became connected to an American sense of a common civic duty (or virtue), and, second, the explicit connection between the perceived moral uniqueness of America with an underlying millennialism that put the thirteen American colonies at the center of God's unique purpose for the world.

The birth of America's national government, modeled upon a balance between federal and state rights, was a politically secular event, largely shaped by men whose connection to traditional forms of Christianity was often marginal. Yet there is no doubt when one looks at the American system of national government that led to the ratifying of the U.S. Constitution in 1788 and the Bill of Rights in 1791, that religious themes represented a significant concern for the nation's national leaders. The culmination of their efforts was realized in the ratification of the First Amendment to the U.S. Constitution. In effect, a handful of words in that amendment transformed the place of religion in America and set the stage for how American Christianity would develop in ways that probably would have both pleased, and displeased, America's "founding fathers."

GOD'S COVENANT REDEFINED

Popular understandings of the concept of "liberty" often look to groups such as the Pilgrims and Puritans to underscore an American tradition of religious freedom. Clearly, however, these groups of staunch Calvinists were not concerned with promoting liberty as the freedom to do what one pleased. True freedom was to follow God's word in such a way that affirmed one's duties to both God and to the community. When one looks at the relationship of this earlier Christian tradition to the political developments leading up to and following the American War of Independence, one can see how aspects of this earlier tradition were transformed into a unique national ideology. By the end of the eighteenth century, this ideology spoke of America in terms of what has been called republicanism. Broadly understood, republicanism was more than a model of democratic government; it was a philosophy that spoke to the responsibilities that American citizens had to their government and to one another. Regardless of the colony of one's birth, Americans were a people who held a special obligation to practice virtuous living in all aspects of their collective lives.

Jonathan Edwards died at the very moment when mounting political circumstances created the buildup that would lead to American independence from England. However, his theology served as a template for many of his followers to explore how the age-old Puritan understanding of covenant related to the changing political circumstances of the late eighteenth century. As a theologian and church leader, Jonathan Edwards was hardly an expositor of any sort of republican political ideology. His writings largely carry an apolitical tone, and in large measure he held to a perspective that took a dim view of various Enlightenment models of political democracy. Yet Edwards struck upon themes that dovetailed with nascent arguments touting American national uniqueness and a sense of divine providence whereby God was working in unique ways among the English-speaking European settlers of the New World. Not long before he died, Edwards wrote one of his enduring classics, *The Nature of True Virtue*. Picking up on theological issues he wrestled with in his earlier writings, Edwards struggled to bridge the gap between his Calvinist understanding of God's sovereignty and his revivalist view of how conversion awakened the believer to a true understanding of God's purposes for humanity. For Edwards, conversion was nothing short of loving the world with all of one's being. "Nothing is of the nature of true virtue . . . in which God is not the *first* and the *last*." He asserted that "true virtue most essentially consists in benevolence to Being in general."[1] From Edwards' perspective, this benevolence was only possible when the believer centered his or her thoughts entirely on God's love for creation.

While Edwards saw virtue chiefly connected to individual conversion, many of his theological heirs expanded upon his theology, applying his understanding of virtue to broader questions of societal reform. Among the most prominent theologians to articulate this perspective was Samuel Hopkins (1721–1803). Hopkins' name figures prominently in a Calvinist theological legacy of "the New Divinity" that had a major impact on American theology after the Revolutionary War. Spending the majority of his career in two pastorates in Housatonic, Massachusetts, and Newport, Rhode Island (where Sarah Osborn was one of his parishioners), Hopkins, like many theological apologists, saw part of his mission as having to clarify the thoughts of his mentor, Jonathan Edwards.

Hopkins characterized individual acts of Christian charity as "disinterested benevolence," whereby all of one's life was devoted to serve God's creation without regard to the self. Expanding on Edwards' notion of virtue, Hopkins saw Christian conversion not just as a means for the individual to serve God, but to contribute toward the betterment of society. "Love to God, and love to our fellow-creatures, is of the same nature and kind," he wrote in 1793. "It consists most essentially in benevolence or good will to being in general. . . . Disinterested benevolence is pleased with the public interest,—the greatest good and happiness of the whole."[2] Hopkins fully articulated his perspective on virtue after the American War of Independence. However, his view captured what would become one of the dominant motifs for understanding Christianity's role in the context of the American Revolution. For Calvinists such as Hopkins, the concept of liberty was not about being left alone to do as one pleased or, from a religious perspective, to be guided by no doctrinal standards (theologically what was commonly called antinomianism). For Christians to believe in liberty was to live virtuous lives whereby all people were committed to serving the greater public good.

Hopkins and other Calvinists of his era also believed that the efforts of Protestant churches to evangelize America were indispensable to the welfare of the nation. While many American evangelicals by the early nineteenth century rejected Hopkins' Calvinism, they embraced his theological orientation that saw Christian virtue leading churches and the nation closer to the kingdom of God. One of the key consequences of this theological orientation upon nineteenth-century American history would be the rise of religious volunteerism.

Part of what one sees in the progression from Edwards to Hopkins is that virtue became one of the significant qualities of individual liberty. For the Puritans, liberty was primarily a means to keep the faithful from misbehaving, making sure that the baser elements of human nature didn't destroy the civil and religious order that the Puritans envisioned. By the time of American independence, however, liberty was seen in a far more positive light as an expression of God-given attributes of righteous living. Liberty was freedom of conscience, but more than that it was the ability of a person to stand firm against religious *and* political tyranny.

This evolving view of virtue tied into another important component resuscitated from America's Puritan past: the idea of a divine covenant between God and His chosen people. The earlier belief that the Puritans were a chosen people in covenant with God had been under siege in the American colonies for a long time. The Great Awakening of the mid-eighteenth century, in which personal conversion was often placed above the idea of God's covenant with a "chosen" community, appeared to signal a further diminishing of the Puritan ethos. However, the vestiges of covenant theology still remained part of New Light/New Divinity theologies (reflected partly by Jonathan Edwards' decision in his Northampton church to rescind the open communion policy of his grandfather, in favor of a view that the Lord's Supper was meant only for the truly converted). In the decades leading up to the Revolutionary War, New England ministers were reemphasizing the historical covenant between God and New England. However, while early Puritans hoped their religion would reform the churches of Europe, mid-eighteenth-century clergy sharply differentiated their American-born faith from that of Europe. These ministers "presumed the New England tradition to be both Christian and free, and their covenant terminology fused together church, state, and society into an undifferentiated godly community set apart from the British forces of sin and tyranny."[3]

A key factor in the ways this covenant theology carried over into a distinctive type of American ideology is how these theological themes played off an earlier tradition of millennialism. As we have seen, generations of Puritans believed fervently in the idea that their holy experiments were helping pave the way for the return of Christ (and eighteenth-century clergy such as Edwards continued to emphasize this theme in many of their sermons). In the seventeenth century, New England postmillennialism was characterized by the belief that Christ would return after they had created a truly righteous society on earth. In many respects, part of the reason why New England Calvinists (as well as Christians in other parts of the American colonies) gravitated to these millennial themes was the pattern of constant warfare that engulfed Europe during that time period (often waged on religious grounds). By the time of Jonathan Edwards, some of this millennial fervor had dissipated but not disappeared. However, as the colonies became involved in a drawn-out military conflict, first with the French and then the British, it corroborated the sentiment of many colonial religious leaders that God's covenant was not simply about isolated Christian communities in the colonies. Rather, it was a covenant that extended to all godly people in America who strove to stave off the decadence of European nations who were not only politically corrupt, but in some fashion, ungodly.

In many respects, the theology that contrasted the virtues of the New World with the vices and corruptions of the Old World was a continuation of a distinctive tradition of New England theology from the seventeenth century. By the mid-eighteenth century, however, larger political events helped connect this theological heritage to an emerging national ideology.

AMERICAN POLITICAL MILLENNIALISM

The French and Indian War (or the Seven Years' War as it was known in Europe) between 1756 and 1763 was part of a larger European war between England and France over which power would exert primary political and military control over North America. French control was primarily in the Canadian province of Quebec, yet French encroachments upon New England and the desire to establish permanent settlements in the Upper Great Lakes region were common. The French and Indian War was a decisive event that saw many themes derived from New England Calvinism crafted into a form of national religion whereby the thirteen colonies were seen as united in their stance against European tyranny, and was epitomized by the military threats posed to English North America by Catholic France. One of the most significant figures to help make that connection was the Virginian Presbyterian leader Samuel Davies. During the French and Indian War, Davies preached numerous sermons that drew a sharp contrast between the righteousness of the Americans and the "Superstition and idolatries" of French Catholicism. "Our religion, our liberty, our property, our lives, and everything sacred to us are in danger," he asserted.[4]

However, another component of Davies' orations is that he turned up the heat on earlier American views on millennialism. The conflict with France was not simply a military event; it was a struggle between the cosmic forces of good and evil, God and Satan. Davies saw the war as "the grand decisive conflict between the lamb and the beast."[5] Numerous clergy equated France with the evil Babylon depicted in Revelation, and ultimately the French defeat was celebrated in pulpits as a sign of Babylon's fall. Many colonial ministers not only characterized the conflict as a struggle between good and evil, but, using biblical texts from Revelation, equated France with the antichrist. However, by the end of 1760s, Great Britain had replaced France in this dubious role.

In the decade leading up to the American War of Independence, the intermingling themes of divine covenant, virtue, liberty, and America's millennial destiny formed a potent combination. As the colonies found themselves politically and economically impacted by the foreign policies enacted by the British Parliament, colonial clergy spoke more fervently of American uniqueness, merging both secular and religious language. In the aftermath of the French and Indian War, accounts reached American ears about the low morals of British army "regulars" (soldiers in the British army) who served in America during the conflict with France. "Profane swearing seems to be the naturalized language of the regulars," noted a chaplain with a Massachusetts regiment, who also disdained the British penchant for gambling and other assorted vices that helped shape a growing perception of both political and moral corruption among the British.[6] As British political and economic pressure increased on the colonies after 1765 (in particular, after the British government unilaterally imposed higher taxes upon the colonies), the connection of England with the demonic became more pronounced.

On the eve of the American Revolution, numerous clergy raised concerns about the political and moral tyranny of the British, characterizing the difference between the colonists and the British through a distinctive series of jeremiads. "Liberty . . . is the native right of the *Americans*," proclaimed the Boston Baptist minister John Allen in 1772, "it is the blood-bought treasure of their Forefathers; and they have the same essential right to their *native laws* as they have to the air they breath in, or to the light of the morning when the sun rises: And therefore they who oppress the *Americans* must be great enemies to the law of nature, as they who would . . . , if it were in their power, vail the light of the sun from the universe."[7] At the time of the signing of the Declaration of Independence in 1776, Samuel Sherwood made the logical link between the theme of God's covenant with America to the idea that Americans (or at least those who embraced the teachings of Christianity) were a chosen people. Sherwood reminded his congregation of their sacred past while warning them of the dangers of falling away from the true faith of the past amid the turmoil of war. Yet Sherwood concluded by noting that God's blessing was truly upon the American colonies. "Liberty has been planted here; and the more it is attacked, the more it grows and flourishes. The time is coming and hastening on, when Babylon the great shall fail to rise no more; when all wicked tyrants and oppressors shall be destroyed forever."[8] Sherwood's proclamation emphasized Americans as a chosen people who were not only part of an unfolding providential plan, but also as a people who were striving to stave off the evil tyrants of British Babylon.

This emerging concept of America as a divinely anointed land served as the basis for what scholars would later term "civil religion." At its most basic, civil religion refers to the fusing of sacred and secular symbols in ways that create an ideology that, in quasi-religious fashion, speaks to a shared national mission or purpose. By the time of the American Revolution, America's destiny was intricately linked to a belief not only that God had somehow anointed the new nation, but that this righteous people carried a chosen status that set them apart from all other nations on earth. The idea of civil religion has played a defining role in understanding Christianity's role in American history, for better and for worse.

A unique dimension of this emerging tradition of American civil religion can be seen in the ways that the legacy of George Whitefield was recast after his death. Like other revivalists of the Great Awakening era, Whitefield was often apolitical, and his position on many social issues tended to be on the conservative side. For example, while his evangelicalism had a major impact on the subsequent development of African American Christianity, unlike John Wesley, Whitefield never advocated for the abolition of slavery. Yet Whitefield always displayed a profound sense of identity with the colonies and developed close friendships with several American political leaders, including Ben Franklin. Whitefield's death in 1770 during his final revival tour in North America was greeted by a shared sense of loss among citizens in all of the colonies. Unintentionally, he became a symbol of American liberty.

Perhaps the most revealing (and macabre) acts related to Whitefield's identity with the American political cause occurred not long after the Revolutionary War began. In 1775 a revolutionary chaplain and a group of officers (including one of the colonies then most promising military leaders, Benedict Arnold) entered Whitefield's tomb in Newburyport, viewed his corpse and actually handled parts of the dead man's clothing. This "cult of Whitefield's body" continued among many "pilgrims" for many years, extending beyond the end of the war.[9] Whitefield came from a Protestant tradition that scorned faith in relics, which was often associated with Catholicism. For many Americans, faith in relics was also associated with the discarded theological legacy of Old Europe. However, these pilgrimages to Whitefield's crypt reflected that in death Whitefield had become in the colonies more than a great man. He had become an American patriot.

It is important to note that America's religious heritage was one contributor to an emerging national ideology that saw America as a land of chosen people. In the aftermath of the Revolutionary War, numerous artists depicted the nation's founding fathers in ways that mixed religious symbols with an Enlightenment-based appreciation for the classics of antiquity (especially reflected in a growing American fascination with Greco-Roman art, literature, and architecture). However, the shadow of New England Calvinism that marked the founding of the Massachusetts Bay Colony in 1630 had served as a foundation for a shared theme that would be reinterpreted and misinterpreted for generations to come. Mainly, the greatness of America was in a shared moral foundation that not only separated the new nation from Europe, but by implication marked its religion as the purest that the world had ever seen. The difficulty that the new nation would face at the end of the American Revolution, however, was what type of Christianity would serve as the model for the new nation to follow.

THE CHURCHES AT WAR

In the course of the war, numerous clergy volunteered for military service, and in many ways association with the Patriot cause did largely break out along denominational lines. While the vast majority of Congregational, Presbyterian, and Baptist leaders supported American independence, there were always exceptions, as some of these denominations included clergy who supported the Tories. In the aftermath of the war, several clergy and laity sympathetic to the British cause either emigrated to Great Britain or to Britain's colonies in Canada. One of the most unusual developments during the war years were the small number of independent Baptist congregations that developed in the South that were made up and led by free African Americans. In a period in the late 1770s when many southern colonies were under firm British control, seaboard towns in South Carolina and Georgia experienced a rise in their free black populations. With the surrender of the British army at Yorktown, Virginia, in 1781 and the Treaty of Paris in 1783 that formally ended hostilities, many of these African Americans fled the South for northern cities, or in many cases, a life in Canada. One large contingent of African Americans under the leadership of a former slave, David George, led his congregation from Silver Bluff, South Carolina, to Halifax, Nova Scotia—establishing what many believe to be the first independent African church in Canada. Ultimately, disillusioned by the racism he experienced in Halifax, George moved to Sierra Leone, Africa, spending the rest of his life as a missionary in that country.

Not surprisingly, the one American church most prone to support the British was the Church of England, and it was this tradition that suffered the greatest losses during the war. Numerous Anglican clergy returned to England or immigrated to Canada, while those clergy who attempted to remain in America struggled to hold congregations together. In several former colonies, state legislatures no longer recognized the establishment privileges of the Church of England, and several churches found themselves without pastoral leadership due to the shortage of clergy (and the absence of any Anglican bishops in America to ordain them). At the end of the war the Anglican Church found itself struggling for survival as it sought not only to reaffirm its ecclesiastical connections to the Church of England, but also to reconstitute itself in ways that aligned its clergy to the realities of the new American republic.

Perhaps the groups that suffered the most persecution during the American Revolution were the colonies' various Anabaptists and other churches that advocated pacifism. In particular, Quakers were often singled out for harsh treatment for their refusal to fight (although some Quakers did serve in the Continental Army). While these groups often faced harassments from local communities, many state legislatures during the war passed measures of toleration aimed to protect the rights of religious minorities such as the Quakers.

In parts of New England and upstate New York, some authorities became aware of a tiny group of religious dissenters who were often dubbed "Shaking Quakers" for the ways they engaged in excessive shaking in their worship. While this sect would never be very large, this group, the United Society of Believers in Christ's Second Appearing, commonly known as the Shakers, would be at the vanguard of the innovative new religious movements that would hit the new nation in full force in the decades following American independence.

Another group adversely affected by the war was the Methodists. Although a small group, Methodist societies had been making inroads within several colonies on the eastern seaboard such as Delaware and Virginia. During the war, the backlash against Methodism was not only because of its association in many colonists' minds with the Church of England (although few Anglican parishes in the colonies welcomed the Methodists), but the fact that Methodism's leader, John Wesley, was a staunch Tory. Just prior to the start of the American Revolution, Wesley published "A Calm Address to Our American Colonies," a letter that both praised the British monarchy and castigated the colonists for their faith in the misguided principles of American republicanism, associated with figures such as Thomas Paine. For example, Wesley had no use for the colonists' complaint of "taxation without representation," believing that this so-called God-given right was a farcical notion (and for support, Wesley pointed out the fact that the same Americans who rallied to the cause of political liberty did not extend that privilege to the slaves they owned). By 1777 most British-born Methodists who had been sent to America to help organize the fledgling Methodists returned to England out of concern for safety. The only one to remain was forced to go into hiding for several years and would not be able to reestablish any contact with Wesley until after the war. This man, Francis Asbury, would transform the Methodists into one of the most dominant religious movements of the nineteenth century.

Although Anglicans and Methodists were hit the hardest during the war, other American churches suffered precipitous membership declines, especially in the Mid-Atlantic and the South, which was where the bulk of the Revolutionary War battles were fought after 1778. Although several religious leaders in the 1770s and 1780s relied on various forms of the jeremiad stressing Americans as a chosen people, the war years saw a precipitous decline in church attendance throughout the colonies—in fact, one could argue that the war years represented the historical nadir of American religious participation. By some estimates, less than 20 percent of the American colonial population was actively involved in their respective faith communions.[10] Obtaining precise data on colonial religion requires some guesswork. However, if one looks at American religion on the basis of actual congregations during the period around 1775–1776, then one receives an indication of some of the dilemmas that would be faced by national leaders concerning religion's role in the war's aftermath.

In 1775, based solely on the number of congregations, the Congregational churches appeared to have a near-hegemonic dominance in the Americas with approximately 730 churches (the next largest group, the Presbyterians had 450 churches). However, Congregational influence outside of New England was almost nonexistent. By contrast, Presbyterian Churches, a tiny minority in New England, had a number of churches throughout the Mid-Atlantic and into the South. Although Anglicans were strongest in the South, with the majority of their strength in Virginia, they also had a number of "dissenting" churches in Connecticut and Massachusetts—the stronghold of Congregationalism. The group that enjoyed the most immediate impact from the Great Awakening, the Baptists, was increasingly prevalent throughout the geographical spread of the colonies, and during the war their numbers grew, especially in rural areas of the South. Meanwhile, a small variety of different sects ranging from Quakers, Mennonites, and Moravians also represented a presence, although sporadic, within many colonial areas.

With the exception of the Congregationalists in New England, no colonial region possessed an overwhelming majority favoring one particular church over another. Presbyterians constituted a majority in places such as New Jersey, but also competed with other Reformed Calvinist denominations. Anglicans hung on to a majority in Virginia, but their establishment status was challenged by a large number of Presbyterians. Throughout most of the colonies, the Baptists emerged as a strong movement of churches that repeatedly echoed Roger Williams' century-old lament about the need to remove government from offering any form of legal support for any one religious group.

During the war, colonial legislatures passed what amounted to oaths of allegiance to the new United States, and one's religious preference was often seen as central to that loyalty. By the formal end of the war in 1783, many state assemblies and legislatures had passed laws that attempted to support religious diversity by passing guarantees of religious liberty while also being careful to define government support of those religious groups deemed acceptable as properly "Christian." Many colonies (later states) passed laws generally favoring traditions historically associated with Protestantism. Yet some colonies, such as Delaware, went further by passing a 1776 statute asserting that state office holders had to take an oath professing "faith in God the Father, and in Jesus Christ His only Son, and in the Holy Ghost," and "acknowledge the holy scriptures of the Old and New Testament to be given by divine inspiration."[11]

As the war drew to a close, many national leaders saw the question of religious preferences to be a matter best left to individual states. In 1781 the first attempt to craft a model for the new American government resulted in the Articles of Confederation. The Articles did not directly address the issue of religious establishment, leaving the question of religious establishment in the hands of the state. Yet it became clear to some religious and secular leaders that answering the question of which forms of Christianity to recognize and which to leave out was increasingly difficult. It was one thing to do as Delaware did during the war to insist that public officials affirm common standards of Christian doctrine, but how did this translate in terms of which churches were worthy of state support? In the minds of several leaders, this left a choice between Presbyterians, Congregationalists, or (perhaps) Anglicans. Yet immediately questions arose. Did this legal protection of religion extend to groups such as the Baptists, Quakers, or other Christian sectarian groups that shared Quaker-like sentiments (such as pacifism)? The Roman Catholics, at this point a tiny religious minority largely consigned to cities on the eastern seaboard, didn't even factor into the equation.

Yet even with the collapse of the Articles of Confederation, many political leaders still believed that matters of religion were best left to the states. By the same token, figures such as Thomas Jefferson were deeply concerned that whatever form of government Americans chose, it needed to avoid the older political and religious patterns of Europe. Jefferson greatly valued aspects of European culture, but looked with disdain at the larger history of Europe, in which state battles for religious control were often responsible for a variety of protracted wars, especially during the seventeenth century. Even as the nation's political leaders wrestled over the question of how government should relate to religious groups, an eclectic group of leaders, spearheaded by Jefferson, led a campaign for a new model of national government that ultimately transformed the shape and character of American religion.

A GODLESS CONSTITUTION?
The Coming of Religious Disestablishment

Perhaps no more contentious idea exists in American history than that America is somehow a de facto Christian nation. Since the ratification of the U.S. Constitution in 1788 and the Bill of Rights in 1791, debate has raged among politicians and religious leaders over the extent to which religion should play a role in the larger body politic of the United States. One particular way of measuring the claims of America's Christian origins is to reflect on the language of the First Amendment to the U.S. Constitution: *"Congress shall make no law respecting an establishment of religion, or prohibiting the free exercise thereof."* The language of the First Amendment owes a great deal to the legacy of two Virginians, the future American presidents Thomas Jefferson and James Madison.

Much has been written about the religious beliefs of these two men. While they did share similar beliefs on religion (with both leaning toward deism), they also were united in their belief, characteristic of the late eighteenth-century American political mindset that looked with both disdain and fear at the European model of religious establishment. As governor of Virginia, Thomas Jefferson in 1779 introduced a bill to the Virginia Assembly calling for a guarantee of religious liberty. Jefferson considered this document and the Declaration of Independence to be his most important public contributions, and while the religious liberty bill was defeated in the state assembly, it served as a prototype for future successful efforts.

Jefferson's declaration made two basic points. First, people should be free to worship as they choose; second, no person should feel coerced to pay taxes to support a religious tradition that was not his or her own. Although the document appeals to divine providence, these appeals were phrased in a way that they support reason and despise religious intolerance.

> *Well aware that the opinions and belief of men depend not on their own will, but follow involuntarily the evidence proposed to their minds; that Almighty God hath created the mind free, and manifested his supreme will that free it shall remain by making it altogether insusceptible of restraint; that all attempts to influence it by temporal punishments, or*

burthens [*sic*], or by civil incapacitations, tend only to beget habits of hypocrisy and meanness, and are a departure from the plan of the holy author of our religion, who being lord both of body and mind, yet chose not to propagate it be coercions on either, as was in his Almighty power to do, *but to extend it by its influence on reason alone.*[12]

Jefferson was no orthodox Christian, and he looked with disdain toward the "religious enthusiasm" that characterized the Great Awakening. Yet he affirmed the sanctity of personal opinion in one's choice of religion, in ways that echoed the sentiments of Roger Williams from an earlier era. Jefferson's call was for government to do no harm to people by making persons support a religious tradition with which they disagreed. He wrote ". . . *that the opinions of men are not the object of civil government, nor under its jurisdiction*; that to suffer the civil magistrate to intrude his powers into the field of opinion and to restrain the profession or propagation of principles on supposition of their ill tendency is a dangerous fallacy, which at once destroys all religious liberty."[13]

Jefferson's campaign for religious liberty was eventually picked up in the Virginia Assembly several years later by James Madison. Using many of Jefferson's arguments, Madison argued that disestablishment would not only promote religious freedom, but establish the means by which dissenting forms of religion could flourish. In 1785 Madison's "Memorial and Remonstrance" asserted that an argument that Christianity could not flourish without the power of the state underestimated the power of God. To argue that Christianity could not survive without formal religious establishment "is a contradiction to the Christian Religion itself, . . . for it is known that this Religion both existed and flourished, not only without the support of human laws, but in spite of every opposition from them, and not only during the period of miraculous aid, but long after it had been left to its own evidence and the ordinary care of Providence."[14]

Part of the reason that Madison's disestablishment bill succeeded in the Virginia Assembly was that many Virginian evangelical Christians recognized that it was impossible to determine exactly which type of Christianity the government should support. By the mid-1780s, American Anglicans were in disarray, and it would take several years for the reconstituted Episcopal Church to rebuild itself. In 1784 Patrick Henry offered a bill in Virginia that proposed multiple religious establishments, recognizing the equality of all Christian denominations (a proposal that prompted Madison to write his "Memorial and Remonstrance"). While this bill initially received some support, especially from Presbyterians, the question of which groups should count as Christian and which ones should not proved unanswerable (few members in the Virginia Assembly, for example, would have been willing to give tax-based support to the state's fledgling population of Baptists and Methodists). Virginia's debate on religious disestablishment served as a prism for other state discussions on this issue. Most state legislators took for granted that American society was going to permeate with the values of Protestant Christianity, yet the diversity of Protestant groups throughout the former colonies made it impossible to develop any consensus upon which groups to support. Further, Madison's assertion that religion could flourish without the support of the government had a number of supporters from within the more evangelical churches, in particular, the Baptists.

THE RELIGIOUS CASE FOR DISESTABLISHMENT
The Example of Isaac Backus

Nathan Hatch notes that one of the direct consequences of the American Revolution was the explosion of what he terms "vulgar democracy."[15] While political leaders such as John Adams and Thomas Jefferson differed on the government's role in relation to American political democracy, they shared common assumptions that the nation's political and moral leaders needed to be drawn from elite educational and social institutions. This worldview was shared by the majority of clergy who represented churches from the old religious establishments of the colonial era, in particular, the Congregational and Presbyterian churches which, after the war, often made up the majority of members in many states. However, the Revolutionary War provided impetus for a new explosion of popular religion that largely hastened the demise of earlier religious establishments. The career of Isaac Backus (1724–1806) is illustrative of this process.

Backus' life is a significant bridge between events of the Great Awakening in the mid-eighteenth century with the type of popular religion that would soon be unleashed upon America in the aftermath of American independence. As a youth, Backus grew up on a farm in Norwich, Connecticut. While his parents were members of the local Congregational church, Backus took little interest in religion until he attended a revival led by George Whitefield. Backus later attested to a conversion experience that changed his life. At first Backus joined his parent's church, but he soon grew disillusioned with the lack of an authentic Christianity in the parish. In 1748 he became pastor of a separatist New Light Congregational Church in Middleborough, Massachusetts, and in

1756 he became a Baptist. Over the next several decades he was a major revivalist leader in New England.

Part of what Backus' life shows is the inevitable consequences of what had been started by Whitefield and other Great Awakening revivalists. On one hand, Backus expressed his conversion in language similar to other American New Light evangelicals. Like John Wesley's "heart strangely warmed" experience, Backus saw himself at a point of spiritual crisis whereby conversion had resolved his inner religious doubts. As he later recounted, God's power gave him assurance of his salvation "and of the infinite fullness that there is in Christ to satisfie [sic] the wants of such a helpless creature as I was . . . that my whole heart was attracted and drawn after God and Swallowed up in admiration in view of his Divine glories."[16]

Backus' conversion, however, did far more for him than just give him a secure feeling about his salvation. It empowered him to preach the good news of God's salvation to others. With little formal education, Backus began a remarkable career in the Baptist ministry, spending most of his active ministry as an itinerant preacher. In addition to building several Baptist churches in New England, Backus is most remembered for his campaign waged against the New England Congregational establishment. In 1777 he published A History of New England, arguing that the Baptists, not the Congregationalists, were the true theological architects of the great Puritan tradition (and, in the process, helping to resurrect the legacy of Roger Williams).

Not surprisingly, Backus' attacks against Congregationalism did not go unnoticed, and on many occasions he was arrested for his failure to pay church taxes. At the same time that deists such as Jefferson were mounting their arguments for disestablishment, Backus was making similar assertions, but following the line of reason used by Roger Williams that government had no business dictating how the Christian Gospel should be preached and taught. In a Massachusetts declaration of rights written in 1779, Backus used language reflective of the Enlightenment rationalism of Jefferson. "All men are born equally free and independent, and have certain natural, inherent and unalienable rights, among which are the enjoying and defending life and liberty, acquiring, possessing, and protecting property, and pursuing and obtaining happiness and safety."[17] Backus' concern for liberty was not just to prevent political and religious tyranny, but also to ensure that authentic expressions of Christianity would not be tainted by state interference. He showed his Puritan side when he noted in 1783 that authentic liberty is achieved through service to God. "Christianity is a voluntary obedience to God's revealed will, and everything of a contrary nature is antichristian." While Backus echoes the rhetoric of Jefferson, he also made clear that tradition and Scripture warranted his understanding of religious liberty. Citing passages from Romans 13 and 14 that deal with the relationship of Christians to civic authority, Backus argued with an Enlightenment twist: "Reason and revelation agree in determining that the end of civil government is the *good* of the governed by defending them against all such as would work *ill to their neighbors* and in limiting the power of rulers there. And those who invade the religious rights of others are *self-condemned*, which of all things is the most opposite to *happiness*, the great end of government."[18]

Although many evangelical leaders would later turn on Jefferson, seeing him by the time of his presidency as a godless person out to discredit Christianity (not the last time in American history that evangelical Christians would level these assaults against the nation's political leaders), the turn toward disestablishment proved to be a godsend for many dissenting evangelical groups. By the 1790s, as the first wave of post–Revolutionary War settlement led to new communities in western New York, Ohio, Kentucky, and Tennessee, these settlers brought with them their own iterations of Christianity.

New England Calvinism, a heritage indispensable to shaping the religious ethos of the United States, would still produce many important religious figures in the nineteenth century. However, few Congregational clergy in the early 1800s wanted to acknowledge not only that the geographical center of the country was moving away from New England, but the religious center as well.

IS AMERICA REALLY A CHRISTIAN NATION?

Since the earliest days of their nation, Americans have attempted to read their history back through the lens that the nation was founded as a form of Christian republic where its founders made decisions (much like the early Puritans) with an eye toward Scripture. When Robert Baird wrote his pioneering history of American religion in the 1840s, much of his narrative was crafted with the view that American greatness was ultimately related to its unique heritage of Christianity, centered upon the development of colonial New England. It is true that many of America's political founders did revere the Bible and had no desire to degrade it as a "wise" book. This did not mean, however, that figures such as John Adams, Thomas Jefferson, and James Madison did not take exception to what they often felt were the superstitious teachings of the Bible that went against the contours of the modern world—and of what they felt a religion should teach.

Yet even amid overwhelming historical evidence, claims of America's unique founding as a Christian nation persist. In the latter half of the twentieth century, some have argued the case that the disestablishment of religion does not mean that the founding fathers didn't intend for America to be Christian. One such author, John Eidsmoe, has written a spate of books that advance arguments that the "founding fathers" chief intention was to promote America as a moral republic grounded on Christian biblical suppositions.[19] Eidsmoe and others have largely viewed American history as a form of benign theocracy that has increasingly been corrupted by later generations of secularists and anti-Christian forces. For Eidsmoe, America's founders were men who believed in the moral authority of the Bible to guide the nation. In many ways figures such as Eidsmoe promote a view of history not unlike Robert Baird's that sees America not only as a Christian country, but more specifically, as a Protestant country.

There is no doubt that from a political standpoint, the First Amendment supports the concept of what one scholar called a "Godless Constitution."[20] Jefferson's concept of a "great wall of separation" between religion and government was seen as a way to make sure that the dominant posture of a religious group (or groups) would be unable to manipulate and control the ministrations of government. While it is true that one of the primary political leaders of this period was the Presbyterian minister John Witherspoon (the only clergyman to sign the Declaration of Independence), the key political architects (and icons) of American independence, Benjamin Franklin, John Adams, Thomas Jefferson, James Madison, and George Washington, leaned heavily toward deism and were often highly critical of what they considered to be the theological meddling of orthodox churches such as the Presbyterians who, in their judgment, tried to saddle the new nation with their doctrines.

By the same token, if Jeffersonian political ideals were the substance of the bricks used to build the political model of American republican democracy, religion played a vital role in shaping the nation's mortar. Although there have been voices in American history that have seen the wall of separation concept as a means to restrict the religious voice in the public square, the First Amendment has never restricted how one's religious preferences shape the nation's public voices and opinions. Although people such as Madison and Jefferson were worlds apart from an evangelical Protestant such as Isaac Backus (and Roger Williams from an earlier era), their worlds met in a shared belief that religion would do best when not connected to the meddling of the government. This reality would be readily apparent at the beginning of the nineteenth century as new iterations of evangelical Christianity would form and prosper out of the free market of American religion.

For all their foresight, neither Jefferson nor Madison or perhaps even Isaac Backus could have foreseen how wide reaching and effective religious disestablishment would be. For all the visionary aspects of his thinking, Thomas Jefferson fervently believed in the rational goodness of humanity, and for him the value of religion was primarily predicated on its ability to lead humans to a moral and ethical life. After he left the presidency in 1809, Jefferson created his own version of the Bible, in effect, eliminating parts of Scripture that supported supernaturalism and what he considered to be irrational thinking, keeping only sections of the Old Testament and parts of the gospels that supported a more ethical type of religion. A few years before his death in 1826, Jefferson predicted that the future of American religion did not rest with the superstitions of evangelical churches, but rather, he wrote, "I confidently expect . . . that the present generation will see Unitarianism become the general religion of the United States." Jefferson believed that God-given reason would lead Americans to reject "the hocus-pocus phantasm" associated with teaching surrounding traditional church doctrines such as the Trinity and "that there is not a young man now living in the U.S. who will not die an Unitarian."[21]

In hindsight, never has a prediction about America's future been so off course than Jefferson's. However, American Christianity would produce figures in the nineteenth and twentieth centuries many who would make similar arguments. While not necessarily casting their lots with Unitarianism, many religious leaders after Jefferson would make the case that in order for Christianity to survive it must abandon the otherworldly in favor of a more rationalist model of religion.

Ironically, at the time that Jefferson appended his hopeful appraisal of Unitarianism, America was already caught up in torrents of religious enthusiasm that made the original Great Awakening seem tame by comparison. Secular leaders such as Jefferson and Madison were absolutely correct. Disestablishment helped religion rather than hurt it. It forced churches to aggressively market their beliefs to a public that, as it turned out, was desirous to hear a wide range of religious voices. Yet the aftermath of disestablishment was not one characterized by greater reliance on religious reason and rationality, but on a quality that people such as Jefferson lamented—the quest for the supernatural.

It is important to remember that the First Amendment only guaranteed religious liberty on a national level. While several states moved swiftly to ratify First Amendment privileges in their states, there were some states, especially in New England, that successfully resisted disestablishment for several years. Perhaps fittingly, the last state to abolish its religious establishment was Massachusetts in 1833, a state whose history contained both the strongest legacies of religious establishment as well as producing many voices that helped shape the intellectual rationale for religious liberty.

As religious establishments died off in America, many clergy lamented what they feared might be the demise of Christianity in America. When another Puritan stronghold, Connecticut, voted to disband its Congregational Church establishment in 1818, a minister from the old "standing order" was distraught. "It was a time of great depression and suffering," he wrote years later. "It was as dark a day as ever I saw. The odium thrown upon the ministry was inconceivable. The injury done to the cause of Christ . . . was irreparable. For several days I suffered what no tongue can tell."[22] This minister would soon get over his feelings of despair. For much of the first half of the nineteenth century, Lyman Beecher not only became one of America's most prominent clergymen, but a noted proponent of the spirit of revivalism that came to characterize what historians have called the Second Great Awakening.

Winthrop Hudson has called the American tradition of the separation of church and state "the great tradition of the American churches." Disestablishment fostered not only a tradition of preserving religious liberty, but also caused an upswing in the rise of popular religious movements in which Isaac Backus and New England Baptists were only a part of a wider phenomenon. By the end of the Revolutionary War, evangelical movements were starting to gain strong followings throughout the colonies. In Virginia, upstart Baptist and Methodist churches were growing in many rural communities throughout the state, prefiguring the spread of these two evangelical denominations in the South and throughout the country. By the 1790s settlers from New England began to migrate through upstate New York, some planting roots while others headed west into the Ohio territory. The events of the American Revolution had dramatically altered the character of American religion, setting the stage for what historian Jon Butler referred to as a "spiritual hothouse."[23] The extent of these changes would become fully visible during the opening decades of the nineteenth century.

PART II
The Evangelical Empire and Its Critics, 1800–1865

Writing in 1897 Leonard Bacon looked back on the nineteenth century as a historical epoch filled with trying moral tests for the American people. In a century marked by explosive population growth, immigration, western settlement, urbanization, industrialization, and technological advancement, Bacon believed that America stood poised at century's end to enter a new era marked by social and moral prosperity. Leading the way in this emerging vision were the nation's churches, which would provide for Americans a beacon leading into the future. Almost fifty years after Robert Baird and Philip Schaff first spoke of a providential form of Protestant Christianity taking shape in America, Bacon echoed these historians' unflinching confidence that God's hand was still at work in the nation. Not only did Bacon see the nation's churches working toward a common purpose in terms of providing an increasingly diverse population a sense of national and cultural unity, but he confidently saw American Christianity at the center of the Christian world. He believed that the nation's churches would be responsible for the revival of Christianity worldwide. "The vital strength of the American church, as of the American nation, has been subjected to the test of the importation of enormous masses of more or less uncongenial population, and has shown an amazing power of digestion and assimilation. Its resources have been taxed by the providential imposition of burdens of duty and responsibility such, in magnitude and weight, as never since the early preaching of the gospel have pressed upon any single generation of the church."[1] From Bacon's perspective, not only did American Christianity weather the massive social, political, and cultural

107

changes of the nineteenth century, it thrived in this environment. While historians such as Baird and Schaff had attempted to explain the peculiar workings of American Christianity to a European audience, Bacon surmised without hesitation that the dominant forces within the Christian world now emanated from the United States.

Yet underneath Bacon's confident veneer lurked signs of trouble. At the same time that he spoke confidently of the ecclesiastical and cultural muscle of the nation's churches, he recognized that the country was divided by numerous sects that threatened the future vitality of American Christianity. Bacon conceded that sectarian divisions were inevitable in American Christianity given the fact that America did not recognize one exclusive government-sponsored church. Yet he remained hopeful that what he saw as inherent qualities of Americans for cooperation and goodwill could overcome these divisions. "There are many indications, in the recent history of the American church, pointing forward toward some higher manifestation of the true unity of the church than is to be found in occasional, or even habitual, expressions of mutual good will passing to and fro among sharply competing and often antagonist sects."[2] Despite the annoying perpetuation of sects in nineteenth-century America, Bacon looked back at American religious history and saw clear signs that the nation's churches would ultimately heal these divisions.

Bacon did have reason to be confident. While America witnessed unprecedented change since the early national period, many of the same Protestant churches so favored by Robert Baird and Philip Schaff appeared to be winning the day. In the years leading up to the Civil War, Protestant churches such as the Presbyterians, Congregationalists, Methodists, and Baptists showed an ability to build not only churches, but scores of colleges and universities that put these traditions at the cultural center of American life. Amid periods of social turmoil, these churches mobilized Americans into "voluntary societies" that addressed at local and national levels a wide range of social ills, including temperance, education, and antislavery reform, setting the stage by century's end for massive institutional growth among several Protestant denominations. In the aftermath of the Civil War, American Protestant churches blanketed the world— and America—with missionaries, including clergymen and laywomen who felt called to a life of evangelism in Africa, Asia, and the growing inner-city slums of American cities. Most especially, Protestant churches were showing clear signs by the 1890s of crafting a burgeoning ecumenical movement that would ultimately lead divided Christendom to reunite.

But behind Bacon's sense of Christian unity, the nineteenth century broke with a spirit of religious rage that splintered the nation's churches into scores of competing religious sects. As the new century began in a spirit of religious revivalism, it soon witnessed the emergence of new Christian sects and denominations that radically transformed the nation's religious map. Furthermore, as the nineteenth century progressed, even the most ardent believer in the argument that America was a Protestant nation could not ignore that not all Americans were evangelical Protestants. While Bacon helped craft a perception that the nineteenth century was a Protestant century, the largest Christian movement in America by the end of the century was the Roman Catholic Church, a tradition whose ecclesiastical structure and theological orientation often clashed sharply with the nation's Protestant caretakers.

Even more difficult to explain for Bacon was the proliferation of synergistic religious movements. These were religious groups who identified themselves exclusively as representing the true incarnation of "primitive" Christianity but who embraced belief systems that often had little relationship to long-standing Catholic and Protestant ecclesiastical traditions. Amid this whirlwind of religious sectarianism, at the center of the century was the specter of a violent civil war, a conflict that ultimately points to the failure of the Protestant churches so exalted by Leonard Bacon to deal constructively with the greatest moral failure in American history: slavery.

≪ 5 ≫

METHODISM AND THE RISE OF EARLY NINETEENTH-CENTURY POPULAR EVANGELICALISM

In 1810 Jesse Lee published the first history of the church that became the dominant American religious movement in the first half of the nineteenth century: Methodism. Like the earlier Puritans, Lee's account permeates with a strong sense that God's hand was at work among the Methodists, whereby "the Lord has, from very small beginnings, raised us up to be a great and prosperous people."[1] Comparable to other Methodist historical narratives written during the first half of the nineteenth century, the story of Methodism is told through a yearly record of ecclesiastical gatherings, revivals, and, most especially, accounts of personal conversion.

However, the Methodist interpretation of providence had its own unique theological orientation that in many ways differentiated it from older Protestant movements in America. In the early years of the republic, Methodism spearheaded an unprecedented explosion of evangelical Protestant Christianity that contributed to a transformation of American society, in ways that altered the social and political world of the nation in the years following the Revolutionary War. In 1776 Congregationalists, Presbyterians, and Anglicans were the chief religious groups in the colonies, and their authority was largely secured through their protection as religious establishments. The Great Awakenings in the 1740s and 1750s challenged many church leaders to wrestle with the place of revivalism within the parameters of specific churches and denominations. However, early nineteenth-century evangelicalism erupted on a far more massive level that rewrote the rules for religious engagement and crafted forms of popular theology and revivalism that an earlier generation of preachers such as George Whitefield would scarcely recognize. The tone of early nineteenth-century revivalism was set by the meteoric growth of Methodism. The emergence of American Methodism signaled an explosion of popular religion that transformed belief patterns across the United States, influencing the development of American Christianity in ways that would carry forward into the twenty-first century.

On one hand, Methodism's historical and theological imprint certainly owed a great deal to the theological developments that shaped western Protestantism in the aftermath of the sixteenth-century reformations. Coming as it did out of the Anglican Church, Methodism carried imprints of that tradition's theological heritage into its numerous North American iterations. However, its genetic code was also programmed to make it fit the emerging democratic ethos of post–Revolutionary War America. Methodist adherents accepted that they were a movement whose beliefs and practices represented the most authentic form of Christianity since apostolic times. While Puritans such as John Winthrop were intent on establishing "a city upon a hill" in the context of seventeenth-century New England, American Methodists envisioned their mission, like the first Christians, more as a perpetual sojourn in the wilderness. The movement succeeded not because of the intellectual rigor of its theology, but because of how Methodists grafted a unique theological blueprint upon the popular imagination of many segments of American society. In the process, this tradition helped contribute to the demise of the elite religious and cultural world that had existed up to the time of the American Revolution. Put another way, Methodists and other evangelical Protestants embraced what they believed to be the true practices of primitive Christianity and merged these beliefs into emerging social and cultural models of life in post–Revolutionary War America.

FRANCIS ASBURY AND THE SPRIT OF AMERICAN REVIVALISM

No person epitomizes the soul of the American Methodist vision more than its undisputed early leader, Francis Asbury. As the primary spokesperson of the movement from his election as a bishop in 1784 until his death in 1816, Asbury not only shaped the early ecclesiastical structure of American Methodism, but for many not connected with the movement, he represented the most prominent public face of this new style of American revivalism. While John Wesley had provided the theological and ecclesiastical blueprint for Methodism in the eighteenth century, it was Asbury who adapted it to the context of life in the United States in the late eighteenth and early nineteenth centuries. Born in Birmingham, England, in 1745 to a working-class family, Asbury served as a trade apprentice until he was converted at a Methodist revival at the age of 14. Like Wesley, Asbury embraced the Arminian message of free grace that stood as the cornerstone of much Methodist theology. Following the themes of John Wesley, and echoed for subsequent generations by the hymns of John's brother, Charles, Methodists challenged Calvinist assertions behind theologies of predestination and election, asserting that God's grace was a gift offered to any sinner who came to God with a penitent heart and an openness to receive God's divine mercy. There was certainly continuity between Asbury's theology to that of the Calvinist revivalists who influenced the contours of the Great Awakening in the American colonies. Asbury shared George Whitefield's belief that true Christians needed to go through a conversion experience and provide public testimony of that conversion. However, Asbury and many other evangelical Protestants who emerged in the late eighteenth and early nineteenth centuries hammered home the classic Wesleyan theme that salvation was as much a lifelong quest as it was a once-and-for-all gift. Like Wesley, Asbury and other early American Methodists did not view the doctrine of original sin with the same degree of finality as did their Calvinist counterparts. While the Methodists saw sin as a corrupting and tainting of human nature, they downplayed the Augustinian doctrine of total depravity so central to many Calvinist traditions. Keeping with the spirit of Wesley, they believed that the converted could grow in God's grace in such a way that one's actions would manifest the perfect will and intent of God.

This belief in the doctrine of sanctification, or Christian perfection, in which individuals were saved from the power of inward sin became a cornerstone for the Methodists and helped explain the efforts undertaken by John Wesley and British Methodists at social reform throughout the eighteenth century. Central to this progressive vision of salvation was the emphasis that the Methodists placed on small group piety. Asbury's rise as a leader in British and American Methodism was paradigmatic of the path followed years later by many American Methodist converts during the heyday of Asbury's leadership in post–Revolutionary War America. After his conversion, Asbury was immediately placed into a class meeting made up of anywhere from ten to twelve members who undertook a weekly examination of each other's faith. His early taste of leadership came as a class leader who entreated followers to grow in grace and in their knowledge of

God's love. By the late 1760s, he had emerged as one of the principal lay preachers in British Methodism, assisting Wesley with the organization of Methodist preaching societies in England. In 1771 Wesley sent Asbury to the American colonies to help provide organizational leadership to the fledgling Methodist movement. By 1777, as the American Revolution entered its third year, Asbury was the only British Methodist leader sent by Wesley who remained in America. Because of Methodism's historical connection to Anglicanism, the movement's leaders were often suspected of being British sympathizers. Consequently, Asbury spent much of the Revolutionary War in hiding, while at the same time emerging as the undisputed leader of the small number of Methodists living in the American colonies.

By the time of the British surrender at Yorktown in 1781, American Methodists consisted of a few thousand followers mostly concentrated in rural locations in Virginia and along the eastern seaboard. After failing to find bishops in the Church of England who would ordain priests to send to the Methodist societies in the United States, Wesley took the step of ordaining ministers for the purpose of constituting an independent Methodist church in North America. In December 1784 the Methodist Episcopal Church was founded in Baltimore, Maryland, with Wesley, Asbury, and Thomas Coke (a priest in the Church of England and a close associate of John Wesley's) designated as "general superintendents" of the new church.

Theoretically, Asbury's designation as a general superintendent of the Methodist movement made him equal partners with Wesley and Coke in the administrative oversight of the new church. In the early years after its founding, however, Asbury was the undisputed leader of the American Methodists. Although Wesley's and Coke's beliefs were solidly grounded in many aspects of the Anglican theological and liturgical tradition, Asbury used these traditions selectively. As Nathan Hatch observed, American Methodism succeeded in large measure because it emphasized three distinctive themes: "God's free grace, the liberty of people to accept or reject that grace, and the power and validity of popular religious expression."[2] These themes not only capture the success of American Methodism, but describe the central ideals behind what many religious historians commonly label "the Second Great Awakening."

THE SECOND GREAT AWAKENING

Historians differ about the dating of this event, but much like the mid-eighteenth-century Great Awakening, the so-called Second Great Awakening is a term that describes a general pattern of religious revivalism as opposed to an organized singular movement undertaken by Protestant churches. By the same token, the patterns of religious revivalism that broke out in America roughly between 1795 and extending through the first quarter of the nineteenth century served as a model for future generations of American evangelicals. What distinguished the Second Great Awakening from the First Great Awakening was not only the larger scale of revivalism that broke out throughout the country, but the way these revivals were connected to patterns of popular religion that went way beyond the revivals staged in the pre–Revolutionary War era by the likes of George Whitefield and Gilbert Tennent.

American society in the decades following the Revolutionary War was confronted by unprecedented social mobility triggered in large measure by population migrations out of New England and the eastern seaboard. The consequence of this shift, as many historians have pointed out, was that earlier gentry and upper-class groups were unable to regulate politically the new religious movements (and emerging forms of religious expression) brought on by religious disestablishment and an increasingly mobile and expanding population. At the center of these migrations was an explosion not only of fledgling religious movements such as the Methodists, but new and innovative forms of religious practice. At the center of this transformation was the revivalist phenomenon known as the camp meeting. Building on an earlier tradition of eighteenth-century Protestant revivalism represented by the likes of Whitefield and Tennent, the camp meetings became the primary means by which once-marginalized religious groups such as the Methodists, built powerful religious movements that impacted the subsequent development of the American revivalist tradition that extends into the twenty-first century.

In 1801 the Presbyterian minister James McGready conducted what many consider to be the first American camp meeting in Cane Ridge, Kentucky. Although preachers of an earlier generation gained popularity due to the extemporaneous nature of their sermon styles, revivalists of the Second Great Awakening took this style of preaching even further. While Whitefield and other revivalists of his generation tended to focus their energies in cities, early nineteenth-century revivalism, at least initially, focused on the growing frontier regions of a geographically expanding country, with Kentucky, Tennessee, western New York, and the newly opened Ohio territory being popular staging areas for revivals. Forms for camp meetings varied, yet most held several factors in common. Camp meetings tended to be held over several days and were, in many respects, forms of popular entertainment. Individuals and whole families would often travel to the camp meeting grounds encircling the revivalists with their wagons and prepared to spend several days listening to preaching and actively receiving the revivalists' calls for conversion by singing and praying together.

What characterized the camp meetings, much to the dismay of their critics, was the high degree of emotionalism. Earlier revivalists such as Whitefield had cracked the door of religious enthusiasm, but revivalists associated with the Second Great Awakening kicked those doors down. In the opening years of the nineteenth century, hundreds of camp meeting revivalists entreated their audiences to accept Christ and to receive the gift of salvation. Spurring the decorum of formal liturgies and church buildings, outdoor revivalists would often engage in vivid and colorful histrionics in their sermons. Often, sermons were received by displays of spiritual ecstasy that shocked many observers unaccustomed to these gatherings. The newly converted would often engage in strange behaviors, including massive groaning, barking, or jerking uncontrollably. For many Protestant churches that embraced the camp meetings, these physical manifestations were a sign of their success because they gave evidence to the workings of the Holy Spirit.

Although the Presbyterians were largely responsible for designing the blueprint for the earliest camp meeting revivals, it was the Methodists who perfected it. While John Wesley encouraged a degree of religious enthusiasm, the emotionalism associated with the camp meetings would have likely horrified him. This was not so for Francis Asbury. For Asbury, camp meetings were akin to "fishing with a large net," representing a means of attracting converts to the Methodist movement. He also recognized the ways that camp meetings differentiated the Methodists from their religious competitors. Writing to a colleague in 1805, he noted "that these campmeetings [sic] will bring on great opposition and I should not wonder if some of us should lose our lives, but I am sure they will storm still and shake the formality of religion out of the world."[3] For Asbury, camp meeting revivalism represented a necessary assault upon the citadels of false (or indifferent) forms of Christianity. While he was not inherently hostile toward other Christian churches in America, he was concerned that other churches had failed in bringing the gospel of Christ and the word of salvation to the masses not simply because of poor theology, but because churches had lost an ability to communicate to the masses. One of the primary responsibilities of Methodist ministers on the frontier was to organize camp meetings. While the spirit of spontaneity prevailed over these gatherings, most were well-organized affairs, and to conduct a successful camp meeting became one of the major requirements for any- one who became a Methodist minister. Jesse Lee, himself a prominent leader of early American Methodism, concluded his history of American Methodism with a primer on how to conduct an effective camp meeting, laying out the following schedule:

> We proceed in our religious exercises as follows: soon after the first dawn of day, a person walks all around the ground in front of the tents, blowing a trumpet as he passes; which is to give the people notice to rise; about ten minutes after the trumpet is blown again with only one long blast; upon which, the people in all their tents begin to sing, and then pray, either in their tents, or at the door of them, as is most convenient. At the rising of the sun a sermon is preached, after which we eat breakfast. We have preaching again at 10 o'clock, and dine about one. We preach again at 3 o'clock, eat supper about the setting of the sun, and have preaching again at candle light. . . . The people being continually engaged in sing- ing, praying, preaching, or exhorting without any cessation.[4]

Part of what also made the camp meetings both novel and effective was their use of music. In the eighteenth century, Methodist revivalists in England had developed the practice of setting "sacred" lyrics (many writ- ten by Charles Wesley) to popular melodies. This practice became a feature not only in the revivals of the Second Great Awakening, but a consistent theme adapted by future revivalists (as well as twenty-first-century church growth enthusiasts).

By 1810 Methodist camp meetings were a feature of religious life, in both rural and urban areas of the country. Yet the success of Methodist camp meetings went beyond the religious and social novelty of the events. One of the reasons Asbury embraced the title of bishop (despite Wesley's furious objection) was that it expressed his belief that he was invested with an authority like bishops in the early church to organize and hold the Methodist movement accountable to his central leadership. In the decades following the Revolutionary War, American society found itself in what Nathan Hatch called "a crisis of authority."[5] On the eve of the American Revolution, America was made up of colonies in which the majority of people lived in cities lining the Atlantic coast. The nation's secular leaders were largely made up of men of privilege and wealth, while the nation's churches were predominantly ministered by well-educated clergy who saw themselves as upholders of clearly defined historical and theological heritages. In the two decades following the ratification of the American Constitution, however, this model of religious authority was starting to disintegrate. On the eve of the Revolutionary War, the Anglican Church, which competed against the Congregationalists and Presbyterians for religious establishment privileges, faced the specter of reorganizing itself in the aftermath of religious disestablishment. While Congregational churches attempted to organize revivals in New England and actively promoted "western missions" into the American frontier, they shared with the Anglicans a reliance on a professional core of highly educated ministers. These settled clergy, who often spent their entire ministries in one congregation, contrasted with the spirit of the Second Great Awakening, focused on extemporaneous preaching, a clear focus on personal conversion, and a populist theology that became an ongoing characteristic of religious movements in America long after the fires of the Second Great Awakening died out.

METHODISM AND EARLY NINETEENTH-CENTURY POPULAR THEOLOGY

Perhaps more than any other factor, understanding the Second Great Awakening revolves around understanding how evangelical theology gave power to a cross section of people to speak with religious authority. Unlike Protestant revivalists of the eighteenth century that revolved around the authority of clergy, Asbury was leader of a fledgling religious movement that gave power to everyone. Early American Methodism held its followers in a paradoxical tension that emphasized the authority of Asbury's leadership *and* a democratic spirit that encouraged a variety of Americans, whether male or female, black or white, slave or free, to devote their lives to the service of God. At the center of the Methodist movement was the circuit rider whose rise in American popular culture crafted the dominant image of American evangelism for generations. To be an ordained Methodist minister was to commit oneself to a life on horseback, spending months traveling hundreds of miles back and forth among any number of preaching stations on a circuit. Asbury also expected Methodist preachers to be single-mindedly devoted to the work of saving souls and had no use for ministers who sought the urbane life of a "settled" minister. In particular, Asbury discouraged Methodist clergy from marrying, believing that family responsibilities would rob preachers of their zeal for ministry. Behind Asbury's zeal, however, was a clear-cut theology that saw American Methodists fighting a decisive battle against the forces of sin and wickedness. Writing to a friend to describe a recent Methodist revival in Lynn, Massachusetts, Asbury notes the Methodist gains in a way that suggests that he viewed himself as a Pauline figure of benevolent authority, recounting the sacrifices of the Methodists to win converts. "O Glory! Superstition falls in New England. I look for great persecution: all hell is in motion. I think some of us shall be martyrs yet, we make such conquests in every direction."[6]

Methodism's growth was more than just the result of dedicated clergy and popular revivalism. What anchored the movement was its grounding in small-group class meetings, adapted from British Methodism, which relied almost exclusively on the leadership of lay men *and* women. In juxtaposition to the First Great Awakening era in which the fires of revival often died out once a revivalist left a city or town, Methodist circuit riders employed a system of lay preachers and lay leadership that took responsibility for organizing churches in the absence of clergy. In this regard, Methodism was a very democratic movement. While Wesley had sanctioned lay preaching in the Methodist revivals in Great Britain, laity played an even more vital role in the spread of American Methodism. The extent of this lay involvement can be seen in terms of Asbury's unequivocal support for the class meeting. Originally arising out of British Methodism in the 1740s as a means of collecting money to support impoverished Methodist families, the class meeting had evolved in both Great Britain and North America as the primary means of nurturing Methodist spiritual discipline and, as had been the case with Asbury, identifying and cultivating future religious leaders. In the early years of the nineteenth century, one could not be a Methodist without joining a class meeting, and these classes helped craft a level of religious commitment that was likely as important to the movement's success as were the highly publicized revivals conducted by Methodist preachers. Within a short time frame, Methodist circuit riders, lay preachers, and class leaders were successful not only on the rural frontier but also within communities that had previously been strongholds of older religious establishments, such as New England and Virginia.

This taut organization helped separate Methodists from many of their evangelical competitors in the early nineteenth century. Their closest rivals were the Baptists, who also thrived in this climate of revivalism. However, the Methodists had two advantages in the early nineteenth century over the Baptists. Baptist communities continued to engage in long-standing theological battles between factions that favored a Calvinist theological orientation (Particular) and those who emphasized an Arminian free grace theology (Free Will). While Methodists often stereotyped Baptists as staunch defenders of predestination, in truth Baptist communities remained fervently divided on these questions, and these theological divisions would lead to further theological divisions among Baptists as the nineteenth century progressed. Second, although Baptist ministers often enjoyed a great deal of flexibility to establish new churches, especially in frontier regions of the country, they lacked the type of denominational support that characterized the Methodists. Baptist ministers on the frontier were often bivocational, supplementing their ministry by farming or teaching school. Methodist circuit riders did not suffer these constraints and Asbury made it clear that these men had one mission: "to spend and be spent in the work of ministry." While the image of the circuit rider would become romanticized later in the nineteenth century through popular lithographs, the life of these itinerants was far from glamorous. Most received an annual salary of less than $100, and few received their full salary allotments. While few Methodist preachers matched the peripatetic pace of Asbury's travels, most circuit riders in the early nineteenth century could count on a life where they could expect few amenities. Many of these preachers suffered from chronic poor health and many circuit riders died at a young age. In the early nineteenth century, it was the rare circuit rider who lived into his forties.

The success of Methodism was staggering. At the outbreak of the American Revolution in 1775, there were approximately 3,000 Methodists in the colonies. Twenty years later, the number was over 60,000, and in 1815 there were over 211,000. The success of Methodism continued after Asbury's death. By 1850, 1.5 million Americans, one-third of the nation's population that belonged to a church, was Methodist.[7] By the time of Asbury's death in 1816, the Methodists were well on their way to becoming the largest church in the United States, and their numerical status in American Protestantism would remain uncontested for much of the nineteenth century.

JAMES O'KELLY AND THE SPIRIT OF CHRISTIAN RESTORATIONISM

Yet even in the early years of Methodism's rise as a religious movement, it was fraught with controversies that Bishop Asbury could not control.

Methodist camp meetings encouraged a host of popular revivalists who often forsook the ecclesiastical responsibilities of the circuit riders in exchange for advancing their status as popular revivalists. One popular Methodist preacher, Lorenzo Dow, embodied this tension. In the early nineteenth century, Dow's exploits as a preacher made him well known in the United States and Great Britain, yet often put him at odds with Methodist leaders in both nations. While some Methodist leaders worried that Dow was more interested in promoting his own ministry rather than Methodist teachings, other segments of American Methodism were challenging Asbury's authority. In 1792, at the first gathering of the Methodist Episcopal Church's legislative general conference, a group of ministers led by a popular Virginia preacher, James O'Kelly, challenged Asbury's authority to appoint preachers. Reflecting a strong popular democratic spirit, O'Kelly called for a vision of Methodism that reflected the hard-fought values of American democracy and liberty over the Old World monarchical values espoused by "Pope Asbury." O'Kelly did not come by this rhetoric flippantly. Born in 1735, he was a highly respected Methodist leader, even before Asbury's arrival in America. In 1784, at the Baltimore conference that founded the Methodist Episcopal Church, O'Kelly was one of twelve ministers ordained by Asbury and Coke, and his ministry was critical to Methodism's rapid growth in the Tidewater area of southeastern Virginia. Yet even before his formal ordination, his dissent from Asbury was coming to the surface. Before Methodism's beginnings as an organized church, in 1779 O'Kelly was one of the principal leaders who favored a formal break of the Methodists from the Church of England. His efforts to convene a conference of Methodist preachers in Fluvanna, Virginia, in order to ordain clergy as part of a new Methodist church may well have succeeded if not for the efforts of Asbury to stave off this separation. O'Kelly also possessed a passion that also was rampant among the early followers of Methodism: he staunchly opposed slavery.

Many fledgling revivalist groups such as the Methodists initially fostered strong antislavery traditions. When the Methodist Episcopal Church was founded in 1784, it forbade members to own slaves. However, O'Kelly, among others, was sensitive to the fact that the church was not strongly invoking this antislavery provision. While Asbury shared this distaste for slavery, he early displayed a pragmatism characteristic of other American churches, whereby he felt it necessary to tolerate the existence of slavery in order to appease church members who lived in states where slavery was legal, mainly in the South. A few years before his death, Asbury lamented that he saw no way to rid the nation of slavery. "We thought . . . we could kill the monster at once," he reflected in 1812, "but *the laws and the people* were against us, and we had to compromise the matter, or lose the South."[8] Although a southerner, O'Kelly was a Virginian in the late eighteenth century where there was a strong antislavery sentiment. Many burgeoning evangelical traditions in the South saw their ministries as a direct challenge to an aristocratic colonial culture predicated on the authority of wealthy plantation families. In the 1780s, O'Kelly helped usher in a new spirit of evangelical Protestantism that not only challenged this earlier colonial worldview, but displayed a staunch egalitarianism that increasingly viewed the model of episcopal church government, epitomized by Francis Asbury, as antithetical to the spirit of American Methodism *and* American democracy.

What especially bothered O'Kelly was Asbury's almost total monopoly over the Methodist clergy appointment system. For O'Kelly, this was a model of clergy authoritarianism antithetical not only to the spirit of Methodism, but of America as well. As he noted in 1798, "Ah, Francis [Asbury] was born and nurtured in the land of kings and bishops, and that which is bread in the bone, is hard to be got out of the flesh." This sentiment was a not-so-subtle jab at a man whom O'Kelly believed did not truly grasp the spirit of the new nation. "O Heavens! Are we not Americans! Did not our fathers bleed to free their sons from the British yoke? And shall we be slaves to ecclesiastical oppression?"[9] Despite O'Kelly's efforts, the 1792 general conference supported Asbury's (and subsequent generations of Methodist bishops') right to appoint clergy to preaching circuits and churches. This decision led O'Kelly and a group of followers to leave the denomination to establish what was initially called the Republican Methodists. While the new church held onto distinctive Methodist theological teachings, it abolished the episcopal office in favor of a more "democratic" appointment system.

Yet even that formal identity as Methodist was soon abandoned by O'Kelly in favor of an even more authentically democratic name: the Christian Church. O'Kelly argued that the true nature of Christianity extended beyond the polity of any particular denomination or creed. Echoing a theme that would become a staple for evangelical Protestants in the early nineteenth century, he thundered that all churches needed to "submit to Christ, who is the head, and only head of his church; and then we as brethren will walk together, and follow God as dear children." This central theme for O'Kelly served as a dominant emphasis for a wide variety of American evangelicals ever since: the equating of popular American democratic ideals with the mission and purpose of the early church. Ultimately, O'Kelly's solution to the problems of competing religious sects was a simple one: seek what is pure in Christianity by abolishing all creeds and doctrines that divide. "As each church is called by a different name," he explained, "suppose we dissolve those unscriptural names, and for peace sake, and for Christ's sake, call ourselves Christians? This would be—'The Christian church.'"[10]

James O'Kelly's rebellion against the ecclesiastical powers of American Methodism signaled the emergence of another powerful current within early nineteenth-century American evangelicalism: Christian restorationism. Although his own restorationist movement would disappear into obscurity, the impulse he seized upon would permeate the historical landscape of American Christianity, contributing to the formation of countless churches and sectarian bodies during the first half of the nineteenth century. These restorationist churches had much in common with other revivalists coming out of traditions such as the Methodists. They tied together a profound belief in the sanctity of the early church with the unique American populist environment that was emerging in the early nineteenth century. Like many revivalists, they tied together the workings of God to the unique ethos of the American social and political experiment. Yet unlike other evangelists, restorationist movements developed an aversion toward any form of creedal Christianity, seeing creeds not only as a source of theological division, but repelling the faithful from the New Testament religion of Jesus as mediated through the Bible. Since the sixteenth century, Protestant churches of different theological heritages have always elevated the exclusive authority of Scripture. However, the restorationist traditions that were birthed in the early nineteenth century helped spread a popular religious worldview that still resonates with disparate Christian groups in the early twenty-first century: there is no creed but the Bible.

The most prominent of the early nineteenth-century restorationist leaders were Alexander Campbell and Barton Stone. Originally a Presbyterian minister and an immigrant from Ireland, Campbell increasingly grew dissatisfied with the way that Presbyterians were mired in creedal disputes. Eventually his "Campbellite" movement joined forces with the followers of another restorationist minister, Barton Stone, to form what would eventually become known as the Disciples of Christ. Stone also began his career as a Presbyterian; in fact, he was one of the major leaders of the famous Cane Ridge revival of 1801. As Kentucky Presbyterians debated the merits of revivalism, Stone became associated with a faction of disaffected Presbyterians who over time joined forces with splinter restorationist groups from other denominations such as O'Kelly's Christian Church. Followers of Stone and Campbell shared a reluctance to organize a new denomination and, in fact, their congregations were often characterized by a resistance to being labeled as such. Yet the movement shared a unique elasticity of beliefs, including diverse opinions on numerous matters of doctrine and a tendency to emphasize "open membership," welcoming seekers and the disillusioned from a variety of different traditions. Restorationists were staunch supporters, however, of a congregation-based polity and tended to emphasize the necessity of believer's baptism (which made many observers view the followers of Campbell and Stone as Baptists). By the eve of the Civil War in 1860, the Disciples held approximately 200,000 members, yet the spirit of restorationism embraced by Campbell and Stone exceeded the parameters of any one tradition. This spirit of restorationism helped spawn one of the largest and most contentious movements in the history of Christianity: the Church of Jesus Christ of Latter-day Saints, or Mormons.

By 1830 these assorted evangelical and restorationist groups caused a radical change not only upon American religion, but American politics. For all the differences that separated the politics of an Alexander Hamilton and a Thomas Jefferson, both shared a taken-for-granted supposition that the nation was to carry vestiges of an Old World aristocracy, whereby important truths were to be mediated through the talents of educated men. By the 1830s revivalist currents dovetailed with emerging populist currents within American politics, especially as it was represented through the presidency of Andrew Jackson. With his image as a leader of the "common man," Jackson symbolized emerging American political worldviews that sought to challenge the elite social and political cultures of earlier Federalist political leaders (such as George Washington and John Adams). The spirit of Protestant evangelicalism that exploded in the early nineteenth century supported this populist view of America as an egalitarian society and helped provide the means for those at the bottom of the American social hierarchy to become leaders. While it was a spirit that appealed to many evangelicals, it also created tensions among other Protestant traditions that wanted to disassociate themselves from much of the populist ethos of this new style of American revivalism.

Yet even upstart groups like the Methodists found themselves in the early nineteenth century drawn to impart a legacy not unlike the churches that came before them. In the years between 1830 and 1870, Methodists led other Protestant churches in the founding of new colleges and universities. For a movement that initially spurned formal models of university and seminary training for its clergy, Methodists became inveterate planters of higher-education institutions, especially in the South and Midwest. Even as most of these colleges began as underfunded and understaffed institutions, by the mid-nineteenth century, the growth of Methodist colleges was an indication that this church was moving away from the primitive Christianity envisioned by Francis Asbury and James O'Kelly.

PROTESTANT ALTERNATIVES TO REVIVALISM

The spirit of Protestant evangelicalism appeared to be contagious. At the very least, it forever transformed the religious map of the country. Nowhere was this impact more evident than among the older colonial establishment churches in New England. At the dawn of American independence, the Congregational Church was the largest single religious group, with approximately 20 percent of the total religious adherents among its membership. Yet by the middle of the nineteenth century, Congregationalist churches made up less than 5 percent of all religious adherents. Many historians have pointed to the fact that one of the major reasons that the Congregationalists lost ground was an inability to mobilize their clergy in westward expansion, in the same manner as did the Methodists and Baptists. Yet many Congregational leaders, such as Timothy Dwight and Lyman Beecher, were passionate about the need for revivals and issued persistent pleas for Congregationalists to head west (and crafted a tradition of evangelical Calvinism often associated with New England "New Divinity" theology). The Presbyterians, in particular, fought over the place of revivalism in the tradition, recalling earlier eighteenth-century Great Awakening debates among Congregational and Presbyterian "New Light/New Side" versus "Old Light/Old Side" factions. The Congregational and Presbyterian traditions, heirs to the intellectual legacy of Puritanism, certainly valued religious experience. However, one's understanding of experience was traditionally always measured in relation to the larger community of the church. As architects of the camp meeting revival, many Presbyterians stood poised to embrace the revivalist spirit of the age. By the 1830s some Presbyterians openly embraced the techniques of American revivalism. Other Presbyterians, like the noted theologian Charles Hodge, continued to emphasize the doctrinal contributions of Protestantism emerging from the creedal expressions from the Reformation/post-Reformation era. Still other traditions, emerging primarily out of New England Congregationalism, followed the path of the rationalist theology of Charles Chauncy in the mid-eighteenth century. These rationalists split from both the revivalists and orthodox Calvinists, serving as a foundation for American Unitarianism.

The debate over revivalism played out somewhat differently among the heirs of the Anglican Communion in America. In the aftermath of the American Revolution, the Anglican Church was in shambles. The fact that colonial Anglicanism derived all of its leadership from bishops in Great Britain provided no basis for the emergence of a new church in the aftermath of independence. Yet several Anglican laity during the Revolutionary War fought on the side of the patriots and a majority of signers of the Declaration of Independence and drafters of the Constitution were members of the Church of England (albeit, many nominally so).

In the years following the war, fragments of the Anglican Church reconstituted themselves through assemblies within several states. By 1789 three bishops were in place in the United States to oversee canonical oversight of the church, now known as the Protestant Episcopal Church. The Episcopal Church had numerous problems to overcome. Still suffering under suspicion of being hostile to American democratic institutions, the Episcopal Church struggled for decades with slow growth and tensions among Episcopal bishops concerning the best ways to live out their "via media" tradition in America. This fissure was also felt in the church's early history when a division emerged between two pioneer bishops of the church: Samuel Seabury and William White. As Bishop of Connecticut, Seabury had been a Tory during the war, and his presence in New England opened up old wounds in many Congregationalist and Episcopal churches. Yet White supported American independence and was reflective of what became known later in the nineteenth century as the "broad church" tradition within Anglicanism (picking up on earlier strands of Anglican theology that affirmed a wide plurality of theological perspectives within the church). On the other hand, Seabury identified with the "high church" party of Anglicanism and prefigured the growing nineteenth-century theological tensions between Episcopalians who favored greater ties with other evangelical Protestants and those who favored closer ties with the Roman Catholic Church.

Many early bishops of the Episcopal Church, while staunch Americanists, enthusiastically embraced the liturgical renewal movements that paralleled development in the Church of England. Indicative of this trend was the influence of Bishop John Henry Hobart. Consecrated Bishop of

New York in 1822, Hobart had served for years as an influential priest and writer whose theology challenged many of the predominant revivalist assumptions of most Protestant evangelical churches. Hobart shared with many Episcopalians a profound dislike for Calvinist theology and a desire to preserve critical aspects of the Anglican heritage that came out of the post-Reformation era. However, he was drawn to the liturgical practices of the patristic period and like other high-church Episcopalians, Hobart embraced what became known later in the nineteenth-century as the "Oxford Movement," which placed a premium on the theological and liturgical traditions paralleling those of the Roman Catholic Church. Drawing on a rich blending of Anglican theologians from the seventeenth and eighteenth centuries, Hobart and other Episcopalians emphasized a doctrine of holy living, paralleling the Wesleyan tradition's emphasis on the need for a life that blended together piety with acts of charity. However, the cornerstone to the high church, or Tractarian party, in the Episcopal Church was a renewed emphasis on liturgical worship, centered upon the sacrament of communion and a belief in the ways that the church was indispensable toward salvation. For most of the nineteenth century, however, the majority of Episcopalians did not identify themselves with Hobart's high-church party. They were divided among those made up of "American churchmen" who largely identified themselves as Protestant, and an "evangelical" wing that actively associated itself with the revivalist spirit of Protestantism, epitomized by clergyman such as Lyman Beecher.[11] For many evangelical Protestants, high-church Episcopal language of ritualism and the exclusive nature of the church (in which authentic sacramental authority could only come through Episcopal clergymen), bespoke an elitism that did not seem to fit the spirit of the times (especially, the ways that many evangelicals associated some Episcopalians with the Roman Catholic Church). Yet the theological diversity of this tradition prefigured the role that this church would play in fostering the later growth of the Protestant ecumenical movement. Further, by the end of the nineteenth century, the Episcopal Church was one of the earliest Protestant traditions to embrace theological liberalism.

By 1850 the percentage of churchgoing Americans who identified with the Episcopal Church was only 3.5 percent. Methodists were at over 34 percent, and Baptists were over 20 percent. The Episcopal stress on the liturgical and theological world of Old Europe would not be totally eclipsed by the American world of evangelical revivalism. In third place behind the Baptists in 1850 was another tradition steeped in the theological, cultural, and liturgical suppositions of Old World Europe: the Roman Catholic Church.

Numerous historians have noted that the rise of early nineteenth-century evangelicalism paralleled the rise of the ecumenical movement and a whole-scale Protestant commitment to foreign missions. Although there was a connection between Protestant foreign missions and ecumenism, that connection did not become fully evident until the late nineteenth and early twentieth centuries. Prior to the Civil War, Protestant foreign missionary societies were underfunded and direct accountability between missionaries and their respective denominations was often lax. By the same token, these early missionaries helped lay a foundation that would lead to the explosive growth of Protestant foreign missions by the late nineteenth century.

The best-known Protestant foreign missionary in the antebellum period was likely Adoniram Judson. Originally a Congregationalist minister, Judson had volunteered for missionary service to Burma in 1812. While onboard the ship, he encountered a Baptist couple who convinced Judson and his wife, Ann, that the Baptists were the true incarnation of the early church. Forsaking their Congregationalist roots, Adoniram and Ann Judson worked for years as Baptist missionaries in Burma and India, building schools, translating Scripture into indigenous languages, and facing persecution and imprisonment. While Adoniram Judson helped shape a romantic image of the foreign missionary (at least from the standpoint of an American audience who read about Judson's missionary perils), his efforts were greatly aided by his wife, Ann, who labored alongside her husband in his work (as would be the case with Judson's three successive spouses, two would die, the fourth would outlive Judson). Judson also illustrates another facet of the missionary that appealed to many American Protestant women: the role the minister's wife could play as a partner in her husband's ministry. At a time when women were institutionally barred from ordination, the one option often available to women who felt a call to ministry was to marry a minister. Within colonial America, ministers' wives served their husbands as helpmeets who in addition to taking care of their families were expected, if nothing else, not to interfere with their husbands' ministry. The era of the Second Great Awakening transformed this earlier culture concerning the role of women. While the culture of colonial America often saw women as inherently sinful (as daughters of Eve), the emerging "cult of true womanhood" stressed the superior moral attributes of women to serve as wives and mothers. Some women used this ideology as a means to advocate for the wider place of women in church and society by arguing that women's moral attributes would have a positive influence on American moral behavior. In many instances, ministers' wives such as Elizabeth Finney (wife of the revivalist Charles Finney) and the spouses of Adoniram Judson played very public roles in their husbands' successes, serving as teachers, leading prayer meetings, ministering to the sick, and, in some cases, actually preaching.

On one hand, these women were clear that they were seeking to ensure the successes of their husbands' ministries as opposed to seeking to change the institutional structure of churches. However, women such as Ann Judson came to symbolized for other Protestant evangelical women the uniqueness and power of women's piety. As the nineteenth century progressed, other women, married and single, would become bolder in seeking ways to have their voices heard, increasingly challenging earlier theological and cultural beliefs that when it came to religion, women needed to remain silent.

THE SPIRIT OF THE SECOND GREAT AWAKENING
Competition or Cooperation?

Scholars of American religion have identified the era of the Second Great Awakening as inaugurating an era of church cooperation that became a cornerstone of American Christianity. While disestablishment no longer gave legal protection to any one particular church, historians claimed that it necessitated the ideal that the most effective manifestations of Christianity would emerge through cooperative ecumenical initiatives. There is much evidence coming out of the early nineteenth century to support this claim. In the years between 1810 and 1830, Protestant churches created scores of religious voluntary societies staffed by clergy on a national level and largely funded by laity on a grassroots level. These numerous societies had the primary aim to propagate a public vision of evangelical theology as well as addressing a variety of social concerns endemic to the American social-political context of the time. For later historians such as Leonard Bacon, this system of "organized benevolence" represented the genius of American Protestantism. Indeed, many of these voluntary societies, such as the American Education Society (founded in 1815), the American Sunday School Union (1824), the American Tract Society (1826), and the American Home Missionary Society (1826), played a critical role in addressing a wide range of social ills and revealed that despite the differences separating churches in matters of theology and practice, America was a nation in possession of a powerful Protestant evangelical ethos.

Yet these voluntary societies were largely the byproducts of churches, such as New England Congregational churches, that were on the losing end of the popular religious eruption that occurred in the early decades of the century. For many evangelical churches, epitomized by the success of the Methodists, the early nineteenth century was a time whereby competition, not cooperation, was the dominant motif. These evangelical Protestants cared little for cultural respectability; their primary concern was to save souls, accomplished through innovative forms of ministry that utilized men and women in grassroots leadership. While dominant in terms of numbers, pre–Revolutionary War traditions such as the Congregationalists, Presbyterians, and Episcopalians castigated the uncouth tactics used by evangelical churches such as the Methodists and Baptists, it was these former traditions that were left on the short end of "church growth" during the first half of the century.

However, the success of the Methodism was, in many ways, short-lived. By the 1830s Methodist gains caused some in the tradition to embrace the allures of a culturally respectable ministry, and in the process, more and more Methodists abandoned the devices of the camp meeting and class meeting that had been fundamental to the tradition's growth. As Methodism settled, other fissures developed within what has been called "the evangelical empire." In particular, other Americans were taking themes of Christian restorationism and "primitive Christianity" in directions that had permanent consequences on the shape of American religion.

« 6 »

Experimental Christianity

The meteoric growth of evangelical Protestantism during the early nineteenth century makes it easy to accept the conclusion that the majority of Americans were swept up in this phenomenon. However, it is important to keep in mind the ways that American evangelicalism epitomized larger theological and cultural changes that were sweeping across the nation. Despite the popular success associated with the revivalism of the Second Great Awakening, the first half of the nineteenth century produced other responses among other religious communities, causing them to move beyond canonical sources of religious authority and, in some cases, to move beyond the parameters of Christianity altogether.

Historian R. Laurence Moore used the term "religious outsiders" to describe groups that intentionally rejected the predominant religious orientations of their era, preferring (at least initially) to be sectarian groups on the margins of society as opposed to adapting their teachings to fit the values within a wider religious and cultural consensus. When applied to early nineteenth-century religion, the term not only depicts how certain groups stood outside the citadels of Protestant ecclesiastical power, but also reveals how certain theological impulses, often originating in Europe, took on radically new manifestations in the United States. The next two chapters explore a cross section of groups that in unique ways embody the label of "religious outsiders." Some of these groups were noteworthy in terms of how they engaged earlier Christian traditions concerning the end times. Other groups reinterpreted earlier understandings of Christian perfectionism in ways that led to distinctive experiments in communal living.

Finally, as chapter 7 discusses, the early nineteenth-century context provides an opportunity to see how historical traditions of Christianity were
reinterpreted by two disparate groups: immigrant Catholics and African
Americans. For all the differences between the movements covered in the
next two chapters, they served notice that in an era of perceived evangelical Protestant dominance, this spirit of sectarianism would become
an equally dominant theme in the development of American Christianity.

ON THE CUSP OF THE END TIMES
The Shaker Example

Since the earliest days of colonial settlement, American Christianity carried a strong belief that one day the world would come to an end. The belief
that people might live to see the return of Christ was not just a pattern
coming out of New England Puritanism, but one that reflected a persistent current through many colonial religious movements. A number of
Anabaptist groups, such as the Mennonites, and Spiritualists (groups such
as the Quakers), held with varying degrees of fidelity to the idea that they
might be living amid the last days before a final divine judgment would
occur. Part of what fostered this early apocalyptic speculation was not
simply abstract theological speculation, but the ways that these communities identified their mission with the desire to build righteous God-fearing
societies on earth. While the early Puritans had a distinctive sense of being
set apart from nonbelievers, their faith was predicated upon living in a
world in which they would have to interact with saints and sinners daily.

Yet by the early nineteenth century, groups were emerging in America
that not only took the power of their beliefs seriously (often seeing their
own unique iteration of religion as the only valid religious truth), but felt
the only way to maintain that vision of truth was to withdraw from nonbelievers into separatist communities. The United Society of Believers in
Christ's Second Appearing, commonly known as the Shakers, was one of
the first American religious groups in the early national period to follow
this pattern.

Much speculation surrounds the origins of this group. Although the
Shakers were frequently associated with Quakers, their developing theology and, in particular, their worship style, deviated significantly from the
Friends' emphasis on silence and the inner light. Evidence suggests that
those who became Shakers were drawn into the movement through a radical group of French Huguenots, often referred to as the French Prophets.
Followers of this French sect made their way to Manchester, England, in

the mid-1700s and attracted a following among a small group of men and women in that city. The ecstatic behavior of this new sect quickly earned them the name "Shaking Quakers" because of the ways that this new group emphasized the direct intersession of the Holy Spirit and spurned the ecclesiastical legitimacy of other Christian churches. These Shaking Quakers were far more extreme than the Friends, both in their sectarian desire to withdraw from society and in their urgent apocalyptic speculation that the end of the world was occurring soon.

The central figure of the Shakers was an individual that historians know very little, Ann Lee. Lee was born to a working-class family in 1736 and apparently became an early convert to the teachings of the French Prophets. Before her immigration to America in 1774, she had been arrested on several occasions for her public advocacy of her religious positions (and consistent with earlier Quaker practices in the seventeenth century, her behavior included interrupting church services through spoken testimony). However, after she and a small group of other Shakers arrived in the American colonies, Lee dropped off the historical radar for several years. It was not until 1779 that a Shaker community formed outside of Albany, New York, in a village called Niskayuna. For the next several years, Niskayuna became the base where members of the community, including Ann Lee, traveled throughout eastern New York and Massachusetts to recruit followers. The unusual character of Lee's teachings, especially stressing the apostasy of all existing churches, and the imminent end of the world did not go over well with civil authorities and their neighbors given the fact that America was in the middle of its war for independence. After several more imprisonments, Lee's health finally broke and she died in 1784.

Lee's death marked a period over the next four decades during which the movement grew, if not large in size, to be at least prominent in its distinctive theological beliefs, worship practices, and self-sustaining economic enterprises. Lee left behind no corpus of writings, but her example combined Christian hospitality with firm theological convictions anchored the movement, as it spread to other communities in New England and the Midwest. Largely through the mission work of one of Lee's disciples, Lucy Wright, the Shakers experienced modest growth. At its peak membership in the 1820s, there were twenty-three Shaker villages, stretching from Maine to Kentucky, with approximately 5,000 members.[1] On one hand, Shaker lifestyles were even more austere than the earlier Quakers. Practicing strict celibacy, the movement's theology emphasized the rewards of heaven that would befall the believers upon Christ's return. By the same token, Shaker worship was far from austere or dull. While congregants would be segregated by gender, services were characterized by lively music and expressive dances. Many early Shaker hymns (including the popular hymn "Simple Gifts") would be revised and adapted into the liturgies of many churches and denominations in the twentieth century. Most noticeable to an observer, however, was the spirit manifestations of shaking that paralleled the religious vibrancy of the Second Great Awakening, but also anticipated patterns of religious ecstasy of later Christian movements, in particular, pentecostalism.

Shaker communities slowly declined throughout the nineteenth century (which is perhaps, in part, explained by the tradition's strict adherence to celibacy). However, the economic model of Shaker communities, anchored in the making of crafts and furniture, helped many of their communities survive, even as the movement was reduced to a handful of Shaker villages in New England by the end of the twentieth century. Several religious communities that formed in the early nineteenth century often sought to emulate the economic practices of the Shakers—if not their theology.

The Shakers were only one small manifestation of larger movements of apocalyptic theology that swept through America in the early nineteenth century. In the aftermath of the Revolutionary War, however, apocalyptic beliefs became more strident as a number of new religious movements not only followed the example of the Shakers by renouncing all other churches, but made apocalyptic speculation a centerpiece of their theologies. Historians have noted that conditions of the early nineteenth century, including the specter of new lands in the west, the communal egalitarianism of the Second Great Awakening, and a general sense of uncertainty about the new nation's future, contributed to the widespread speculation about the end times. While many Americans ridiculed the practices and apocalyptic pronouncements of groups such as the Shakers, the Shaker phenomenon was only the tip of the iceberg of an emerging range of movements that made apocalyptic speculation central to their identity.

A NEW ERRAND INTO THE WILDERNESS
The Religious Odyssey of Joseph Smith

The use of the term "sect" is often understood as an aberrant label whereby a religious group does not reflect belief patterns that are deemed by the larger society as acceptable by convention and custom. Historically however, religious sectarianism has been a critical part of understanding religious renewal. Scholars have recognized that religious sects are spawned not out of a desire to pervert or destroy a tradition, but to renew it. Many Christian churches historically have been born out of this impulse in which new Christian movements are birthed out of a desire to restore what is perceived to be the waywardness within dominant faith traditions. During the sixteenth and seventeenth centuries, a range of Protestant churches were formed from this impulse. Throughout the seventeenth and eighteenth centuries, America became a sanctuary for several Christian sects that fled persecution in their home countries such as Great Britain and Germany. Yet as the fires of revivalism started to die down by the 1830s, new homegrown sectarian movements were challenging the legitimacy of every other American church. In particular, the restorationist spirit of the Second Great Awakening produced movements that not only claimed the mantle of primitive Christianity, but also sought to sever any sort of theological connection with European religious movements. At the top of the list of new religious movements to emerge in this era, perhaps the most enduring and most uniquely American has been the Church of Jesus Christ of Latter-day Saints (LDS), also known as the Mormons.

In many ways, the growth of the LDS movement can almost be viewed through a lens comparable with various Puritan groups from the seventeenth century who found themselves in a wilderness filled with apostate people. Early Mormons did not view themselves as religious extremists (or fanatics), but as a chosen people who were proclaiming and carrying the revealed truth of God in their mission. Their history was one of unprecedented uniqueness and was, in its own way, quintessentially American. Mark Twain gave one of many caustic summations of Mormonism in the nineteenth century when he referred to the LDS's scripture, the *Book of Mormon*, as "chloroform in print." Leonard Bacon, a historian who tried to cast an irenic posture toward most Christian churches, could not hide his disdain for Mormonism—one shared by most of his Protestant contemporaries. Noting that the movement's founder Joseph Smith was nothing more than "a disreputable adventurer," he marveled "that the silly lies put forth by this precious gang should have found believers."[2] Yet even Bacon had to concede that there was something distinctively American about Mormonism and that the movement was in its own way an inevitable, but unfortunate, consequence of the revivalist spirit of the age.

Mormonism picked up on two significant motifs that emerged in early nineteenth-century America: sectarianism and millennialism. However, the rise of the LDS reflects one of the most unique examples in American history of Christian restorationism. Many restorationist movements of the early nineteenth century vehemently rejected other institutional forms of Christianity. However, Mormons took this impulse a step further by seeking to provide extracanonical means for followers not only to understand the Bible, but to understand why God chose Joseph Smith as the person who would unlock the final mysteries of God's divine plan in ways not revealed in the Bible.

In the early nineteenth century, many evangelicals believed that America stood on the cusp of an era in which the full manifestation of God's kingdom would be revealed. Numerous Protestant evangelists sought the eradication of social evils and believed that their efforts would help usher in the kingdom of God even as they cast a wary eye toward humanity's sinful nature. Mormonism shifted this kingdom equation significantly. While early Mormons shared strong convictions with other evangelical Protestants about the coming of Christ, the Church of Jesus Christ of Latter-day Saints was conceived as the *only* true church whose members lived in a wicked world and where the faithful needed to gather to escape the wrath to come. This fundamental theological stance would come to define many future movements within American Christianity.

As vilified as he would become in the minds of Americans such as Mark Twain and Leonard Bacon, Joseph Smith was nothing but an American original. Smith was born in rural Vermont in 1805 and reared in a family that perpetually lived on the edge of poverty. After the failure of the family farm, the Smiths headed to western New York, settling near the village of Palmyra, outside of Rochester. Here, the family continued to struggle economically, but it was also the context from which Joseph developed his interest in religion. In 1820 western New York was in the midst of massive revivalism, reflecting its identification as "the Burned-Over District" during the Second Great Awakening because of its intense revivalist fervor. The Smith family lived in an area that was on the main thoroughfare for western migration, and in 1825, the opening of the Erie Canal would continue this pattern as countless Americans left New England in search of economic opportunities either in rural agricultural communities in New York, Pennsylvania, and Ohio, or in growing Great Lakes cities including Rochester, Buffalo, and Cleveland. In addition to Methodist revivalists, the region outside of Rochester where the Smith family operated a farm was filled with a number of different churches, including Methodist, Presbyterian, and Universalist churches, all of which competed for the loyalties of the region's population. Put simply, Smith's family was exposed to just about every type and style of Protestantism in existence in the early nineteenth century.

Smith's anxiety over the sheer number of Christian groups led to his first recorded vision. In 1820, while still a teenager, he was visited by two personages who warned him to stay away from all existing churches and sects because all of them were false. Over the next several years, Smith recounted other divine visions that told him of the existence of gold plates buried not far from his home, representing the consummation of the truths proclaimed in the Bible. In 1827 an angel named Moroni, a descendent of a long-forgotten Jewish tribe that had come to America hundreds of years before Christ's birth, revealed the location of these plates on a hillside not far from the Smith farm. Smith unearthed these plates, which appeared to him in an unknown ancient dialect (what he later termed "Reformed Egyptian"), and using the aid of seer stones that accompanied the plates (called the Urim and Thummim), he translated these plates into English. In early 1830 Smith's translation was published as the *Book of Mormon*.

Smith's visions and the ensuing publication of the *Book of Mormon* must be viewed in the context of the historical era that produced them. The fact that Smith was the recipient of divine visions is hardly surprising given that he lived during a time when many Americans were claiming similar manifestations of the spirit. Mormon tradition relied on commonly practiced notions of religious syncretism, bringing together aspects of evangelical Protestantism with a vast array of folk religions that had been long present in America. Like his father, Smith was interested in prospecting, and was constantly on the lookout for devices such as "divining rods" and seer stones that would lead him to unearth gold and other precious minerals. Smith failed in the task of unearthing material wealth, but he prospered in terms of unearthing what appeared to others not just a set of unique religious beliefs, but a whole new manifestation of religious truth. Later generations of Mormons would staunchly argue that theirs is an authentic expression of Christianity, entirely consistent with the religious and theological claims made by other Christian churches and denominations. However, as historian Jan Shipps points out, Mormonism in its early forms emerged in America as a third distinctive religious tradition along with Judaism and Christianity.[3] A major part of this identification rests with the authority that the LDS place upon the *Book of Mormon*.

For nineteenth-century critics, the *Book of Mormon* embodies the fanciful narratives of a crazy man, but for believers, this book represents not just a continuation of the biblical narrative, but provides the basis for the group's claims as a chosen people. The book tells the saga of the tribe of Lehi, a family that escaped ancient Judah just prior to its fall at the hands of the Babylonian Empire in 587 BCE, ultimately to end up on the shores of America. The descendants of the family patriarch split between two sons whose descendants fought for supremacy of the continent. The Nephites represented a dynasty of righteous people, while their rivals, the Lamanites, tended to operate on cunning and deceit. Over hundreds of years, the Lamanites won out, but not before Christ made an appearance before the peoples of the New World. The *Book of Mormon* reflected both a tale of tragedy (via the fall of the Nephites), but also one of hope. The angel Moroni who appeared to Joseph Smith was not only a descendant of the Nephite family, but manifested the belief that Joseph Smith (whose rule as a prophet was foretold by the *Book of Mormon*) would serve as God's prophet for the American people.

The *Book of Mormon* has been analyzed for the ways that it adapted many distinctive American currents of popular religion (including an interest in Masonic beliefs). However, the core of the book's message was centered upon a uniquely American restorationist vision of primitive Christianity. Smith not only lived within a historical context that encouraged supernatural speculation, but spoke to the cultural imagination of many Americans who were seeking to make sense of the social-religious context of the early nineteenth century. In a time that witnessed the collapse of colonial society and the availability of lands for population migration, persons such as Joseph Smith came up with a message that offered a compelling interpretation not simply of religious truth, but of the American experience, in general. As historian Jon Butler noted, one simple reason that the *Book of Mormon* was effective is that it transferred the main arena of God's activity from the Middle East to America. "This new scenario enables the Mormons to transcend the Protestant denomination rivalries that had so repelled Smith. The *Book of Mormon* offered American readers a wholly fresh, wholly novel, and—most important—wholly innocent new Scripture."[4]

In language that harkened back to Old Testament images, the Mormons emphasized their separateness not only from other Christian churches, but from the rest of the world (referring to non-Mormons as gentiles). By 1840 these latter-day saints were in the midst of a decade in which Smith, like Moses, led his followers in a sojourn through the American wilderness. Opposition to Mormons led the movement out of western New York early in 1831, and they settled in Kirkland, Ohio; Independence, Missouri; and finally, in 1839, Nauvoo, Illinois. What characterized Mormon leadership under Joseph Smith and his closest lieutenants, Sidney Rigdon and Brigham Young, was the way in which the Saints openly defied social conventions of the time. Sociologists Luther Gerlach and Virginia Hine note that the growth of social movements is often accelerated whenever it encounters real or perceived opposition from the dominant culture.[5] This reality certainly galvanized the growth of the LDS. As a verse from a popular Mormon hymn in the 1830s asserted:

> We want no cowards in our bands,
> Who will our colors fly:
> We call for valiant-hearted men,
> Who're not afraid to die![6]

Throughout the 1830s Mormon communities that followed Smith west fostered not only religious sectarianism, but like the Shakers, fostered economic and political self reliance as well. Also, by the time the LDS set up the city of Nauvoo in 1839 (which for a time became the largest city in Illinois), Smith's visions had moved further beyond the parameters of conventional Christian beliefs. Through an array of pronouncements during the 1830s and early 1840s, Smith announced the acceptance of the baptism of the dead and, even more controversially, polygamy.

During the Mormons' sojourns in the 1830s and 1840s, Smith was subjected to frequent arrests and beatings, yet he never wavered in his convictions that the LDS represented the true incarnation of God's revealed word on earth, nor did he step away from his role as God's messenger. In the culmination of his tumultuous career as a religious leader, in 1844 Smith announced his candidacy for the U.S. presidency. When a Nauvoo newspaper publically criticized Smith's leadership, he had the press shut down, leading to his arrest. On June 27, Smith and his brother Hyrum were murdered by a mob that stormed the Carthage, Illinois, jail where they were being held.

Smith's death served as a symbol of religious martyrdom to his followers. While a small faction of Mormons split off to form a church based in Independence, Missouri, the mainstream of the movement followed Smith's successor, Brigham Young, west on a thousand-mile trek to Salt Lake City, Utah, arriving at this final destination in 1847. Young's leadership as president/prophet of the Mormons continued the confrontational "outsider" posture employed by Smith, including an embrace of polygamy and an open contempt for American political authority. By 1850, twenty years after Smith introduced the *Book of Mormon* to a small group of associates in western New York, the LDS numbered 60,000 members, with active missionaries in Europe.

By the end of the nineteenth century, many of the most controversial Mormon ordinances had been abandoned, particularly the acceptance of polygamy. When polygamy was dropped as an approved practice of the LDS in 1890, it prefigured the entry into the Union of Utah as the forty-fifth state in 1896. However, the movement's unconventional sectarianism would continue to draw new converts, even as many LDS members during the twentieth century sought to recast themselves within the mainstream of American culture. Yet Smith was far from being the only religious innovator of the early nineteenth century. In the years following Joseph Smith's death, another Vermont native stressed his own unique theological response to the times.

In 1848 John Humphrey Noyes, a former student at the Calvinist-oriented Andover Theological Seminary, led a group of followers from Putney, Vermont, to establish a utopian community in Oneida, New York. Like Joseph Smith, Noyes reached a point of disillusionment with the era's churches, and his theological solution led to one of the most unique religious experiments in the nineteenth century. For the next thirty years, Oneida existed as a utopian community that practiced economic self-sufficiency (ultimately becoming one of the major producers of silverware in the United States), social egalitarianism (where men and women shared in the economics of the community), and religious practices that syncretized Noyes' distinctive views on Christian perfectionism and millennialism. As we have seen, various theological interpretations of the doctrine of sanctification frequently produced wide-ranging efforts in personal morality and social betterment. Yet Noyes' understanding of the doctrine was integrated by a pervasive millennialism and a unique model of social experimentation. Insisting that the second coming of Christ had already occurred, Noyes believed that humans were no longer bound to earlier social institutions, such as marriage, that often suppressed the ability of persons to live lives of perfect devotion to God. Unlike the Shakers, who saw holiness manifested through strict practices of celibacy, Noyes developed highly controversial beliefs in sexual experimentation, epitomized by what he called "complex marriages."

Overseen by Noyes, sexual interactions were regulated between couples in the community (in which older women were often paired with younger men and young women with older men). In an era when pregnancies could be very dangerous medically, Noyes argued that conventional marriage had robbed women of any semblance of social equality because sexual relationships often put women's lives in danger. While later images of the community would often see its values as nihilistic and amoral, community life was strictly regimented and all members (including Noyes) were expected to engage one another in frequent sessions of "mutual criticism" whereby it was hoped that persons would grow in grace as they served God and the community. At the same time, the community had a level of openness with the outside world, as it frequently held visitor days in which Oneida's townspeople, supporters, and critics alike could meet and interact with those in the community (and visitors to the community might have noticed that the women were dressed in a distinctive short-skirted garb that prefigured the popularity later that century of the dress known as the bloomer).

Yet the controversial practices of Noyes ultimately led to numerous legal confrontations that forced him to abandon the Oneida Community in 1878. Many of the children born at Oneida bore a striking resemblance to the community's founder, and a large part of Noyes' vision of Christian perfection was predicated upon what amounted to a form of eugenics. By 1880 Oneida discarded its controversial religious practices to focus solely on its economic functions predicated on the manufacturing of silverware. The pattern of economic innovation outliving religious conviction would be followed by other nineteenth-century experimental communities (perhaps most notably, the German pietist Amana Colonies of eastern Iowa that ultimately become an economic innovator in food refrigeration and air conditioning).

The fate of the Oneida colony revolved around one factor: its millennial vision and radical social practices did not survive its founding generation. Yet there were numerous other groups that filled that void, and the early nineteenth century witnessed the emergence of movements whose legacy of millennial thought carries down to this day. Perhaps the most dramatic example of Christian millennialism in the 1830s and 1840s was the Millerite movement.

PREDICTING THE SECOND COMING
William Miller and the End of the World

Since the time of the first Puritan settlements, American Christianity has fostered belief in the idea of Christ's second coming. In the early nineteenth century, these earlier themes took on a new sense of urgency and perhaps no movement in American history illustrates that urgency more than the Millerites. Like other sectarian Protestant groups such as the Mormons, the Millerites had an unlikely prophet: William Miller. Like Joseph Smith, Miller came from humble origins. Born in 1782, he grew up in Massachusetts and Vermont, and his sustained interest in religion began after his return from the War of 1812, where he was drawn into the spirit of revivalism sweeping the country. Ultimately settling in upstate New York, Miller became a Baptist and like many Baptists of that era, supported his preaching through farming. Like many Americans of the time, Miller was gripped by the spirit of restorationalism and millennialism. The difference in Miller was the specificity in predicting an exact date for the end of the world. Like Christians before him, Miller was fascinated by the cryptic messages contained within the biblical books of Daniel and Revelation. In the twelfth century, a monk named Joachim of Fiore used these books to predict a precise date for the end of the world, and successive generations carried forward this fascination with the apocalyptic speculation in these texts.

The Greek root of the word "apocalypse" means "hidden," and part of the way that Miller approached his interpretation of Scripture was his belief that he had cracked a hidden code. At the same time that Joseph Smith was leading his converts out of Ohio and Missouri in the mid-1830s, Miller was preaching throughout the northeastern United States that his study of Scripture revealed a startling fact: the world would come to an end sometime in 1843 or early 1844. Employing elaborate illustrations to support his arguments, Miller constructed a chronology of biblical and historical events since the time of Genesis and was convinced that the books of Daniel and Revelation pointed to Christ's imminent second coming.

Miller's apocalyptic vision most likely would have come for naught if he had not received the sponsorship of Joshua Himes, a prominent Boston minister and publisher. Himes supported Miller's efforts to publicize his work through the publication of a periodical and sponsored his speaking at a number of camp meeting revivals. The years leading up to Miller's window for the end times led to an increase in national excitement. Convinced in the persuasive means by which Miller used the Bible, citing chapters and verses of Scripture that pointed to the end times, followers began to sell off their possessions and joined one another in a massive assembly of thousands of people on Miller's upstate New York farm in Hampton, New York. When by early 1844 the second coming didn't occur, Miller reasoned that he did not take into account the year zero in his calculations, settling on a new date of October 22, 1844. Again the crowds gathered only to experience what Miller and his followers termed the "Great Disappointment" when Jesus did not return at the appointed time.

Miller lived his final years trying to recalculate his errors, and in the eyes of some followers, he was a disgraced figure. However, his understanding of what came to be known as "Bible prophecy" would become a central theme in American Christianity by the close of the nineteenth century. What constituted Miller's appeal and led to his downfall was his insistence on dating the exact time of the second coming. Since Miller, many Christian apocalyptic movements would continue to read the Bible with an eye toward cracking a hidden code pointing to the end times. Although some apocalyptic Christian communities would still insist on predicting exact dates for the end of the world, many future leaders who picked up on the Millerite cause avoided precise dating while still holding followers attentive to the possibility that the end was near. These apocalyptic movements grew throughout the nineteenth century and, while rooted in different theological traditions, shared faith that the Bible pointed Americans to the path of salvation *and* gave them a clear blueprint for the last days of humanity before the end of time.

SURVIVING THE GREAT DISAPPOINTMENT

The coming of the Great Disappointment shattered the hopes of many of William Miller's followers, but it didn't destroy his dreams. In the years following 1844, some Millerites sought to recalculate Miller's arithmetic, and periodically new dates were set for the end of the world. By the early 1850s, however, many within the Millerite fold needed to redefine their mission, if not their faith. Some Millerites found other millennial groups to join, such as the Shakers. However, many Millerite followers ended up forming a variety of different movements that stayed rooted in the idea of Christ's imminent second coming without deciding upon an exact date. This emerging group of Adventist churches (named after the belief in the second coming, or Advent of Christ) represented a unique blending of theological and practical themes.

Perhaps the most significant of these Adventist groups to form out of the Millerite movement was the Seventh-day Adventist Church. The Seventh-day Adventists argued that what happened (or didn't happen) on October 22, 1844, was a preparation phase that would ultimately lead to the second coming. These Millerites reinterpreted the events of 1844 as a movement of Christ to "cleanse the sanctuary," whereby the truly faithful would be made more righteous prior to meeting Christ.[7] Led by a former Millerite, Ellen White (1827–1915), the Seventh-day Adventists not only continued to speak about the inevitability of Christ's second coming, but established a number of practices that helped define their uniqueness from other Christian movements. Historians note that part of understanding the rise of churches such as the Seventh-day Adventists was not simply a desire to keep the legacy of William Miller alive, but to provide followers a way to hold in tension the inevitability of the second coming with the need to keep living a righteous life on earth. White's response was to stress the moral purity of the community, including faith practices and even one's diet. She created a movement that held in tension care for the body and the soul. One characteristic was the practice of celebrating the Sabbath on Saturdays (akin to Jewish tradition). A wide-ranging cultural impact of the tradition was how this church promoted strict dietary practices, including introducing to many Americans the benefits of vegetarian diets. In the latter part of the nineteenth century, this tradition spawned a number of health sanitariums designed to promote healthy lifestyles centered upon exercise and diets.

The Adventist model proved effective holding in tension an apocalyptic theology within an evolving denominational structure. While the fledgling church initially spurned evangelism, the movement grew steadily throughout the nineteenth century. From approximately 3,000 members in the early 1860s, by the early twentieth century, the Seventh-day Adventists had over 50,000 members. By the end of the twentieth century, that total was closing in on a million members. This church's ability to balance a millennial theology with an institutional framework to back and sustain it would resonate within many other Protestant churches later in the nineteenth century. Perhaps no movement of American Christianity has been as successful, both on a popular and institutional scale, than a form of millennial theology that became prominent in many Protestant churches by the end of the century: dispensationalism.

When one looks at the spectrum of many sectarian movements discussed so far in this chapter, they reflect a strong fidelity to unique forms of communal living and a belief (in some form) that Christ's final judgment upon the earth was coming soon. Yet while America was becoming cognizant of groups such as the Millerites, Adventists, and Latter-day Saints, another manifestation of religious offshoots believed that the power of Christianity was not manifested through its supernaturalism, but on how the power of God was made manifest by how persons could live moral and ethical lives—without worrying about the life to come.

UNITARIANISM AND UNIVERSALISM

As a tradition, Unitarianism has roots that go back to the sixteenth-century Reformation and to individuals such as Michael Servetus who taught that the doctrine of the Trinity was unbiblical. Following the path of Christian rationalism paved by Charles Chauncy, several New England Congregational churches during the late eighteenth century began turning to Unitarian theology. In 1788 King's Chapel in Boston, the oldest Anglican congregation in New England, became the first recognized American Unitarian church, observing aspects of Anglican liturgy devoid of all Trinitarian references. Yet American Unitarianism as a distinctive theological tradition largely took shape in the early nineteenth century as a movement that not only expunged Trinitarian language, but promoted an Enlightenment worldview fundamentally at odds with older Calvinist theologies.

As a formal denomination, Unitarianism was never very large, yet the movement prefigured the theological fissures that would develop in American Protestantism on a much larger scale in the latter half of the nineteenth century. Two events galvanized the formation of Unitarianism as a distinct movement within New England Congregationalism. In 1805 a vacant faculty chair of divinity at Harvard College was filled by a Unitarian minister, Henry Ware. In reaction to this appointment, a coalition of New Light/Old Light Congregational clergy formed the Andover Theological Seminary in 1807 as a rival to Harvard. These events marked a process over the next two decades whereby Unitarian and Calvinist Congregationalists disassociated from one another. While the founding of Andover Seminary not only marked a rupture within Congregationalism (and the founding of America's first theological seminary), it signaled the beginnings in the formation of American theological liberalism.

The most influential figure in Unitarianism in its early American iterations was William Ellery Channing. As the pastor of Boston's Federal Street Church, Channing became the major figure of the Unitarian movement from the late 1810s until his death in 1842. Channing's theology makes evident that he saw himself as a defender of true Christianity predicated on the Bible and scriptural authority. Yet his main critique of Trinitarian theology (in particular, New England Calvinism) was its doctrine of sin that negated, in his mind, any ability of humans to work for individual virtue and the betterment of society. "We object, strongly, to the idea of many Christians respecting man's impotence and God's irresistible agency on the heart, believing that they subvert our responsibility and the laws of our moral nature," he noted in one of his most famous sermons, "Unitarian Christianity" in 1819. From Channing's perspective, orthodoxy made "men machines," in effect making it easy to blame God "of all evil deeds, that they discourage good minds and inflate the fanatical with wild conceits of immediate and sensible inspirations."[8] Channing did become involved in a number of inter-Protestant cooperative ventures in his ministry. Yet unlike their Universalist cousins who often engaged in fervent revivals in the northeast, Unitarianism largely rejected the ethos of revivalism as catering to superstition and irrational fear of divine punishment. Like their Puritan forbearers, however, Unitarianism played a major role in the intellectual development of American theology that was disproportionate to its relatively small size and geographic base in New England.

Closely associated with Unitarianism theologically, but reflecting a more populist orientation culturally, was Universalism. Universalism accentuated the eighteenth-century legacy of Charles Chauncy, emphasizing the theme of universal salvation as the key message of Scripture. Its membership consisted of many disaffected Protestants, including Congregationalists, Baptists, and Methodists. While a small movement, it shared with other evangelical Protestants a desire to expand geographically, and although vastly outnumbered by Methodists, Baptists, and Presbyterians, this small movement thrived in parts of the frontier, competing against many revivalist churches in upstate New York and Pennsylvania. Later in the nineteenth century, it extended its mission to areas of the American West and became one of the few nineteenth-century traditions that ordained women. By the end of the nineteenth century, while social-economic factors tended to keep the two movements apart (with the Universalists leaning toward a more populist base), Unitarianism and Universalism reflected a shared emphasis on liberal theology, the goodness of humanity, and, ultimately, a movement away from the exclusive reliance on the Bible as the sole source of theological truth.

One individual drawn to Universalism was a young man from rural Vermont, Orestes Brownson. Born in 1803, Brownson, much like his fellow Vermonter Joseph Smith, was a religious seeker. While initially trained as a school teacher, Brownson was attracted to many of the theological tenets of Universalism, in particular its understanding that the teachings of Jesus pointed to universal salvation. Eventually, Brownson entered the

Universalist ministry, serving for a time in a rural parish in upstate New York. However, he soon grew tired of parish ministry and longed to pursue a career as a writer. After a stint as the editor of a Universalist newspaper, Brownson ended up in Boston where he threw himself full time into literary pursuits. By the end of the 1830s, he was one of the central figures associated with a distinctive offshoot of Unitarianism, commonly referred to as Transcendentalism.

TRANSCENDENTALISM

Often, the study of history calls upon one to recognize that sometimes the most significant legacies are crafted by movements that did not attract mass followings. This observation is especially true of the rise of the Transcendentalist movements of the 1830s and 1840s. Transcendentalists were not sectarian in the sense that they looked to an apocalyptic end of history, nor did they engage in the quest for religious perfectionism as did many Protestant evangelicals of the era. By the same token, persons associated with what became known as the Transcendentalists believed that their understanding of religion would lead persons to a new way to think about God's relationship to the world.

At its core, Transcendentalism was a movement that emerged out of New England Unitarianism. Although early Unitarians such as William Ellery Channing preached a "liberal" message that emphasized human goodness, they clearly identified themselves as part of the Christian tradition, with many Unitarians holding on to belief in biblical miracles and the miraculous nature of Christ's life, death, and resurrection. By the 1830s, however, a sense of disillusionment settled over many Unitarian clergy who believed that many aspects of traditional Unitarianism were out of synch with the emerging realities of the nineteenth century. By 1840 the first examples of what became known later in the century as biblical criticism found its way to America from Germany. These writings not only questioned the supernaturalism associated with Christ, but drew greater attention to the moral stirrings of Jesus' teaching that increasingly became an important theme in the future development of American theological liberalism.

The tone for much of the Transcendentalist movement was set by Ralph Waldo Emerson. A former Unitarian minister, Emerson became disillusioned with his parish work and advocated a model of faith that spoke more to the power of humans to perceive the divine within the world, as opposed for humans to wait upon God's intervention into the world. The great manifesto of Transcendentalism came in 1838 when Emerson gave an address to the graduating class of Harvard Divinity School. At the time of Emerson's address, Harvard Divinity School was considered the standard bearer of New England Unitarianism. Many of Harvard's faculty had been, or were, well-known pastors in and around the Boston area, who stressed the combination of rationalism and inherited Christianity that had been the cornerstone of clergy like Channing. Yet Emerson, in his short address at Harvard, not only challenged the heritage of Christian Unitarianism, but prompted his audience to envision Christianity and religion in a whole new way. "Jesus Christ belonged to the true race of prophets. He saw with open eye the mystery of the soul. Drawn by its severe harmony, ravished with its beauty, he lived in it, and had his being there." In juxtaposition to classical traditions of Christian thought, one shared by evangelical Protestants and many Unitarians in the 1830s, Emerson asserted that Jesus did not come into the world to show sinners the path to salvation, but to reveal the divine spark that existed within every person. "Alone in all history, he estimated the greatness of man. One man was true to what is in you and me. He saw that God incarnates himself in man, and evermore goes forth anew to take possession of his world."[9]

Emerson's message, that religion was not primarily about inherited tradition but uncovering the natural truth revealed by God in the world, attracted an eclectic network of intellectuals and social reformers. This group included Margaret Fuller, a pioneer nineteenth-century feminist, the abolitionist leader Theodore Parker, and another former Unitarian pastor, George Ripley. In many ways, Transcendentalism was as much a literary movement, as it was a religious one. Highly influenced by several early nineteenth-century English Romantic writers, in particular Samuel Taylor Coleridge, Transcendentalists celebrated the goodness of humanity and the natural world. Part of the literary spirit that spoke to people like Emerson was to find ways to take what was valuable within certain teachings of Christianity (and like Jefferson, emphasizing the moral teachings of Jesus) and to apply these themes practically toward the creation of alternative models of living. Perhaps the figure who most embodied this spirit was a young Harvard graduate and sometime protégé of Emerson's, Henry David Thoreau.

Thoreau's public career embodied many classical Transcendentalist themes, including the idea of the divine within, the veneration of the natural world, and a distrust of many aspects of modern society, including industrialization. Perhaps the classic phase of Thoreau's career occurred in the mid-1840s when he lived in isolation for several months in a tiny cabin on Walden Pond, just outside of Boston. Thoreau's writings display ambivalence toward historical Christianity. As he noted in his book, *Walden*, "Christ was a sublime actor on the stage of the world. He knew what he was thinking when he said, 'Heaven and earth shall pass away, but my words shall not pass away.' I draw near to him at such a time. Yet he taught mankind but imperfectly how to live; his thoughts were all directed toward another world. There is another kind of success than his."[10] While it is true that Thoreau celebrated the virtues of nature, his larger concern was to protest the tenets of modern society that from his perspective had imposed a false framework upon the lives of modern humanity. Foremost for him were his ideas of civil disobedience that asserted the natural right of humans to abstain from participating in any laws that a person deemed unjust. Although Thoreau is not primarily associated with Christianity, his influence on later Christian leaders, most especially Martin Luther King Jr., is unmistakable.

Yet Thoreau's impulse to isolate himself from the world and his almost anarchistic tendencies toward authority were not embraced by the vast majority of people associated with Transcendentalism. In the years leading up to Thoreau's sojourn at Walden Pond, George Ripley and his wife Sophia were the principal founders of an experimental community that sought to apply the transcendentalist vision in a communitarian manner through the establishment of the utopian community Brook Farm.

Brook Farm was one of several short-lived nineteenth-century experiments in community living that, in its own way, sought to integrate a religious vision with a distinctive political model. Established in West Roxbury, Massachusetts (outside of Boston) in 1841, Brook Farm was to offer residents a more simple life that would likewise provide residents with leisure time to engage in learned pursuits. Members of the community, men and women alike, shared equally in labor, and the community established a school that provided both primary and college preparatory courses. The community regularly sponsored lectures by a range of figures sympathetic to Transcendentalism, and many visitors reflected upon the spirit of vitality that occupied Brook Farm. Although Thomas Jefferson may not have agreed with some of the socialistic premises of Brook Farm, he likely would have seen the community's values as a prime example of the type of religion he believed would dominate America's future. (As well as another short-lived Transcendentalist community, Fruitlands, founded in 1843 just west of Brook Farm.)

Yet like many experimental communities of that era, practical considerations destroyed Brook Farm. The agricultural initiatives that were to be the economic backbone of the community were unsuccessful, and the decision in 1845 to align the community's aims more directly with a specific model of political socialism (represented at that time by the French theorist Charles Fourier) caused several defections from the community. Finally in 1847, after the collapse of a major building program, the community closed its doors.

The Transcendentalists from Brook Farm went off in different directions. Some, including Ripley, continued their literary pursuits. Others identified themselves increasingly with a model of Unitarianism epitomized by the antislavery activism of Theodore Parker that looked beyond Christian sources and tradition while also continuing to emphasize the moral model of Jesus to the contemporary world. There were still others, including Ripley's wife, Sophia, who grew disillusioned with the Transcendentalist message and ultimately found solace within more traditional forms of historical Christianity. For Sophia Ripley and two other Brook Farm supporters, Isaac Hecker and Orestes Brownson, this meant a return to what many Americans saw as the discarded faith of the Old World: Catholicism.

RELIGIOUS OUTSIDERS OR INSIDERS?

On the surface, Brook Farm had little to do with other forms of Christian sectarianism during the first half of the nineteenth century. Yet Brook Farm shared with other communities a desire to break away from the emerging social-economic patterns of what America in the nineteenth century was becoming: mainly, a nation that was increasingly urban and industrial. As the nineteenth century progressed, many religious groups such as the Mormons and Seventh-day Adventists would seek ways to accommodate their beliefs to a predominant cultural and religious mainstream. Although Mormonism would splinter into scores of groups that continued to practice polygamy and move further into sectarianism, by the twentieth century, the core of the Mormon movement sought to define itself as part of the cultural and religious center of the nation. Even the proliferation of numerous Adventist groups during the nineteenth century showed how some of these groups, while continuing to believe that the end of the world was near, nevertheless made efforts to accommodate their beliefs to the ways of the world.

Some communitarian experiments like Brook Farm embodied the "enlightened religion" envisioned by many of the nation's founding fathers, such as Thomas Jefferson. Yet, social utopias, predicated upon mixing a vision of liberal religion and political idealism, have had an uneven record in American history. At the same time, these communities are unique because they reflect upon how predominant religious and philosophical values of the Enlightenment have been used to protest the perceived faults of modern industrialized capitalist societies.

By the time of the Great Depression in the 1930s, many rural communities, especially in the American South, founded a number of experimental communities whose ideals were not far removed from Brook Farm. Practicing their own primitive forms of "communism," they were committed to providing economic support to rural communities most heavily affected by the Great Depression while also displaying a concern for the religious and political idealism of Brook Farm.[11] Many of these communities fostered a range of religious activists who protested the capitalism and militarism of twentieth-century America. By the 1950s some of these dissenters explored creative new approaches of communitarian and nonviolent living that were germane to the success of the American Civil Rights movement.

Just as the descendants of the Millerites scattered in many directions, so did those associated with the experimental religion of Transcendentalism. Some, including Ralph Waldo Emerson and George Ripley, continued to carry the banner of Transcendentalism to the larger American public. For others, however, Transcendentalism was a stepping-stone in a longer religious quest. The pilgrimage of Sophia Ripley, Isaac Hecker, and Orestes Brownson led them to embrace what was by the 1850s one of the fastest growing churches in America.

≪ 7 ≫

CONFLICTS OF TWONESS
CATHOLIC AND AFRICAN AMERICAN CHRISTIANITIES

Historian Jay Dolan commented that American Catholics have lived in the paradoxical tension of "two souls," confronting the challenge of being good Catholics and good Americans.[1] A large part of Dolan's argument relates to how the history of the Catholic Church in America has been chronicled. Protestant church historians of the late nineteenth and early twentieth centuries labored to see Catholicism as an important Christian tradition that deserved to be tolerated for its contributions to American life. Even Catholic commentators of that era were prone to stress the way that their tradition fit into Protestant religious and cultural worldviews of being good Americans. Writing at the end of the nineteenth century, Catholic historian Thomas O'Gorman noted how the history of American Catholicism was in accord with inherited national traditions of "American liberty," serving the country as "the strongest moral power for the preservation of the republic from the new social dangers that threaten the United States as well as the whole civilized world."[2]

Yet both Protestant and Catholic historians in the United States were clear about one point: the Catholic Church didn't quite fit the Protestant pattern of being an American church. For one thing, Catholicism's history did not connect to the religious narratives of Protestant English colonization that occurred in the seventeenth and eighteenth centuries. In the early nineteenth century, Catholicism possessed a theological and liturgical orientation that often put it at odds in some way with the dominant evangelical Protestant vision of American society. In particular, Protestants were disturbed by the hierarchical nature of Catholicism and by the fact that ultimate church authority rested in a foreign oligarchy of clergy headed by the pope. For all the ways the Catholic Church flirted with culturally dominant understandings of Americanism, this was a faith tradition that literally spoke a different language than the traditions represented by evangelical and sectarian Protestantism. Nineteenth-century evangelical Protestantism largely defined its mission in ways that echoed the early Puritans. Mainly, evangelicals believed that they were carrying their mission beyond the church in ways that would sanctify and redeem the nation (and later in the nineteenth century, the world). American Catholic history, however, largely stems from a history of the Catholic Church *in* America. This theological orientation is more than a matter of semantics, but represents a style of ecclesiastical and (ultimately) cultural identity that inevitably brought this tradition into conflict with the majority Protestant culture throughout the nineteenth century and for much of the twentieth century. In other words, the Roman Catholic Church, from a Protestant perspective, did not fit the accepted pattern of being an American church.

Although Catholic missionaries from France and Spain were responsible for establishing the first colonial settlements in North America in the sixteenth century, the history of American Catholicism began in earnest in the first half of the nineteenth century. From the standpoint of many Anglo-Americans at the time of the American Revolution, Catholicism was seen as a remnant of an Old World European order that Americans had thankfully escaped. But in a remarkably short period of time, the nature of American Catholicism changed drastically. From only a few thousand Catholics living primarily in New York, Rhode Island, Maryland, and Pennsylvania in 1800, the total number of Catholics jumped to approximately 300,000 by 1830. In a forty-year period between 1830 and 1870, the Catholic population rose by a staggering 800 percent, and by the early 1870s, the Catholic Church rivaled the Methodists as the largest religious body in America, with a membership numbering from approximately 3.5 to 4.5 million adherents.[3] Protestants in the late nineteenth century (like Protestants of later generations) marveled at this growth but found it easy to dismiss in their formal explanations. For most Protestants, Catholic successes could easily be explained by immigration patterns, accentuated by the millions of immigrants who came to America in the early and mid-nineteenth century primarily from Ireland and Germany. Late nineteenth-century historians such as Leonard Bacon were also quick to point out that if you pooled the largest Protestant denominations together, they would far outnumber the American Catholic population.

Such explanations, however, do little to obscure what has long been evident throughout American religious history: Protestants felt threatened by what they considered to be an alien religious tradition. In some measure, the tensions that existed in the nineteenth century can be seen as a continuation of the battles waged in Europe between Catholics and Protestants in the sixteenth and seventeenth centuries. Yet the issues involved in America were far more complex. American Catholics and Protestants were certainly divided over issues of theology. However, their differences were also marked by divisions over politics, class, and, most especially, ethnicity. These variables created the dualistic distinctions among Catholics that Jay Dolan noted about being both Catholic and American. The history of American Catholicism reveals how a tradition took its status as a religious outsider and crafted a whole new way of being an American.

The Catholic Church became one of the most prominent targets for Protestant vitriol in the decades leading up to the Civil War. However, most Protestants *and* Catholics were blind to the rise of perhaps the most innovative religious movement in American history, what has commonly been called the "black church." Within the context of free African American communities in the North and slave communities in the South, new understandings of Christianity were being shaped that crafted faith traditions that by the mid-twentieth century would produce some of the most visionary movements of Christianity in American history.

JOHN HUGHES AND THE BATTLE
FOR A CATHOLIC CONSCIOUSNESS

In 1838 John Hughes, a prominent Roman Catholic cleric, was consecrated bishop in the diocese of New York. Hughes' ascension to the order of bishop was symbolic of the way that it signaled an important shift in Roman Catholic consciousness in America. The pattern that Hughes embodied within American Catholicism would remain salient in one form or another for well over a hundred years. Born in Ulster County, Ireland in 1797, his family immigrated to the United States in 1817. When his family settled in Chambersburg, Pennsylvania, Hughes, like Francis Asbury before him, might very well have spent his life learning a trade, or helping his family run their small farm, if not for his religious zeal. In 1820 he began his studies at Mount St. Mary's College in Emmitsburg, Maryland. Mount St. Mary's was part of a small number of Catholic colleges that had been founded in the United States since 1800. Although Hughes was an Irish immigrant, he represented a rarity among Catholics in America during the first half of the nineteenth century in that he received his theological training in the United States, as opposed to a European seminary. After his ordination as a priest in 1826, Hughes served in the Diocese of Philadelphia where he became rector of St. Mary's Church in Philadelphia until his consecration as a bishop.

Hughes' early career was a time of marked transition for American Catholicism both in terms of how the church defined itself and how it was perceived by the Protestant majority. During the first third of the nineteenth century, for some Protestants their chief encounters with Catholicism came for those fortunate enough to have the means to travel to Europe. Many upper- and middle-class Americans began to travel regularly to Europe, and the Catholic Gothic cathedrals of Italy, France, and Spain represented some of their favorite destinations. These structures were seen by Protestants in a paradoxical fashion. On one hand, they represented relics of an era of religious superstition that Americans had thankfully thrown off. Americans in the first half of the nineteenth century (such as the historian Robert Baird) were constantly seeking ways to define what was unique about America, compared to Europe. The ornate cathedrals of Europe represented for many Americans the trappings of cultural and ecclesiastical elitism that the young nation had escaped. And yet these cathedrals represented the tip of the iceberg of a religious culture that for many Americans was dangerously alluring. The expansive sanctuaries, prayer chapels, and, in particular, catacombs of these churches became a point of fascination that would capture the popular imagination of many Americans who traveled to Europe (or read about these cathedrals in various literary accounts).

For many American Catholics in the early nineteenth century, it was this type of Old World image of their faith that they sought to counter. For decades after the American Revolution, Bishop John Carroll represented the public face of American Catholicism. Carroll was the product of a prominent Maryland family who stood firmly in support of American independence (his brother Charles was a signer of the Declaration of Independence). From his appointment as the first American Catholic bishop in 1789 until his death in 1815, Carroll frequently emphasized that there was nothing within Catholic tradition that put it at odds with America's cultural, political, and religious values. As Bishop of Baltimore, he worked diligently to foster a sense of connection with his Protestant neighbors and allowed Catholic parishes in his diocese significant latitude in controlling the internal affairs of their churches. In short, Carroll's ministry stressed the compatibility between Catholicism and the American democratic experience.

However, the Roman Catholic tradition operated under historical, theological, and ecclesiastical precepts that differentiated it from genres of American Protestantism. Steeped in the theological heritage of Augustine and Thomas Aquinas, Catholicism was a global religion that stressed a powerful historical tradition that was unbroken and, in many instances, unbending. Protestantism's strength historically was that fidelity to the centrality of Scripture gave these traditions a freedom to develop theologically, often independent of external authority (and as we saw earlier, one thing that characterized American Protestantism was the constant presence of charismatic leaders who instead of accepting the doctrines of preexistent churches felt compelled to start new ones). However, Protestantism's curse, as Catholics since the sixteenth century have been quick to point out, is that human nature would make it impossible to discern once and for all what religious interpretations were from God and what interpretations came from human folly.

While Protestants in the first third of the nineteenth century were spinning off into sects such as the Mormons and Millerites that seemed to be convinced that the world was ending, Catholics saw in their church a sacred place that not only provided pastoral comfort, but a promise of salvation in the life to come. For most evangelical Protestants, salvation came either through individual conversion or the ability to interpret the truths contained in the Bible. For Catholics, however, the Church was *the* path to salvation and to be outside of its gates was to risk your very soul. While the historical and theological orientation of Catholicism proved an attractive option for many Americans who immigrated to America during the middle third of the nineteenth century, it increasingly alienated many native-born Protestants who saw the hand of the devil at work in the Catholic Church.

In the half-decade prior to John Hughes' consecration as Bishop of New York, the nation witnessed the first major outbreak of anti-Catholic rioting. The worst of these riots occurred in Boston in 1834 when a mob attacked and burned an Ursuline convent. A catalyst for subsequent Catholic hostility was an exposé published by a young woman named Maria Monk that provided a sensationalist account of her "escape" from a convent school in Montreal. Monk's book, *The Awful Disclosures of Maria Monk* (1836), played upon emerging Protestant fears of Catholicism, especially highlighting the perception that the secret rituals of Catholicism were a means to conceal the sexual promiscuity of priests and nuns in religious orders. As worsening economic conditions in Ireland and Germany in the 1830s and 1840s brought increasing numbers of Catholic immigrants to America, Protestant prejudices continued to soar. While some Protestant clergy condemned the sensationalist exposés of persons such as Monk, subsequent "captivity narratives" remained popular in America through the middle third of the century (bringing to mind some of the themes used by Mary Rowlandson in her captivity narratives). As immigration from Germany and Ireland increased, so too did the fear of native-born Protestants that their republic was being overrun by undesirable foreigners (epitomized in the 1850s by the establishment of what was called "the Native American" or "Know Nothing" Party, which was largely devoted to an anti-Catholic, anti-immigrant political agenda).

Hughes, like other Catholic leaders, condemned acts of Protestant violence toward Catholics, arguing that Catholics were as American as any other religious group in the nation. Yet his leadership was devoted to one primary goal: the strict enforcement of Catholic doctrine within his archdiocese. Two issues that Hughes battled reflect, in microcosm, the larger struggles of the American Catholic Church in this era: lay trusteeism and the role of Catholic parochial schools. Part of the Americanist orientation of Bishop Carroll had been his support of lay trustees in a local parish in which parishioners were allowed a degree of administrative latitude in the governance of the congregation. In particular, many Catholic churches were able to appoint office holders in the parish, which was in direct violation of long-standing Catholic precedent that focused more on the unquestioned authority of bishops and priests. In the early 1800s, Bishop Carroll operated within a culturally precarious context in which the number of Catholic churches was small and the financial generosity of wealthy lay Catholics was a necessity to sustain a tradition that was largely isolated from the church hierarchy in Europe. But by Hughes' tenure in New York, this pattern of trusteeism that had spread primarily to wealthier parishes in major eastern cities was under assault. Hughes himself had come of age as a Catholic leader as a staunch ally of Bishop Francis Kenrick. As bishop of Philadelphia, Kenrick was determined to bring into line several parishes that had been involved in the 1820s in protracted battles over trusteeism. Hughes' pastorate at St. Mary's Church was in part a reward for his stand in support of Kenrick's authority over the lay trustees of that congregation. Within the New York archdiocese, Hughes threatened to censor any church that engaged in the practice, and in one case, when a congregation refused the bishop's appointment of a

Sunday school teacher, Hughes issued a pastoral letter that, in effect, told the congregation to accept his authority or face excommunication.

Hughes came to symbolize what was for many Protestants the dogmatism of Catholic ecclesiastical authority. While an earlier generation of Catholic bishops such as Carroll saw lay trusteeism as an embodiment of a democratic spirit at work in the church, the Catholic hierarchy, embodied by Hughes, was a reassertion of the Old World authority of the church. Hughes always maintained his loyalty to the United States, asserting his own pride in being an American. However, he was quick to point out that democratic political principles had nothing to do with being a Catholic. This tension in the early nineteenth-century Catholic experience is evident in Hughes' defense of Catholic parochial schools.

In the 1830s American public school education was in its infancy, and the idea of compulsory education for children was not universally embraced. Many affluent Americans often chose to send their children to private schools and some Protestants actually sent their children to Catholic schools. (The irony of the 1834 attack on the Boston Ursuline convent is that the school that was destroyed by the mob taught Protestant as well as Catholic youth.) Throughout the nineteenth century, most backers of public school education took for granted that religious education was to be central to the curriculum, but their views of religious education were heavily biased toward a Protestant worldview. Hughes attacked New York City public school leaders for their Protestant biases, including the use of the Protestant King James Bible, and he won the support of many of the city's Catholics who increasingly represented working-class Irish immigrants who had no desire to associate themselves with the English-Protestant bias of the city's public schools. Hughes even went as far as to suggest that if Protestants could ask for public funding for their public schools, he was well in his right to ask for public funding for the Catholic parochial schools. As R. Laurence Moore wryly asserts, Hughes "stressed the theme that Catholics did not have to become American. They already were."[4]

In the short run, Hughes largely lost his political battle with the New York City. However, his effort helped lead to a flourishing of Catholic parochial school education in the United States. As immigrants from Ireland and Germany continued to pour into America, Catholic churches increasingly evolved into the model that would mark the continued growth of Catholicism in the years following Hughes' death in 1864: the ethnic parish.

For over a hundred years, from the mid-nineteenth to the mid-twentieth century, the Catholic parish represented the backbone of American Catholicism and showcased that church's diverse ethnic and cultural character amid a fixed ecclesiastical structure. In cities and small towns throughout America, Catholic immigrant communities flourished; the parish was a means by which different ethnic groups could preserve their unique languages, cultures, and liturgical customs under the umbrella of ecclesiastical unity. In addition to worship, parish priests and nuns served as caretakers of these communities, providing pastoral care and support for individuals in the parish. The parish schools, staffed by various orders of priests and nuns, served the needs of the parish's children, including instruction in Catholic doctrine *and* fostering ethnic identity in the American context.

The shift from the early nineteenth-century Catholicism of John Carroll to the mid-nineteenth-century Catholicism of John Hughes displays how this faith tradition moved from a small homogeneous movement that sought cultural inclusion with English Protestants to a heterogeneous one that stressed cultural diversity amid a unified doctrinal tradition. As the nineteenth century progressed, these ethnic parishes increasingly reflected the immigrant diversity of the nation. While Catholicism was seen by many Protestants as a church made up of "foreign" immigrants, many "native" Protestants were being drawn to the tradition, including individuals who would be responsible for crafting distinctive models of American Catholicism.

BECOMING AN AMERICAN CATHOLIC
The Example of Orestes Brownson

John Hughes' leadership symbolized what Jay Dolan describes as the turn of American Catholicism from a spirit of democracy to one of Romanization. Hughes made clear throughout his extensive correspondence that he viewed American Catholics as living in a hostile land in which persecution and damnation awaited those who strayed from the Catholic fold. In an 1858 letter, he described how his archdiocese reflected a conglomeration of Catholics from many lands who lived in constant peril of being snared by the evils of a Protestant world. "I had to stand up among them as their bishop and chief; to warn them against the dangers that surrounded them; to contend for their rights as a religious community; to repel the spirit of faction among them; to convince their judgment by frequent explanations in regard to public and mixed questions; to encourage the timid, and sometimes to restrain the impetuous; in short, to knead them up into one dough, to be leavened by the spirit of Catholic faith and of Catholic union."[5] For many Protestant nativists, comments such as Hughes' affirmed their worst fears about the antidemocratic character of the Catholic Church. Yet at a time when nativist tensions were high in the 1840s and 1850s, Catholicism proved an attractive religious option among several "native" Americans.

The greatest fear of some Protestants was that Catholicism not only would pollute the social fabric of American society, but that vulnerable, weak-willed individuals would be tempted by the mysteries of Catholicism to do the unthinkable: convert. In looking at nineteenth-century statistics, it is evident that the majority of Catholics were not primarily drawn from native-born Protestants and, in fact, many Catholic leaders were reluctant to actively seek Protestant converts. Yet several Protestants did convert, and their zeal for their adopted faith played a significant role in the development of American Catholicism. In 1805 Elizabeth Ann Seton of Baltimore, who was raised an Episcopalian, embraced Catholicism after her husband's death, and in 1809, established the Sisters of Charity, the first Catholic religious order established in the United States. Seton and her order's activism and care for the poor of Baltimore led to the proliferation of her legacy after her death in 1821. In 1975 she became the first American-born saint in the Roman Catholic Church. A generation after Seton, Isaac Hecker, an individual who passed through a number of different Protestant religious movements (and like Sophia Ripley and Orestes Brownson was a one-time Transcendentalist), converted to Catholicism and later established the Paulist Fathers, a religious order that focused upon outreach and evangelism to the non-Catholic community (that is, Protestants). By far, however, the most significant and vocal of these nineteenth-century converts was Orestes Brownson. A biographer characterized Brownson as an "American religious weathervane" because of the ways he embodied so many different currents of American religion during the first half of the nineteenth century.[6] Like his contemporary and friend Isaac Hecker, Brownson explored a number of religious options before converting to Catholicism.

Brownson's true passion was as a writer, and by the end of the 1830s, he not only identified with the Transcendentalist movement, but was one of the movement's most eloquent literary voices. As the editor of the *Boston Quarterly Review*, Brownson became one of the most prominent literary defenders of the movement and his commentaries helped attract wider interest to the movement's cause by the late 1830s. In 1841 several Transcendentalist leaders established the Brooks Farm community in West Roxbury, Massachusetts, where Brownson was a frequent visitor.

By 1843, however, Brownson was showing signs of discontent with his Transcendentalist colleagues. The utopian experiment at Brooks Farm revealed how Transcendentalists divided over questions of politics, with some followers more interested in experimenting with models of political socialism as opposed to exploring the religious ideals at the center of the community's founding. Brownson's editorials in the *Review* began to bemoan what he considered to be the failure of the utopian ideals of the movement, and he increasingly lamented the sectarian fragmentation of Protestantism. In 1844 much to the dismay of his friends and allies, he converted to Catholicism and until his death in 1876, threw his efforts into arguing the case that Catholicism was the best, indeed, only hope for the country's future. Although Brownson was more enthusiastic than Hughes to note the compatibility between American democracy and Catholic thought, Brownson remained thoroughly orthodox in his outlook. Like Hughes, he saw Catholic doctrine as permanently fixed and unaffected by changing historical circumstances. Drawing on his own previous literary background, Brownson argued that Catholicism was the only reasonable religious faith that offered Americans social stability in the face of archaic Protestant sectarianism.

> The Roman Catholic religion, then, is necessary to sustain popular liberty, because popular liberty can be sustained only by a religion free from popular control, above the people, speaking from above and able to command them,—and such a religion is the Roman Catholic. It acknowledges no master but God, and depends only on divine will in respect to what it shall teach, what it shall ordain, what it shall insist upon as truth, piety, moral and social virtue.[7]

Brownson never succeeded in his hope that American Protestants would accept the reasonableness of Catholic doctrine and thereby convert. Yet his efforts to present Catholic apologetics as an alternative religious and ethical model for American culture would resurface in American Catholic thought generations after his death, including more recent traditions of Catholic social ethics.

THE SPREAD OF CATHOLIC PARISH MISSIONS

At the same time that Brownson was espousing his beliefs in the compatibility between traditional Catholicism and American democratic values, American Catholicism continued to draw much of its leadership from Europe. Even as more American-born priests were entering service as secular priests or as members of religious orders, several

European-born Catholics were playing a significant role in the church's success in America. The career of Francis Xavier Weninger (1805–1888) is instructive in this regard.

An Austrian, Weninger was a Jesuit who had received his theological training at the University of Vienna. After years as a theology professor in Innsbruck, in 1848 Weninger immigrated to the United States, following many German and Austrian immigrants who left those countries in response to political instabilities. For decades, Weninger and other Jesuit priests conducted the Catholic equivalent of revivalist crusades, holding services throughout the country and reinforcing the work of numerous Catholic parishes. Weninger helped pioneer a practice of parish missions, whereby priests often spent several days in a parish preaching and instructing laity in strengthening the work of the parish church. In some ways embodying characteristics of camp meeting preaching, many missions were used both to stir the hearts of the faithful and to bring new converts into the fellowship of the Catholic Church. In 1854 alone, Weninger not only conducted numerous revivals, but heard 30,000 confessions, preached 900 sermons, and converted fifty Protestants. What is more remarkable is that even though Weninger primarily held parish missions among German immigrants, he often held preaching services for multiple ethnic groups in multiple languages. As he recounted,

> I myself gave ordinarily two set sermons. . . . When, as was frequently the case, the congregation was a mixed one, of English, German or French, I had to preach eight times a day, or upwards of sixty times in eight days. If it happened that all three nationalities were present in large numbers in a congregation, the leading points had to be put before each nationality. Then, of course, each sermon is considerably shorter, the three taking an hour and a half. Such a mission, in the three languages, is very taxing upon the missionary, but the effect is far greater than when a special mission is given to each nationality.[8]

To his audiences Weninger left little doubt about the central thrust of his teaching: eternal truth was to be found only within the teachings of the Catholic Church. "For, first of all, the faithful everywhere, but especially in America, should clearly understand, and be in a condition to instruct others, that there is but one religion revealed by God and that there is but one church founded by Christ, viz the first Christian Church, the Roman Catholic Church which is the only saving Church." Through sermons and religious instruction, Weninger and other priests proclaimed the message that "Catholics must believe without any admixture of error in their faith, hence they should admit the infallible teaching authority of the head of the Church."[9]

CATHOLIC PLURALISM

The overwhelming problem that faces any student of American Christianity is that the history of the American Catholic Church does not easily fit into the boxes constructed by Protestant historians. The traditions of American evangelicalism emanating from the Second Great Awakening led to the creation of new models of religious leadership and broke the power of an older ecclesiastical Protestant order in the early nineteenth century. These diverse movements often succeeded by stressing the claim that they were separating themselves from discarded European practices to achieve a purer form of Christianity. While Catholics did emulate Protestants in some aspects (as the example of Francis Weninger's preaching suggests), in some ways, the growth of American Catholicism was counterintuitive to the approach taken by many evangelical Protestants.

First, and of primary significance, Catholic leaders such as Hughes were unapologetic in articulating a belief that they were not part of an American church, but of a global one. Catholic authority was centrally located in the papal office, and as the nineteenth century unfolded, assertions of papal supremacy became more strident. While Protestants were driven by a desire to cut ties with Europe, asserting the uniqueness of their homegrown Christian traditions, Catholics took pride on the centrality of their faith and that ultimately how one's Catholicism reflected upon their own European ethnic identity.

Second, as the nineteenth century progressed, American Protestant churches were increasingly wrestling over the relationship between inherited faith traditions with what scholars have labeled "modernity." From a theological standpoint, modernity (or modernism) often refers to the compatibility between religion and the natural world. Heavily influenced by Enlightenment rationalism, numerous Protestant movements were able to thrive by questioning the value of inherited theological wisdom. Increasingly, as the nineteenth century progressed, Protestants believed that Christian theology could be reconciled with a reliance on reason and scientific discovery. Later in the century, many Protestants embraced new traditions of theological liberalism and biblical criticism that emerged primarily from Germany, seeing these traditions as essential for uncovering the true meaning of religion (often at the expense of earlier traditions). Within the Catholic Church, however, by and large, doors were shut upon this modernist worldview. In keeping with the mandates emerging from the Council of Trent in the sixteenth century, and reinforced by numerous church councils in the nineteenth century, Catholic tradition was permanent and not conditioned in any way by historical factors. One could argue that this intellectual insulation hurt American Catholicism in successive generations, denying the church the benefit of the intellectual leadership that marked the development of Protestant theology by the late nineteenth century.

Yet the Catholic Church embodied something largely missing from every denominational form of Protestantism in America: theological unity in the midst of cultural diversity. From a small number of English Catholics in 1800 to a growing mosaic of ethnic groups that would include by the end of the century Irish, German, Italian, and a host of other immigrant groups, Catholicism succeeded for many years in providing sacred space for communities to be ethnically and cultural different from the dominant culture. Amid the diverse languages spoken among different parish communities, the liturgy of the Latin mass still emanated from every single parish in America. Theories of pluralism often see religious diversity as a form of harmonious coexistence between different religious and cultural groups. The American Catholic experience underscores that religious diversity in American history often arises out of deeply contentious historical contexts. The discordant tones struck by Catholics not only disturbed Protestants, but actually galvanized them to unite their denominational forces. In 1846 the Evangelical Alliance was formed in London, signaling an important chapter in the wider development of a transnational Protestant movement of global Christianity. Conceived as a Protestant interdenominational movement among European and North American Protestants, the movement was essential in encouraging a growing international missionary movement among Protestants. By the same token, the American chapter of the Evangelical Alliance was conceived not only for the purpose of trying to heal sectarian divisions within American Protestantism, but also out of the hope that Protestant churches could combine their moral muscle to stave off the corrupting influences of Catholicism.

The irony of Catholic growth is that it not only revealed antagonisms among different groups of Protestants, but it represented a potentially combustible mixture of Catholics. The parish system reflected its own stratification, in which the Irish for years controlled the American church hierarchy and often found themselves at odds with other ethnic-Catholic communities. Further, many ethnic parishes resisted any efforts toward assimilation, and by the end of the century a hierarchical battle was waged between those who followed the assimilationist model of John Carroll and the sectarian orientation of John Hughes. By the last third of the nineteenth century, these tensions spilled over in terms of how Protestants sought to mobilize their resources to stave off the perceived Catholic threat.

RICHARD ALLEN AND THE RISE
OF THE BLACK CHURCH

The history of African American Christianity reflects a range of theological and cultural perspectives that serves as a microcosm of American religious diversity. However, the history of what later twentieth-century scholars would call "the black church" is inseparable from one persistent evil: slavery. Throughout much of colonial history, slavery was legal in the majority of colonies, although from the earliest years of colonial settlement, free African Americans lived in cities such as Boston, New York, and Philadelphia. By 1800 the northern states had passed legislation barring the holding of slaves and in 1808 American participation in the Atlantic slave trade legally came to an end. Yet the institution of slavery continued to thrive in the American South, where large cotton and tobacco plantations saw the perpetuation of slavery as an economic necessity.

During the colonial period, religious leaders in both the northern and southern colonies largely took an ambivalent view toward efforts at evangelism toward slaves. Although many enslaved Africans who worked on slave plantations on the Caribbean islands and French colonies in present-day Louisiana were drawn to Catholicism (often incorporating Catholic teachings into various African religions and Caribbean practices of Voodoo), English Protestant efforts at evangelism were usually haphazard and ineffective.

On the surface, the colonial-era Great Awakening did not have an immediate impact upon slaves. However, even before the beginning of the Revolutionary War, African Americans were caught up in the revivalist ethos of that era. In New York City, free African Americans participated within fledgling evangelical groups such as the Methodists, and the Awakening's stress on spiritual equality spawned numerous responses from African Americans. Yet the full manifestation of this earlier revivalist ethos became evident by the way both slaves in the South and free African Americans in the North were caught up in the evangelical furies of the Second Great Awakening.

Scholars have long debated the relationship between earlier African religious traditions and the appeal of emerging eighteenth- and nineteenth-century models of Protestant evangelism. However, it is evident that many aspects of evangelical culture resonated with the social and cultural context experienced by many African Americans in the early nineteenth century. For many African Americans, the appeal of evangelicalism was both practical and deeply theological. On one hand, the extemporaneous nature of revivalism and its openness to a wide range of worship medium resonated with many African Americans, who received from the tradition glimpses of an African religious past that centered upon similar models of religious spontaneity and spiritual ecstasy. Not surprisingly, the Christian traditions that fared best in this particular historical context were the evangelical-minded Baptists and Methodists. "The Methodists were the first people that brought glad tidings to the colored people," the African American Methodist Richard Allen wrote in 1793. "We are beholden to the Methodists, under God, for the light of the Gospel we enjoy; for all other denominations preached so high-flown that we were not able to comprehend their doctrine; Sure am I that reading sermons will never prove so beneficial to the colored people as spiritual or extempore preaching."[10] The egalitarian spirit of the Second Great Awakening penetrated the social fabric of many African American communities, both in the South and the North. However, years before American political and religious institutions divided over the issue of slavery, African American faith communities in the North were recognizing the existence of what W.E.B. Du Bois referred to as the "twoness" of African Americans who early in the nation's history experienced the racism that drew sharp distinctions between black and white America.

Paralleling larger events taking place in American society, the nation's churches in the late eighteenth and early nineteenth centuries offered few opportunities for free African Americans to exercise religious leadership on par with whites. The most remarkable exception during the early national period was the career of Lemuel Haynes. In 1785 Haynes was ordained into the Congregational ministry and served for many years as pastor of a white congregation in Rutland, Vermont. Haynes was also a gifted theologian whose writings put him squarely in the tradition of New England New Divinity theology represented by men such as Jonathan Edwards, Samuel Hopkins, and Timothy Dwight. He also employed theological arguments of "disinterested benevolence" to assert that Christians ought to employ all of their moral resources to eradicate the sin of American slavery. Yet Haynes' example is rare and the story of his Vermont ministry is tainted by the fact that ultimately he had to resign his pulpit because of racial tensions in the community.

However, the post–Revolutionary War period witnessed the growth of independent churches founded by and for African Americans. David George, a former slave, led a free African Baptist church near Savannah, Georgia for a short time. At the end of the American Revolution, other former slaves followed George's lead by either immigrating to Canada or to cities in the North, including Philadelphia, New York, and Boston, where they either joined white congregations or founded a range of independent black churches. Many of these churches were associated with a variety of Baptist groups. That tradition's emphasis on "believer's baptism," in which the individual was free to make a decision to accept or reject Christ, struck a responsive note for many former slaves. Throughout the eighteenth century, many churches made feeble efforts to evangelize to slave communities, often relying on catechisms and formal instruction. Baptist tradition, however, gave room for religious experience as well as individual autonomy to accept the gift of salvation. Baptist polity, which recognized congregational autonomy, also allowed for a degree of innovation that was not allowed within other traditions, especially recognizing the authority of a preacher's "call" to assemble believers into a church. By the same token, the years following America's independence witnessed an effort by many white denominations to restrict and undermine the activities of African American churches, in both the slaveholding states of the South and the free states of the North. No individual or movement better represents the paradoxes faced by African Americans than the emergence of the African Methodist Episcopal (AME) Church and its principal founder, Richard Allen.

Allen's story serves to illustrate the prejudices that free African Americans needed to overcome and the innovations they undertook to empower other African Americans to survive the assaults of racism. Allen was born on a Delaware plantation in 1760 and after his conversion as a teenager (through the preaching of a Methodist revivalist), he felt a call to preach both to his fellow slaves and to his slave master—ultimately compelling his owner to grant Allen freedom. After he was emancipated, Allen settled in Philadelphia, which in the 1780s contained one of the largest concentrations of free African Americans in the United States, and become the recognized leader among the African American parishioners of St. George's Methodist Episcopal Church in that city. American

Methodism at its founding was unique among the nation's Protestant churches for its staunch stance against slaveholding. This stance, however, did not prevent churches in the North from creating structures segregating blacks and whites in various congregations. Allen and his colleague at St. George, Absalom Jones, were disturbed by the fact that the theology from the pulpit at St. George (preached by white ministers) emphasized a message that all Christians stood in equal judgment before God, while at the same time blacks were relegated to the church balcony.

Around 1786–1787 Allen and Jones led a group of black congregants to the altar rail to pray, resulting in their forced removal from the church by white trustees. This event caused Allen and Jones to lead African American congregants out of St. George. Allen and Jones established the Free African Society that many historians recognized as one of the first independent organizations funded and run exclusively by African Americans in American history. The organization's purpose was to provide blacks in Philadelphia not only with spiritual resources, but worked to foster economic autonomy among the city's African American community. The Free African Society served as a model for future generation of African Americans, not only in terms of understanding the rise of future black-church traditions in America, but how African American Christianity was often inseparable from political and economic empowerment.

Eventually, Jones and Allen moved into different spheres. In 1794 Jones was ordained as the nation's first African American Episcopal priest and became senior pastor of St. Thomas Episcopal Church in Philadelphia, which is recognized as American's first black Episcopal Church. Allen was more reluctant to leave his Methodist roots behind, but events in that tradition in the 1780s and 1790s gave him little cause for hope. The tone for Methodist race relations was set by Francis Asbury, who encouraged African Americans to preach to white audiences at camp meeting revivals. For a number of years, Asbury traveled with a former slave named Harry Hosier. Hosier's reputation as a preacher gained him notoriety not only among blacks, but whites as well. Although he couldn't read or write, Hoosier's preaching invoked in his audience deep emotions and convictions that for a time gained him a reputation as one of the nation's leading evangelists. Upon Hosier's death in 1806, Asbury's colleague, Thomas Coke, remarked that no history of American Methodism could adequately be told without mentioning the contributions made by Harry Hosier.

At the same time, Asbury was following a policy that largely turned a blind eye to the movement's strong antislavery emphasis and undercut its egalitarian spirit. Like Wesley, Asbury detested slavery, and his close friendships with Hosier and Richard Allen demonstrate his commitment to the cause of many African American Methodists. In 1799 Allen was ordained a Methodist deacon at a time when the Methodist Episcopal Church's polity did not allow for the ordination of African Americans. In the end, however, Asbury chose what appeared to be the only pragmatic course. In his mind, fighting slavery in the South and racism in the North would ultimately destroy the Methodist movement by alienating the church's base. Many southern states enacted laws prohibiting the manumission of slaves, and Asbury realized that to enforce the church's antislavery position would likely lose the Methodists large support in the South. As Methodism grew exponentially throughout the country, and particularly in the slaveholding South, the appeal of numerical gains became more of a priority for Asbury and other white Methodist leaders who succeeded Asbury in the episcopal office.

Richard Allen felt these tensions in Methodism acutely. Allen appreciated the model of Asbury's leadership and recognized the ways that Methodism spoke to the ethos of many African Americans. However, he increasingly recognized the fact that his adopted tradition provided no place for his voice in white America. In 1794 Allen established the Bethel African Methodist Episcopal Church as a worship center for many black Methodists in Philadelphia. While Asbury himself presided over the dedication of the Bethel church, within a few years, local white Methodists engaged in legal efforts to wrest control of the church from Bethel's trustees. Finally, in 1816 Allen and his followers established the African Methodist Episcopal (AME) Church, electing Allen as that church's first bishop. The AME Church was the most prominent in a series of black Methodist churches founded between 1809 and 1821. Over the next several years, the AME Church sprouted a number of innovative leaders who helped grow the fledgling church. Many of the most influential leaders of the AME were women. Three of the most prominent evangelists in the church's early years were Jarena Lee, Zilpha Elaw, and Rebecca Jackson. These women were noted not only for their preaching, but for their unique roles as prophetesses, recounting to both black and white audiences the extraordinary visions they had received from God. Allen initially had reservations about the role of these women "exhorters," but like many other Protestant revivalists of the era, he was forced to examine the fruits of these women laborers and judged them of God.

Membership in various black Methodist churches grew steadily before the Civil War. Initially confined to urban areas in the North, these churches nevertheless offered a blueprint for a more dramatic rise in African American Christianity after the Civil War. By the time of Allen's death in 1831, black religion in America was entering a new phase of crisis and development.

TWO SOULS

In 1861 a prominent American religious leader made the following observation about the evils of impending Civil War and American slavery:

> ... if this nation has a future, if its destiny is, as we have hitherto boasted, to prove what man may be when and where he has the liberty to be himself, uttered by one or the other it ere long will be, and in tones that will ring out through the whole Union, and through the whole civilized world now anxiously listening to hear it. The Union is and must be sacred to liberty. Here man must be man, nothing more, and nothing less.[11]

These words were not written by an abolitionist leader, but by a major Roman Catholic spokesperson, Orestes Brownson. Brownson shows how the historical American conceptualization of the concept of liberty could conjure a shared meaning, even as that term meant different things to different segments of Americans.

A major dilemma for many free African Americans in the early nineteenth century was the question of whether to stay in predominantly white churches and denominations, as did Absalom Jones, or follow Richard Allen into independent black churches. For various reasons, African Americans chose both paths. By the same token, one persistent theme that connected the emerging black church experience in America was that African Americans received from the message of evangelical Christianity empowerment and the possibility of divine liberation in ways that were both otherworldly *and* worldly—and very different from the ways most white evangelicals understood the message of Christian salvation. In 1808, in a sermon that celebrated the abolition of the African slave trade (but not slavery itself) by the U.S. Congress, Absalom Jones struck a tone that would become a major theme for future iterations of African American Christianity. Just as God led the Israelites out of slavery to freedom, so did God share a similar covenant with African Americans as they struggled to find an identity in a land dominated by racism and slavery. "The history of the world shows us that the deliverance of the children of Israel from their bondage is not the only instance in which it has pleased God to appear in behalf of oppressed and distressed nations," Jones asserted. "He has heard the prayers that have ascended from the hearts of his people; and he has, as in the case of his ancient and chosen people the Jews, *come down to deliver* our suffering countrymen from the hands of their oppressors."[12] Jones articulated a theological theme that would continue to inspire various forms of African American Christianity over the next two centuries and challenge politically dominant voices in America that God would not tolerate the sins of white America.

The stories of American Catholicism and what would later become known as the black church tradition reflects different historical traditions from two groups that had radically different religious narratives for understanding their presence in America. Whereas many Catholic immigrants who came to America did so out of economic necessity or to escape political persecution, the struggles of African Americans connects with the ongoing perpetuation of chattel slavery whose origins in America predate the founding the Massachusetts Bay Colony. Sadly, immigrant Catholics and "native" Protestants alike were guilty of the sins of racism, a fact that would be exacerbated during the Civil War when antidraft riots in the North were often centered within Irish Catholic immigrants that had no desire to fight a war to liberate black slaves.

Yet in subsequent years, both groups would embody a tension that in some fashion represents the struggle of all religious "outsider" movements in American history: that is, to what extent should religious minorities stay distinct and in tension with the dominant culture and to what extent should these groups seek assimilation? For American Catholics who challenged the theological and cultural suppositions of the Protestant evangelical empire and for African Americans whose faith in the early nineteenth century was shaped by the realities of slavery and racism, those responses would be varied and at times contentious. As subsequent chapters of this book discuss, these issues of differentiation and assimilation would not be easily answered by either group.

≪ 8 ≫

THE PERFECTION OF CHRISTIAN AMERICA
FROM HOLINESS TO CIVIL WAR

In 1837 Elijah Lovejoy, a Presbyterian minister and abolitionist leader, wrote that slavery was not only morally incomprehensible, but also "a sin against God, whose prerogative as the rightful owner of all human beings is usurped, and against the slave himself, who is deprived of the power to dispose of his services as conscience may dictate, or his Maker require."[1] Months later, after several attempts to publish an abolitionist newspaper in Alton, Illinois, led to mob action that destroyed his press, Lovejoy was murdered. Lovejoy's example reflects one view of slavery represented by American Christianity in the years preceding the American Civil War. While many white Americans in both the North and the South viewed slavery as a political issue they hoped would go away, it proved a lightning rod that led to denominational schisms in the decades leading up to the Civil War—a war that both defined and divided Americans for generations to come.

For many white evangelicals, the slavery debates preceding the Civil War were predicated on a central theme: the interpretation of Scripture. In the 1840s and 1850s, denominational publications churned out editorials and articles from many prominent leaders who argued chapter and verse from the Bible to advance either pro- or antislavery arguments. For white abolitionists such as Lovejoy and for many African American Christians, the relationship between Christianity and slavery was framed differently. For them, the perpetuation of slavery in America was a great evil that would ultimately serve as a harbinger of divine judgment.

Later generations of Americans, in both the North and the South, would see the Civil War in providential terms. The lyrics of Julia Ward Howe's 1862 hymn, "Battle Hymn of the Republic" would be seen by many in the North to epitomize how the war served as a divine cleansing whereby God's wrath destroyed evil (embodied by the South) and set the stage for the divine reign of God on earth.

> Mine eyes have seen the glory of the coming of the Lord;
> He is trampling out the vintage where the grapes of wrath are stored;
> He hath loosed the fateful lightning of his terrible swift sword;
> His truth is marching on.

Southern churches were the equal match for their northern counterparts in seeing the hand of God behind the war. In the South, no less than in the North, ministers preached that theirs was the true nation blessed by providence. With southern secession and the formation of the Confederate States of America in 1861, its Constitution explicitly proclaimed the new nation a Christian country—the true heirs of the legacy of the American Revolution. As one southern church leader noted, the South fought "to drive away the infidel and rationalistic principles which are sweeping the land and substituting a gospel of the stars and stripes for the gospel of Jesus Christ."[2]

The triumphant millennial spirit embraced by many churches in the North and South can obscure a complex historical context confronted by mid-nineteenth-century Americans leading up to the Civil War. While it is true that many American churches and church leaders were invested in the moral arguments over slavery and often strained to attach theological meaning to the Civil War, the generation leading up to the war witnessed larger theological developments that went hand in hand with the moral arguments used in relationship to slavery. These theological fissures were especially acute within the mainstream of the evangelical Protestant churches that emerged as the predominant religious groups in the aftermath of the Second Great Awakening, in particular, Baptists, Presbyterians, and Methodists.

The years leading up to the Civil War witnessed renewed debates over the future of Protestant revivalism in the United States. At issue for many Christians was not just the question of whether or not revivalism was a good thing for churches, but what the desired outcomes (doctrinally and practically) one sought from the converted. As churches that embraced a revivalist ethos gained more and more converts, inevitably some of their members found themselves invested with a new social and material status, putting them at odds with others in their fellowships who believed that the quest for material prosperity compromised gospel zeal to reform the nation.

These debates not only led to divisions and schisms in American Protestantism on the eve of the Civil War, but raised in a new way a fundamental question throughout American religious history: who has authority to speak in the name of God? Leonard Bacon noted hopefully that the "religious lesson" learned by northern and southern churches during the Civil War "was the lesson of Christian fellowship as against the prevailing folly of sectarian divisions, emulations, and jealousies."[3] Bacon is accurate in the sense that the aftermath of the war gave many Protestant denominations (at least in the North) a theological rhetoric of unity that would recast earlier theological language of Protestant providence in ways that provided Americans with a shared sense of the nation's unique mission to the world. However, the theological confusion that permeated the main currents of American Protestantism in the mid-nineteenth century reveals that few American Christians were united in their central theological and moral commitments. The theological divisions that emerged before the war set the stage for even further divisions within the nation's Protestant churches in the war's aftermath.

THE PROTESTANT QUEST FOR PERFECTION

The Second Great Awakening stressed two themes that became ongoing emphases in the development of American popular religion: an Arminian "free grace" stress on the importance of a conversion experience and the role of the individual in accepting (or rejecting) that gift of unearned grace. Methodist successes during the first third of the nineteenth century reflected a larger push within American Protestantism that saw the displacement of an earlier Calvinist theological hegemony in America. On a purely intellectual level, Calvinist theologians continued to gain a hearing for their ideas throughout the nineteenth century. In the era of the Second Great Awakening, New England Calvinist "New Divinity" theologians such as Samuel Hopkins, Timothy Dwight (the grandson of Jonathan Edwards), and Lyman Beecher debated with antirevivalist theologians who emphasized the importance of adherence to historical Reformation doctrines and practices coming out of the Reformed tradition. By the 1830s Princeton Theological Seminary had emerged as the intellectual center for this latter movement, spearheaded by the seminary's longtime professor of systematic theology, Charles Hodge. This tension between what was known in the Presbyterian Church as "New School" and "Old School" adherents fractured the unity that had existed between the two traditions that served as the primary caretakers of Reformed theology: the Congregationalists and Presbyterians. Confident in the early years of the century that they could stave off both the theologically uncouth revivalism of the Methodists and Baptists, as well as the heterodox teaching emerging from New England Unitarianism, the Congregationalists and Presbyterians entered into a plan of union in 1801, not to create an organic merger, but as a means by which both traditions might pool their clergy and financial resources together. This arrangement was shattered as debates over revivalism eventually led to a schism among Presbyterians in 1837.

By the time of the 1837 Presbyterian schism, however, similar tensions were brewing among the two most successful revivalist traditions during the Second Great Awakening: the Baptists and Methodists. Long fractured along divisions between Calvinist and Arminian theologies, Baptist congregations and regional associations increasingly divided over the issues of slavery, eventually leading several southern churches to form the Southern Baptist Convention in 1845. Developments within American Methodism embodied comparable tensions as other evangelical traditions. However, they also raised a question that many other churches had to face historically: what happens to a religious movement when the fires of revivalism start to die out?

In the 1820s and 1830s, a variety of Methodist leaders railed against the evils of Calvinism. Yet the issue that became critical for Methodists at this point was no longer simply staving off the challenge of Calvinism, it was discerning the proper understanding of John Wesley's doctrine of sanctification, or Christian perfection, within the tradition. While many sectarian leaders such as John Humphrey Noyes saw the doctrine of perfection as a means to transform the social conventions of the day, the majority of Protestant evangelicals such as the Methodists defined the doctrine in terms of individual holiness and how the spiritual perfection of the individual could bring about a righteous society on earth.

This heightened emphasis on the doctrine of sanctification was not unique to Methodism. In 1821 an upstate New York lawyer underwent a conversion experience and proceeded to enter the Presbyterian ministry. By the early 1830s, this minister, Charles G. Finney, was on his way to becoming one of the most prominent revivalists in American history.

While Finney emerged out of a tradition of Calvinism revivalism associated with New School Presbyterianism, his theological leanings were decidedly Methodist in orientation. He was the classic embodiment of a strong tradition of antebellum postmillennial revivalism whose larger mission was to make America a morally righteous society. While always clear that his goal in life was to preach for personal conversion (and he did not shy away from warning sinners of the consequences to their souls if they did not repent and died unconverted), he emphasized the importance of one receiving the "second blessing" of Christian perfection, whereby the sanctified were converted to live in "perfect obedience to the law of God."[4] Picking up on Samuel Hopkins' notion of "disinterested benevolence," Finney captured the spirit of Protestant optimism that believed that personal conversion, and the cooperation of the churches, would lead to a better society—and eventually a triumphant second coming of Christ. "As saints supremely value the highest good of being, they will and must take a deep interest in whatever is promotive of that end. . . . War, slavery, licentiousness and all such evils and abominations are necessarily regarded by the saint as great and sore evils, and he longs for their complete and final overthrow."[5] In 1835 Finney, now a Congregationalist minister, became a professor, and later president, of Oberlin College in Ohio, a college that became noteworthy for being coeducational and for harboring a spirit of social reform, particularly in relation to abolitionism.

Finney's success as a revivalist and popular theologian revealed how Wesleyan and Arminian ideals were spreading outside of Methodism, finding footholds within Presbyterian, Congregationalist, and Baptist churches. Within the eighteenth-century Methodism of John Wesley, sanctification was seen mostly as a goal one strived for in this life as opposed to actually obtaining. Yet the idea that one could actually be made perfect in this life, whereby one was made free by God's grace from the power of sin, increasingly captured the imagination of many religious seekers in the 1830s and 1840s. The most famous of these seekers was a New York City woman who spent the early part of her adult life wrestling over the state of her soul.

PHOEBE PALMER AND THE WAY OF HOLINESS

Ironically, as Finney and other New School Presbyterians and Congregationalists flirted with Wesleyan notions of sanctification, by the 1830s, the doctrine appeared to be waning within American Methodism. In the aftermath of Francis Asbury's death in 1816, the fires of camp meeting revivalism slowly began to die out. Increasingly, Methodist preachers began to prefer the model of ministry enjoyed by Congregational and Presbyterian ministers, desiring to serve churches in settled areas in major cities such as New York and Philadelphia as opposed to the lifestyle of an itinerant circuit rider.

The career of Nathan Bangs (1778–1862) reflects this transition in American Methodism. Like most early nineteenth-century circuit riders, Bangs was a self-educated man. Beginning his career as a circuit rider in upstate New York, in 1818 he took up the position as head of the tiny Methodist publishing operation in New York City. By 1850 Bangs had transformed the Methodist Book Concern into one of the largest publishers in the country. The press produced a variety of publications, ranging from Sunday school materials and women's magazines to its own scholarly journal. The success of the publishing house also reflected the ways that Methodists became obsessed with higher education. Beginning in the 1830s and extending to the end of the nineteenth century, Methodists blanketed the nation with colleges, leading American Protestantism in the establishment of denominational colleges and universities. This spirit eventually led Methodists to do what would have been unthinkable during the heyday of Bishop Asbury: establish theological seminaries. By the 1870s Methodist seminaries such as the Boston University School of Theology, Drew Theological Seminary, Vanderbilt Divinity School, and Garrett Biblical Institute were attempting to match the intellectual pedigrees represented by older Presbyterian and Congregational seminaries such as Princeton, Andover, Bangor Seminary in Maine, and Union Seminary in New York City.

These "worldly" developments were not embraced by all Methodists. Peter Cartwright (1785–1872), perhaps the most well known in legends of popular early nineteenth-century circuit riders, bemoaned the loss of Methodism's "white hot" zeal. Following the tradition of Asbury, Cartwright advocated throughout his ministry the importance of the class meeting, prayer groups, and, in particular, camp meetings to stoke the fires of religious zeal, lamenting what he saw as Methodism's desire to accommodate its theology to the world, thus sacrificing its mandate to save souls. "I am sorry to say that the Methodist Episcopal Church of late years, since they have become numerous and wealthy, have almost let camp meetings die out."[6] Cartwright's comment goes beyond a lament for Methodists to return to the good-old days of camp meetings. It reflects his concern that Methodists were becoming indistinguishable from other churches in America in their desire to build extravagant church buildings and (increasingly) rely on seminary-trained clergy. Increasingly, this debate about the proper role of revivalism hinged on how various Methodists interpreted the doctrine of sanctification.

The Methodist debate over the doctrine of sanctification preceding the Civil War would spill over into other Protestant traditions in the latter half of the nineteenth century. Ultimately, it would lead to schisms that created a number of churches devoted to the pursuit of holiness. These holiness churches and denominations eventually served as a foundation contributing to the founding of the largest global movement of Christianity by the early twenty-first century: pentecostalism. In many ways, the future course of these religious currents can be traced to one Methodist laywoman, Phoebe Worrall Palmer.

Palmer was born in New York City in 1807 and raised in a pietistic Methodist family. She married John Palmer, a city physician, and settled into life as a wife and mother. Almost from the outset of her marriage, however, Palmer's life was filled with tragedy. Three of her children died in infancy and one daughter was killed in a house fire. These events made Palmer examine the state of her soul and convinced her that these tragedies were a mark of her own faith deficiencies. Palmer took solace in two sources. First, she read a number of spiritual biographies of pious Protestant women, a genre that held great popularity for many American women during the first half of the nineteenth century. In particular, Palmer was drawn to the life story of Hester Ann Rogers, an English Methodist who, in addition to the distinction of providing one of the most public accounts of John Wesley's death in 1791, gave vivid testimonies of her own quest for entire sanctification. Palmer resonated with accounts of Rogers' own worldly suffering but felt compelled by the fact that Rogers' strove for a life marked by entire sanctification. The example of Rogers' life gave Palmer not only a theological rationale for her own tragedies but also provided her with a growing conviction that sanctification was the primary goal for the converted Christian to strive.

The second reassuring factor for Palmer was her sister, Sarah, whose family shared a home with Phoebe and Walter Palmer. By the mid-1830s, Sarah hosted a small women's prayer meeting in their New York City home that devoted itself to the pursuit of Christian holiness. Phoebe not only took comfort in these gatherings but shared, along with a number of other evangelicals such as Finney, a belief that the only valid form of Christianity was realized through the individual quest for entire sanctification.

Phoebe Palmer's emergence on the historical stage coincided with a moment when Methodist leaders began to place a renewed emphasis on promoting holiness within their churches. In 1835 Sarah announced that she had received the blessing of entire sanctification. Two years later, Phoebe herself received this same gift. Unlike Finney's view of the doctrine, however, Palmer's theology of entire sanctification was predicated not so much on a feeling of assurance, but on the act of willingly devoting one's life entirely to God. Her sanctification rested not on emotionalism, but on a personal decision to devote her life to God. As she explained, "the covenant was consummated between God and my soul, that I would live a *life of faith* . . . though I might be called to endure more complicated and long-continued trials of my faith than ever before conceived of . . . I would still believe, though I might *die in the effort*, I would hold on in the death struggle."[7]

Palmer's understanding of sanctification touched upon aspects of the tradition practiced by Finney (both, for example, stressed the importance of Matthew 5:48: "Be ye perfect, even as your Father which is in heaven is perfect"), yet her view also typified developing gender ideologies in the early nineteenth century. For Palmer, all of her suffering had a purpose: to lead her to place total trust on God's grace in her life. After Sarah and her husband moved to upstate New York, Palmer was ready to act out her hard-won convictions.

Phoebe Palmer's leadership of what became known as the Tuesday Meeting for the Promotion of Holiness represented a turning point in her life. By the early 1840s, the group that met in the Palmer's home was attracting not only women, but men and several evangelical Protestants outside of the Methodist fold. Meetings at the Palmer home were crowded affairs and included testimonies, prayer, and singing. "In these meetings the utmost freedom prevails. The ministry does not wait for the laity, neither does the laity wait for the ministry."[8] Palmer's reflection indicates how she built upon a legacy of earlier Protestant evangelical women in North America and Great Britain. Not dependent upon the official sanction of clergy leaders, Palmer acted on her faith because there was a pragmatic need for her to do so. By the 1840s and 1850s, comparable prayer meetings were being held by evangelical Protestants modeled after Palmer's Tuesday Meeting throughout the northeastern United States.

Palmer witnessed to a unique theology that was indebted to earlier Wesleyan theology but also went beyond the tradition. She referred to her beliefs as an "altar theology," whereby penitent sinners might leave their sins on the altar for Jesus and become entirely sanctified. While many Methodist leaders, such as Wesley, tended to see sanctification as a process of spiritual growth, Palmer stressed that holiness could and should be achieved in an instantaneous fashion. She came to believe that conversion was a rational ascent to the power of God to cleanse an individual from the power of sin. This "shorter way" toward salvation became the cornerstone of Palmer's theology, and by the mid-1840s, she started holding revival meetings in the northeastern United States and Ontario, Canada. Her 1843 book *The Way of Holiness* became one of the major religious works of the nineteenth century. Like Charles Finney and other male revivalists of the era, Palmer engaged in a successful series of revivals in Great Britain during the 1850s and stayed active as a revivalist until her health caused her to withdraw from public life in the 1860s.

Palmer contributed to a larger evangelical tradition that emphasized two themes that echoed throughout the subsequent history of American evangelicalism: the power of God through Jesus Christ to make a person sinless and the centrality of the Holy Spirit as the primary mediator for salvation. Many Methodist (and non-Methodist) critics of Palmer pointed to the fact that John Wesley saw sanctification as a process of development as opposed to an instantaneous conversion to a sinless life (although Wesley did not discount the reality of entire sanctification being achieved in this lifetime). While Palmer certainly believed in the importance of Christian charity (she helped establish a mission in the Five Points slum of New York), her "altar theology" contributed to an evangelical Protestant idiom that helped shape the larger tradition of holiness theology in the late nineteenth century. "Holiness is an entire salvation from sin; a redemption from *all* iniquity. The soul through faith having laid upon that altar that sanctifieth the gift experiences continually the all-cleansing efficacy of the blood of Jesus; and through this it knows the blessedness of being presented faultless before the throne and, . . . gaining new accessions of wisdom, power, and love, with every other grace, daily."[9] In the second half of the nineteenth century, the gospel hymns of Fanny Crosby conveyed a model of American evangelicalism that speaks to the theology of Palmer. As a verse in one of Crosby's hymns affirmed: "O perfect redemption, the purchase of blood, to every believer the promise of God; the vilest offender who truly believes, that moment from Jesus a pardon receives."

Popular evangelicalism in the nineteenth century increasingly latched onto a language of Christian conversion expressed through the idea that salvation came through exclusive faith in a personal savior. Earlier traditions of revivalism tended to stress the role of God's sovereignty (Calvinism) or God's grace (Arminianism), but the growing motif in the nineteenth century was on *the person* of Jesus and on the role of the Holy Spirit in the conversion process. In language that echoed other millennial traditions of the time, Palmer believed that the account of Pentecost in Acts 2 was a sign of how the Holy Spirit was preparing Christians for Christ's second coming. Describing her experience of attending a holiness convention in an Episcopal Church, she exclaimed, "It was a season of Holy Ghost power. Male and female disciples participating with unreserved freedom. Congregational, Episcopal, Baptist, and Methodist ministers, as one, witnessing to the great salvation."[10] Some fifty years later, similar language would be used to describe the enthusiasm that ushered into being the pentecostal revivalism that began in Los Angeles in 1906.

WOMEN AND THE CALL TO PREACH

Within her lifetime, Palmer's ministry ignited a public debate not just on a proper understanding of sanctification, but on whether or not women should preach. Like John Wesley, Palmer drew a distinction between preaching as a gift of ministry and ordination. Preaching, she argued, was a gift of the spirit and should not be deterred, regardless of who was exercising the gift. "We have nothing more to do than Mary, when, by the command of the Head of the Church, she proclaimed a risen Jesus to her brethren. . . . We occupy the desk, platform, or pulpit, as best suited to the people in order that all may hear and see."[11] Like other women in American religious history, Palmer took a pragmatic view toward her work: if ministry needed to be done, it should be undertaken by persons who were called out by God (or put another way, if men were not willing to do the work, why not the women?). Like other women of that time, Palmer stopped short of advocating for women's ordination, but the themes of her theology would echo within the tiny minority of women who sought ordination in the mid- and late nineteenth century.

At the height of Palmer's public fame as a revivalist in the early 1850s, a small number of women refused to differentiate between the call to preach and the call to ordained ministry. The most prominent of these women was Antoinette Brown, who is recognized as the first woman to be ordained by a Protestant church in America in 1853. Brown grew up in upstate New York and attended Oberlin College, where she convinced Charles Finney of her sincerity in attending the theological college (although the school would not award her a degree). After a stint as a suffrage speaker in western New York, she was called to the pulpit of a small Congregational church in South Butler, New York. Her ordination in 1853 featured a sermon in support of women's ordination given by a Methodist minister named Luther Lee. Lee's sermon surmised theological positions that would be picked up by other women seeking ordination in the twentieth century, particularly Paul's words from Galatians 3:28: "In Christ, there is neither slave nor free, male nor female."

Yet Brown's pastorate in South Butler was short-lived. Unable to receive the support of other Congregational churches, and finding herself increasingly under siege for embracing a call preserved for a man, she left the Congregational ministry and went on to a successful career as a writer, woman's rights advocate, and, late in life, as a Unitarian minister. A final and painful irony of her departure from South Butler was when Brown appealed to Luther Lee for his support that hers was a valid ordination and he refused assistance, noting that he had only been asked to preach a sermon in support of a woman being ordained, not specifically speaking on the validity of Brown's ordination.

Phoebe Palmer was both typical and atypical of many women who ventured into the public sphere of ministry in the nineteenth century. On one hand, Palmer witnessed to the uniqueness of women's special gifts to prophesy, in effect setting aside conventional arguments articulated by St. Paul that women should keep silent in church. In effect, these women carried forward on the arguments made by Anne Hutchinson in the 1630s. By the same token, Palmer was careful to work within the parameters of an emerging Victorian society. As would be the case with other Protestant women in the late nineteenth century, Palmer stressed the importance of social convention and never questioned the emerging "separate spheres" view of the mid- and late nineteenth century that saw women as the moral caretakers of America. Her life stood not only as a unique model for women in ministry, but as an individual who helped birth a theological orientation that served to polarize many in American Protestantism in the years preceding and following the Civil War.

EVANGELICALISM AND THE SINS OF WEALTH

Part of the ramification of Finney and Palmer's emphasis on entire sanctification was to reinvigorate a strong tradition of evangelical social action. While Palmer herself tended to be apolitical on many social issues of the day, other Protestant leaders who were drawn to Palmer's example carried their understanding of entire sanctification to a more thorough critique of the social issues of the time. One practice that was becoming increasingly controversial among affluent Protestants was pew renting. By the 1840s the success of Methodism had led to the construction of large church buildings that resembled the architectural designs of older Congregational, Presbyterian, and Episcopal churches. As a consequence, many of these churches followed the lead of other Protestant churches by adapting the long-held practice of pew renting as a means of raising money.

Pew renting was seen as symptom of how evangelical Protestants were accommodating their mission to worldly standards and as a measure that violated the egalitarian spirit so characteristic of many postmillennial Protestant movements. Within northern churches, the debate surrounding pew renting mirrored a growing disillusionment over the church's acquiescence to the evils of slavery. In 1842 an antislavery holiness faction left the Methodist Episcopal Church in protest to the denomination's reluctance to embrace an antislavery position (as well as picking up on James O'Kelly's antiepiscopacy themes). This movement prefigured the larger schisms over slavery that would divide the Methodists (1844) and Baptists (1845), setting the stage for larger national debates over the slavery issue in the 1850s.

While some white Protestant evangelical leaders spoke prophetically against slavery in the decades leading up to the Civil War, they were in a clear minority. James Thornwell, a prominent southern Presbyterian, captured a sentiment shared by many in the South (and likely many in the North) that slavery was providential in that it provided an opportunity for African slaves to be exposed to the positive influences of Christianity. "We cannot but accept it as a gracious Providence that [slaves] have been brought in such numbers to our shores, and redeemed from the bondage of barbarism and sin."[12] While some church leaders were firmly committed to abolitionism in the North, many remained equivocal about abolition. Charles Hodge, the most well-known Old School Presbyterian theologian before the Civil War, probably captured the sentiment of many white Americans when he observed in 1836 that "if we are right in insisting that slaveholding is one of the greatest of all sins; that it should be immediately and universally abandoned as a condition of church communion or admission into heaven, how comes it that Christ and his apostles did not pursue the same course?"[13]

As the slavery issue grew in public intensity by the late 1830s, several Protestant leaders became invested in the goal of gradual emancipation of slaves in exchange for financial remuneration to slave owners and the return of former slaves to Africa. The American Colonization Society represented the most visible voluntary organization in the antebellum era with this expressed goal. The tenor of most who advocated colonization within the evangelical Protestant churches was one largely predicated on a paternalistic view toward slaves. Although slavery was seen as morally reprehensible, few white Protestants could envision a society in which blacks and white could live together as social and political equals.

The majority of radical abolitionist leaders to emerge prior to the Civil War possessed a decided antagonism toward institutional Christianity. In Boston, Theodore Parker had left the Unitarian ministry not only because of its theological conservatism, but out of his sense that organized Christianity was incapable of addressing the moral complexity of the slavery issue. Although many abolitionist leaders such as Parker and William Lloyd Garrison used the moral language of Christianity to speak against slavery, they were largely alienated from church denominations. In the end, few white Americans had a clear grasp of the moral issues at stake in the debate over slavery preceding the Civil War. Within nineteenth-century antebellum African American Christianity, perhaps the most incisive critique of American slavery and racism was represented by Frederick Douglass.

TOWARD A PROPHETIC AMERICAN THEOLOGY
The Example of Frederick Douglass

Douglass' life demonstrates a powerful example of a prophetic African American Christian tradition that extends to the present day. Born around 1817 on a Baltimore plantation, Douglass received a modest degree of religious instruction as a child. After escaping the plantation in the mid-1830s, he settled initially in Massachusetts where he had the opportunity to meet some of the key abolitionist leaders in Boston, including William Lloyd Garrison. Within a few years, Douglass made his way to Rochester, New York, where he became editor of his own abolitionist newspaper, *The North Star*. As had been the case a generation earlier during the heyday of the Burned-Over District, Douglass found himself in the right place at the right historical moment. While Rochester itself had virtually no African Americans residents, the city had a core of secular and religious activists who engaged in a number of social reform causes. Among those who became close friends with Douglass were Susan B. Anthony and Elizabeth Cady Stanton. Furthermore, the Underground Railroad that carried escaped slaves north into Canada had many "stopovers" in the western New

York region, becoming a base of operations for leading African American abolitionist crusaders such as Sojourner Truth and Harriet Tubman.

Douglass' work for social justice extended beyond slavery and included support for women's suffrage (he attended the landmark women's rights convention at Seneca Falls, New York, in 1848). Yet his staunchest advocacy was directed toward the abolition of slavery, and his writings repeatedly relied on Christian themes to support his arguments. Douglass directly challenged southern (and northern) clergy who used proof texts from Scripture to justify slavery. To those who would cite chapter and verse to justify slavery, Douglass retorted, "It would be insulting to Common Sense, an outrage upon all right feeling, for us, who have worn the heavy chain, and felt the biting lash, to consent to argue with Ecclesiastical Sneaks who are thus prostituting their Religion and Bible to the base uses of popular and profitable iniquity. They are of their father the Devil, and his works they do, not because they are ignorant, but because they are base."[14]

The themes of Douglass' writings reflected the unique realities of how African American Christianity was developing in the slaveholding South in the years between 1820 and 1860. In 1808 the United States officially ended the importation of slaves from Africa. In reality, however, slaves were still smuggled into the country as the demand for plantation labor in the agriculturally dominated southern states stoked the demand for more slaves. By 1861 the ten million African slaves living in the United States reflected religious practices as diverse as the regions of African where they were born. Enslaved Africans brought to these plantations a mix of religious traditions, including traditions steeped in practices of magic ("conjuring"), as well as indigenous African traditions of Christianity brought to America. Like their free counterparts in the North, African Americans in the South were attracted to the extemporaneous nature of Protestant evangelicalism. Matching the reputation of late eighteenth-century black preachers such as Harry Hosier, hundreds of slave preachers emerged in the early nineteenth century, preaching to slaves and slave owners their own unique genres of evangelical Christianity.

The currents of black plantation religion represent one of the most remarkable developments in the history of American Christianity. Often through the tacit approval of their slave masters, plantation slaves began to preach a theology that reflected critical themes central to the development of African American Christianity. On one hand, the message of slave preachers was otherworldly, emphasizing the glories of heaven and the rewards awaiting the forgiven sinner. However, the preaching also contained a radical edge in which societal values would be reversed, where the last (the slaves) would be first, and the first (slave owners and, more generally, white Americans) would be last. Like other forms of early nineteenth-century popular Christianity, slave religion had its own apocalyptic edge. Christ's second coming was not symbolized by a peaceful return of the Savior, but in many cases by a violent overthrow of white oppression. In the early nineteenth century, aborted slave uprisings had been fueled by this apocalyptic theology. Early in the century, inspired by the recent slave revolution in Haiti led by Toussaint L'Ouverture, Gabriel Prosser planned an aborted slave revolt in Richmond, Virginia. Prosser's cause was picked up in 1822 by Denmark Vesey, a former slave who had worked out a carefully planned revolt among slaves in Charleston, South Carolina (both Prosser and Vesey strongly identified with the antislavery theology of early American Methodism). Vesey's plan might well have succeeded, at least initially, had not a slave informant alerted authorities at the last minute.

By far the most consequential slave insurrection in American history occurred in 1831, when a slave plantation preacher named Nat Turner led a rebellion that ended with over fifty whites killed in the Tidewater region of southeastern Virginia. Turner, a Baptist-oriented slave preacher, was filled with a belief of his own anointing from God. After 1831 southern states swiftly passed laws forbidding slaves to preach. After the Turner rebellion, major Protestant denominations such as the Methodists and Baptists sponsored "plantation missions," whereby white ministers traveled to plantations preaching to slaves a message of submission to slave masters and to await the rewards of heaven. It was this early nineteenth-century context in which many African American slaves crafted what has been called "the invisible institution," reflecting the ways in which slave Christianity developed in secret outside the eyes and ears of slave owners. White ministers would preach submissive and obedient behavior on the part of slaves. Later in the evening, however, slaves would "steal away" into the woods, "hush harbors," or their quarters, preaching, singing, and praying in whispers to a God who proclaimed a theological message vastly different than the one preached by white ministers. This nascent black theology centered not only on the promises of heaven, but the assurance that slaves, like the Israelites of old, would be led out of their bondage to a promised land. "In the ecstasy of worship [slaves] reenacted the trials and triumphs of God's chosen people and so reaffirmed their own value and dignity, as they kept up their hope for freedom."[15]

The political developments in the South brought out a mixture of responses from northern churches. Even as slavery caused schisms among Methodists and Baptists in the 1840s, grassroots support for abolition among whites in the North remained low. Yet many antislavery activists were engaged in Protestant voluntary groups such as the American Anti-Slavery Society, an organization that provided a forum for many abolitionist leaders, including Douglass, Sarah and Angelina Grimke, and Henry Ward Beecher and his sister Harriet Beecher Stowe. Both of the Beechers were tied to the legacy of their father, Lyman Beecher. Following his career as a New England revivalist in the Second Great Awakening era, Beecher moved to Cincinnati in 1833 where he became one of the founders of Lane Theological Seminary. While Lyman Beecher preached a moderate antislavery theology, he represented a clear majority of white northerners who saw the ultimate solution to the slave issue as returning expatriated slaves to Africa. Despite his identification with various measures of revivalism, Beecher frequently campaigned to stave off the excesses of revivalism and worried about the impact of abolitionist-oriented revivalists like Charles Finney. In 1835, tensions boiled over at Lane as a faction of students left that school for abolitionist-leaning Oberlin Seminary.

Both Henry Ward Beecher and his sister Harriet possessed a greater affinity for the cause of abolitionism. After a pastorate in Indianapolis, Henry became pastor of Plymouth Congregational Church in Brooklyn, New York in 1847 and was a staunch supporter of the antislavery cause. Although the vast majority of white northerners still reflected varying degrees of sympathy for the abolitionist movement, national events during the 1850s were pushing more northerners to oppose the advancement of slavery, and the moral imperative to work for its eradication. As a response to the Kansas-Nebraska Act of 1854, allowing popular sovereignty in Kansas to determine whether that territory would enter the Union as a slave or free state, Beecher used his Plymouth congregation to raise funds to purchase weapons for pro-Union settlers. Beecher would go on to greater fame and notoriety in the years following the Civil War as one of the country's best-known pulpit orators. However, it was his sister, Harriet, who gained the greatest fame before the war with the publication of her 1852 novel *Uncle Tom's Cabin*.

For later generations of Americans, *Uncle Tom's Cabin* epitomized the perpetuation of harmful racial stereotyping, especially the image of the submissive slave character Uncle Tom. Yet a large part of the success of Beecher Stowe's novel was the fact that she underscored the prevailing racial and gender ideologies of white America in the mid-nineteenth century, especially the theme that white women needed to be aroused to the plight and suffering of slaves and respond with moral vigor to attack the evils of chattel slavery. Her conclusion echoed millennial themes that Christianity needed to lead the country through the wilderness of sin in hope of a day when slavery would be abolished. "Both North and South have been guilty before God," she summarized, "and the *Christian Church* has a heavy account to answer." For Beecher Stowe, the only way for the Union to be preserved was not through politics, "but by repentance, justice, and mercy; for, not surer is the eternal law by which the millstone sinks in the ocean than that stronger law, by which injustice and cruelty shall bring on nations the wrath of Almighty God!"[16]

The apocalyptic tones of *Uncle Tom's Cabin* echoed with greatest force in 1859, when John Brown, an abolitionist leader who had conducted many raids against southern settlers in the Kansas territory in the 1850s, raided the federal army arsenal at Harper's Ferry, Virginia. While Brown was captured and quickly hanged, his message of a God who judged without mercy evil sinners soon became an archetype for a theological rhetoric that characterized the North and the South during the Civil War.

What was unique about Frederick Douglass' voice is that while echoing sentiments of the radical abolitionist movement he helped shape a legacy of African American religious thought that castigated the biblical literalism of pro-slavery forces and the myopic outlook of certain white abolitionist leaders. Like many abolitionist leaders, Douglass repeatedly made a distinction between what he saw as the true Christianity of Jesus and the false Christianity sanctioned by American churches. "I love the religion of our blessed Savior," Douglass noted in an 1846 tract. "I love that religion that is based upon the glorious principle of love to God and love to man; which makes its followers do unto others as they themselves would be done by." Yet when compared to the practices of southern slavery, he surmised, "it is because I regard the one as good, and pure, and holy that I cannot but regard the other as bad, corrupt, and wicked. Loving the one I must hate the other; holding to the one I must reject the other."[17]

Douglass repeatedly attacked what he saw as the hypocrisy of American churches for emphasizing personal salvation without addressing the sins of slavery. Using arguments that would be adapted by many African American church leaders later in the twentieth century, Douglass asserted, "I believe the grand reason why we have slavery in this land at the present moment is that we are too religious as a nation, . . . we have substituted a form of Godliness, an outside show for the real thing itself."[18] Douglass was one of the few Americans of that era, black or white, who saw Christianity as a means of transforming *both* black and white Americans. As a moral leader, he was not above entering the fray in terms of engaging in biblical interpretation. (For example, he refuted the long-standing argument that African American slaves were directly descended from Noah's son, Ham, in the book of Genesis, and thus doomed to carry the sins of Ham for eternity.) Also, like the radical abolitionist John Brown, Douglass did not discount the right of slaves to use force as a means of liberation from slavery. Yet Douglass recognized that the moral crisis facing the country on the eve of the Civil War could not be solved solely through injunctions to Scripture, and that merely abolishing slavery would the problems of race be solved. Douglass, perhaps more than any other American of that time, noted that the question that faced the North and South was not simply predicated upon whether the South seceded from the Union, or, for that matter, if slavery was abolished. The issue was to what extent America was willing to become a society in which blacks and whites could live in community with one another in a spirit of equality. Even as political forces were pushing the nation closer toward war, Douglass offered a providential hope that God's justice would prevail upon the nation. "I have only to go on in His fear and in His spirit, uttering with pen and tongue the whole truth against Slavery, leaving to Him the honor and the glory of destroying this mighty work of the devil. I long for the end of my people's bondage, and would give all I possess to witness the great jubilee; but God can wait, and surely I may."[19]

CIVIL WAR FAITH

Ultimately, few religious leaders in the North or South embraced Frederick Douglass' vision of justice and equality when the Civil War began in April 1861. From the onset of the war at Fort Sumter, South Carolina, until the Confederate surrender at Appomattox, Virginia in April 1865, Christian leaders in the North and South engaged one another in political and religious jeremiads in defense of their own "sacred" causes. The concept of America as a divinely chosen nation represents one of the most historically engrained ideas in American history. As was discussed in the first section of the book, this concept of America as blessed by God has roots that go back to the Puritans, with these themes taking on a strong millennial current by the time of the American War of Independence. The irony of the Civil War is that both the North and the South spoke from the same historical and theological reservoirs that identified themselves as God's chosen people. The fulfillment of each nation's divine mission would be realized when the enemy (either in the North or the South) was defeated.

An especially tragic dimension of this Civil War faith, however, is that these millennial themes got stronger on both sides as the war dragged on. As each side did in the years leading up to the war, northern and southern Protestant spokespersons relied on the Bible for the justification of their cause. In the South, church leaders proclaimed the hope that every southern victory was a sign of God's providential blessing, while northern theologians noted that battlefield bloodshed was a form of divine cleansing for the sins of the nation. Horace Bushnell was typical of many northern clergymen who saw the war as both punishment for the nation's sins and a sign that God had blessed the nation (the North). "In these rivers of blood we have now bathed our institutions, and they are henceforth to be hallowed in our sight. Government is now becoming Providential,—no more a mere creature of our human will, but a grandly moral affair."[20] However, what is evident is that Protestant evangelicalism, which earlier in the nineteenth century had sought to craft a vision of America as a postmillennial republic, was unable to empower Americans to see the moral ambiguities surrounding the conflict. In the end, it was President Abraham Lincoln, a man whose commitment to Christianity has long been debated by scholars, who give a theological assessment of the war in ways that separated him from many of the church's leaders of that time.

In March 1865, when Lincoln gave his second inaugural address, he acknowledged that while America was guided by a spirit of divine providence, it was difficult to discern where that spirit of providence was leading the people of the South and the North. "Both read the same Bible, and pray to the same God; and each invokes his aid against the other. It may seem strange that any men should dare to ask a just God's assistance in wringing their bread from the sweat of other men's faces; but let us judge not, that we be not judged. The prayers of both could not be answered—that of neither has been answered fully." As opposed to a theology of righteous indignation and moral certainty, Lincoln used religion to reflect critically on the terrible causes of the war while also looking to providence in hopes that the wounds of the nation might be healed—and the nation reunited. "With malice toward none; with charity for all; with firmness in the right, as God gives us to the right, let us strive on to finish the work we are in; to bind up the nation's wounds, . . . to do all which may achieve and cherish a just and lasting peace among ourselves, and with all nations."[21]

While many northern ministers identified God's plan with Union victory, they ignored the ambiguity in Lincoln's words that called upon Americans to discern the presence of God as a healer amid a time of national tragedy. Nor would the majority of America's religious leaders in 1865 heed Frederick Douglass' hope that the Civil War might lead to an America that could truly become a just society for all of its citizens. It would be the responsibility of future African American church leaders to remind the nation of that hope.

A PROTESTANT KINGDOM?

The major blemish that Robert Baird confronted in his account of American religious history was how to handle the issue of slavery. Writing at the conclusion of the 1856 edition of his history, Baird conceded that he wasn't sure how the slavery issue would be solved in America, only that he knew that the evil institution would die out—through God's power. "Great wisdom will be requisite to carry the country safely through the difficulties which surround this great question. Our trust must be in God, that with patience and prudence, slavery will be done away in time, in a way consistent with the best interests of all concerned."[22] A generation later, without any hesitation, Leonard Bacon was able to view the war as an event that put the nation's Protestant churches on a road that he hoped would bring unity to American Christianity.

By his own calculations, Leonard Bacon reasoned that 143 Christian sects existed in the United States by the late 1890s. However, he was confident that negotiations could reduce these to four (the Roman Catholic Church, plus a merger of the Protestant churches down to three). Further, Bacon dared to hope that the twentieth century would witness an eventual setting aside of sectarian differences and that the major Protestant communions could merge into one church. He reasoned, if America could be reduced to two churches (Protestant and Catholic), perhaps a basis for a long elusive Christian unity could be established.[23] As the next section of the book discusses, the late nineteenth century fostered a new spirit of optimism that the nation's churches (spearheaded by Protestant churches) could foster the goal that had been elusive since the Protestant reformations of the sixteenth century: Christian unity. "It begins to look as if in this 'strange work' God has been grinding up material for a nobler manifestation of the unity of his people," he surmised. "When next some divine breathing of spiritual influence shall be wafted over the land, can any man forbid the hope that from village to village the members of the disintegrated and enfeebled church of Christ may be gathered together 'with one accord in one place' not for the transient fervors of the revival only, but for permanent fellowship in work and worship?"[24]

In a sense, Bacon's prediction for the future of American Christianity came to pass. The years after the Civil War would witness a renewed sense of hope around the idea that the nation's churches could find a basis for a shared unity (although that unity was primarily defined on Protestant terms). Yet amid these hopes, the historical realities of what had exploded upon the American landscape in the early and mid-nineteenth century were impossible to eradicate. In the years after the Civil War, the South was turned into a northern-occupied territory, and efforts at restoring the South to the Union in the conciliatory fashion envisioned by Lincoln gave way to heightened regional animosity, setting the stage for the coming of Jim Crow segregation. For all of Leonard Bacon's hopefulness about the future, he was typical of most northern secular and religious leaders of the time who viewed the South as a backward place that did not fit into the increasingly late nineteenth-century worldview of national unity, social progress, and hope for a new Christian millennium.

And yet, for all of his hopefulness, what Bacon did not see was how American Christianity's divisions during the first half of the nineteenth century reflected its remarkable adaptability to the unstable social and political contexts of American society. Historians have noted the dramatic transformations that America underwent from the early years of nationhood to the eve of the Civil War, a transition marking a movement from an agrarian society largely controlled by social elites to an industrial, urban society characterized by competing visions of political and economic power. In examining these changes, one would be remiss to overlook the role played by religion, and Christianity in particular. Christianity's growth in the United States was important not only in helping Americans cope with larger societal changes, but, as the first half of the nineteenth century demonstrates, to show how religion gave people a voice amid a whirlwind of societal changes.

In some ways, the scars of the Civil War have never healed in America, as reflected in the ongoing struggles of Americans to come to grips with issues of race. Yet the war also led to the emergence of a growing mythology that bespoke the prophetic nature of the American experience to the world. In the years since the Civil War, this rhetoric has symbolized at its worst a harmful parochial sense of the country's zeal to be a millennial superpower, seeing its own national purpose as God's purpose. Yet that tradition has at various times called the nation to repentance and accountability with its own best self. As Martin Luther King Jr. remarked in his 1963 March on Washington speech, America stood under God's judgment to live out the meaning of its sacred creed that all persons are created equal. This rhetoric that held in tension the idea of God's judgment and providential blessing upon America formed the basis of what represents the best aspects of this tradition of prophetic civil religion.

> So I say to you, my friends, that even though we must face the difficulties of today and tomorrow, I still have a dream. It is a dream deeply rooted in the American dream that one day this nation will rise up and live out the true meaning of its creed—we hold these truths to be self evident, that all men are created equal. . . .
>
> With this faith we will be able to hew out of the mountains of despair a stone of hope. With this faith we will be able to transform the jangling discords of our nation into a beautiful symphony of brotherhood.[25]

As the nation pushed into the years following the Civil War, Christianity would continue to be a key factor contributing to the creation of an ideology of national unity that in large measure was shaped by the nation's evangelical Protestant traditions. By the same token, the religious sectarianism so much in evidence during the first half of the nineteenth century continued to manifest itself within all sections of the expanding country. In the final decades of the nineteenth and early years of the twentieth centuries, the legacies of persons such as Charles Finney, Phoebe Palmer, Frederick Douglass, and Abraham Lincoln provided the impetus for the ways that Christianity sought to anchor Americans in the memory of the past while creating patterns for future manifestations of Christianity in a divided land.

PART III
American Christianity in Tumult, 1865–1920

Just over thirty years after Leonard Bacon's study of American religious history first appeared, in 1929 H. Richard Niebuhr published one of the classic studies of American Christianity, *The Social Sources of Denominationalism*. While late nineteenth-century historians were convinced that providence and manifest destiny were the predominant themes for understanding the unique nature of American Christianity, Niebuhr lamented what he believed was the historical and sociological inability of churches to live out Jesus' teachings. Looking back on over two hundred years of American Christianity, Niebuhr saw repeated examples of how Christianity, manifested through the continuous rise of numerous sects, had failed as a unified ethical movement. Yet unlike Bacon who reflected the largely accepted wisdom that Christian sectarianism was responsible for undercutting the power of the gospel, Niebuhr judged sectarian Christianity as the primary source for Christianity's historical vitality in the West. "The rise of new sects to champion the uncompromising ethics of Jesus and 'to preach the gospel to the poor' has again and again been the effective means of recalling Christendom to its mission."[1] For Niebuhr, it was denominations, bodies of churches that had grown into culturally dominant institutions, that accentuated the failure of Christianity, because they represented how institutional Christianity had become captive to dominant secular norms in religious history. Denominationalism "represents the moral failure of Christianity. And unless the ethics of brotherhood can gain the victory over this divisiveness within the body of Christ it is useless to expect it to be victorious in the world."[2]

Niebuhr's analysis primarily focuses on American Christianity from the time of the First Great Awakening through the Civil War, yet one cannot help but read events that occurred in American religious history in the late nineteenth and early twentieth centuries into his narrative. Niebuhr came of age in a society that still largely believed that America's future would be guided by the moral force of Protestant Christianity. On one hand, the years roughly between 1865 and 1920 appeared to offer hope in the goal of church unity. This period witnessed the birth of what became the modern ecumenical movement and saw numerous efforts undertaken to bring together the various denominational forces of American Protestantism. In what many have seen as one of American theology's great contributions to world Christianity, numerous theologians and church leaders offered provocative, some argued heretical, views on Christianity's relationship to modern political and economic life, crafting distinctive theologies of what has been called "social Christianity" that carries down to our time. The late nineteenth century also witnessed an explosion in Protestant missionary zeal whereby numerous churches sent missionaries not only throughout the world, but also galvanized young single women to undertake unique ministries to America's urban poor. Indeed, by the time of the international missionary conference held in Edinburgh, Scotland in 1910, hope abounded among church leaders that American Protestant churches were going to lead the way in a new movement of social and moral reform that was referred to by many as "Christianizing the social order."

But beneath this portrait of Protestant cultural unity, the emerging picture of American Christianity was far from idyllic. The major Protestant denominations, as Niebuhr observed, were raked by numerous schisms that continued a process of Protestant fragmentation that has been an ongoing part of American religious history. Debates in Protestant churches raged over age-old questions of defining salvation and understanding how Christian conversion should be manifested in the world. Christians argued over the meaning of recent scientific discoveries and attempted to reconcile these discoveries with time-tested propositions of inherited Christian truth. Immigration patterns begun earlier in the nineteenth century continued to accelerate in the last third of the century. These changing patterns not only brought millions of non-Protestant immigrants to the United States, but for the first time, immigrants who did not easily fall into the descriptive categories of "Protestant" or "Catholic." In the context of these changing historical circumstances, new indigenous forms of Christianity took root in America.

For all the ways that Niebuhr broke from past traditions in his analysis of American Christianity, he couldn't quite give up on the earlier Protestant vision of America. Post–Civil War Protestantism spoke hopefully about the type of nation they hoped their churches would build in America during the last third of the nineteenth century. In the aftermath of World War I, American Protestant leaders still echoed some of this optimism that God was leading His Church in a unique mission. Like many American Protestant leaders of his generation, Niebuhr longed for a church in which the radical commission of the gospel would find a way to forge denominational unity. "The road to unity is the road of sacrifice which asks of churches as of individuals that they lose their lives in order that they may find the fulfillment of their better selves. But it is also the road to the eternal values of a Kingdom of God that is among us."[3]

The following section asks the reader to make a judgment about what forms of Christianity dominated the American religious landscape between the end of the Civil War and the end of World War I. While a strong case can be made that this was a period when evangelical Protestants succeeded in their quest to unite Christianity under shared missional banners, the era also suggests that religious sectarianism went far beyond what Niebuhr described.

« 9 »

DEFENDING THE PROTESTANT EMPIRE

In 1885 a minister named Josiah Strong published a book entitled *Our Country: Its Possible Future and Its Present Crisis.* Perhaps more than any church leader in late nineteenth-century American history, Strong helped fashion an ideology of manifest destiny whereby American political, cultural, and religious principles would come to dominate world affairs. For future scholars, *Our Country* came to symbolize the worst aspects of an American Protestant tradition of ethnocentric, if not racist, Protestant ideology. While it is certainly difficult interpreting *Our Country* through the eyes of a twenty-first-century reader, the book effectively captures many of the tensions and transitions that impacted America following the Civil War. In the two decades after the assassination of Abraham Lincoln, America entered an unprecedented period of social-economic, cultural, and political change that had a deep impact on the development of American Christianity. Between 1860 and 1900, the size of America more than doubled from a population of approximately 31 million to 76 million. In the North, urban areas grew at a staggering pace, and the accompanying industrialization created new social conditions that became a focal point of concern for religious and secular leaders. Central to these changes were the continued patterns of immigration that began prior to the Civil War. By some estimates, an average of one million immigrants arrived in the United States annually during the 1880s, and by 1910, that figure had doubled.

In some ways, religious patterns that had been established prior to the Civil War remained intact, yet new immigrant patterns gave these traditions a new accent. While pre–Civil War immigration was confined mostly to Ireland and Germany, the years after the war saw the majority of immigrants coming from countries in eastern and southern Europe. For the first time in American history, sizeable pan-Asian immigrant communities took root in America, particularly on the West Coast, fueling what would become a growing Western fixation with Eastern religious traditions. Further, new immigration patterns introduced for the first time faith communions coming from the traditions of Eastern Orthodoxy, as well as a variety of numerous ethnic Protestant traditions that flourished for a time in the final quarter of the nineteenth century.

When one looks at this map of historical change, it allows one to understand the significance of a book like *Our Country* to the larger history of American Christianity. The book sounded a warning that an earlier Protestant worldview was under assault from alien religious, cultural, and political forces. Yet, the book offered many of the nation's Protestant churches the assurance that their heritage was still firmly in control of the nation's religious, cultural, and political destiny.

JOSIAH STRONG'S AMERICA

Josiah Strong (1847–1916) can be viewed as a transitional figure in American Protestantism who reflected how many of the nation's largest churches were moving away from the religious volunteerism of the early nineteenth century. When *Our Country* was first published, Strong was a little-known Congregational minister who had served a number of pastorates in the West and Midwest. The publication of *Our Country* turned Strong into one of the most recognizable leaders in American Protestantism. Strong originally published the book under the auspices of the American Home Missionary Society (AHMS). In the aftermath of the Civil War, the AHMS began as an effort of many northern Protestant churches to evangelize to former slaves in the South, but increasingly the AHMS focused its mission upon the nation's growing cities. As some Americans became more aware of decaying social conditions in urban America, numerous church leaders took to the pulpit and platform to address these concerns. In many ways, Strong's analysis was foundational to the liberal theological movement that later generations called "the social gospel." However, the book's initial success needs to be seen in the context of larger Protestant crusades to bring the gospel to the lost and destitute within America's growing cities.

Strong's theology reflected upon the growing organizational sophistication that anchored many efforts of post–Civil War American Protestant revivalism, embodied within the career of Dwight Lyman Moody

(1837–1899). While Moody's status as a revivalist was characterized by his straightforward theology of personal conversion and his association with developing forms of late nineteenth-century conservative Protestant theology, it is often forgotten how his influence galvanized numerous efforts of Protestant mobilization that transcended theological differences. Moody's life fits well the Horatio Alger, Gilded Age paradigm of an enterprising individual who through hard work achieves unimaginable status and recognition. Originally working as a salesman in his uncle's shoe factory, Moody was reared in New England and nurtured in an environment of evangelical Calvinism. Later he moved to Chicago where he took up full-time work with a new Protestant organization, the Young Men's Christian Association (YMCA). From the middle of the nineteenth century through the first third of the twentieth century, the YMCA served as one of the most important Protestant ecumenical organizations in North America. The YMCA, and the women's equivalent the YWCA, would be responsible for producing future ministers, missionaries, and Christian lay leaders who engaged in a wide range of ministries. By the early 1900s, these men and women represented many of American Protestantism's most significant leaders.

Moody first gained fame as a lay revivalist during a series of urban revivals in 1857–1858 (what some historians have labeled "the business-men's revival"), but his real fame came in the 1870s when he led a series of well-publicized urban revivals throughout North America and Great Britain. Together with his musical partner, Ira Sankey, Moody entreated his audiences to accept Christ and offered a plain-spoken message of the Christian gospel. Moody frequently made the analogy that he was in a lifeboat and his mission was nothing more than rescuing sinners from drowning. Yet what is often overlooked about Moody's success was his irenic view toward Christians of differing theological commitments and his organizational genius.

By the 1880s Moody centered his operations in his hometown of Northfield, Massachusetts, where he was responsible for building a network of evangelical organizations whose influence would be felt well into the twentieth century. In addition to a number of urban schools that were designed to engage in inner-city mission work (including what would become known as the Moody Bible Institute in Chicago), he was one of the central figures behind the establishment in 1886 of the Student Volunteer Movement (SVM), one of the major conduits of American Protestant foreign missions in the late nineteenth and early twentieth centuries. The SVM soon became one of the most powerful vehicles for the recruitment of young missionaries, and several of its early leaders, including a young Methodist layman named John R. Mott, would help forge the worldwide ecumenical movement in the first half of the twentieth century.

Although Josiah Strong is identified more with theological liberalism than the traditional Moody, both strived for similar ends of Christianizing America along decidedly Protestant lines. Strong and Moody championed a vision of global Protestantism that emerged from the crucible of older revivalist Protestant traditions. For Strong and other Protestants of his generation, the concept of Christianizing America had as much to do with a view of cultural, as opposed to a theological, worldview. He discussed a number of challenges facing the country, noting in particular immigration, urbanization, and use of western lands, and ended by issuing a plea that the values of an Anglo-Saxon, Anglo-American civilization might assimilate groups that previously resisted being Americanized. While Strong had harsh words for political socialism and vigorously condemned the sins of Mormonism, his greatest worry was American Catholicism.

Strong restated arguments that Protestant nativists had leveled against the Catholic Church at the height of the Know-Nothing hysteria in the 1850s and would be raised repeatedly against Catholicism by Protestants through much of the twentieth century, mainly, that the church represented theological and ecclesiastical traditions that were antithetical toward the American democratic tradition. As an individual who believed that certain Protestant churches represented and reflected the best attributes of American democratic life, Strong had reason to worry. He was not blind to the rapid growth of the Catholic Church in the United States. By the early 1870s, the Roman Catholic Church had become the largest single religious body in the country, with a membership of approximately 3.5 million. Less than twenty years later, in 1890, the number rose to seven million, and by 1910, the membership of the Roman Catholic Church totaled approximately 15 million members, or almost 30 percent of all religious adherents in the country.[1] To get a sense of the Catholic Church's numerical dominance at this point, it is important to note that the second largest church in the United States in 1910 was the Methodist Episcopal Church (the major northern branch of Methodism) with a membership of approximately four million members.

However, Strong and other Protestant leaders had a solution to address the problem of the Catholic Church in America: mobilize the nation's Protestant resources. Not long after the first edition of *Our Country* was published, Strong became the General Secretary of the American chapter of the Evangelical Alliance. Founded in Great Britain in 1846 as an effort of Anglicans to stave off the influence of the high church Oxford Movement in the Church of England, the Alliance strove to promote unity among various denominations. From its inception, the organization took a strong "anti-popery" position and sought to promote means by which various Protestant churches could cooperate through shared missions.

Part of Strong's argument, one used by many of his contemporaries, was that when one pooled the numerical resources of the "evangelical churches," they outstripped the resources of the Catholic Church. He gave expression to a sentiment prominent among many Protestant leaders who feared that Catholics would overrun the country. Such a development was unacceptable because it would undermine American democratic institutions. "It is the theory of absolutism in the church that man exists for the church. But in republican and Protestant America it is believed that church and state exist for the people and are to be administered by them."[2] At the very moment that Strong made this assertion, the heirs to the Catholic legacy of John Carroll and John Hughes were wrestling over the implications of being both a Roman Catholic and an American.

In the mid-nineteenth century, Catholic apologists such as Isaac Hecker and Orestes Brownson tried to articulate a vision of Catholicism that was compatible with American democratic values (while at the same time insisting upon the authority of the Church). In the second half of the nineteenth century, that issue played out over the question of how far a Catholic should assimilate into the dominant Protestant culture of the time. By the 1880s a clear system of ethnic parishes was in place throughout the United States. While the majority of the Catholic Church hierarchy was made up primarily of Irish Americans, the arrival of immigrants from Germany, Italy, and a variety of Eastern European countries helped make the Catholic Church something that Protestant leaders such as Strong disdained: the most ethnically diverse church in the country.

For all the ways that many Protestants (and some Catholics) frowned upon the ethnic parish, in its own way this model was quintessentially American. In large urban centers throughout the country such as New York, Boston, and Chicago, parish communities were established along the lines of ethnicity. What made these communities unique was not only the fact that they were communities where people worshiped, but where they lived and worked and where the language and culture of the Old World was preserved. Each parish had a parochial school in which parish children were educated by religious orders staffed by nuns and priests.

While Protestants such as Strong looked with fear to the rising tide of non-English Catholics pouring into the country, many Protestant churches were also attempting to organize and support their own ethnic congregations. When German immigration to the United States exploded in the 1850s, Baptists and Methodists established German-language congregations and conferences that, much like their Catholic counterparts, were designed to provide both a cultural buffer and a means for cultural assimilation. In 1858 northern Baptists established a German department at Rochester Theological Seminary. This school not only trained German immigrant pastors to serve German-speaking congregations in the United States, but many of the seminary's graduates returned to Germany where they established Baptist parishes. By the end of the nineteenth century, evangelical Protestant mission churches had also been established with modest success among Swedish and Italian immigrant communities.

One of the great Protestant mission disappointments throughout the nineteenth century was the continued uneven record of evangelization toward Native Americans. The chronicle of Protestant and Catholic missions to Native Americans reveals some success. Some early nineteenth-century missionaries, in the spirit of toleration preached by William Penn and Roger Williams, insisted that native tribes were entitled to their land and rejected the paternalistic views imposed upon these groups by government and religious organizations. Yet by and large, the sense of divine providence, in which white colonization was seen as part of God's divine plan of salvation, continued to dominate the thinking of most Protestant and Catholic missionaries (epitomized by how many church leaders either acquiesced to or openly supported the government's reservation system that confined Native Americans to certain territorial lands).

By far the largest growth among ethnic Protestants in the late nineteenth century occurred within the Lutheran Church. While modest Lutheran growth had occurred in sections of the American colonies (largely attributed to the effort of German Lutheran immigrant pastors such as Henry Muhlenberg), growth of the tradition remained relatively small during the first quarter of the nineteenth century. As immigrants came to the United States toward the middle of the century from Germany and Scandinavia, however, Lutheranism experienced significant growth, especially in the Midwest and Upper Midwest. Like the Catholic Church, Lutheran churches tended to be defined by ethnicity and numerous synods were formed often defined around whether one was Swedish, Danish, Norwegian or German. Like Catholic ethnic parishes, Lutheran parishes were places where Old World culture could be preserved, including languages and religious customs. By 1850 a movement largely associated with the leadership of Samuel Schmucker toward cultural assimilation began to take shape within American Lutheranism. A professor at the Lutheran seminary in Gettysburg, Pennsylvania, Schmucker's mission was dedicated to strengthening Lutheran doctrine and encouraging Lutherans to become Americanized. At the same time as Schmucker argued for an assimilationist Lutheranism, other Lutherans, especially in the Midwest, dissented not just on matters of ethnicity, but theology as well. Two prominent examples birthed at the end of the nineteenth century include the Missouri Synod and Wisconsin Synod Lutherans whose theologies in many respects echoed an emerging antimodernist perspective.

The tensions concerning whether to embrace a uniform standard of American culture would be repeated over and over again in American Christianity during the second half of the nineteenth century. It was one thing for many Christians to embrace English as a primary language, but it was quite another for immigrants to abandon customs and religious practices cultivated for generations. By the 1880s this uneasiness caused many churches to fight battles not only over what it meant to be an American church, but over the larger question of how Protestant and Catholic communions defined the meaning of theological orthodoxy.

CATHOLICISM AND AMERICANIZATION

Josiah Strong argued in *Our Country* that an Americanized Catholicism was not possible, stating succinctly that "there is no such thing as an American or Mexican or Spanish Catholic Church. It is the Roman Catholic Church in America, . . . having one and the same head, whose word is law, as absolute and as unquestioned among Roman Catholics here as in Spain or Mexico."[3] There is no question that Strong's analysis of Roman Catholicism came in the midst of an era where historical claims of papal authority were being exercised upon American Catholics in unique ways.

By the end of the Civil War, the papacy was on the eve of reasserting its authority in ways that directly impacted the American Catholic Church. For much of the first half of the nineteenth century, the papal hierarchy largely had a hands-off approach in the Catholic Church in America. Deferring to the leadership of bishops such as John Carroll, American Catholics initially found no inherent tension between being Catholic and being American. Yet throughout the first half of the nineteenth century, the papacy witnessed political revolutions that rocked Europe, especially in countries with large Catholic populations such as Germany, France, and on the papal doorstep itself, Italy. From the perspective of the Vatican, these democratic revolutions represented political and social chaos that undercut the historical authority of the church. In 1864 Pope Pious IX issued a declaration that denied the cherished American principle of free-dom of religion, reaffirming that the Roman Catholic Church was the only valid expression of Christianity.

Protestant fears were fueled by the First Vatican Council held between 1869 and 1870 (and the first Roman Catholic Church council since the Council of Trent convened in the mid-sixteenth century). This council assertion of the pope's infallibility on matters of church law and doc-trine helped corroborate Protestant fears that the Catholic Church was an anti-American religious body. While the church had its adherents for Americanization, the majority of immigrant Catholics after 1860 followed the model of ethnic parishes that, in the eyes of many Protestants, only reinforced the alien nature of the Catholic Church. However, within the hierarchy of the American Catholic Church there emerged a group of leaders who sought to reintroduce an assimilationist vision more consis-tent with the Catholic Church envisioned by Bishop Carroll.

The major figures in this effort to Americanize the Catholic Church in the late nineteenth century were Archbishop John Ireland and James Cardinal Gibbons. As archbishop of St. Paul, Minnesota, Ireland bemoaned the fact that many priests serving in the United States were European born (a fact that had plagued the Catholic Church in America since the founding of the Maryland colony in the seventeenth century). Ireland and Gibbons were strong advocates for the development of Catholic seminaries in the United States and supported efforts in higher education, most notably in the establishment of the Catholic University in Washington, D.C. in 1889. Also, Gibbons was a strong advocate for the rights of American workers, setting a pattern that would characterize the development of what became known by the end of the nineteenth century as social Christianity.

In the end, the papacy could not completely curtail the currents of Americanization within the Catholic Church, epitomized by the contin-ued growth of Catholic institutions of higher education that by the early twentieth century were competing against the best Protestant universities in the country in terms of academic prestige. Yet the sense of grassroots fidelity to Old World Catholic traditions remained strong in Catholic par-ish life. It would not be until after World War II when new historical devel-opments would not only open up American Catholics to new movements of Americanization, but expose on a popular level rich traditions of centu-ries of Catholic tradition to millions of Americans Protestants.

The cause of Americanization faced a major setback in 1899 when Pope Leo XIII's encyclical *Testem benevolentiae* rebuked the idea that the Catholic Church might adapt its teachings to the tenets of American secular society. Although this encyclical did not stop the advocates of Americanism, it did reflect the strong sentiment in the American Catholic Church to uphold traditional Catholic teachings. One of the chief opponents of the Catholic Americanists was the Bishop of Rochester, New York, Bernard McQuaid. In his own way, McQuaid's ministry echoed themes of Catholic identity expressed a generation earlier by John Hughes. For the traditionalists, the question was not one of loyalty to the United States (conservative leaders took this for granted). The real question was where the Catholics placed one's ultimate loyalties—in the teachings of Catholic Christianity or in the secular state? In his own way, conservatives such as McQuaid shared the fears of Protestants such as Strong that one of the chief dangers to America was represented by agnosticism and socialism. However, for Strong and other Protestants, the chief difference was their faith that American democracy would lead to the fullest expression of Christianity, not its negation.

At the end of the nineteenth century, many Protestant leaders saw themselves as standing on the side of an American democratic tradition that was in firm opposition to the antidemocratic tendencies of the Catholic Church (as well as a variety of sectarian religious movements including Mormonism). Figures such as Strong and Moody represented a shared consensus in the idea of America as an Evangelical Empire, mobilizing its resources for the purposes of not just personal conversion, but to promote a strong front of denominational unity to convert (or stave off) non-Protestant influences. Yet even as a book such as *Our Country* appeared to offer common ground for many Protestants to agree upon their mission, the Protestant theological landscape was shifting in ways that by the early twentieth century would make it difficult for the theological heirs of Strong and Moody to share the same worldview.

PROTESTANT THEOLOGICAL SHIFTS

In 1874 America was on the verge of marking its centennial. Amid growing preparations for this celebration in Philadelphia, uneasiness settled over many parts of American society. The post–Civil War experiment of southern reconstruction was a failure, and by 1877 federal troops were removed from the former states of the Confederacy. In the North, cities swelling with growing immigrant populations teemed with social tension, reflected increasingly by economic disparities between the rich and the poor. While many urban revivalists such as Dwight Moody preached on behalf of the poor, their theology tended to emphasize the importance of individual salvation as the primary anecdote to the problems of modern life. Elsewhere, some Protestants picked up on earlier theological themes that had first become evident in American Unitarianism earlier in the century. One Presbyterian minister's commitment to that tradition ignited a controversy that mirrored American Protestantism's future.

Many historians see the years between 1865 and 1900 as a period of theological transition in American Protestantism. It was during this time that American Protestants en mass encountered and debated the merits of what many contemporaries called "the new theology," what would later be known as "theological liberalism." In the eyes of later generations, the term "liberal" would become attached to a variety of different meanings and connotations. But applied to a discussion of nineteenth-century theology, liberalism denotes the ways that theological beliefs and traditions could be adapted to the contours of the natural and social world.

Prior to 1865, the majority of American Protestant churches were largely tied together around shared intellectual suppositions. This faith, as it had during the time of the Reformation, centered upon fidelity to Scripture. The judgment of most Protestants around the year 1850 was that the Bible was *the* book of God's revealed truth, containing no errors or contradictions. Many Protestants coming out of Reformed denominations, such as the Presbyterians, continued to affirm post-Reformation documents of belief, such as the seventeenth-century Westminster Confession. Developed as a platform of English Calvinist theology, the Westminster Confession became the bedrock for many Calvinist communities in the Western world for generations. For many churches such as "Old School" Presbyterians, adhering to a literal interpretation of the Confession was deemed absolutely essential for church membership.

While it is true that Calvinism was losing its hold as a popular religious movement by the end of the nineteenth century, the intellectual underpinnings of Reformed theology were evident within a large cross section of evangelical Protestants. Central to this intellectual worldview was an eighteenth-century philosophical tradition known as Scottish Common Sense Realism. Building upon the work of the seventeenth-century English philosopher Francis Bacon, eighteenth-century Scottish philosophers such as David Reid were reacting to what was seen as the moral subjectivism of Enlightenment philosophers such as John Locke, David Hume, and ultimately Immanuel Kant. Common Sense thought affirmed a view of the natural world that saw no incompatibility between the claims of religion and science. While the majority of Protestants were not hostile to science, scientific developments were always secondary to one's commitments as a Christian—especially because ultimate truth was defined and taught in the Bible. In fact, divine revelation was as inherently natural to the cosmos as was the existence of gravity, and such reasoning was foundational for most interpretations of the Bible and theology for much of the nineteenth century.

This convergence between Common Sense reasoning and Christianity largely held until the middle half of the nineteenth century. The contributions of biblical and theological scholarship in Germany, combined with post-Enlightenment religious movements such as liberal Unitarianism and Transcendentalism, represented a challenge to taken-for-granted assumptions such as the doctrine of original sin and the literal truth of Scripture. In particular, Charles Darwin's theories on evolution served as a direct scientific challenge to historical dating, questioning long-accepted notions concerning the historical accuracy of Scripture (for example, claims made in the Book of Genesis that the world was created in seven days). This shifting intellectual landscape caused inevitable conflict among different traditions in American Protestantism.

By the early 1870s, fidelity to various forms of theological liberalism was confined primarily to small groups of clergy and academics (the latter having spent time studying in many German universities, such as those of Berlin, where liberal theology had deep intellectual roots). Yet a popular form of liberalism was beginning to hold sway in a few large urban churches in the Northeast and Midwest, with many liberal preachers, such as David Swing, becoming easy targets from more orthodox theological constituencies.

David Swing was both an unlikely and logical person to be caught up in this developing theological chasm. Since 1866 he had served as pastor of Chicago's Westminster (later Fourth Presbyterian) Church. By his own admission, Swing was not a fiery orator, yet his intellectual temperament spoke to many well-educated, middle-class Americans, who embraced changing social and scientific models of knowledge yet still wanted to hang on to their Christianity. William Hutchison goes as far as to suggest that Swing was the first so-called modernist to emerge out of evangelical Protestantism.[4]

The term "modernism" is often used interchangeably with "liberalism," although it is probably more accurate to see liberalism as an outgrowth of a modernist worldview. Generally speaking, modernism refers to an intellectual orientation that places a premium on the values of the Enlightenment, stressing the centrality of new scientific discovery and human capacity to address the social, political, and cultural problems in society. Although the task of liberalism was to find ways to accommodate Christian teachings to an emerging modernist orientation, the consequences of this theological adaptation was that liberals called into questions many time-honored assertions made by earlier Christian traditions.

The issues Swing raised that caused the Presbyterian Church to charge him with heresy in 1874 foreshadowed theological conflicts that would be waged for decades to come. Swing's sermons emphasized a view that theology was historically constructed. While he saw creeds and church confessions as important signposts for the believer, they had to be measured in the context of the time periods in which they were written. More importantly, Swing was on the vanguard of a movement in liberal theology that attempted to ascertain the exact words and actions of Jesus, not just what others had to say about him. This emphasis on the "Jesus of history" became a cornerstone for just about everyone caught up in the liberal movement. In the early nineteenth century, discerning the ethics of Jesus as opposed to the doctrines formed throughout church history became the cornerstone to Unitarianism and its more radical cousins. This debate had caused radical Unitarians such as Theodore Parker to reach a point at which they felt doctrinal emphases on original sin were misplaced. The real issue for these early proponents of American liberal theology was to create conditions for human beings to use their God-given faculties in service to the world. Traditional Protestant theologies during the Second Great Awakening era, whether Calvinist or Arminian, presupposed that sin was the eternal problem that humanity sought to overcome through faith in Christ. However, liberal theology tended to reverse the equation: faith in Christ enabled humans to make sense of a world that was inherently just *and* change the world. As opposed to saving individuals from the hell fires of eternal damnation, liberalism emphasized the inherent goodness of humanity that gave individuals the power to overcome sin.

It is this final point that helps explain the popularity of many late nineteenth-century Protestant "pulpit princes" who preached to large, upper- and middle-class congregations in major cities in the North and Midwest. The most prominent of these pulpit princes were Henry Ward Beecher, long-time pastor of the Plymouth Congregational Church in Brooklyn, New York, and Phillips Brooks, rector of Trinity Episcopal Church in Boston. While both men are rightly identified with an emerging generation of post–Civil War liberal thinkers, their theology, like Swing's, was not meant for the subject of academic scrutiny or systematic study. Rather, their intent was largely pastoral, and in many respects, they offered a message that would be picked up by liberal preachers well into the twentieth century: how can the message of Christianity help a person make sense of modern life? One biographer referred to Beecher as the "most famous man in America" in the second half of the nineteenth century, an assertion that has a great deal of merit.[5] While connected to one of the most famous families in the history of American Protestantism, Beecher shaped his own theological course, first as a Congregational minister in Indianapolis, and later as the pastor of Plymouth Congregational. Beecher's sermons, widely reprinted and read by millions of Americans, stressed the idea that Christianity was a faith not primarily about judgment, but grace. Although he had been identified with the abolitionist movement during the Civil War (and was also a supporter of women's suffrage), Beecher's preaching was often apolitical, stressing the ways that the message of Jesus provided a means to confront the issues of modern life. A similar theme echoed from Phillips Brooks, who, as pastor of Trinity Church in Boston, drew large crowds to his services and enjoyed wide popularity through his published sermons.

These liberal ministers were not paradigmatic of what was occurring on a grassroots level in American Protestantism, nor did they necessarily reflect the official theological perspectives within their respective denominations; they were, however, a reflection of how larger theological and cultural currents were being integrated into the fabric of influential urban congregations. Liberal theology attracted attention in part because many of its major adherents after the Civil War were ministers of prominent American pulpits whose sermons were regularly published in both religious and secular periodicals. In 1874, at a point when Swing's popularity was on the rise, he was accused of heresy by a young professor at the Theological Seminary of the Northwest in Chicago (later to become president of Princeton University), Francis Patton. Patton's accusations against Swing mirrored the charges that would be made by orthodox against liberals well into the twentieth century: the need to stand by the sanctity of Christian doctrine, as revealed through Scripture.

Patton was a graduate of Princeton Theological Seminary, which had a long-standing reputation as the major defender and upholder of traditional Calvinist orthodoxy within the Presbyterian Church (and the Reformed tradition in general). This tradition, represented by the school's longtime professor of theology, Charles Hodge, had already fought extensive battles over doctrine prior to the Civil War, epitomized by attacks against Lyman Beecher and other New School preachers in the 1830s. Hodge and younger Princeton theologians such as Patton argued that part of what gave theology its force was that it remained committed to the time-honored traditions of Scripture and affirmed key doctrinal themes emerging from church history (in particular, fidelity to historical Reformed Protestant documents such as the Westminster Confession). Historical conditions might change, but the teachings of Christianity did not. The theological worldview of Princeton Seminary was one of the contributing factors to what would become known by the 1920s as "fundamentalism."

Swing was not convicted of heresy charges by the Chicago Synod of the Presbyterian Church. However, he soon left the denomination, opting to preach in an independent Chicago pulpit for fear that Patton and his supporters would come after him again. Yet Swing's heresy trial was the first of several to impact the Presbyterian Church and other Protestant churches that would extend through the first quarter of the twentieth century.

Popular conceptions of liberal theology frequently see the movement as obsessed with religious experience at the expense of historical doctrine. While liberals such as Swing did place a great emphasis on an individual's experience, consistent with the currents coming out of Germany and, in particular, the more radical movements emerging out of New England Unitarianism, the larger issue for most late nineteenth-century liberal ministers was predicated on finding ways to preserve Christian tradition in the face of the complexities of a modern era. At the same time as Swing was on trial for heresy, the writings of a minister relatively unknown outside of New England were starting to find a following. By the twentieth century, this minister, Horace Bushnell, would be considered one of the main architects of American theological liberalism.

HORACE BUSHNELL'S POSTHUMOUS LEGACY

Bushnell lived most of his life in relative obscurity despite being a prolific writer. Born in Connecticut in 1802 and educated at Yale Divinity School, Bushnell spent the bulk of his ministry as pastor of a Congregational church in Hartford, Connecticut (where he also worked as a city planner, reflected in the design of a city park that bears his name to this day). In many ways, Bushnell maintained a theological outlook consistent with an earlier generation of New England Congregationalists. He looked favorably on the history of religious establishment in that state and was concerned with preserving a Congregational hegemony in Connecticut. Yet Bushnell's theology pushed beyond the parameters of what his clergy colleagues saw as sound orthodoxy. After surviving charges of heresy in the 1840s, Bushnell continued to expand many of his ideas, especially in his views on Christian conversion. Well read in both German theology and the literary romanticism that increasingly moved from Unitarianism into numerous Protestant churches with greater regularity after the Civil War, Bushnell emphasized that discerning ultimate theological truth was difficult, if not impossible, because of the subjective nature of language. For Bushnell, the primary means to understand doctrine and theology was through metaphor. From his perspective, the use of language and metaphor did not invalidate the historical creeds of the church, but rather affirmed that there were limits upon human-constructed language to fully ascertain the nature and meaning of God.

In some ways, Bushnell did not refute traditional Calvinist views of divine sovereignty. In fact, he viewed his discussion of language and its limits as part of the fundamental problem facing humans who attempted to interpret the meaning of Scripture and church tradition: the effort to know a God who was for all intents and purposes unknowable. Yet Bushnell's own assertions of orthodoxy were undercut even more with the publication in 1847 of his most influential work, *Christian Nurture*. This work had a major impact among many Protestant leaders after the Civil War (including Josiah Strong), and the suppositions of this and his other works proved foundational to later generations of liberal theology. Bushnell directly challenged age-old concepts of the doctrine of the substitutionary or ransom view of the atonement. This belief held that Christ's death on the cross paid a divine debt for the forgiveness of sins, whereby those who believed in Christ would be guaranteed (by virtue of their faith in Christ) eternal salvation. This doctrine of the atonement had long-standing roots in Christian theology extending back to the Middle Ages, and increasingly the impact of revivalism in the eighteenth and nineteenth centuries had lifted this view of the atonement to a central place in American academic and popular theologies. Bushnell picked up on another medieval tradition, one commonly referred to as a "moral influence" view of the atonement. While he stressed the centrality and uniqueness of Christ's sacrifice, Bushnell saw in Christ's death the means by which humanity came to an understanding of God's saving grace. This moral influence view of the atonement had a major impact on how Bushnell rethought matters of conversion. In juxtaposition to an instantaneous change in the believer, Bushnell saw conversion as part of stages of faith, whereby the fellowship of the church had a responsibility to nurture and cultivate Christian discipleship within the believers.

In articulating these views, Bushnell drew heavily on what he saw as the historical precedents in both Protestant and Catholic traditions. However, the presuppositions of his theology set the stage for future liberal

Protestants to reassess the meaning of Christian doctrine in the years following Bushnell's death in 1876. His impact can be seen in the theologies of a number of ministers who rose to prominence in the 1870s and
1880s, especially influential Congregational ministers including Theodore
Munger, Newman Smyth, and Washington Gladden. Increasingly, these
theologians stressed the need for churches not to emphasize a unitary conversion experience, but to stress the importance of Christian education as
a means to develop faithful disciples.

The post–Civil War Sunday School movement in American Protestant was a major arena where many of Bushnell's ideas took root, both
within individual churches and increasingly within the structures of
formal denominations. By the 1870s many churches were architectur-
ally designed on what was called "the Akron Plan," whereby sanctuaries
were segmented into specific areas for religious instruction. Increasingly,
denominations created formal structures to support Christian education
that included by century's end a growing network of both denominational
and ecumenical youth and young-adult organizations. Part of the philosophy of many Christian education professionals was that the movement
needed to cultivate faith within the church and provide opportunities of
learning to the wider society. In 1871 a Methodist minister named John
Vincent established a Sunday school academy on Chautauqua Lake in
western New York for the purpose of offering religious education training for Methodist clergy and laity. By the end of the nineteenth century,
the Chautauqua Institute had moved beyond this early mission by offering a variety of forums where religious leaders, politicians, professors, and
social activists could present public lectures and offer short-term classes
for the thousands of middle-class Americans who flocked to the Institute
annually. Increasingly, Chautauqua stressed the relationship between religion to the political-economic problems of modern life, thus becoming a
principal conduit for what became the social gospel.

EMMA RAUSCHENBUSCH CLOUGH
AND FOREIGN MISSIONS

Josiah Strong's *Our Country* appeared at a key moment in American
Protestantism. For all the perils facing American Protestantism, the
book echoed a triumphal spirit that the virtues of Anglo-American
Protestantism would be felt worldwide. In no area was this spirit revealed
more acutely than in the explosive growth in Protestant foreign missions. Prior to the Civil War, many efforts of Protestant foreign mission
were often sporadic and funding depended largely on voluntary efforts

on a local level. Although most denominations possessed foreign mission societies, and several denominations cooperated together to sponsor joint missionary efforts, missionary service was seen as a vocation reserved for an elite few (i.e., male clergy and their spouses). By the end of the Civil War, women's activism would play a major role in the boom of foreign missions. By the early 1870s, women's foreign missionary societies emerged in several Protestant churches. These groups were largely spearheaded and led by the wives of prominent ministers. These organizations were not only a major source of funding for denominational missionary causes, emphasizing the historical role played by women as fundraisers for religious organizations, but also provided numerous volunteers who pledged themselves to missionary service. Through denominational missionary societies and through organizations such as the YMCA, YWCA, and SVM, large numbers of women and men pledged to lead lives of service to Christ as missionaries.

These developments reflected the heyday of American Protestantism as the global leader in international foreign missions. Between 1870 and 1900, hundreds of successful missions, primarily Baptist, Methodist, and Presbyterian, were established in Africa, Asia, and India, and by 1910 there were over a hundred mission boards operating in North America. While most of these boards grew out of the historic Protestant churches that emerged prior to and following the American Revolution, they also included smaller churches that formed in the midst of the holiness movement of the late nineteenth century.

Critics of foreign missions often cite the way that some missionaries exported the worst characteristics of Protestant Christianity. Denominational missionary magazines often gave myopic accounts of how missionaries struggled to spread Christianity to the heathen in places such as Africa, chronicling the exploits of heroic missionaries to save souls. Yet behind this romanticism rests another story. Many foreign missionaries actively worked with indigenous populations to build schools and improve the economic quality of life within a given community. (This is especially evident of missionaries in India who worked with the Untouchables, those who socially and economically were at the bottom of the Hindu caste system.) Yet even within the explosive institutional growth of missions, the theological differences accentuated by the David Swing trial began to play a role in the mission field. Many leaders of the mission movement, including the Presbyterian minister A. T. Pierson, embodied conservative theologies, and, while working passionately to ameliorate the sufferings of indigent populations, never lost track of their ultimate mission to save souls. Yet a new generation increasingly struggled with this formulation of missions. The life of Emma Rauschenbusch Clough provides an insightful case study for how mission theology began to shift by the late nineteenth century.

She was born to a German American family in 1858, and her father August was the head of the German department at the Baptist seminary in Rochester, New York. Emma's older sister, Frieda, married a German Baptist minister and the two later went on to work among fledgling Baptist communities in Germany. Emma's younger brother, Walter, went on to a career as a Baptist minister (and years later became one of the major American representatives of the theological tradition known as the social gospel). Like many women of her generation who chose to enter missionary service in the 1880s, Emma became a missionary as a single woman. Initially a German teacher in the Chicago public schools, in 1882 she was accepted as a missionary to the Baptist Telugu mission in south India, working over the years as a teacher primarily among Indian women. In 1894, Emma married the mission's principal founder, John Clough, and remained in India until her husband's death in 1910. During her years as a missionary, she also received a Ph.D. from the University of Bern in Switzerland, writing on the significance of Mary Wollstonecraft's work for women's rights.

Emma Rauschenbusch Clough reflects a larger tension that impacted foreign missionaries by the late nineteenth century. While most Protestant missionaries were united in their conviction to win souls for Christ, some also came to believe that meeting the material needs of people was equally important, if not more important, than soul saving. In an autobiography on her late husband published in 1914 (a book that although written in John Clough's voice was actually written by Emma), Rauschenbusch Clough sought to reconcile traditional Protestant theme of "Christianizing" non-Christian societies with the need to embrace the indigenous practices emerging out of these cultures. What Rauschenbusch Clough observed became a pressing theme for many in the foreign mission field in the early decades of the twentieth century, mainly, "the American type of Christianity did not fit in all cases into the conditions which [missionaries] found."[6] More than the account of her late husband revealed, Emma Rauschenbusch Clough's theological struggles went beyond mission theory. In her final years in India, she became a convert to the synergistic teachings of theosophy, a movement that combined elements of Hindu, Christian, and nontraditional religions. Emma's struggle represented a tension that would grow more acute by the early twentieth century: was the goal of foreign mission predicated on conversion along Western lines or could Christianity adapt itself to the religions and cultures that it encountered? Although Emma Rauschenbusch Clough was an extreme case, her life reflected the tensions that some American Protestants were starting to have with inherited forms of evangelical Christianity.

CHRISTIANITY AND NEW THOUGHT
The Creative Synthesis of Mary Baker Eddy

At the same time that many American Protestants felt comfortable in flexing their institutional muscles, a disparate series of movements were creating alternative forms of religiosity, especially in the Northeast and Midwest. The term most often used to define these movements is "New Thought." Generally, the term New Thought is used to describe a con- sortium of philosophical streams and "folk" practices that stressed the ability to use the mind to cure diseases. Christianity as a religious move- ment stressed a tradition of physical healing, predicated on many of the gospel accounts of Jesus in the New Testament. While many New Thought movements sought to reclaim this early Christian tradition, many also relied upon an eclectic range of movements that came out of Europe in the eighteenth century that gained popular expression in America during the nineteenth century. The origins of New Thought are often associated with Emanuel Swedenborg, an eighteenth-century philosopher who stressed ways that the mind was involved in the promotion of health and wellbeing. Another eighteenth-century figure, Austrian physician Franz Mesmer, took these ideas further by stressing how individuals could actively par- ticipate in the healing of others (hence the use of the term "mesmerism" often associated in the late nineteenth century with those who could use the power of the mind for both curing and inflicting illness upon others).

Some practitioners of New Thought, while not hostile to Christianity, stressed range of solutions to cure diseases and often were not specific in terms of codifying their methods through published writings. Typical of this phenomenon was a native of Portland, Maine, Phineas Quimby. A self-educated man, Quimby embarked on a career that combined homeo- pathic treatments with a range of teaching that stressed the role of the mind to cure diseases. His example was emulated by a wide range of fol- lowers. None, however, achieved the stature in late nineteenth-century society as one of Quimby's former pupils, Mary Baker Eddy.

Born in rural New Hampshire in 1821, Mary Baker Eddy's family was steeped in the traditional religion of New England Calvinism. Yet a series of personal tragedies, including the death of her first husband, the subsequent adoption of her son by another family, her abandonment by a second husband, and frequent poverty, increasingly brought her to despair manifested in a series of physical maladies. Yet far from subscribing to any doctrine of nineteenth-century Victorian womanhood, Eddy searched for ways to use her talents that molded together one of the most successful and controversial religious movements to emerge in American history: Christian Science.

The dramatic turning point for Mary Baker Eddy occurred one day in the winter of 1866 after she fell on ice in Lynn, Massachusetts. In good biblical fashion, she arose from her injuries on the third day, and over the next several years, despite many setbacks, built a reputation as both a healer and as an exponent of what she saw as the key to understanding Christianity. In 1875 Eddy published her first edition of *Science and Health*. Over the years, this book was expanded and refined to articulate her belief that in Christian Science one not only could find health, but understand that the essence of Christianity was in Jesus' healing of body and mind. As more and more practitioners gathered around Mary Baker Eddy's teachings, her organization rose with a growing number of Christian Science churches that extended from Boston to Los Angeles by 1900. After consecrating a large neo-gothic "mother church" in Boston in 1894, the fledgling movement soon began plans for an even larger building adjacent to that church that would be built at a cost of two million dollars.

Eddy's view of Christianity modified numerous traditional understandings of doctrine. She held to what her critics saw as a Gnostic view of theology that denied the reality of Jesus' humanity. Yet her writings reflect a remarkable intellectual awareness of differing theological and popular religious currents of the day (and in many respects, a strong rejection of her own Calvinist upbringing). As she summarized in *Science and Health*,

> When we possess a true sense of our oneness with God, and learn we are Spirit alone, and not matter, we shall have no such opinions as these, but will triumph over all sickness, sin, and death, thus proving our God-being. That we are Spirit, and Spirit is God, is undeniably true, and judging by its fruits, . . . we should say this is not only science, but Christianity.[7]

Many assessments of Mary Baker Eddy paint her as a religious fanatic and a paranoid, vindictive person who systematically built a wall of secrecy around her and mercilessly drove out all dissenters. As one of Eddy's biographers observes, however, Eddy was a far more complex person who saw within Christianity the resources to escape the physical pain caused by illnesses. She was a woman who repeatedly overcame personal setbacks and found in religion both comfort and empowerment. Like earlier nineteenth-century religious innovators such as Joseph Smith, Eddy showed an ability to craft a theological worldview centered upon an engagement with contemporary understandings of science and metaphysics, synthesizing these resources toward her quest to find religious meaning. By the time Eddy died in 1910 at the age of 89, she had crafted a movement that not only continues to thrive, but remains rooted in her religious vision as founder and guiding spirit.

The ramifications of Eddy's ideas would not only live on in movements in Christian Science, but increasingly in the twentieth-century ideas linking religion to personal health would become commonplace within a wide range of more "orthodox" Christian churches. One of the most noteworthy examples in the early twentieth century was the Emmanuel Movement, centered upon the ministry of Elwood Worcester, rector of the Emmanuel Episcopal Church in Boston. Worcester's theology combined a largely liberal orientation and a New Thought emphasis on mind-body health. Although the Emmanuel Movement lasted only a few years, the legacy of linking Christianity to personal health *and* ultimately economic prosperity would become an enduring theme in what became known in the late twentieth century as the prosperity gospel.

LATE NINETEENTH-CENTURY AMERICA
A New Religious Pluralism?

The size of New Thought and Christian Science movements were small in comparison to the numerical growth within various evangelical Protestant and Catholic churches. However, these movements reinforced the fears of clergy such as Josiah Strong that old-stock religious values were under assault. In the face of these fears, however, many Protestant leaders could allow a level of tolerance for non-Protestant and heterodox faiths while also asserting the superiority of their own beliefs.

In 1893 the World's Parliament of Religions was held in conjunction with the Columbia Exposition in Chicago. Designed to celebrate the 400th anniversary of Christopher Columbus' "discovery" of America, the exposition was largely an occasion to celebrate America's technological and cultural sophistication. In addition to the attractions that brought thousands of Americans to the Exposition during the summer and fall of 1893, the World's Parliament of Religions represented one of the first sustained efforts by American Christian leaders to grabble with what would be known by the end of the twentieth century as religious pluralism.

Featuring an array of Hindu, Buddhist, Jewish, and Muslim leaders, the Parliament attempted to showcase not just how religious diversity was affecting the nation, but also in its own way to show the superiority of an emerging liberal Protestant ethos. In 1893 adherents to Eastern religions were extremely few in the country, and many Americans attracted to Eastern religions came to them through synergistic movements such as theosophy. At the same time, Jewish immigrants from Eastern Europe were coming to the United States in record numbers by the late nineteenth century, as were a small number of immigrants who came out of the historical churches associated with Eastern Orthodox Christianity.

At the conclusion of *Our Country*, Josiah Strong summed up the mission facing American Protestants. "Ours is the elect nation for the age to come," he surmised. "We are the chosen people. We cannot afford to wait. The plans of God will not wait."[8] Many Protestant Americans heard Strong's appeal; this is not only reflected in his book sales (over 175,000 copies were sold in its early printings), but in terms of how the book came to define the way many Protestants fused their church's mission with that of the nation. Robert Handy has noted that the ideological shift that occurred in American Protestantism after the Civil War was one that moved from a sense of mission to reform America to one where the mission was nothing short of converting the world.[9] More than any other Protestant leader of his time, Josiah Strong gave expression to that hope and to that vision. Ironically, at the very moment in which Strong and other Protestant leaders expressed hope that their vision of ethnocentric evangelicalism would reign supreme, the theological worldview that undergirded that vision was collapsing. On one hand, it was easy for many Protestant leaders of that time to point to the evils of the Catholic Church or the proliferation of groups such as the Mormons or Christian Scientists who claimed the mantle of Christianity. On the other hand, it was becoming increasingly clear to many orthodox Protestants that the teachings of liberals such as David Swing were only the tip of the iceberg.

« 10 »

SOCIAL CHRISTIANITIES
AND SOCIAL GOSPELS

Despite the effort of Protestant churches to affirm a shared unity, the fissures of division that were widening by the end of the nineteenth century split open in the early twentieth century. Many of these divisions
centered upon ongoing developments within American liberalism, as a
rising number of theologians and church leaders continued to raise questions about the nature of biblical miracles and the reliability of trusting
the Bible as a divinely inspired book. While one dimension of theological
liberalism increasingly allied itself with emerging traditions of philosophy, others saw within liberalism the keys to understand the relationship
of Christianity to what was called by some in the early twentieth century
"the social awakening." Liberal theology was not only seen as a means
to move beyond what was perceived as Christianity's misguided focus on
the apocalyptic and otherworldly, but as a means to bring the heart of
Jesus' teachings to bear upon the conditions of social-economic inequality
in America. For all of the blatant imperialism within Josiah Strong's *Our
Country*, the book was a key harbinger of what initially was called "social
Christianity" and later the "social gospel."

Dating from approximately the early 1880s to the early 1920s, the
social gospel was never a singular movement either organizationally or
theologically, and in some ways the term is more applicable to its period
of greatest public notoriety in the early decades of the twentieth century.
However, its theological moorings influenced a cross section of religious
leaders who attempted to reinterpret Christian teachings in light of the
contemporary social problems brought on by late nineteenth-century

urbanization, immigration, and industrialization. While it was associated in the public's mind, and in the judgment of later historians, with issues of social-economic reform (and a desire on the part of some social gospelers to experiment with democratic socialism), the social gospel had a deeply spiritual side, embodied in devotional works and popular hymns.

In the early 1920s, Shailer Mathews, one of the chief liberal spokespersons of the time, made the assertion that the social gospel was nothing more than "the application of the teachings of Jesus and the total message of the Christian salvation to society . . . as well as to individuals."[1] Mathews' definition could be applied to earlier evangelical efforts of social reform, especially as it took the form of "Christianizing" America by means of eradicating alcohol abuse, promoting Sabbath observance, and most especially in antislavery crusades before the Civil War. In many ways, the social gospel can be seen as a continuation of an earlier tradition of nineteenth-century evangelicalism that had as its goal the perfection of society. Yet the chief distinction between the social gospel and earlier forms of evangelicalism was how the former emphasized the need for Christians to demand *systemic* change to the nation's economic and political structures.

What is often forgotten about the rise of the social gospel, however, as historian Sidney Mead pointed out, is that it was chiefly a movement that arose out of the major denominations within institutional Protestantism.[2] While many of its leaders spoke boldly about the need for America to undergo a dramatic reorientation of social-economic power, the primary spokespersons for the social gospel represented denominational interests of what later historians called "the Protestant establishment." By the end of the nineteenth century, Protestantism moved away from an earlier nineteenth-century model of voluntary churches to one made up increasingly of centralized denominational boards and a growing network of ecumenical organizations. These groups were often tied together into networks of church leaders, philanthropists, politicians, and business leaders who, despite theological differences, shared a common concern that Protestant Christian values be spread throughout the nation.

In a broad sense, the social gospel carried on an earlier evangelical tradition of postmillennialism, believing that it was possible to transform the world through the power of Christian conversion. Yet those who came out of the social gospel movement carried forth a postmillennialism with a difference. While many social gospelers did express the importance of a personal conversion experience, this reality was secondary to how *society* was to be converted. The social gospel was closely tied to the precepts of the Progressive Era, a time when many Americans were caught up in a desire to work for measures of economic and political reform. The social gospel was an example of something old and something new in American Christianity. Its radical side was reflected in the ways that many of its more visionary leaders spoke unequivocally on behalf of the poor, offered insightful and systemic critiques of American social-political institutions, and, most especially, made compelling theological arguments for the intersection between Christianity and the social-political realities of the modern world.

Conversely, the vast majority of social gospelers maintained a strong connection to the white Protestant middle-class culture of the late nineteenth century. Theirs was a vision often predicated on familiar themes of anti-Catholicism, Christian triumphalism, and, like most white Americans, a tendency to ignore issues of racism. As the movement matured by the second decade of the twentieth century, many of its chief proponents embodied the tension between radical social-economic reform and preserving cherished Protestant ideals, perhaps no one more acutely than the individual who became most identified with the subsequent legacy of the social gospel in America: Walter Rauschenbusch.

GILDED AGE DISSENT
The Origins of the Social Gospel

In 1890 a Philadelphia Baptist minister, Russell Conwell, preached a sermon that became one of the most widely reprinted addresses in American religious history. This sermon, "Acres of Diamonds," fit well the Gilded Age vision that many Americans, at least in theory, wanted to believe about their nation. Born in 1843, Conwell's life seemed to embody the popular notion that hard work and perseverance would be met by success, if not material wealth. A Civil War veteran, Conwell initially practiced law before being called into the Baptist ministry. As pastor of one of the largest churches in Philadelphia, Conwell's theology mixed together the revivalism of Dwight Moody, with a self-help liberalism embodied by Henry Ward Beecher. "Acres of Diamonds" combined a prototype model for many future preachers, especially those associated with what would become known later in the twentieth century as the prosperity gospel. For Conwell, the essence of the Christian story was not just about personal success, but achieving wealth as well. "Money is power, and you ought to be reasonably ambitious to have it," he asserted. "Money printed your Bible, money builds your churches, money sends your missionaries, and money pays your preachers ... I say, then, you ought to have money. If you can honestly attain unto riches ... it is your Christian and godly duty to do so."[3]

Conwell was giving expression to a deeply engrained theology of wealth that had been embedded in Protestantism in one form or another since the Reformation. In the eighteenth century, John Wesley was noted for his admonition "earn all you can, save all you can, give all you can," reflecting a widely held sentiment that wealth was essential to a Christian's personal and moral wellbeing. In his own way, Conwell embodied a logical extension of certain aspects of late nineteenth-century Protestantism's cultural ambitions. Like many prominent business tycoons of that era, Conwell used his wealth (much of it generated from money earned through the "Acres of Diamonds" sermon) to fund a variety of Protestant ministries and philanthropic enterprises, his crowning achievement being his role in the founding of Temple University. At the same time, many people who would become associated with the later social gospel carried a strong connection to the social world of Conwell. Many proponents of social Christianity were tied to denominations such as the Northern Baptists, who relied on the financial support of many affluent Americans to fund their ministries (not the least being the president of the Standard Oil Company, John D. Rockefeller). Yet those who became connected with the social gospel increasingly could not accept Conwell's theology. For them, although wealth in and of itself was not a sin, the ways that wealth was utilized could have adverse consequences—on individuals and society.

For many Protestants who were drawn to the social gospel, Christianity had a two-pronged mission: it carried a deeply evangelical message of personal conversation that would make the nation more righteous *and* would lead Americans to reexamine the social structures of the nation in the realms of business and government. Some of the first stirrings of what became the social gospel not only came from clergy, but through the efforts of an emerging network of women's organizations.

WOMEN'S SOCIAL REFORM
Frances Willard's America

As women mobilized their efforts into a variety of denominational foreign missionary programs, a parallel movement of women's organizations took root for the purpose of evangelizing the inner cities of the United States. Perhaps the most significant outgrowth of this call to national conversion was the rise of the woman's home missionary movement from approximately 1880 to 1900. The antecedents of the home mission movement can be traced to earlier nineteenth-century Lutheran women in Germany, where women were responsible for ministries of care primarily within hospitals (specifically as nurses). From a biblical standpoint, the home mission (or deaconess movement) was seen as a connection to the Apostolic Church, whereby deaconesses had primary responsibilities for care of the poor and destitute. The deaconess model caught on in many American Protestant churches, in particular among the Baptists and Methodists. By 1900 deaconess groups were responsible for establishing "training schools" to educate and prepare women for service as inner-city missionaries; they also created urban settlement houses to care for the material needs of immigrant communities, and, like the earlier model in Europe, worked as nurses in denominationally sponsored hospitals.

Many deaconess groups projected an appearance that they were a Protestant religious order, often dressing in clothing resembling a nun's habit. Unlike previous models within American evangelicalism that stressed the role of the minister's wife as a helper or assistant to her husband, deaconess groups were made up mostly of single women. Many historians of women and American religion have pointed to the connection between the rise of deaconesses and the ways that many Protestant churches in the late nineteenth century reinforced prohibitions on ordaining women and restricted the right of women to preach. Yet to serve as a deaconess or home missionary was to find oneself on the frontlines of the urban landscape described by Josiah Strong. The bulk of the deaconess ministry was within cities such as New York and Chicago that teemed with poor, immigrant populations.

Women home missionaries offered spiritual care to their flocks, but they also became experts at what was initially dubbed "Christian sociology" or "applied Christianity" by the early twentieth century. Most deaconesses who attended ministry training schools were exposed to the latest writings of influential sociologists and economists such as Richard Ely, whose writings in the 1880s stressed the interconnection between Jesus' social teaching and modern economic theory. Often, home missionaries integrated a socially conservative (and nonthreatening) model of women's leadership, with a radical critique of social-economic conditions that frequently showed sympathy for models of democratic socialism. Reflecting what historians have called "domestic feminism,"[4] deaconesses worked under the banner of preserving cherished American values (such as the family), while also being outspoken about the social misery that they encountered in their ministries.

One of the best models of this late nineteenth-century paradox can be seen in the example of the Woman's Christian Temperance Union (WCTU) and its charismatic leader, Frances Willard. Founded in 1873, the WCTU committed itself to continuing earlier nineteenth century Protestant crusades in favor of a temperance amendment banning the sale of alcoholic beverages. The temperance movement is often depicted as a myopic campaign by overly moralistic Protestants to enforce Puritan values upon the country (this depiction is a misnomer considering that many seventeenth-century New England Puritans were not above drinking a pint or two of ale). The WCTU was an organization that depicted Protestant organizational transitions from the first to the second halves of the nineteenth century. Early nineteenth-century Protestant volunteerism centered upon the effort of organizations to function on a grassroots level. While Protestant voluntary societies often had national offices, the bulk of mission (including fundraising) occurred at a local level. This form of advocacy continued into the second half of the nineteenth century, however, increasingly the spirit of volunteerism was being supplanted by a growing professionalism within official denominational boards and inter-church groups.

The history of the WCTU reflects this process of transition that began in earnest in 1879 when Frances Willard became president of the WCTU. Like Phoebe Palmer from an earlier generation, Willard's impact in American history would be largely forgotten by later generations. However, from the time she took over the WCTU until her death in 1898, she was one of the best-known and beloved figures in the United States. Born in upstate New York in 1839, Willard moved to suburban Chicago as a young girl and, after a stint as a school teacher, became president of a women's college in Evanston, Illinois (which later merged with Northwestern University). Willard was raised a staunch Methodist and her diary reveals many of the agonies she felt about being a woman who felt called to preach the gospel—yet was barred by the church from doing so. Prior to becoming president of the WCTU, Willard worked as an assistant for Dwight Moody as an organizer for his revivals. Within a few years after taking over the WCTU, Willard lifted that organization to a new level of prominence in America, with a strong network of WCTU chapters flourishing in both North America and Great Britain.

For later generations, the WCTU would be famous (or infamous) for the so-called "pledge" that it insisted that all temperance-loving Americans take to forsake the consumption of alcohol. Such moralistic pledges were part of the culture of post–Civil War revivalism. In this regard, Willard's name became associated with a rather bucolic and conservative social vision of American culture, epitomized in the early twentieth century by a Methodist minister who remarked on his childhood that he grew up schooled in the belief that "God, Buffalo Bill and Frances Willard were the three most wonderful people on the earth."[5]

Yet there was another side to Willard that was far more controversial. Like Phoebe Palmer, Willard believed that women, as well as men, had a right to preach. Unlike Palmer, however, Willard went the next level and advocated for the ordination of women. In the 1880s and 1890s, only a handful of churches had ordained women as clergy, the majority of them coming out of the Universalist Church and a limited number of churches primarily within smaller evangelical churches (in particular, out of the holiness and pentecostal movements). However, the largest Protestant churches in the country—Presbyterian, Episcopalian, Baptist, or Methodist—refused to ordain women. In the 1880s, the Methodist Episcopal Church was the largest Protestant denomination in the country, but it reflected the attitude of the vast majority of Protestant men who saw women's leadership both as unscriptural (citing familiar texts from the Apostle Paul) and socially unorthodox (for the ways that ordination violated conservative views of gender, in which women were seen as the natural caretakers of Christian homes).

Willard directly challenged these views, citing not only pragmatic arguments related to women's gifts to preach but also searching scripture for views to counter traditional Pauline perspectives on gender. Her activism also led her increasingly to sympathize with numerous utopian political movements that emerged in the 1880s (she developed a keen interest in various movements of political socialism), and she attempted to get the WCTU to lend its support to a variety of political causes such as the support of labor unions and advocate for legislation to curtail business monopolies. Most importantly, Willard threw the WCTU into the women's suffrage movement, and her work helped pave the way for the eventual passing of the Nineteenth Amendment to the Constitution in 1920, which granted women the right to vote.

One may view Frances Willard's life as inspiring Protestant women (and men) to commit their lives toward the service of Christ in the country. While organizations such as the SVM, YMCA, and YWCA were primary conduits for recruiting foreign missionaries, the WCTU was a means of mobilizing the moral forces of the nation's churches to wipe out the evils of alcohol. Yet Willard's life reveals a complex portrait of late nineteenth-century Protestant women. The fact that Willard promoted the WCTU as an organization that saw its members as "the mothers" of America indicates how she carefully relied on a conservative view of gender. While she helped solidify a strong base for the women's suffrage movement, like many white feminist leaders of that era, Willard tended to ignore issues of racial justice. In the 1890s, at a time when prominent African American activists such as Ida B. Wells attempted to bring attention to the rise of lynching in the South, Willard largely turned a blind eye to such issues—a reality that ties her story to most white Americans of that time. By the same token, Willard attempted to push the WCTU to embrace what she called a "do every-thing" agenda that would expand the public role of women in church and society. Her activism helped set the stage for the ways that many Protestant churches entered the twentieth century.

SOCIAL EVANGELICALISM ASCENDING
The Coming of Social Christianity

The rise of women's home missionary societies and the WCTU was one example of how Protestants sought to mobilize their efforts to address the needs of society. In the years following the Civil War, many Protestant evangelical groups continued a legacy of reform through the establishment of inner-city missions, one of the most enduring being the Salvation Army. Established in London by William Booth, a former Methodist preacher, the Salvation Army emerged by the early twentieth century as a movement that stressed hands-on evangelicalism in the context of urban squalor. Booth's 1890 book *In Darkest England* provided readers a grim view of the poverty faced by thousands in the streets of London and offered a plea to many Christians to respond with compassion and outreach to those who were poor.

Yet Booth's evangelicalism was predicated primarily on earlier models of Protestant conversion centered upon personal salvation (and increasingly, as will be discussed in the following chapter, a theological emphasis on what has been called premillennialism). While many persons drawn to the social gospel would look positively at evangelical movements such as the Salvation Army, they did not go far enough in their calls for societal change. In the years after the Civil War, Americans wrestled with growing unrest between business owners and their workers, and numerous voices emerged not only critiquing the abuses of big business, but advocating for workers' rights to form unions. As early as the 1870s, a small group of church leaders began to raise questions about how Christianity needed to take a more vigorous role in responding to pressing social-economic questions of the day, the most prominent being Washington Gladden.

Gladden was born in 1836 and spent his formative childhood in rural upstate New York. After graduating from Wesleyan University, he embarked on a career as both a reform-minded minister and journalist. Deeply influenced by the theology of Horace Bushnell and by his early exposure to labor-management tensions that surrounded his North Adams, Massachusetts parish, Gladden developed a firm commitment to what would be called by the early 1880s social Christianity. Although Horace Bushnell showed little interest in matters of systemic social reform, Gladden represented a vanguard of Protestant leaders who would reveal their indebtedness to Bushnell's theology, in particular his understandings of Christian nurture and social development. Like his contemporary, Josiah Strong, Gladden affirmed a theological outlook that stressed the progressive character of Christian theology, and in Gladden's case this theme was embodied in his early writings by an insistence that social-economic reform and a just society could be obtained through fidelity to the ethical principles of Christianity. Gladden was one of the first Protestant leaders to call for models of economic cooperation between labor and management, including a support for labor unions. While critical of socialism, he was an advocate for worker cooperatives that would enable models of mixed ownership between businesses and their workers.

Yet always in the back of Gladden's theology was his fidelity to the idea that Christianity was essential for the creation of the ethical worldview for a just outcome between capital and labor. "For let no one fail to see that cooperation is nothing more than the arrangement of the essential factors of industry according to the Christian rule, 'We being many are one body in Christ, and every one members one of another.' It is capital and labor adjusting themselves to the form of Christianity; and like every other outward symbol, is a false deceitful show, a dead form, unless filled with the living spirit of Christianity itself."[6]

Gladden first made his mark in the 1870s as an editor of the popular periodical, *The Independent*. However, he found a wider public audience in 1882 when he was called to the First Congregationalist Church of Columbus, Ohio. First Church served as a paradigm for many future social gospel preachers that would extend through the first half of the twentieth century. While Gladden's Columbus church did not carry the stature of the East Coast churches pastored by liberal ministers of that era such as

Henry Ward Beecher's Plymouth Congregational Church in Brooklyn, New York, or Phillips Brooks' Trinity Church in Boston, Gladden went beyond these earlier paradigms of liberalism by introducing a separate Sunday evening service devoted entirely to the question of "the church and the social problem." In his years in Columbus, Gladden involved himself in city politics, even serving a term on the Columbus City Council, and published over thirty books dealing with questions of how Christian theology had a fundamental duty to address pressing social-economic issues. By the time Gladden retired in 1912, he was recognized as one of the leading figures of American Progressivism and, in the eyes of future historians, became known as "the father of the social gospel."

The themes within Gladden's theology would increasingly resonate on a popular level. In 1894 William Stead, a prominent British journalist, published a scathing indictment of the political-economic environment in Chicago with his book *If Christ Came to Chicago!* The book combined a sociologist's detail in analyzing the economic corruption of that city with a clear moral mandate that the city's (and nation's) churches were not exercising their ethical muscle to put an end to Chicago's vice. Stead's analysis perfectly captured the social milieu that gave rise to the social gospel, focusing on urbanization, corporate and political greed, and the huge wealth disparities between Chicago's rich and poor.

Many of the themes within Stead's work would find a wider audience in the United States in 1897 when a Topeka, Kansas, Congregational minister, Charles Sheldon, published a novel that later would be seen as a classic expression of the social gospel entitled *In His Steps*. Sheldon had already published works of fiction that revealed his sympathies with aspects of the teachings of social Christianity (most notably his 1890 work *The Crucifixion of Philip Strong*). However, *In His Steps* introduced to America the enduring slogan, "What would Jesus do?" that a hundred years later would be claimed by many American evangelicals as their own.

For many, the theological themes of Sheldon's novel came to epitomize the idealistic naiveté of the social gospel. Set in a fictitious Midwestern city within a prosperous congregation, the church comes to question its commitment to Christianity after a "tramp" interrupts a church service. Recounting the ways in which he and his family had been adversely impacted by industrial capitalism, he sets before the congregation a challenge, later taken up by the church's pastor, to live lives in accord with the teachings of Jesus—embodied by the tramp's question to the church, "What would Jesus do?" Sheldon's persistent message in the book (and in his other novels) was that the core message of Jesus' teachings could overcome the inequalities of a corrupt, unchristian society. What was needed, however, was the heroic and unselfish commitment of Christian men and women to follow those teachings.

Gladden and Sheldon are instructive of a critical aspect of the social gospel's rise in American Protestantism. Although many historians identified the social gospel primarily as a response to late nineteenth-century industrialization, the major spokespersons for the tradition, in particular clergy, acted more as evangelists who advocated from the pulpit, classroom, and lecture circuit as opposed to being social scientists who worked out specific programs of reform. The rise of social Christianity was marked by a decidedly liberal theological emphasis in the belief that the essence of Christianity was not predicated on its doctrines, but on its practices. Central to the emerging social gospel was how Christians responded to the conditions of economic inequality, urban poverty, and moral listlessness. William Stead captured this tension at the conclusion of *If Christ Came to Chicago!* when he asserted, "If Christ came to your city would He find you ready? If so you will not have long to wait. For the least of these, My brethren, are a numerous tribe, and an hour will not pass . . . before your readiness will be put to the test."[7]

The early proponents of the social gospel saw themselves as lonely prophets in the wilderness fighting an uphill battle against vice and economic greed. At the same time, however, the rise of the social gospel paralleled the growth of Protestant churches into large institutional networks. By the early 1900s, these networks would include official denominational boards, ecumenical agencies, educational assemblies such as the Chautauqua Institute, and even Protestant youth organizations that provided speaking venues for many rising social gospel leaders. The growing network of public lyceums within several American cities (forums that often brought together prominent secular and religious leaders of the day) created a context for more radical iterations of social Christianity that moved outside of institutional Christianity. The most controversial was Midwestern Congregational minister George Herron.

RADICAL SOCIAL CHRISTIANITY

For all the appeal of figures such as Charles Sheldon and Washington Gladden, those men reflected a view that accentuated the inherent goodness of American society and its institutions. As Gladden and Sheldon stressed the possibilities of the "Golden Rule" to reform society, another segment of social Christianity centered its appeal under the banner of "Christian Socialism." The legacy of George Herron is perhaps the most revealing of a strong undercurrent of late nineteenth-century social Christianity that would reemerge within a number of later theological movements, most notably within late twentieth-century liberation theology. Herron was born in 1862, and while he possessed little formal education, he developed a reputation as a spellbinding orator that led him first into the Congregational ministry and then to a professorship at Iowa (later Grinnell) College in the field of Applied Christianity.

Herron's inspiration came from a number of intellectual trajectories; however, he reflected a growing fascination with emerging European models of political socialism. In the first half of the nineteenth century, a few Anglican clergy experimented in England with what they termed "Christian Socialism." This tradition, embodied in the careers of Frederick Robertson and F. D. Maurice, reflected a belief that true Christianity not only spoke about the poor, but rose up righteous persons willing to live and work among them (what would be called in the late twentieth century as being in solidarity with the oppressed). A generation later, urban settlement houses in America continued to embody these practices, and in many large cities a new form of Christian ministry was taking root. The Institutional Church movement centered on congregations that often built facilities designed to offer a range of activities throughout the week. Many of the largest of these congregations had programs aimed to meet the needs of the urban poor, including civics classes, food preparation courses, daycare for working mothers, and gymnasiums for exercise and recreation. The theme of healthy recreation became a cornerstone within American Christianity by the early twentieth century and was mirrored in the fitness programs that became central to organizations such as the YMCA.

Yet, for radicals such as Herron, these measures did not go far enough. By the 1880s a small number of American clergy and laity were wrestling with emerging theories of democratic socialism such as was embodied by the Italian politician Giuseppe Mazzini (who combined the languages of Christianity and popular democracy in his campaign for a united Italy) and, to a lesser extent, Marxist theory. The relationship between political socialism and Christianity was engaged by a spate of influential theorists such as the economist Richard Ely, the Episcopal clergyman W. D. P. Bliss, and even the beloved president of the WCTU, Frances Willard. Yet Herron gave a new urgency for his calls to reform. Herron's theology was a blend of influences that included a love for Mazzini and Christian ascetics such as

Francis of Assisi. While the mainstream of the social Christian movement was represented by persons such as Strong and Gladden who saw social reform primarily through the moral influence of the nation's Protestant churches, Herron believed that the problems of society required something more than moral suasion—it required national repentance. Although Herron did not discount that part of the Christian message was to love one's neighbor, he stressed that the central thrust of Jesus' message was to advocate for a complete reversal of societal values, in which Jesus' blessing of the poor in Matthew 5 needed to be taken literally. For Herron, Jesus' blessing of the poor was increasingly embodied through political socialism.

In a period from approximately 1894 to 1899, Herron stood at the vanguard of a small group of Protestant leaders who saw within models of political socialism the key that would bring economic and moral reform to the nation. While Iowa College was a tiny college, it became associated with what became known as the "kingdom movement," and drew visits from some of the leading proponents of social Christianity in North America and Europe, including settlement house pioneer Graham Taylor and British reformer William Stead. Herron also drew large crowds when he gave addresses at some of the largest universities in the country. Although Herron went beyond most mainstream social Christians in his embrace of socialism, he tended to see Christian conversion in highly moralistic terms. Like more conservative social gospelers, personal sacrifice and regeneration were needed if the nation was to be redeemed for placing too much emphasis on the gospel of wealth rather than the gospel of Christ. At the center of this change, as in the novel *In His Steps*, was the need for individual repentance and a willingness to suffer for others as Christ suffered for us. Ideally, a Christian's hope was realized in a situation whereby "individuals would sacrifice their selfish acquisitive instincts so that institutions could be changed from their protective, paternal, individualistic purposes to redemptive, fraternal, collectivist ones."[8]

Despite the initial appeal of Herron, his message often ran afoul of the majority of social Christians who were rooted institutionally within the denominational structures of American Protestantism. By 1900 the major public phase of Herron's career was over. After an affair with the daughter of the benefactor of his Iowa College faculty chair was exposed, Herron's popularity waned. Initially, he cast his lot with the American Socialist Party, but by the time of his death in 1925, he was living in exile in Europe, where he had served as a consultant to the American delegation at the Versailles Peace Conference after World War I. Herron's career, however, spotlighted an issue that future Christian leaders in the tradition of the social gospel would have to wrestle: to what extent could Christian theology be identified with *specific* social-political models of reform? Even as Herron's star was rising, there were many signs that America was being ripped apart by a class struggle between rich and poor. Although some social Christians such as Josiah Strong and Charles Sheldon viewed social-ism as a potential menace to national order, others were calling for a reas-sessment of socialism in ways that embraced aspects of Herron's teachings but that could also be reconciled with the institutional role of American Christianity. In a growing number of popular lecture programs such as Chautauqua, leading religious and political figures began to debate the merits of applying the teachings of Jesus to the issues of modern society. While many individuals would rise to prominence in the early twentieth century as proponents of what became commonly known in the 1910s as "the social gospel," none was more influential than Emma Rauschenbusch Clough's younger brother, Walter.

THE SOCIAL GOSPEL COMES OF AGE
The Impact of Walter Rauschenbusch

Of all the figures associated with the social gospel, none has drawn the interest of scholars as much as Walter Rauschenbusch (1861–1918). A con-temporary of George Herron, Rauschenbusch shared Herron's interest in finding ways to radicalize the teachings of Jesus in ways that attacked the power structures of big-money capitalism. Also, Rauschenbusch was strongly rooted in a unique background that included the influences of German pietism, classical theology (including a fondness for certain fig-ures of Christian mysticism), and an eclectic assortment of late nineteenth-century political theorists (including Mazzini). Unlike Herron, however, Rauschenbusch shared the hope of more conservative and moderate social gospelers such as Josiah Strong and Washington Gladden that the nation's Protestant churches could lead the cause of Christianizing America.

Rauschenbusch spent his formative years as pastor of a German-immigrant congregation in the Hell's Kitchen section of New York City in the 1880s and 1890s. The exposure to the social misery of his church galvanized Rauschenbusch's desire to devote his ministry to addressing questions of social justice, even as his health broke under the strain of his ministry (including losing most of his hearing by the time he was thirty). In 1897 he was appointed to the faculty of Rochester Theological Seminary where Rauschenbusch's father had served on the seminary's German department. In 1907 Rauschenbusch's first major book *Christianity and the Social Crisis* not only brought him fame but helped give the social gospel an organizational center. In December 1908 the Federal Council of Churches was formed in Philadelphia, consisting of thirty-three Protestant denominations. The Federal Council was unique in its mission that was not so much predicated on doctrinal unity as it was defined in terms of social action. For much of the twentieth century, the Federal Council and its successor, the National Council of Churches, would develop a strong association with propagating the legacy of the social gospel.

While he never associated himself with the ministry of George Herron, Rauschenbusch picked up and fleshed out Herron's central passion for the theological ideal of the kingdom of God. Trained in many of the currents of late nineteenth-century German liberalism (in particular, the pioneering work of the German historian Albrecht Ritschl), Rauschenbusch believed that understanding the nature of Christianity in the contemporary context was to seize hold of how the first-century Christian communities understood this "conquering ideal" of the kingdom within Christian theology. Central to Rauschenbusch, and to many proponents of the social gospel tradition who followed him, was a belief that the church surrendered early in its history the radical ethics of Jesus' social teachings for what became either a pessimistic otherworldly theology (embodied by apocalyptic movements) or the institutional preserving tendencies of the medieval Catholic tradition. In juxtaposition to Herron's tendency to equate the kingdom directly with political socialism, Rauschenbusch saw within socialism an approximation of the gospel's theological conception of a new heaven and a new earth.

Later critics of the social gospel would castigate it for its optimism concerning human progress. Yet Rauschenbusch shared with Herron and more conservative social gospelers a belief in redemptive suffering. A just society required sacrifice, and in a fashion consistent with Christ's suffering, the social gospel placed a high premium on a moral-influence understanding of the atonement. Mainly, Christ's death had redemptive consequences on how His disciples would be empowered to work for a just world. The fact that Rauschenbusch used the term "social crisis" in the title of his first major book also suggests that as the movement matured, disciples would experience resistance to their efforts at reform. As he noted in the book's conclusion, "in asking for faith in the possibility of a new social order, we ask for no Utopian delusion. We know well that there is no perfection for man in this life: there is only growth toward perfection. . . .

At best there is always but an approximation to a perfect social order. The kingdom of God is always but coming."[9]

In the aftermath of *Christianity and the Social Crisis*, Rauschenbusch's writings continued to draw wide attention in America and internationally for the ways he applied Christian teachings to the conditions of modern society. For many Protestant ministers who came of age in that era, Rauschenbusch was a principal influence. In 1912, with the publication of his second major book *Christianizing the Social Order*, Rauschenbusch offered his most detailed analysis exploring the relationship between Christianity and contemporary social-political realities. This book presents a paradoxical picture of Rauschenbusch and the social gospel as a whole. Rauschenbusch expressed a confidence shared by some of his older colleagues that the nation was on its way to being "Christianized." Denominations with their official pronouncements, families and public schools with their structures and values, and even aspects of the political realm were showing the influences of Christian teaching. Yet the economic realm represented the chief "unredeemed" component of the social order. For Rauschenbusch, the prophetic mandate of the church was to make people aware of the sinful nature of the nation's economic system while engaging in systemic reform endeavors to transform it. "The bravest act of faith and hope that a Christian can make is to believe and hope that such a salvation is possible and that the law of Jesus Christ will yet prevail in business."[10]

Yet, by 1917 Rauschenbusch found himself in some ways an outsider within a movement he helped spawn. With the start of World War I in August 1914, Rauschenbusch became suspect both for his defense of American neutrality and for his own German-American background. Although most social gospelers initially opposed the war, the vast majority became enamored by the pleas of President Woodrow Wilson to "make the world safe for democracy," vigorously supporting the war effort upon American entry in April 1917. In part Walter Rauschenbusch rose to fame not just because of his insightful analysis, but because he rode a popular Progressive Era wave of enthusiasm that America was on the verge of eliminating the problems of industrial capitalism. Sadly, much of this same wave of optimism crushed him. His final book, *A Theology for the Social Gospel*, contained no language about Christianizing America, but reflected a chastened outlook that would have a prescient impact on subsequent theological developments in the United States. When Rauschenbusch died in July 1918, his was a notable voice of dissent from the belief held by many social gospelers that Allied victory in the war would create the conditions for a postwar golden age.

At times, Rauschenbusch's theology reflected a deep vein of piety and an irenic spirit toward his theological adversaries. Although he came to identify himself as a socialist, he never joined the American Socialist Party. For Rauschenbusch, socialism was embodied in concrete political models of democratic socialism, but it was also a means of affirming a form of Christian perfectionism that supported a vision of a Christianized America. While supportive of women's suffrage, he clung to a conservative view of women's public roles and, like later generations of conservative Protestants, worried about how changes in societal norms would impact the moral compass of the nation (these tensions were evident in his own family as Rauschenbusch repeatedly argued with his oldest daughter, Winifred, over her choice of a career as well as her rejection of her father's Victorian cultural suppositions of a woman's place). Also, while Rauschenbusch was deeply concerned about issues related to Christian anti-Semitism, he maintained deep-seated suspicions toward American Catholics, employing a logic not far removed from Josiah Strong's. Finally, Rauschenbusch embodied a tension evident within the thought of most white social gospelers. Mainly, he was unable to fully grasp perhaps the most divisive social issue in American history: racism.

ALTERNATIVE VOICES
The Social Gospel Vision of Reverdy Ransom

In the years following his death, Rauschenbusch would serve as a model for many Protestants of a more radical social gospel that pushed beyond its inherited faith in the values and suppositions of middle-class America. By the same token, Rauschenbusch's life shows a clear connection to a larger culture of evangelical Protestantism—even as those connections were drawing to a close by the time of his death. One of Rauschenbusch's earliest publications was an 1888 field report praising the revivalist atmosphere of one of Dwight Moody's summer conferences in Northfield, Massachusetts. In the 1890s Rauschenbusch collaborated with Moody's revivalist partner, Ira Sankey, in publishing a German-language hymnal. Even as his theology attacked the problems of parasitic wealth associated with big-money capitalists, he courted the friendship (and the money) of several prominent business tycoons, including John D. Rockefeller.

In other segments of American Protestantism, however, these sorts of alliances with the rich and powerful were either unspeakable or impossible.

By the end of World War I, small cadres of Protestant ministers influenced by the social gospel left the ministry. Believing that institutional Christianity was unable and unwilling to engage in a thorough revision of social-economic power, these former ministers turned to the creation of political action organizations. Some of these leaders were influential in the founding of the American Civil Liberties Union in 1919. Others threw their efforts headlong to work for the advancement of Rauschenbusch's vision of democratic socialism, the most prominent being a former Presbyterian minister, Norman Thomas, who would become the American Socialist Party's standard-bearer for the next four decades.

For the approximately ten million African Americans who either worshipped within the older European church traditions, or more commonly within historically black churches of their own creation, the social-political ends of the social gospel were quite different. The career of Reverdy Ransom is illustrative in this regard. Born in Ohio in 1861 (the same year as Rauschenbusch), Ransom graduated from Wilberforce College and entered the ministry of the African Methodist Episcopal (AME) Church. From 1890 until 1912, Ransom served parishes in Cleveland, Chicago, Boston, and New York and gained fame through his preaching, writing, and social activism. In 1900 he established an Institutional Church in Chicago, one of several with which he would become involved, and was one of the founders of the all-black Niagara Movement, spearheaded by W.E.B. Du Bois. Along with Du Bois, in 1909 Ransom was a co-founder of the National Association for the Advancement of Colored People. In 1912 he became the editor of the *AME Church Review* and in 1922 until his death in 1952 he served as an AME bishop.

Ransom's career reflects upon the realities of racial segregation that have marked America's story. Like other social gospelers, Ransom supported democratic socialism, and in the early twentieth century he shared with white social gospelers a level of jingoism about the uniqueness of the American religious and political experience. Yet Ransom's central focus was to address the sufferings of African Americans, chiding white America for its inability to address issues of race. A spellbinding orator and prolific writer, Ransom in his later work emphasized that the future of humanity, including its religion, would come from the oppressed voices of Africa, noting bluntly, "the African and his descendants are the last spiritual reserves of humanity."[11]

Ransom represents another "lost voice" of history. However, his legacy would be embodied later in the twentieth century by a number of African

American Christians who would expose many Americans to the rich historical and theological themes of black Christianity. For all the ways that white Americans remained blind to the work of African Americans such as Ransom, most Protestants initially paid little attention to the iterations of social Christianity coming from the Catholic Church, in particular the work of one Midwestern Catholic priest.

CATHOLIC SOCIAL CHRISTIANITY

While late nineteenth-century American Catholicism was caught in struggles over papal authority, various aspects of Catholic social teaching found a wider audience in the latter half of that century. In 1886 Henry George, an economist and author of one of the most influential texts of Progressive Era economic theory *Progress and Poverty*, ran for mayor of New York. One of his chief supporters was Father Edward McGlynn, a Catholic priest who stressed the relationship between Jesus' words in the Lord's Prayer to contemporary social conditions. Later in his career, Rauschenbusch would cite both George *and* McGlynn as pivotal figures in his own social awakening.

Catholicism in the late nineteenth and early twentieth centuries had its own parallels and complements to the Protestant social gospel (and as mentioned in the previous chapter, James Cardinal Gibbons was an example of a major Catholic voice that defended the rights of labor). While leaders such as McGlynn could sound almost Protestant in their stirrings about the kingdom of God, Catholic social teaching was centered in the authority of the Catholic Church. Papal pronouncements against Americanism, reflected this model of the church's authority (represented through the papal office). What is often forgotten, however, is how these papal statements were accompanied by support for organized labor in the United States. Papal pronouncements such as Leo XIII's 1891 encyclical *Rerum Novarum,* although critical of various understandings of Americanism (including American democracy), acknowledged the ways that church teachings needed to address the need for social-economic equality in modern life, whereby Catholics needed to promote the physical and spiritual wellbeing of the individual.

By the early twentieth century, Catholic and Protestant social teachings often advocated for similar ends, such as federal and state legislation to protect worker rights and the right to form labor unions. The means by which the two traditions arrived at these conclusions, however, were far different. Protestant theologies of the social gospel tended to derive from a wide range of intellectual sources, with many social gospelers grounded in the suppositions of German, English, and American secular and religious liberal philosophies that emerged in the latter half of the nineteenth century. Although social gospelers spoke of the important role of the church, their understanding of authority was rooted in an individualism that increasingly stressed how individuals could model "the personality of Jesus" in their actions (that is, in the sense of how one's ethical and moral behavior might manifest Christlike love for a suffering world).

Catholic social teaching did embrace aspects of Protestant social analysis. For example, many Catholics were well versed on different dimensions of modern economic theorists, such as taught by the economist and Episcopal layman Richard Ely. Yet they came at social reform from a distinctively post-Reformation theological outlook. The Council of Trent in the mid-sixteenth century largely established parameters for Catholic doctrine that would be in place until the Second Vatican Council of the early 1960s, and in this respect, Catholic doctrine was largely seen through the theological lens of Thomas Aquinas. Just as mid-nineteenth-century American Catholics, such as Orestes Brownson, were able to integrate Thomist theology into distinctive patterns of American democracy, so was a new generation of Catholic leaders in the early twentieth century able to apply that tradition to contemporary social problems. One of the most enduring figures to come out of this particular tradition of social Christianity was Father John Ryan (1869–1945).

Born and raised in an Irish Catholic immigrant community in rural Minnesota, Ryan's education was marked early by a strong fidelity toward traditional Catholic teaching. Yet, as a seminarian, Ryan studied both Henry George and Richard Ely, and was especially captivated by Ely's insistence that Jesus' teachings on wealth and property could speak with conviction to the realities of modern economic life. However, Ryan did not share the enthusiasm for socialism of Protestant social gospelers, and saw government intervention in the private sector more as a method of last resort as opposed to being a sign for the kingdom of God. In 1906 he published one of the lost classics of the social gospel era, *A Living Wage*, a work that would serve as a model for many Catholic social reformers well into the twentieth century. Basing much of his argument on the philosophies of Aquinas and Leo's *Rerum Novarum,* Ryan argued that workers receiving a just wage was a natural human right and the means by which humans could achieve their God-given potential within society (including traditional Catholic responsibilities of marriage and raising a family).

If these rights could not be achieved through private measures, then the state had a moral obligation to create the conditions that would promote human freedom. *A Living Wage* was one of the first works to advocate for a minimum wage, and in successive works, Ryan pressed the argument that government had to play a role in the process of social amelioration. For years, Ryan taught at the Catholic University in Washington, D.C., where his work attracted attention and some scorn from many in the Catholic Church. While his critics castigated him for moving the Catholic Church into the realm of secular politics, Ryan countered that he was simply being faithful to the papal teachings of *Rerum Novarum*. His work was firmly rooted in a model of Catholic social teaching, and at points he blamed the problems of industrial society partly as an outgrowth of Protestant individualism caused by the Reformation. The remedy for this individualism ultimately was not from the secular world, but came from Catholic teaching. "In a word, all free human actions, whether without or within the field of industry, come under the control of the moral law; and the teaching and application of the moral law is the business of the Church," he noted in 1927.[12]

Ultimately, Ryan's influence would extend beyond the Catholic Church, and in the 1930s he became a principal advisor to President Franklin Roosevelt. The paradox of Ryan's social gospel, holding in tension Catholic Church tradition and social praxis, would continue to resonate with Catholic reformers throughout the twentieth century and influence many religious and secular social theorists, both inside and outside the Catholic tradition.

THE SOCIAL GOSPEL
Something Old and Something New

In January 1920 the Eighteenth Amendment to the U.S. Constitution, banning the sale of alcoholic beverages, went into law. The coming of Prohibition appeared on the surface to be a singular triumph for American Protestants. For over a hundred years, moral crusades against the sale and use of alcohol served as a central cause by which American Protestantism measured its moral influence. Yet the Prohibition amendment marked a symbolic, if not literal, end to any semblance of Protestant theological and cultural unity. For decades Protestants of different theological backgrounds were able to maintain a degree of missional connection, largely centered upon the belief that they were working toward the creation of a unified Christian culture in America. By the time that the Prohibition amendment was repealed in 1933, any sense of missional cohesion was shattered, as the churches of what once constituted the nineteenth-century "evangelical empire" moved in a variety of different directions—theologically and missionally.

For all the ways that the social gospel would later be lauded or stigmatized as something radically new in American Protestantism, it was partly rooted in a desire to preserve an earlier culture of Protestant privilege. By 1916 the largest Protestant denominations in the North, and to a lesser extent in the South, were increasingly controlled by leaders who were in sympathy with aspects of the social gospel agenda, expressed in the ministries of popular preachers, academicians, and, most certainly, spokespersons such as Walter Rauschenbusch. Yet even at this moment of institutional triumph there were signs that the nation's churches were coming apart. In 1914 Rauschenbusch noted that historical moments for social change rarely last long and the coming of World War I marked a point of crisis for those within the social gospel coalition. By the time of American entry into the war, followers of the social gospel, along with more conservative Protestant groups, embraced the war as a holy crusade. At times, conservative and liberal Christians accentuated shared themes of patriotism and American exceptionalism. However, for many within the social gospel coalition, the war represented a necessary evil in which an Allied victory would create the circumstances for a postwar world in which the nation's churches would be at the forefront of ushering in new iterations of the kingdom of God. As part IV reveals, the collapse of this myopic vision had a distinctive impact upon those who took up the mantle of the social gospel.

To a degree, social gospelers were able to garner the support of influential figures from politics and business, yet largely failed to make a lasting impression on the one group for whom they advocated the most: working-class Americans. For all of its subsequent influence in shaping the theological direction of American Christianity, the social gospel had difficulty finding popular support, in ways characteristic of conservative movements within American Protestantism at that same time. Religious leaders such as Gladden and Rauschenbusch were aware of this gap and attempted in various ways to bridge it. Charles Stelzle, a prominent early twentieth-century Presbyterian minister, employed popular entertainment and music in his mission church in New York, and even Rauschenbusch used similar tactics in his efforts to build a so-called "people's church" in Rochester, New York. Yet the success of the social gospel was largely institutional, even though individuals such as Gladden and the Methodist social gospeler and ecumenical leader Frank Mason North were responsible for writing popular hymns that found their way into the mainstream culture of American Protestantism.[13]

One way to understand the rise of the social gospel is to see its connection to the rise of the Progressive Era in the United States. Cresting during the years preceding American entry into World War I, a variety of politicians, journalists, academicians, and church leaders served as the vanguard of legislative reform that in various ways advocated for a number of social reform measures. It is even appropriate to suggest, as some historians have, that the social gospel was the religious wing of American Progressivism, as both movements had many shared goals of political reform and a desire to maintain certain cultural values associated with a late nineteenth-century Protestant worldview.

One interesting example of this connection occurred in 1911 and 1912 when many progressives and social gospelers supported the Men and Religion Forward movement. This campaign had a twofold purpose; first, it encouraged men to become more involved in the life of the nation's churches (reflecting the fear of both conservatives *and* liberals that churches were becoming too feminized), and second, it provided a means by which churches could raise funds for the purposes of social evangelism. While the movement represented another example of how liberals and conservatives could still come together to support common causes in the early twentieth century, it displayed a public posture that increasingly became central to how the liberal, or mainline, Protestant churches would define themselves by the middle and latter parts of the twentieth century. For much of the twentieth century, many Protestant leaders assumed that their voices spoke to a wide-ranging constituency, both inside and outside the churches, and that the larger public wanted to hear what Protestants had to say about the major social, cultural, and intellectual issues of the day. The social gospel influenced this twentieth-century model of what has been called "the public church" that has remained a fixation for many Christian leaders, even as the historical realities to support this model have faded.

However, the focus on the cultural conservatism of the social gospel overshadows the fact that it was an innovative theological tradition. Part of what united all of the social gospelers was certainly a belief that collective action on the part of Christians could change history. Yet it was also a profoundly theological belief that *individuals* could change their ethical behavior because they were fundamentally good, not sinful. The rise of Progressivism and the social gospel coincided with the popularity in America of the social philosophy of Herbert Spencer. His ideals, associated chiefly with what became known as "Social Darwinism," stressed the role of one's social environment in shaping human adaptability (or what has been referred to as "survival of the fittest"). Social gospelers fought against these theories and, like many earlier traditions of Christian revivalism, insisted that Christian faith offered people the ability to change both their inward and outward behavior.

Clearly, social gospel leaders had many blind spots, especially with regard to questions of racism, sexism, and (in the Protestant case) a tendency to see their churches as the embodiment of the best qualities of American democracy (in contrast to their Catholic neighbors). By the early 1920s, the major theological voices that had given expression to the social gospel in the early twentieth century, including Rauschenbusch, were dead. The heirs of the tradition were left trying to plot a course within a post–World War I cultural climate that appeared to be moving further away from the progressive dreams of the social gospelers.

By the same token, the theological foundations of the social gospel served as cornerstones for emerging iterations of American theology that would carry the movement's legacy well beyond the cultural context of the late nineteenth and early twentieth centuries. The staying power of the social gospel is perhaps best indicated by Martin Luther King Jr., who later affirmed his debt to Walter Rauschenbusch by noting that "It has been my conviction ever since reading Rauschenbusch that any religion which professes to be concerned about the souls of men and is not concerned about the social and economic conditions that scar the soul, is a spiritually moribund religion only waiting for the day to be buried."[14]

Yet for all the influence of the social gospel upon the shaping of American theology, even Rauschenbusch could see that it was threatened by what a popular hymn of the day called "that old-time religion."

≪ 11 ≫

Dispensationalism, Pentecostalism, and the Origins of Fundamentalism

In the years prior to American entry into World War I, American Protestantism had witnessed seismic changes. Numerous spokespersons of theological liberalism and social Christianity strove to articulate a vision of Christianity that could confront the challenges of a rapidly changing era, and on the surface these movements appeared to be succeeding. While northern denominations such as the Methodists, Presbyterians, and Baptists were no longer growing at a pace comparable to that of the first half of the nineteenth century, these churches enjoyed a prominent place at the center of emerging institutional matrices that historians later called "the Protestant establishment." The ecumenical currents budding at the beginning of the twentieth century related in large measure to the effort of these churches to unite under the banner of what some called "the Christian Century," giving many church leaders a new purpose to strive for Protestant union. At its founding in 1908, the Federal Council of Churches affirmed not only its desire that all American Protestant denominations be part of its fellowship, but that the Council was "profoundly impressed with the present opportunity for coordinating the churches in the interest of wider and larger service for America and the Kingdom of God."[1]

Yet this perceived Protestant consensus was disrupted by emerging conservative movements that continue to play a major role in the development of Christianity in America. Although these movements emerged from disparate theological sources, ultimately they would converge around a shared desire to stave off the influence of liberal-modernist forms of Christianity. Many of these conservatives were later responsible for creating coalitions of clergy, laity, academicians, and popular revivalists who would frequently be categorized under the label "fundamentalism."

The term fundamentalism has often been used as a catchphrase to define a wide range of disparate (and often unrelated) theological movements that emerged by the early twentieth century (the term itself did not come into wide use until the early 1920s). Yet many churches that were erroneously labeled by some as fundamentalist often reflected a wider conservative reaction against liberal-modernist forms of Christianity. This historical context not only gave birth to churches that are historically connected to fundamentalism, but also to pentecostalism. While possessing distinctive roots and theological emphases, many varieties of these theologically conservative Christians shared a common link to what has become perhaps the most resilient popular theological movement in American history: dispensationalism.

UNDERSTANDING FUNDAMENTALISM

Perhaps no term conjures up more misunderstanding and, in certain quarters of American society, contempt than the use of the term fundamentalist. For many, the term caricatures a pejorative image of a Bible-thumping uneducated minister who preaches to a congregation of equally uneducated backwoods congregants (or images of television preachers predicting the end of the world while simultaneously asking for donations). Since the late twentieth century, the term has been applied to many religious groups—including Christians, Muslims, Jews, and Hindus—who embody an antimodernist theology and call upon their followers to return to what they see as the basic tenets of their faith traditions.

However, the origins of the term fundamentalist in America emerged from prominent northern clergymen who came out of Protestant denominations that were historically connected to theological Calvinism, in particular Presbyterian and Baptist churches. While liberal theology stressed the need to adapt Scripture and theology to the conditions of modern life, preachers who later identified with the fundamentalist movement, such as William Bell Riley and I. M. Haldeman, attempted to hold modern society accountable to what they saw as the timeless teachings of Scripture. Most especially, however, church leaders and movements that later became associated with the rise of Christian fundamentalism in the twentieth century preached a decided pessimism that emphasized the necessity of personal conversion and a view that modernist Christianity was misguided in its efforts to improve worldly conditions. Chapter 12 of this book tells the story of the struggle for control among the major Protestant denominations that broke out in the 1920s and has been labeled the "fundamentalist-modernist controversy." Yet to understand fully that struggle, one must first examine how conditions for that division were well on their way to formation prior to American entry into World War I.

Historians have noted that what became known as fundamentalism by the 1920s was represented by individuals, churches, and movements that stressed five basic principles:

1. Biblical inerrancy, that is the idea that the Bible was a book of divine origin whose human authors gave an accurate historical account;
2. The virgin birth of Christ;
3. Substitutionary atonement, that is the belief that Christ's death "paid a price" for repentant sinners, offering them salvation;
4. Christ's physical resurrection from the dead; and
5. The factual reality of biblical miracles.

All of these "fundamentals" did carry the weight of Christian tradition on their side, but as we have seen, the weight of new scientific discoveries in the nineteenth century and emerging models of biblical higher criticism had a major impact upon the worldview of late nineteenth-century Protestantism. Although Charles Darwin's teachings on evolution shook the faith of many evangelicals (especially by challenging long-accepted wisdom that the earth was only thousands, not millions, of years old), the dual onslaughts of German liberalism and biblical higher criticism were at the frontline of contention. Debates over liberal theology led to heresy trials in several Protestant churches. In the early 1890s, Charles Briggs, a professor of biblical theology at Union Seminary in New York, was put on trial by the Presbyterian Church for his denial of the church's doctrinal authority. Briggs was one of several academics accused of heresy by various Protestant denominations, for espousing not only liberalism but also German higher criticism.

Biblical higher criticism would take on many forms, but central to the work of many biblical scholars like Briggs was the conviction that Scripture represented the work of numerous authors who wrote from the perspectives of different historical periods in the ancient world. Instead of a unified worldview, Scripture represented a multiplicity of historical and theological perspectives into what life was like in ancient Israel (e.g., one of the common themes challenged by proponents of higher criticism was the long-accepted wisdom that Moses was the sole author of the first five books of the Old Testament, asserting that many views espoused in the Scripture were formed through centuries of oral and written traditions).

Part of the counterarguments used by traditionalists was that biblical criticism, as well as most liberal-modernism, was anchored in erroneous intellectual suppositions. The origins of fundamentalism go deep into the intellectual roots of nineteenth-century American Protestantism. For much of the century, the majority of evangelical traditions were rooted in some fashion in the theology of Scottish Common Sense Realism. As was discussed in chapter 9, this theological movement had a tremendous hold on most evangelicals for the first two-thirds of the nineteenth century. Common Sense Realism was predicated on the harmony between religious teachings and science, especially emphasizing the compatibility between divine revelation and reason. While most adherents to this tradition accepted scientific discovery, the natural world took a back seat to the world of Christian revelation. Their message was direct: any type of scientific knowledge that contradicted Scripture was false.

In many ways, the institution most associated with preserving this tradition of fundamentalist Christianity was Princeton Theological Seminary. Since its founding in 1812, Princeton had become a symbol for a long-standing intellectual tradition of Old School Calvinist orthodoxy. For much of the nineteenth century, Princeton was the premier American seminary within the Reformed tradition, whose students went on to pastor prestigious churches throughout the country. Many of the staunchest critics of theological liberalism came from Princeton Seminary, and Princeton would indirectly play a significant role in the theological battles between liberals and conservatives in the 1920s.

At the same time, Princeton theology was not theology for the masses. Its mission was to educate and train a learned clergy for a learned ministry, and many of its leaders looked with disdain not only upon the rise of theological liberalism, but also at some of the theological developments going on among more traditional evangelical Protestants. In particular, for those who allied themselves with the theological orthodoxy of Princeton and its fidelity to the historical faith articulated by Calvin and his successors, the post–Civil War rise of a theology called dispensationalism was especially distasteful. Dispensationalism is perhaps the single most important type of popular theology to emerge in American religious history. While dispensationalism did arise primarily within segments of Protestant Calvinism, its popularity spread broadly throughout American

Protestantism, and by the early twentieth century many of its core tenets were embedded in non-Calvinist Arminian movements, perhaps most notably within pentecostalism.

Pentecostalism emerged out of a distinctive theological heritage and needs to be seen separately from what would become known by the 1920s as fundamentalism (in fact, many persons associated with the fundamentalist movement looked disparagingly upon pentecostalism). Yet the wider popularity of dispensationalism helped form a glue that often linked together distinctive streams of evangelical thought. Even as social gospel liberals such as Walter Rauschenbusch spoke of social salvation on earth, a range of disparate evangelicals became more convinced that humankind was living amid the last days on earth.

THE PREMILLENNIAL URGE

Prior to the Civil War, American evangelical theology was primarily postmillennial. Since the time of the Puritans, Protestant ministers and theologians had taught that Christ's second coming would occur *after* the millennial age foretold in the Book of Revelation. This belief held that the churches through aggressive evangelism and mission would be responsible for a rise in social righteousness that would set the context for Christ's return (and as discussed in the previous chapter, the social gospel can be seen as a liberal form of postmillennialism). As Protestant churches institutionalized, many segments within these churches abandoned these earlier millennial themes, either viewing the concept of a millennial future as metaphorical or as a misguided concept, taking a position that many later theologians referred to as amillennialism.

This tradition of amillennialism was always strong in the Roman Catholic Church, which in many ways held onto Augustine's notion that the church represented an end in itself. While not denying the idea that history would have some type of final consummation in the future, the important issue was how a person lived out their faith within the communion of the church. The Catholic social gospel tradition lacked the same type of Protestant fidelity to the ideal of the kingdom of God, seeing social reform largely as a way to apply the moral precepts of Catholic doctrine to society at large. Within Protestantism, some conservatives held to a position of amillennialism (such as some of the professors at Princeton Seminary) and it also became prominent in many traditions of theological liberalism that were not especially interested in speculating at all on questions of eschatology or the end times.

Yet the late nineteenth century witnessed a rapid increase in a movement known as premillennialism. Premillennialism has always been a
powerful influence in church history, and the context of post–Civil War
America gave new expression to this perspective. Unlike postmillennialism, premillennialism believes in the idea that Christ would return *before*
the millennial era in the Book of Revelation, and that events leading up to
this return would be marked by social distress and a widespread rejection
of Christ's message of salvation—especially among the vast majority of
churches. Many Americans in the early nineteenth century believed they
were living amid the last days on earth, reflected most dramatically in the
Millerite movement, but also in a variety of Adventist groups that leaned
toward premillennialism. In a post–Civil War context marked by massive
population shifts to cities, non-Protestant immigration (accompanied by
worries over anarchist movements and political socialism), and economic
peril (marked by two major economic depressions in the 1870s and 1890s),
the ground was ripe for new forms of premillennialism to take root.

One dramatic example of the shift away from earlier postmillennialism was a small group initially called the Russellites that would later
become known by the name Jehovah's Witnesses. Influenced by the earlier
Millerite and Adventist movements, the Russellites would become identified with a distinctive type of sectarian Christianity whose members,
comparable with earlier Anabaptist movements, stressed ambivalence, if
not outright hostility, toward the wider culture—including in the twentieth century a refusal to participate in the military. Associated with the
preaching of an Adventist minister, Charles Taze Russell, the Russellites
believed that Christ had returned secretly in 1874 and that the world was
literally controlled by the devil and in the throes of its last days. Like earlier millennial movements, the Russellites placed great fidelity upon the
Book of Revelation (and initially took the reference in Revelation 7 to the
144,000 "sealed saints" as a literal reference for those who would be saved).
However, they differed from other premillennialists in their insistence
that Christ had already returned and that 1914 would mark the end of the
millennial age and inaugurate the galvanic battle of Armageddon (and
the fact that World War I began that same year seemed to corroborate for
many Russellites that their teachings of the end times were on target).

This distinctive theology not only made Russellites hostile to the doctrines taught by other churches (both liberal *and* conservative); it crafted
a movement that took a negative view of what were seen as the unbiblical
trappings practiced by the majority of Christians (for example, Russellites

refused to celebrate birthdays, Christmas, or even the validity of Easter). Over the course of the next several decades, as the movement defined its core beliefs and practices, marked by a rejection of many aspects of modern culture (for example, blood transfusions), the movement would later be at the forefront of numerous lawsuits over the extent to which the group's religious practices could be regulated by the state (a theme shared with another religious movement with completely different theological roots, the Christian Scientists).

Groups such as the Jehovah's Witnesses represented an extreme expression of Adventist-millennial thought in the late nineteenth century. Most other Adventist groups lived in an interesting paradox within the wider society. On one hand, their theologies were apocalyptic in that they looked with expectancy not just for the return of Christ, but believed that the second coming meant judgment upon the earth. At the same time, these groups lived in creative tension with the culture in which they existed. In the final decades of the nineteenth century, many Adventist communities formed rest spas that promoted healthy nutrition (for example, they promoted vegetarian diets), and the Kellogg cereal empire emerged out of a Seventh-day Adventist sanitarium in Battle Creek, Michigan. One of the most unusual of these communities, also located in Michigan, was the House of David, a group that practiced strict celibacy and where men, keeping with codes contained in the Book of Leviticus, refused to shave their beards. Yet in the early decades of the twentieth century, The House of David fielded an amateur baseball team whose players regularly carried on exhibitions with Major League all stars.

Compared to other Protestant churches, these varied Adventist groups were not numerically large. However, they reflected upon the fact that apocalyptic theology that had been present in American theology in one form or another since the seventeenth century was very much a part of the nation's religious landscape. However, the primary groups that carried forth the most popular currents of premillennialism emerged from churches that saw themselves as being faithful to a legacy of evangelical Protestantism. The central movement that would unite numerous Protestants across theological and denominational boundaries was dispensationalism.

DISPENSATIONALISM AS AN AMERICAN FOLK THEOLOGY

Of all the forms of premillennialism that emerged at the end of the nineteenth century, the most influential was dispensationalism. This tradition is most often associated with the Irish clergyman John Nelson Darby (1800–1882). Originally a priest in the Church of Ireland (connected to the Anglican communion), Darby left that church and joined a small dissenting movement called the Plymouth Brethren. Darby's theological orientation and that of the Brethren emphasized an apocalyptic reading of history, stressing to believers not only the importance of personal conversion, but, in the tradition of William Miller, the importance of "Bible prophecy" as a means of understanding God's divine plan for humanity. Like Miller, Darby's view toward the end times was strongly apocalyptic. However, unlike Miller and most future apocalyptic Christians, Darby avoided precise dating of Christ's return. His theology of Bible prophecy in large measure remains in place for many Christians today, serving as the template for his theology called dispensationalism.

The basic premise behind dispensationalist theology is that church history is divided into stages, or dispensations, that reveal an unveiling of God's purposes for human history. While liberal interpretations of church history emphasized the way that humans could shape the contours of history, dispensationalists carried an unbroken sense of the Bible's continuous and unchanging authority over history. Quite simply, if the true believer wanted to understand the past, present, and future of humankind, one must not look to church history as a guide (as social gospelers such as Walter Rauschenbusch did). Rather, one needed to read and interpret correctly the teachings of the Scriptures.

By far the most well known of Darby's theological innovations was his teaching about "the Rapture," whereby God's faithful would suddenly be taken off the earth to dwell with God and Christ. For William Miller, the second coming was seen as a straightforward affair, one in which Christ's return would mark the salvation of all true believers and the end of the world. For Darby, however, understanding of the second coming was predicated on an even more intricate reading of the Bible. According to his view, humankind was currently living through a period, or dispensation, in church history known as the "church age," a period that would be characterized by intermittent times of prosperity as well as religious and civil discord. This period would end suddenly with an event that remains to this day a centerpiece for dispensationalist theology: the Rapture. The Rapture represented a moment when all true believers would disappear from earth in order to dwell in heaven with Christ. Darby took 1 Thessalonians 4:16 as his primary text for the Rapture:

> For the Lord himself will descend from heaven with a cry of command, with the archangel's call, and with the sound of the trumpet of God. And the dead in Christ will rise first, then those who are alive who are left, shall be caught up together with them in the clouds to meet the Lord in the air.

This idea of being "caught up" by God in the clouds was central to the idea of the Rapture. Darby believed that converted Christians would be taken up by God at an unknown future time to receive the joys of heaven. The Rapture, however, was not seen by dispensationalists as the actual second coming of Christ. Rather, the removal of true Christians from earth signaled the beginning of a new dispensation called the "tribulation," a period of time that would witness the rise of the antichrist upon the earth. Using the biblical books of Daniel and Revelation as guides, Darby believed that the end of this period of conflagration (which many dispensationalists saw as a seven-year window) would be followed by the second coming of Christ and the beginning of the millennial age of peace on earth. Finally, at the end of time, Satan would wage one final battle on earth and be defeated by Christ, marking the final reign of God's heavenly kingdom on earth.

Darby's teachings began to gain a following in North America after the Civil War through a series of "Bible Prophecy" conferences held throughout Great Britain and the United States. The Keswick movement, a series of prophecy conferences that began in Great Britain and then spread to the United States, attracted a diverse cross section of evangelicals interested in the relationship between the Bible and current events. While American dispensationalists would add their own unique wrinkles to his theories, the basic structures of Darby's teachings, specifically the idea of the Rapture, remain a centerpiece in American dispensationalist theology to this day.

Dispensationalism has been dismissed over the years as heretical and fanatical. However, these labels fail to capture the reasons for why the movement gained such a powerful hold on many Americans, a hold that has been ongoing since the movement arose at the end of the nineteenth century. First, dispensationalism tapped into a deep-seated American Protestant tradition that emphasized the fact that anyone in America could read and interpret the Bible. Not accidentally, the majority of dispensationalist leaders who emerged in American Protestantism by the early twentieth century tended to come out of the northern Presbyterian and Baptist churches. Both these traditions were rooted in strong Calvinist traditions that emphasized the centrality of Scripture and the worldview of Scottish Common Sense philosophy that fit well into the logic of dispensationalism. Dispensationalism not only allowed Christians a means to understand God's purposes, but affirmed that anyone could discern these purposes directly by reading and studying the Bible.

Second, despite its rather grim view of history, the movement also affirms a discernible pastoral edge that offered an appealing alternative to what appeared to many to be the apostate and equivocal beliefs of religious modernism. Within the dispensationalist worldview, faith in Christ gave the believer comfort in this life and salvation in the life to come. In subtle and not-so-subtle ways, dispensational themes resonate in many of the gospel hymns that emerged between 1870 and 1900. While many Protestant hymns of that period such as "We've a Story to Tell to the Nations" spoke confidently of the postmillennial missionary advance of Christianity that would set the stage for Christ's great kingdom to come upon the earth, hymns with more premillennialist themes, such as Horatio Spafford's "It Is Well With My Soul," spoke of worldly sin and the comfort believers who were prepared to meet Christ either in death or upon Christ's return would receive. Yet unlike some Adventist groups or Jehovah's Witnesses that lived constantly with the sense that the world was evil and the ways of the world should be avoided, dispensationalists felt called to live, work, and evangelize in the world. Simply put, dispensationalist ideals reached well beyond their theological points of origins, and its messages of biblical interpretation, its supernaturalism, and its critique of modernist Christianity reached a wide audience that yearned for the old-time gospel message of salvation through Christ.

Contrary to common stereotypes, dispensationalism initially gained some of its biggest audiences not among the poor and uneducated, but within urban middle-class congregations. Just as some middle-class Americans turned to liberal preachers such as Henry Ward Beecher and Phillips Brooks for solace in the face of urban living, others turned to dispensationalism as a means to cope with the struggles of modern life. While not necessarily the defining theme of his ministry, Dwight Moody became a committed dispensationalist, and the major leaders who carried on his work after his death in 1899 were all dispensationalists. This urban side of dispensationalism's rise is evident in the careers of two of America's best-known ministers in the early twentieth century: I. M. Haldeman and William Bell Riley.

PREPARING FOR THE SECOND COMING
Haldeman, Riley, and the Logic of Dispensationalism

As pastor for over three decades of New York City's First Baptist Church, Haldeman reflected many classic features of dispensationalism. Like other well-known dispensationalist ministers who rose to prominence in the United States between 1890 and 1910, Haldeman was a northerner who pastored a large middle-class urban congregation. For Haldeman, dispensationalism was not just a matter of reading the Bible the right way; it was a matter of drawing the only possible conclusion from Scripture: "The Second Coming is mentioned from one end of the Bible to the other," he wrote in 1906. "It is bound with every sublime promise; with the promise of likeness to Christ, satisfaction of soul, victory over death, victory over sin and Satan, and deliverance of the earth from the bondage of corruption."[2] The evolution of dispensationalism, like other theological forms of what would later be termed fundamentalism, conformed to a certain logical design. Haldeman and other dispensationalists believed that the truths of Scripture would be confirmed by events of the modern world. Unlike the social gospelers, their view of current events gave them pause to believe that the world would get better. While dispensationalists avoided setting precise dates for the end of the world, they did not back away from viewing contemporary events through the lens of Scripture. For Haldeman, as for other dispensationalists, the conclusion was clear: things in the world were growing worse. "Let the man who dreams or has been taught to dream that we are marching to the purple and gold of millennial days through the gradual betterment of society, the advance of the church to higher spiritual grounds, look at this world, at the cold facts which honest examination reveals, and then say whether he can conscientiously and honestly believe that we have any evidence of a millennium to-day, or any prospect of it by Gospel preaching."[3]

William Riley's career followed a similar trajectory. Riley was the longtime senior pastor of the First Baptist Church in Minneapolis and would later become one of the central figures associated with the fundamentalist-modernist controversy in the 1920s. Although the cords of Riley's dispensationalism were perhaps not as strident as Haldeman's, he shared a common belief that a dispensationalist reading of Scripture was the only logical reading of God's word. In part, both men shared the suppositions of Common Sense Realism, yet they also reflected a belief, strong among groups later pegged as fundamentalists, that liberal theology, epitomized by trends that emerged in Germany, had substituted vague theoretical analysis for the inherent truths of Scripture. This was especially evident in the ways dispensationalists decried liberalism's use of history both in terms of emerging models of biblical criticism and the ways that liberal theologians undercut the reality of biblical miracles, Christ's sacrificial atonement, and a belief that faith in Jesus Christ was the *only* path to salvation.

Haldeman's critique of well-known liberals such as University of Chicago professor Shailer Mathews and social gospel leader Walter Rauschenbusch repeatedly made the point that liberalism preached and taught a gospel grounded not in Scripture, but upon the false claims of German rationalism. For Haldeman and Riley, the liberal stress that Christianity was a historically formed tradition was a movement away from the straightforward truth of the gospel. Increasingly, dispensationalists such as Haldeman and Riley were attacked by liberal clerics for what they saw as their otherworldly pessimism. While most men and women who leaned in the direction of theological liberalism or social Christianity tended to view some form of human perfectibility as a desired end, dispensationalism viewed such thinking as being contrary to the true ends of Christianity.

At the same time, many dispensationalists engaged in their own ministries of reform and supported a variety of mission outreaches to the poor even though they believed personal conversion was their ultimate goal. For later twentieth-century commentators of American Christianity, theological differences between "liberal" and "conservative" were often reduced to the difference between questions of "personal" versus "social" salvation. However, dispensationalism reflected that these theological differences by the early twentieth century struck much deeper. Although dispensationalists (and other conservative Protestants) believed strongly in the need to give aid and comfort to the poor, they felt that the social gospel's stress on social improvement was misguided. Personal salvation was not simply affirming the uniqueness of Christ; it was assenting to the truths contained in Scripture that the world was a dying vessel, with faith in Christ serving as one's only hope of survival. Haldeman captured this sentiment when he affirmed, "I have no time to spend in idle pleasure and careless indifference, not only because of my own soul and individual things at stake, but because of my fellow being who has no life of God and Christ in his soul; for his sake, surely, I ought to be up and doing, and crying in his ears the invitation of the Gospel of peace, warning him that he has no time to waste, that any moment the door of grace may be shut and the door of judgment swing open on its brazen hinges."[4]

Some late nineteenth-century conservatives such as Dwight Moody carried an irenic posture toward individual liberal church leaders and were more concerned with matters of cooperation and practical evangelicalism. After Moody's death in 1899, however, that spirit of cooperation rapidly disappeared and the rise of the social gospel in the early twentieth century only made that cooperation more difficult. Before the Civil War, a generation raised on the sermons of Charles Finney would have agreed with later premillennialists that the purpose of Christianity was to save sinners from Hell, bringing the converted to Christ. Yet Finney's postmillennial orientation emphasized the idea that the second coming was predicated on social conditions improving. In many ways, the social gospel tradition picked up on this theme by asserting that the church, while not synonymous with the kingdom of God, had the potential to be an agent of the kingdom's coming. Dispensationalists categorically rejected this rationale. For Haldeman and other dispensationalists, the key to understanding the mission of the truly converted church came through the ability for Christians to unlock the meaning of Scripture. No figure in American dispensationalism represents this theme more than Cyrus Scofield, whose impact on the development of premillennial dispensationalism carries down to the twenty-first century.

A former faculty member at Dwight Moody's Northfield Bible School, Scofield wanted to make the teachings of dispensationalism accessible to a mass audience. In 1909 Scofield published the first edition of a Bible that accomplished that goal. Throughout the twentieth century, and numerous editions, the *Scofield Reference Bible* was one of the bestselling books in the world. While it made use of the popular King James translation of the Bible, its popularity came through its annotations, providing the reader with clear insights into the workings of premillennial dispensationalism throughout the teachings of Scripture. For all the nuances among different dispensationalist ministers and writers, the contours of the movement were well in place by the early twentieth century, setting the stage for an explosion of popular theology that swept America with a new spirit of revivalism. The most prominent of these popular dispensationalist preachers was Billy Sunday. A former professional baseball player for the Chicago White Stockings in the 1880s, Sunday left the game after undergoing a conversion experience and, after a period of study at Dwight Moody's Chicago Bible Institute, began a career as an itinerant revivalist (while also finding a way to be ordained by the Presbyterian Church). Originally working through the auspices of the YMCA, Sunday served for a time as an assistant to the revivalist Wilbur Chapman before striking out on his own.

Academic proponents of theological orthodoxy, such as Princeton Seminary's Benjamin Warfield, tended to deemphasize the apocalyptic character of Scripture and were largely disdainful of the tactics of emotionalism that characterized "sawdust trail" revivalists such as Sunday. Yet Sunday's growing reputation as a popular preacher and revivalist would come to symbolize a growing separation in American Protestantism between liberal and conservative Christianities. In the early years of the twentieth century, attacks by dispensationalists against liberalism grew more strident, as did the attacks by liberals against dispensationalists. Yet even as liberals (and some conservatives) dismissed the logic of dispensationalism, the movement's impact carried beyond its initial points of origin. Ultimately, dispensationalist beliefs would impact preexisting and emerging forms of American Christianity. However, at the same time that dispensationalism was rising at a popular level in the late nineteenth century, another American-born movement was being birthed that would change the face of Christianity in America.

WILLIAM SEYMOUR AND PENTECOSTALISM

Although the two traditions would increasingly find common cause as the twentieth century progressed, theologically and culturally, the roots of pentecostalism and those of fundamentalism are worlds apart. Although both emphasized the primacy of personal conversion, each movement saw the nature and the marks of conversion differently. The origins of what would become known in the 1920s as fundamentalism primarily grew out of churches with strong Calvinist roots, mainly within Presbyterian and Baptist traditions. Keeping with the tenets of the Reformed theological tradition, the fundamentalist stream stressed the primacy of the Bible as the means to personal conversion. Those associated with what would become known as pentecostalism certainly believed in the centrality of scripture. However, they emphasized the ways in which the Holy Spirit empowered individuals to manifest the gifts of ministry—in ways that often bore witness to the biblical record through the practice of what became known as speaking in tongues. While many fundamentalists, at least initially, had their stronghold within middle-class congregations and the matrixes of institutional organizations such as the YMCA and the SVM, Pentecostals emerged from a context of social and cultural marginalization, oftentimes emerging out of storefront churches and, unlike the fundamentalists, initially drawn together within interracial congregations.

What is ironic about the rise of pentecostalism is that despite its meteoric rise and subsequent impact on the development of American Christianity, those within the more liberal theological traditions, and even within orthodox Calvinist traditions, largely ignored the movement. In the period between 1890 and 1910, as some Protestants moved toward ecumenical dialogue and social Christianities and others moved toward defining Christianity along the biblical lines of what became fundamentalism, the spiritual forces of pentecostalism were building.

The roots of pentecostalism largely reside within holiness churches coming out of various Methodist and Wesleyan traditions in American Protestantism. However, like many other sectarian movements that emerged in American history, the early pentecostals had a profound sense of wanting to recover the ethos of the early church. Key to the emergence of the pentecostal movement was its emphasis on the necessity of achieving "the Second Blessing," that is, the goal of Christianity was to achieve a sinless state of entire sanctification, or holiness. At the end of the Civil War, a new generation of revivalists was determined to keep this doctrine in the forefront of American Methodism. As an earlier generation of holiness preachers such as Phoebe Palmer passed from the scene, new ministers and revivalists continued to preach this doctrine to both Methodists and non-Methodists. Many who would be drawn to the holiness movement were influenced by the Irish Methodist William Arthur, whose 1856 book *The Tongue of Fire* stressed the primacy of the Holy Spirit in purifying the believer (ironically, this book was also read and appreciated by some liberals, most notably Walter Rauschenbusch).

One outlet for holiness preaching and theology was the National Camp Meeting Association for the Promotion of Holiness, founded in 1867 by a Palmer disciple named John Inskip. This movement reflected a desire to promote the doctrine of holiness, and by the 1870s it emerged as a form of protest against what was perceived as the growing worldliness of American Methodism. By 1880 American Methodism had moved far from its years of meteoric growth associated with the camp meeting revivals of the Second Great Awakening. Many Methodists no longer judged the church's effectiveness in terms of souls saved, but through its cultural and social affluence. Like other Protestants, some Methodists embraced the tenets of liberal theology, and many bemoaned the fact that Methodism ceased to be a religious movement that preached a "white-hot" message of personal conversion. In the 1880s and 1890s, many Methodists and members of other Protestant churches were swept up in what was called a "come outer" movement. Influenced both by holiness Methodists and the Keswick movement (which tended to be centered more on a Calvinist theology of revivalism), thousands of Christians formed a variety of holiness churches that were devoted to the task of seeking the "Second Blessing" of entire sanctification. These come outers took their cue from Paul's first letter to the Corinthians that argued that true disciples needed to come out of any unholy assembly of apostate churches to form holy assemblies of righteous believers. While many of these "come outers" did emerge out of Methodism to form distinctive holiness denominations (such as the Church of God in Anderson, Indiana), the Church of God in Christ (an African American holiness denomination), and the Church of the Nazarene, many holiness preachers and churches tended to work in loose networks of churches and organizations that proliferated throughout the country in the final decades of the nineteenth century.

One person who traveled this path within the holiness movement was an African American preacher named William Seymour. Born in 1870 to parents who were former slaves, Seymour initially joined a Methodist church in his native Louisiana. By the late 1890s he had spent many years sojourning through a variety of holiness groups in the South and Midwest. Around 1905 Seymour ended up in Houston, Texas where he studied with one of the primary holiness preachers of the day, Charles Fox Parham. Like many come outers, Parham was originally a Methodist who emphasized a theological orientation that would become critical to the later emergence of pentecostalism. Parham and other holiness ministers emphasized the idea of "the Latter Rain," that is, they believed that the earth was in its final days and that this event called upon Christians to recognize the manifestations of God in a new way. These Latter Rain advocates were not initially attracted to the themes of Bible prophecy that characterized dispensationalism. Rather, they emphasized the power of the Holy Spirit to bring about a phenomenon that was largely scorned by many in American Christianity: speaking in tongues.

Associated with the account of Pentecost in Acts 2, the phenomenon of speaking in tongues, whereby the Holy Spirit enabled the apostles to speak different languages and yet understand one another, became a cornerstone of early twentieth-century pentecostalism. The phenomenon of speaking in tongues never completely disappeared from the history of

Christianity and well in advance of the twentieth century, ecstatic utterance was often a manifestation of popular revivalism. However, the reality of speaking in tongues for Parham and Seymour became a sign that the church was on the verge of the second coming. Just as the birth of the Church was announced in Acts 2 with the speaking of tongues, the days before the final judgment of the world would be marked by this phenomenon. On January 1, 1901, the very beginning of the twentieth century, Parham led a watch-night service in Topeka, Kansas, that climaxed with the congregation speaking in tongues, an event that many see as the key spark for the pentecostal movement.

For all of Parham's stress on the Latter Rain, he was not immune from many sins of the world, most especially a virulent racism. He was a sympathizer of the Ku Klux Klan, and in subsequent years he took a dim view of Seymour and his ministry. While Parham allowed Seymour to attend lectures at Parham's Houston school, Seymour was forced to sit out in the hall and listen to Parham speak with the door ajar. On the other hand, Seymour's vision of the Latter Rain was characterized by the belief that social relationships would be turned upside down; in this context it meant that the true church would be characterized by an interracial fellowship. By early 1906, Seymour found his way to Los Angeles and with a multiracial following occupied a building on Azusa Street that had housed a former African Methodist Episcopal Church. In April 1906, Azusa Street became the center of an outbreak of revivalism that would continue for almost three years.

Many who view the Azusa Street revivals between 1906 and 1909 as the "birth" of pentecostalism often emphasize the fact that the movement centered upon the speaking in tongues. In fact, some scholars have argued that the massive religious revivals that broke out in Wales between 1904 and 1905 could have served as a model for Azusa Street and other related pentecostal revivals in the United States. Yet the emphasis on speaking in tongues alone does not do justice to how extraordinary this revival was to the larger history of American Christianity. In the early twentieth century, most forms of American Christianity, whether Protestant or Catholic, were primarily defined by racial-ethnic parameters. Even the Progressive-era movements of liberal social Christianity often accepted these racial dividing lines as a regrettable but unavoidable fact of American life. Yet Seymour's vision of revivalism was so sensational in part because it was unique from other forms of American Christianity. For Seymour, the fact that blacks, whites, Hispanics, men, and women could worship and prophecy together was a sure sign that true Christian folk had achieved a union that could only be made possible through the power of God's spirit.

The Azusa Street revivals were not necessarily paradigmatic of all later Pentecostals, but many future contours of the movement were shaped by these revivals. The key to understanding early pentecostalism was the way that it was able to create its own construct of time. As Seymour's publication *The Apostolic Faith* announced in the fall of 1906, the revivals were seen as a clear sign of the end times. The worshipers at Azusa Street were not approaching this end with dread, but with a sense of joy and purpose for the gifts of the Holy Ghost. It was not only this sense of belief in the end times that brought many individuals to Azusa Street between 1906 and 1909, but a sense of opportunity to participate with fellow believers in the joy and ecstasy of this magnificent baptism of the Holy Spirit.

One reason why the Azusa Street revivals were sustained for so long was the steady flow of men and women who ended up in Los Angeles who later carried the seeds of that revival to other locations. Like earlier traditions of American revivalism, and a key factor in the earlier rise of the holiness movement, Azusa Street gave authority to men *and* women who were not necessarily ministers in any formal sense other than they were baptized with the power of the Holy Spirit to proclaim and testify to God's presence in their lives. Like camp meeting revivals of an earlier time, worship services were marked by times of fervent prayer, singing, and the emotional outbursts of religious enthusiasm that led many of the movement's detractors, conservative and liberal alike, to assign to the Pentecostals the pejorative label, "holy rollers." Just as significantly, however, Azusa Street stressed William Seymour's belief that the end times would be characterized by a fellowship that not only freed itself from the false teachings of apostate churches, but also stressed racial-ethnic equalitarianism.

Like earlier iterations of American revivalism, however, this multiracial fellowship did not last. Many holiness preachers attacked the movement both for its uncontrollable ecstasy and for its multiracial fellowship (often arguing that both realities were the result of Satan's deception). Similar criticism came from conservative theologians and dispensationalist ministers who objected to what they believed was the movement's circumvention of scriptural authority. Ultimately, the fate of Azusa Street, consistent with H. Richard Niebuhr's analysis in *Social Sources of Denominationalism,* was an illustration of how a sectarian movement birthed out of a desire to renew the church ultimately gave way to various forms of denominationalism.

Seymour's leadership of the fledgling movement was hampered by a series of internal scandals. In 1910 he lost control of the movement's periodical *The Apostolic Faith* after a disgruntled follower stole the subscription list and operated the publication from a new base in the Pacific Northwest. The unique interracial fellowship of the movement proved too radical to maintain. Charles Parham worked actively to undermine Seymour's authority in the movement, and in numerous publications cast doubts on the desirability of Azusa's racial mixing.

By the time the Azusa Street revivals drew to a close, the pentecostal movement was well on its way to forming numerous denominations. In 1914 the Assemblies of God, a predominantly white pentecostal church was formed and to this day represents the largest pentecostal church in America. While the Azusa Street fires still burned, Charles Mason, leader of the African-American holiness Church of God in Christ, spent time at these revivals in the spring of 1907. His experience in Los Angeles inspired him to lead the Church of God in Christ into a full embrace of pentecostalism. Mason would serve as leader (bishop) of this pentecostal denomination until his death in 1961, and the Church of God in Christ remains the largest African American pentecostal church in the United States.

In the ensuing years after Azusa Street, many pentecostal leaders attempted to provide a sense of unity to the movement, forming a number of umbrella organizations that attempted to define parameters for the fledgling movement. These efforts, however, not only resulted in numerous splits over doctrine, but also over the claims of racial equality generated by William Seymour. By the time of Seymour's death in 1922, pentecostalism was becoming a global phenomenon, and mission churches were sprouting in Europe, South America, Asia, and Africa. While pentecostalism as a movement fragmented, many of its churches shared with other conservatives a belief that liberal-modernists were apostate churches guilty of false teachings and incorrect interpretations of central Christian truth claims. These contentious divisions were especially evident in Protestant battles over the role of foreign missions.

THE FUNDAMENTALS OF FAITH AND THE STRUGGLE OVER FOREIGN MISSION

In the early nineteenth century, one of the primary theological divisions within American Protestantism was between churches that adhered to a Calvinist theology (primarily Presbyterians and certain Baptists) with those that held to an Arminian theology (primarily Methodists, Episcopalians, and other groups who affirmed a free grace theology).

While these divisions were still evident at the end of the nineteenth century, fidelity to certain aspects of traditional Christian doctrine was increasingly important for conservatives, as opposed to beliefs about divine sovereignty and free grace.

By 1920 the landscape of conservative Christian movements in American Protestantism can be generalized within three groups. These groups were characterized by the presence of dispensationalism in varying degrees:

1. *Traditional Conservatives.* These were people rooted in the suppositions of their individual church's heritage (and in particular, fidelity to the five fundamentals outlined at the beginning of this chapter). Traditional Conservatives represent a wide constituency that extended across the terrain of evangelical Protestantism, including grassroots membership as disparate theologically as the Methodist Episcopal Church (in the North), and the Southern Baptist Convention. Although wary and suspicious of liberalism, these conservatives were not necessarily separatists and were represented by pre-, post-, and amillennial perspectives.

2. *Antimodernist Conservatives.* These were the factions who shared the sentiments of the traditional conservatives, but increasingly saw their traditions as threatened by the teachings of liberalism. They were more strident in their opposition to liberalism. Largely premillennial, these conservatives were most evident within northern denominations such as the Presbyterians and Baptists.

3. *Holiness and Pentecostal Conservatives.* These were groups that mostly separated from Methodism and other Wesleyan traditions after the Civil War to form networks of new denominations and churches. While viewing liberals as apostate Christians, they were also viewed with scorn by other conservatives for undercutting biblical authority and overemphasizing spiritual ecstasy.

Although dispensationalism was one factor in helping to create divisions within American Protestantism, there were other practical issues afoot that made it easier for disparate groups of conservatives to find common ground. One of the most significant arenas for a developing unity was in the field of foreign missions.

Foreign missions went through an explosive growth following the Civil War. By the early 1870s, numerous women's foreign missions societies were formed in many of the major Protestant denominations that played a critical role not just in terms of fundraising to support mission work, but also through sending out women for missionary service. In 1886, at the time that leaders like Dwight Moody and A. T. Pierson sent out a call for young Americans to take up foreign mission service that led to the formation of the SVM, Protestant mission work was not just a vocation for men, but increasingly for single women.

Although the various women's foreign mission movements had a wide-ranging impact on the development of Protestant missions, they also reflected the ways in which foreign mission was becoming a central factor in the institutional push among several church leaders for ecumenical unity. The world missionary conference held in Edinburgh, Scotland, in 1910 on one hand represented both a culmination of Protestant cooperative ventures of the nineteenth century and the beginnings of the global ecumenical movement of the twentieth century—especially in terms of how mission practitioners had to increasingly wrestle with the relationship of Christianity to the non-Western world.

Protestant foreign missions since the early nineteenth century were often split between a stress upon personal conversion and a desire to promote the values of Western cultural Protestantism. By the early twentieth century, however, this issue was being reframed in an important way. Many missionaries coming out of the cultural school of mission were increasingly exposed to the writings of social gospel writers such as Rauschenbusch. This impact caused some in the mission movement to examine how the ideas of social Christianity could apply to their mission sites. In the aftermath of World War I, many in the mission field started to raise questions not only about the role of missions, but whether or not the conversionary premise behind foreign missions was misplaced.

The debates over conversion and indigenization continued to play out throughout the twentieth century. In the short run, however, the fact that leading figures in the mission movement were starting to question if the kingdom of God was dependent upon the ministrations of Western churches helped pave the way for how some Protestants, especially coming out of traditions of theological liberalism, questioned the theological *and* cultural suppositions of Western Christianity—especially its ability to address the indigenous needs of people living outside of the West.

Even during World War I, this liberal emphasis on accommodating Christianity to non-Western cultures and religions served as a wedge between those who carried the outlook of the social gospel and those who worried that Protestant churches were losing the thrust of nineteenth-century missionary zeal, epitomized by the motto of the SVM: "to offer them Christ in this generation." Augustus Strong, Baptist theologian and longtime president of Rochester Theological Seminary, accentuates these tensions. In the late nineteenth century, Strong was considered one of American Protestantism's most prominent and orthodox theologians. Yet he sought to provide a means to accommodate aspects of liberalism in his role as President of Rochester Seminary—this is indicated by his hiring of Walter Rauschenbusch and other theological liberals to the faculty. By 1918, however, he expressed dismay at the direction of Protestant foreign missions, especially its tendency to emphasize social service at the expense of conversion. For Strong, the entire missionary enterprise was "not preaching the Gospel," but "passing . . . religious doubts on to others."[5] Strong's critique was affirmed by many persons within the Protestant mainstream and increasingly reflected how different theological outlooks led to different missionary goals. Quite simply, was the purpose of Christianity to save the world, as the advocates of the social gospel argued, or was it to save souls through the exclusive truth of the Gospel, as conservatives argued?

H. RICHARD NIEBUHR'S "CHRISTIAN AMERICA"

In 1929 H. Richard Niebuhr saw sectarianism as both a blessing and curse. On one hand, sectarianism deprived Christianity from achieving its theological mandate to work for the unity of the church and in many ways kept the church from actualizing the mission of its founder to be one body of faith. Yet religious sectarianism also was the means by which Christianity renewed itself, in effect, by reigniting the hope that the full force of primitive Christianity would be restored. Ironically, for all of his insights into American Christianity's sectarian history, Niebuhr completely ignored the one movement that perhaps most epitomized this renewal of Christianity in his lifetime: pentecostalism. Niebuhr could not abandon hope that Protestant Christianity could find a way to unify its theological currents into one common purpose, and in many ways Niebuhr's chief focus was not upon the biblical hermeneutics espoused by dispensationalists, or the supernaturalism espoused by pentecostals, but on the church's ability to act ethically and uniformly as one body. Although the rise of fundamentalism and pentecostalism represented distinctive developments, their eventual convergence related to a shared concern that modern liberalism had taken away the core essence of Christianity: its otherworldliness.

Even though pentecostalism didn't pop up on his scholarly radar, the pentecostal experience symbolizes the growing discord among the nation's Christian communities, even as efforts were underway among many churches by the early twentieth century to heal these divisions. Niebuhr himself noted in his reflections on the sectarian nature of American Church history, "the accord of Pentecost has resolved itself into a Babel of confused sounds; while devout men and women continue devoutly to confess, Sunday by Sunday, 'I believe in one, holy, catholic Church.'"[6]

Eight years later in 1937, Niebuhr appeared more optimistic in his assessment of American Protestantism when he published *The Kingdom of God in America*. While not refuting all of his earlier arguments, he believed that the greatness of American Christianity (epitomized by traditions coming out of the Reformed Protestant heritage) was characterized by the postmillennial vision of the kingdom of God, presenting Americans with the double-edged sword of a God who judged Americans for their sins (epitomized by Jonathan Edwards), but also offered them forgiveness of sins. At a time when some liberal theologians appeared willing to abandon the historical legacy of the Protestant heritage, Niebuhr delivered what was for some the most famous indictment of theological liberalism, "A God without wrath brought men without sin into a kingdom without judgment through the ministrations of a Christ without a cross."[7] For all of the ways that liberalism's future critics would echo Niebuhr's sentiments, Niebuhr was not thinking about pentecostalism, fundamentalism, or dispensationalism as paradigms of the kingdom that he envisioned. The latter years of the nineteenth century and the early twentieth century clearly saw the Protestant intellectual heritage of an earlier era under full assault, and while the intellectual heritage of Reformed Protestantism would not (and has not) disappeared from the landscape of American Protestantism, it had been marginalized by the early twentieth century through the appearance not only of liberalism, but evangelistic alternatives to an older Protestant intellectual heritage so loved by H. Richard Niebuhr.

Between 1910 and 1915, a series of short pamphlets were published by a disparate group of theologians and popular revivalists under the heading *The Fundamentals*. Financed by a wealthy southern California business tycoon, the authors included an eclectic mix of academicians, mission executives, Bible Institute leaders, pastors, and popular revivalists. Approximately three million of these tracts were sent to denominational executives, pastors, and leaders of a wide range of interdenominational groups. *The Fundamentals* accentuated what were identified at the beginning of this chapter as the five touch points that later generations of evangelicals would unite: biblical inerrancy, the virgin birth of Christ, substitutionary atonement, the bodily resurrection of Christ, and biblical miracles.

One of *The Fundamentals* pamphlets written by J. J. Reeve, a professor at the Southwestern Theological Seminary in Fort Worth, Texas, captures a sentiment that united the authors regardless of whether they came out of Reformed Calvinist, dispensationalist, postmillennial, or amillennial perspectives. Liberal theology and all that it stood for (such as modern biblical scholarship) were false not simply because the basis of their intellectual inquiry was wrong, but because it stripped Christianity of its essential truth claims that were centered upon the Bible. "Christianity is beginning to see that its very existence is at stake in this subtle attempt to do away with the supernatural," he lamented. "I have seen the Unitarian, the Jew, the free thinker, and the Christian who has imbibed critical views. . . . They can readily hobnob together, for the religious element becomes a lost quantity; the Bible itself becomes a plaything for the intellect, a merry-go-round for the mind partially intoxicated with its theory."[8] Reeve's summation comes down to a central core idea that increasingly would unite many conservatives as the twentieth century progressed: Christianity is the *only* true religion because it is the only religion that teaches divine truth.

By 1920 one of the central questions that many leaders of American Protestantism had to deal with was how much supernaturalism one could take out of Christianity while still calling it Christianity. As the next section reveals, twentieth-century commentators on American Protestantism could draw sharp distinctions between so-called fundamentalists and modernists, reflecting a culmination of Protestant infighting that arguably began in earnest with the trial of David Swing in 1874. Yet the struggles that occurred in American Christianity in the years following World War I represented a continuation of earlier historical and theological battles that revealed new forms of sectarianism and new types of popular theology and reopened age-old questions about how the story of American Christianity should be chronicled for future generations.

PART IV
American Christianity and Modernity, 1920–1965

In 1953 Winthrop Hudson published *The Great Tradition of the American Churches*, a book that came to symbolize a dominant historical perspective on American Christianity in the latter half of the twentieth century. Like his historian predecessors of the nineteenth and twentieth centuries, Hudson believed that the key to understanding the uniqueness of American religion was its Protestant heritage, and that what clearly marked that heritage were two factors: religious freedom and volunteerism. For Hudson, it wasn't only that American Protestantism stood for religious liberty, but for how its churches helped shape the American intellectual life essential to a democratic society. "In a democracy there is no substitute for an informed public opinion, and consequently there can be no substitute for a church which seeks to stand apart from the culture with something to say that is distinctly its own. . . . Only thus can an informed Christian public opinion be created."[1]

Hudson's vision of American Christianity was not just one dominated by intellectually rigorous forms of Protestant theology; it was one that heralded the triumph of a modernist theological worldview. The theological divisions that were occurring in the late nineteenth and early twentieth centuries were often characterized by divergent emphases, often causing huge chasms among various evangelical Protestants (as the differences between Princeton conservatism and holiness pentecostalism would have reflected). By the end of World War I, however, many of these disparate conservatives shared a common enemy in liberal modernity.

269

By the early 1920s, the stage was set for a battle for control that effectively tore apart whatever semblance of unity remained in American Protestant's largest denominations. Contrary to the verdict of many later commentators and scholars, these divisions did not necessarily solve the question of who "won" and who "lost" these battles for control. Although conservatives did by and large leave many of these denominations to the liberals, those within what would commonly be known as "mainline Protestants" struggled to redefine their mission in the context of a century that witnessed massive societal changes. Even as mainline Protestant churches found themselves in a position of perceived power and influence at midcentury, some voices, both inside and outside of the churches, raised questions about the effectiveness of the church to offer prophetic insight to the nation. Perhaps no figure embodied this prophetic critique more boldly, nor showed the possibilities of a prophetic Christian witness more heroically, than an African American Baptist minister named Martin Luther King Jr.

≪ 12 ≫

CHRISTIAN REALIGNMENTS BETWEEN THE WORLD WARS

Many scholars frequently mark Walter Rauschenbusch's death as a symbolic, if not literal, end of the social gospel era in the United States. The period between the world wars is often viewed as a time of retreat both from the idealism of the social gospel and a time when Americans retreated inward away from earlier desires to realize a kingdom of God on earth. However, the historical realities of the period between the world wars are far more complicated. The 1920s represented an era when many Protestants sympathetic to the progressive themes of the social gospel were challenged to rethink their idealism in the face of a national mood that showed little interest in the internationalist vision of many social gospelers. Additionally, the heirs of the social gospel found themselves struggling with how to make their message relevant in the face of a post–Progressive Era context. Idealism in American Protestantism didn't die in the years after the war. However, it was chastened not only by resistance to their message within their own ranks, but by an emerging generation of theologians who challenged liberal theological suppositions concerning social and economic progress. This emerging theological movement, sometimes called neo-orthodoxy or crisis theology, would become a staple of American theological discourse with the onset of the Great Depression in the early 1930s and remained a dominant tradition well into the 1960s.

By the time of American entry into World War II, liberal Protestant denominations no longer spoke with the same confident language of "Christianizing the Social Order" that characterized America during the height of the Progressive Era. However, they took for granted that many

Americans, including members of the political, economic, and intellectual elite, were willing to listen to what they had to say. Meanwhile, even as many of the liberal denominations seemed to recover from the political and economic upheavals of the interwar years, there were other Christian voices that continued to offer alternative visions of Christianity in America.

THE AMBIGUITIES OF TRIUMPHALISM

In 1919 representatives of major Protestant denominations launched the Interchurch World Movement (IWM) with the financial backing of many wealthy patrons (including John D. Rockefeller Jr.). Much of the IWM's mission was designed to advance many of the goals of the social gospel, beginning with a number of social service surveys that were to put forth recommendations in support of a range of social-economic programs spearheaded by member churches. World War I was seen by many social gospelers as a galvanic struggle between worldly forces of good and evil. In the aftermath of the war, many IWM leaders believed that the Allied victory had cleared the way to enact their reform agenda. In some respects, this optimism was corroborated by the enactment in January 1920 of the Eighteenth Amendment to the U.S. Constitution outlawing the sale of alcohol. The prohibition amendment was seen by many Protestants (conservative and liberal alike) as the grand realization of one of the great moral crusades of the nineteenth century, and in some ways it was one of the few issues that still could serve as a bridge between many disparate traditions within American Protestantism.

Yet, by 1921 the IWM had collapsed. In part, this collapse reflected the unrealistic goals of many of the IWM's founders, who in their own ways were drawn to their own versions of late nineteenth-century Protestant triumphalism. Yet it also was a reflection of how the ambitions of the IWM clashed with the realities of the postwar world. Many social gospelers were enthusiastic supporters of Woodrow Wilson's plan for a League of Nations, seeing in the League's blueprint the key to creating unprecedented levels of international cooperation that would prohibit the onset of further international wars. Yet, in 1920 Congress not only voted against America joining the League of Nations, but later that year, Americans elected Warren Harding as president. Harding campaigned largely on a platform of international isolationism, noting in his campaign that America's duty should be to bask in the glory of American nationalism.

Yet even as a spirit of isolationism and a "return to normalcy" reflected a strong public sentiment, America was being torn apart by social unrest.

As wartime industries downsized and cut wages, many industry workers went on strike, which often resulted in violence. The most prolonged and violent labor clash occurred in the U.S. Steel Corporation, virtually crippling the nation's steel industry for several months. In the early years of the twentieth century, increasing numbers of African Americans left the South for northern cities, causing an outbreak of race riots in cities such as Chicago (racial tensions were often exacerbated by the fact that many company owners employed African Americans as strikebreakers). Finally, the Russian Revolution of 1917 launched the first (but not the last) "Red Scare" period in American history, in which many Americans saw the threat of communism as a direct challenge to the American way of life, including religious values.

In 1920 Francis McConnell, a Methodist bishop and a major leader of the Federal Council of Churches, chaired an IWM task force that investigated the tactics used by the U.S. Steel Corporation during the national steel strike of 1919–1920. While the McConnell Commission report was critical in leading to federal legislation establishing an eight-hour work day, the report's scathing indictment of the steel industry was too much for many moderate progressives (and their financial backers) to support. Within a matter of months of the report being made public, financial support for the IWM plummeted.

In microcosm, the IWM shows what happened to the social gospel after World War I. The social gospel splintered among those who wanted to carry forth an earlier progressive vision of reform, working within preexisting political and economic structures, as opposed to more radical voices that were strong advocates for various forms of democratic socialism. This latter current represented what one historian called "social gospel radicalism" and developed a following among Christian youth organizations, denominationally sponsored campus ministries, and even within interdenominational organizations such as the YMCA and the SVM. However, a component of the social gospel legacy did stay rooted within the fabric of middle-class urban America. One of these emerging social gospel figures, Harry Emerson Fosdick, would serve as a major player in one of the most significant theological controversies of the twentieth century.

THE FUNDAMENTALIST-MODERNIST CONTROVERSY

Common caricatures of 1920s America depict a time when Americans embraced a carefree, if not narcissistic, posture in relationship to the rest of the world. The sense of isolation, while it did foster a degree of focus away from the world's problems, was not reflected in the activities of the nation's Protestant churches, which continued to look for ways to carry their understandings of social salvation to the outside world. Despite the collapse of the IWM, the ecumenical movement was growing, represented not just by the world missionary movement that had led directly to the 1910 Edinburgh Conference, but now by a new emphasis on Christian social action manifested in 1925 by the international Stockholm Life and Work Conference. With six hundred delegates from thirty-seven countries (mostly Western) the tone of the Stockholm Conference continued to carry earlier themes of the social gospel, stressing the role of churches applying Christian teachings "in all realms of human life—industrial, social, political and international."[1]

The Stockholm Conference reflected that an earlier tradition of social gospel liberalism had survived the war, and in no place was it stronger than within a series of large, upper-middle-class urban pulpits in the Eastern and Midwestern United States. In 1925 *The Christian Century*, a popular liberal Protestant periodical edited by a Disciples of Christ minister named Charles Clayton Morrison, published a reader survey of the twenty-five most influential preachers in the United States (based on a sample of 20,000 ballots). While the survey catered to the *Century*'s liberal audience (only a few conservative ministers such as Billy Sunday and Russell Conwell made the list), the vast majority of preachers included in the "Century 25" were liberals of large, affluent congregations (the South was largely ignored).[2] Like their late nineteenth-century predecessors, this new generation of liberals used their statue as "pulpiteers" to preach their message not only to their congregations, but also to a broader audience through print and, ultimately, by the 1930s and 1940s, through radio. The standard bearer for this new generation of preachers was Harry Emerson Fosdick.

Born in Buffalo, New York, in 1878, Fosdick epitomized how various traditions of theological liberalism impacted many within his generation. Educated at Colgate University (where one of his mentors, William Newton Clarke, was one of the pioneers of late nineteenth-century theological liberalism), Fosdick enrolled in 1901 at Union Theological Seminary, New York, and was ordained into the Baptist ministry. After a successful pastorate in Montclair, New Jersey, Fosdick began to develop a national reputation as a preacher and author. By the early 1920s, he was not only a respected professor of homiletics at Union but represented the high-water mark of a type of middle-class liberalism that held sway in American Protestantism from the 1920s through the 1950s.

Fosdick was clearly a product of a tradition of evangelical liberalism represented by his mentor William Newton Clarke and the social gospel of Walter Rauschenbusch. Like many clergy of his generation, Fosdick served as a YMCA chaplain on the frontlines of France during the latter months of World War I. These experiences led Fosdick and many clergy who shared his experiences in Western Europe, to come home from the war as pacifists; their ministries were marked by a strident antimilitarism during the 1920s and 1930s. Additionally, Fosdick and many of the prominent liberal pulpiteers of that time moved beyond earlier social gospelers by increasingly drawing attention to issues of racial justice, helping to establish a legacy within many liberal denominations that would become more evident during the Civil Rights era a generation later.

For all of Fosdick's activism, however, much of his popularity came through his ability to apply aspects of theological liberalism to the conditions of modern life in ways that integrated the prophetic language of Rauschenbusch with a therapeutic model of Christianity. Like "pulpit princes" of an earlier generation such as Henry Ward Beecher, Fosdick was able to touch a nerve of many middle-class Americans who viewed advances in the modern world positively and believed that Christianity had something prophetic to say to that world. Throughout his extensive career, he published numerous books, including many that sought to address how Christianity brought aid and comfort to those trying to make sense of twentieth-century modernity. In his 1956 autobiography, *The Living of These Days*, he spoke candidly about having a nervous breakdown as a seminarian, and stressed that one of his chief goals as a preacher was to relate the teachings of the Bible to concrete personal life problems. "Every sermon should have for its main business the head-on constructive meeting of some problem which was puzzling minds, burdening consciences, distracting lives, and no sermon which so met a real human difficulty, with light to throw on it and help to win a victory over it, could possibly be futile."[3]

At the same time, Fosdick symbolized how the gap between conservatives and liberals had reached an impasse. In the early twentieth century, the desire for churches to assert their cultural muscle on issues such as Prohibition had provided a degree of unity between disparate theological factions. The publication of *The Fundamentals* pamphlets between 1910 and 1915 signaled a widening chasm. Yet the 1920s hit conservatives with a renewed sense that the soul of Christianity was under assault. Some historians have pointed to the changing social-cultural norms of the decade, especially pertaining to youth during the so-called "Jazz Age." In particular, conservatives reacted to the perceived cultural laxness surrounding the changing roles of women (one example was the symbol of the short-skirted "flapper"). Although battles between conservatives and liberals were acute in all of the major Protestant denominations, the stakes were highest within two denominations in which Fosdick had formal and informal connections: Baptists and Presbyterians.

These two traditions were the chief heirs of an extensive doctrinal legacy of Calvinism. Following a Presbyterian schism largely fought over the place of revivalism in 1837, Baptists divided in 1845, largely reflecting a sectional division over slavery that also impacted the Methodists at the same time. Northern and southern branches of Methodism eventually merged in 1939 (although not without lingering and painful divisions over the place of African Americans in the new denomination). However, northern and southern Baptists remained regionally and, increasingly, theologically separated. While the Southern Baptist Convention tended to gravitate toward a theological conservatism associated with the influence of Common Sense Realism, Fosdick represented a strong tradition of liberalism within the Northern Baptist Convention, carrying forth the legacy of Baptist stalwarts Clarke and Rauschenbusch.

Yet the Northern Baptist Convention was also the denomination of I. M. Haldeman and William B. Riley, and many fellow Baptists shared not only their beliefs in dispensationalism, but embraced the core tenets of *The Fundamentals* pamphlets. At the Northern Baptist Convention in 1920, the term fundamentalist was used for the first time to identify a faction that stood in opposition to the modernist drift occurring within the Baptists. Soon that term also became associated with many conservative voices within the Presbyterian Church.

In 1920 Fosdick, who had been a professor of homiletics at Union since 1915, became the preaching minister at First Presbyterian Church in New York, and found himself attacked by a coalition of conservative Presbyterians who charged that because Fosdick did not subscribe to classical Presbyterian creeds (such as the Westminster Confession), he should not occupy a Presbyterian pulpit. In 1922 Fosdick countered by preaching a sermon that came to embody the liberal creed, "Shall the Fundamentalists Win?" While the tone of the sermon harshly criticized his enemies for their polemics, it also reflected a theme that has remained popular within many tenets of liberal theology ever since. Mainly, Fosdick argued that Christianity must adapt itself to the changes in culture if it was to survive.

Although he tried to strike an irenic tone in his message, Fosdick saw fundamentalism (particularly premillennialism) as a message that was completely foreign to the spirit of modern Christianity. "The question is—Has anybody a right to deny the Christian name to those who differ with him on such points and to shut against them the doors of the Christian fellowship? The Fundamentalists say that this must be done. . . . If they had their way, within the church, they would set up in Protestantism a doctrinal tribunal more rigid than the pope's."[4] A core issue for Fosdick was that fundamentalist leaders not only were wrong in their theology, but engaged in tactics that sought to drive out of the churches those who disagreed with their narrow interpretations of Scripture.

In many ways, the most eloquent and effective critic of Fosdick was a conservative who personally disliked the fundamentalist label: J. Gresham Machen. A professor of biblical interpretation at Princeton Seminary, Machen represented the continuation of a legacy of Princeton Calvinism represented earlier by Charles Hodge and Benjamin Warfield. Disdainful of popular revivalism (and dispensationalism), he was also one of the few Protestant leaders who opposed Prohibition. Nevertheless, he was terrified by the ways liberalism eroded in his mind the classical doctrines of Christianity. In 1923 his book *Christianity and Liberalism* served as a culmination to years of controversy, when Machen asserted that the question was not simply that liberals were tinkering with Christianity (as Fosdick argued), but that they had created a religion completely foreign from Christianity.

Although *Christianity and Liberalism* gave indications of Machen's fidelity to Calvinist orthodoxy, the book accentuated important themes that conservative Christians from disparate theological traditions could easily agree. Machen eloquently and forcefully gave expression to a range of traditional Protestant convictions. He attacked liberalism's worldview that the acid test of Christianity was measured in a person's deeds rather than one's formal doctrine. While acknowledging that one could be a good person and not be a Christian, Machen insisted that fidelity to Christianity was not only dependent upon a person's code of ethics. In essence, liberalism was a false religion that denied all the key historical precepts of Christianity. Machen's arguments were directed to those such as Fosdick who minimized the importance of doctrine, asserting that one's actions had nothing to do with Christian belief. Put succinctly, he embodied a shared sentiment among conservatives that modernism was replacing Christianity as an alternative religion.

> We are not dealing here with delicate personal questions; we are not pre-
> suming to say whether such and such an individual man is a Christian
> or not. God only can decide such questions; no man can say with assur-
> ance whether the attitude of certain individual "liberals" toward Christ
> is saving or not. But one thing is perfectly plain—whether or not liber-
> als are Christians, it is at any rate perfectly clear that liberalism is not
> Christianity. And that being the case, it is highly undesirable that lib-
> eralism and Christianity should continue to be propagated within the
> bounds of the same organization. A separation between the two parties
> in the Church is the crying need of the hour.[5]

Although Fosdick ended up resigning from First Presbyterian Church
to avoid the specter of a heresy trial in the Presbyterian Church, liberals
did not stand idly by. Presbyterian and Baptist liberals pressed for coun-
termeasures that affirmed free theological inquiry and greater levity in
the interpretation of historical church doctrines and creeds. Most significantly, many conservative leaders, while sympathetic with the fundamentalists, showed a greater willingness to compromise with liberals for the
sake of preserving church unity.

It was probably this desire for unity that helped stave off a fundamentalist takeover in the Northern Baptist Convention. In the early
years of the decade, conservatives allied with William Riley were successful in passing legislation that mandated fidelity to traditional statements of doctrine. Yet the 1922 annual meeting of the Northern Baptist
Convention staved off attempts of further fundamentalist encroachment. The key leader at that meeting was the first woman president of the
Northern Baptist Convention, Helen Barrett Montgomery (1861–1934). A
resident of Rochester, New York (and a friend of Walter Rauschenbusch),
Montgomery was a key leader in the Northern Baptist Women's Foreign
Missionary movement. While sympathetic to aspects of liberalism, and a
strong advocate for women's role in the church, Montgomery saw herself as
a defender of Baptist fidelity to religious freedom, believing that numerous
currents within the Baptist tradition could exist within one fellowship. As
pointed out by one scholar, part of Montgomery's appeal at the 1922 convention was that she stressed the priority of the sacred Baptist principle of
"soul liberty" over the idea of fidelity to particular doctrines.[6] Although
the Presbyterians did not put the same type of historical emphasis on individual liberty as the Baptists, a coalition emerged between liberals (and
some conservatives) that pressed the Presbyterian General Assembly for
leeway in the interpretation of doctrine.

Finally, in 1925 an event occurred that came to symbolize for many liberals the "defeat" of the fundamentalists: the Scopes Trial. On one hand, the Scopes Trial was more of an entertaining sideshow, but its outcome had unintended consequences upon many conservatives. In Dayton, Tennessee, a public school science teacher, John Scopes, was arrested for violating a state law that outlawed the teaching of evolution. The prominent attorney Clarence Darrow, an agnostic, came to Scopes' defense, arguing, in effect, that Scopes was merely opposing an unjust law, bringing to bear the knowledge of the modern world against the outdated suppositions of supernatural religious belief (and, by implication, indicting the state of Tennessee for its backward thinking). The prosecutor for this case was the former presidential candidate and Secretary of State under Woodrow Wilson, William Jennings Bryan. Throughout his career, Bryan had developed a reputation as a populist social reformer (he had resigned as Wilson's Secretary of State over disagreements with Wilson's foreign policy that brought America closer to war with Germany). Bryan was also one of the most influential lay leaders in the northern Presbyterian Church and a staunch advocate for the fundamentalist cause. In the trial, he depicted the case not just as a matter of state law, but placed the case on moral grounds by asserting that the sacred truths of Christianity were under assault.

From the standpoint of many commentators of the time, and the verdict of many future scholars, Darrow humiliated Bryan. In the climax of the trial, Darrow called Bryan to the stand and their bantering back and forth on biblical literalism and divine supernaturalism showed the chasm that existed between Darrow's "enlightened" modernism and Bryan's "backward" religion. In the end, Bryan won the case, and Scopes was found guilty and ordered to pay a small fine. Yet throughout the country, Bryan was depicted as representing an outdated anti-intellectual form of religion that had no place in the modern world (and the sad irony is that a week after the trial ended, Bryan died).

Increasingly, liberals in the North, and a few in the South, moved to solidify their institutional hold on various church bureaucracies and theological seminaries. Finding themselves increasingly marginalized within these churches, conservatives such as Machen left their respective denominations. By the end of the 1920s, Machen and other conservative leaders founded new denominations that upheld rigorous standards of theological orthodoxy. Although these traditions were firmly rooted in the tenets of Reformed theology, over subsequent decades many of these conservatives made connections with other streams of American evangelicalism, sharing a common concern that liberalism was an apostate religion. These emerging networks of evangelical subcultures are critical toward understanding the ways that Christianity has developed since the mid-twentieth century.

CHRISTIANITY TAKES TO THE AIR

Some perceive the 1920s as being an era when many Americans not only turned toward modernism but also against religion. The writings of Sinclair Lewis and H. L. Mencken were critical of what they saw as the ignorance of fundamentalism, and tended to see Christianity on the whole as being made up of bigots, hypocrites, and moralistic windbags (one of the predominant caricatures of 1920s religion was Lewis' hugely popular novel, *Elmer Gantry*, the story of a popular preacher whose downfall is largely the product of his own moral hypocrisy). For all the ways that it is easy to see the story of American Christianity in the 1920s either as a decade of religious retreat or as a modernist victory over fundamentalism, many traditional forms of Christianity showed themselves adaptable to the emerging conditions of modernity. No one exemplified this reality more effectively in the 1920s and 1930s than Aimee Semple McPherson.

McPherson's remarkable career can be seen as a continuation of a pattern of women revivalists from the nineteenth century. She was a person who from an early age felt a call to preach, and who had to overcome male resistance to her call and subsequent ministry. Despite these obstacles, McPherson embodied the successes that many evangelicals would have later in the twentieth century with the media, beginning with radio and later with television.

McPherson was born in Ontario, Canada, in 1890, where his parents were active in the Salvation Army and gravitated toward pentecostalism. In her late teens, she married a pentecostal missionary, Robert Semple, and traveled with him to China. By the age of 20, she was a widow and single parent. After settling in New York City and remarrying, McPherson began her rise as a popular revivalist and staged a number of revivals throughout the country (McPherson might very well have been one of the first Americans to drive across the country, conducting services through the aid of her "Gospel Car"). By the early 1920s, she settled in southern California, where she launched her Church of the Four-Square Gospel (still in existence today as a pentecostal denomination). At the height of the fundamentalist-modernist controversy in 1923, her local church base, the Angelus Temple, was dedicated in Los Angeles, becoming one of the most popular congregations in the nation, drawing thousands through its doors every Sunday.

While her theology was rooted in holiness and pentecostal teachings (as well as a stress on dispensationalism), McPherson was one the first major media celebrities in the twentieth century. Her ministry integrated both the old-time gospel, a dynamic preaching style, and, most importantly, a powerful charisma (supported by an undeniable sexual appeal, accentuated by the fact that McPherson's personal life was often the subject of as much public interest as was her ministry). By the time of her death in 1944, she was a worldwide celebrity whose life underscored how many evangelical Christians understood the power of the growing mass media in ways that escaped more liberal-modernist Christians.

In the mid-1920s, with radio still in its infancy, it was not uncommon for stations to sell or even give away airtime for religious programming. However, few liberal churches took advantage or saw the advantages of the new media (the possible exception being big-steeple preachers such as Fosdick whose Sunday services were regularly broadcast from their urban pulpits). By the early 1930s, the Federal Council of Churches had established guidelines for religious broadcasting that emphasized that religious programming should be nonsectarian and avoid discussion of controversial theological doctrines. Yet in the decades following the advent of radio, many evangelicals such as McPherson bought airtime to preach the old-time gospel in a new way. Just as nineteenth-century revivalism effectively utilized available means of mass culture, in the early twentieth-century preachers such as McPherson displayed the acumen of an emerging generation of evangelicals who built up their ministries through the use of popular media.

For all of McPherson's wide-ranging appeal, perhaps the most unlikely religious celebrity in the 1920s and 1930s was Father Charles Coughlin (1891–1979). A priest of a small Catholic parish in Royal Oak, Michigan, a suburb of Detroit, Coughlin first went on the airwaves in the mid-1920s to counter attacks by the Ku Klux Klan against Catholics in his community. With the coming of the Great Depression in the 1930s, Coughlin's activism grew more radical—and erratic. Critical of President Herbert Hoover's lack of response to the Great Depression, Coughlin moved to the Left, and then to the Right, in his solutions to the nation's economic problems. While originally seeing possibilities with the economic practices of the Soviet Union, Coughlin became a fierce anticommunist and, most notoriously, an anti-Semite, blaming Jews for most of the nation's (and the world's) economic calamities. At his height of his popularity in the mid-1930s, Coughlin could claim a radio audience of approximately three million Americans (as well as the approval of many politically conservative Protestants) before radio networks took him off the air in the late 1930s.

Charles Coughlin's career reflects upon the ideological instability of the times and illustrates the long-standing history of Christian anti-Semitism, channeled through a language of conspiracy theory (in his case, Coughlin recycled long-standing arguments that Jews were part of an international plot to disrupt the world's economy). Beyond Coughlin's rhetoric, however, another Catholic was building upon the earlier foundation of social justice planted by John Ryan.

DOROTHY DAY AND THE CATHOLIC WORKER MOVEMENT

Paralleling developments within the Protestant world, the Roman Catholic Church in the postwar period was represented by a diverse perspective of voices. Debates over Americanism continued in the Catholic Church as heirs to the legacy of Cardinal Gibbons pressed the argument that American Catholicism was compatible with the nation's democratic traditions (with Charles Coughlin representing an extreme example of this). Many American Catholics during the 1930s vigorously opposed the anti-Semitism of Coughlin, and at a time when Father John Ryan served as one of President Franklin Roosevelt's key economic advisors (earning him the nickname "The Right Reverend New Dealer"), Ryan's legacy was being developed in unexpected ways.

One of the most unique Christian reform movements in American history was the Catholic Worker movement, centered upon the teaching and advocacy of its principal founder, Dorothy Day. Born in 1897, Day's early life was characterized by a quest to find personal and vocational meaning. After dropping out of college, she moved to New York City and worked as a journalist and leftist activist for most of the 1920s. Although she identified herself as an agnostic, she found herself battling intense loneliness and struggling to find purpose in her life. After a number of failed relationships, an abortion, and then the birth of a child, she resolved to have herself and her baby baptized in the Catholic Church. Yet even after becoming a Catholic, she still struggled over finding her life's mission. In the early 1930s, as America sank into the Great Depression, she met Peter Maurin, a former member of the Christian Brothers religious order in France, who dreamed of creating a movement in America that combined a radical political vision with Catholic piety (and upon meeting

Day for the first time, Maurin allegedly announced that Day would be the next Catherine of Siena). The two were instrumental in forming the Catholic Worker movement and would publish a newspaper, *The Catholic Worker*. As editor of *The Catholic Worker,* Day had an outlet for her radical politics. However, her interest increasingly turned to the question of how a Catholic should live. For her, the answer was to live and work among the poor. Ultimately, Day's Catholic Worker movement established a number of residences ("hospitality houses") that reached out to the poor and destitute in a number of cities throughout the country, offering hospitality and the opportunity to find support and fellowship among other Christians.

Although Maurin was an important influence, the driving force behind the Catholic Worker movement was Day. While Day lacked the formal grounding in Catholic social teachings that characterized John Ryan's work, her understanding of reform was predicated on her own experience of Catholicism that stressed her belief that a true Christian did not simply talk about the poor, but lived and worked among them to alleviate their suffering. For all the seeming simplicity of Day's vision, over several decades she attracted an eclectic assortment of followers who, if not embracing her Catholicism, were drawn to her moral convictions to love one's enemies and to bless society's outcasts. By the end of the 1930s, Day was a committed pacifist and strongly supported the rights of conscientious objectors during World War II. By the time of her death in 1980, Day's synthesis of Catholicism and social action extended beyond the confines of institutional Christianity. Many former Day disciples such as the socialist writer Michael Harrington and peace activist Father Daniel Berrigan helped shape national social-political debates in the Civil Rights era of the 1950s and, most especially, led opposition to the Vietnam War in the 1960s.

THE GREAT DEPRESSION AND CRISIS THEOLOGY

For all the turmoil within American Christianity in the 1920s, another strong current of popular religion reinforced an earlier theme: Christianity not only offered comfort to the soul, but also the opportunity to gain health, fame, and fortune. One example of this self-help gospel came from the French psychologist Emile Coué, who taught a derivative of New Thought that one could achieve a better life through simple mental exercises (embodied by his slogan, "Day by day, in every way, I'm getting better and better"). Coué's teaching would later serve as one of the foundations to a tradition of self-help blending psychology and Christianity that served as a cornerstone later in the century for the career of Norman Vincent Peale.

Directly related to the tradition of Russell Conwell's "Acres of Diamonds" message was the publication in 1925 of Bruce Barton's *The Man Nobody Knows*. Barton, a successful advertising executive, and later a Republican Congressman, conceived of Jesus not so much as a champion of the poor, but as a prototype of the modern business executive. As one historian asserted, Barton's Jesus was "a virile, aggressive, young executive who picked up twelve men from the bottom ranks and forged them into an organization that conquered the world. He was a champion salesman and the most popular dinner guest in Jerusalem."[7] For all the ways that many church leaders from a variety of theological perspectives castigated Barton's book, *The Man Nobody Knows* was the top selling nonfiction book in America in 1925 and 1926.

Barton's treatment of Jesus embodied the economic prosperity that flourished in America for much of the 1920s. Although most of Western Europe had experienced economic turmoil in the aftermath of World War I, the New York Stock Market crash in October 1929 had devastating consequences for many Americans, both financially and existentially. The resulting unemployment and the near collapse of the nation's financial system found theological expression in numerous outlets.

In 1918 Karl Barth, a Swiss pastor whose education was steeped in the traditions of German theological liberalism, published his *Epistle to the Romans*. Published just prior to the end of World War I, the book served as a theological bombshell against the basic tenets of liberal theology. Barth took exception not just to what he considered to be liberalism's overly optimistic perspective on human progress, but believed that liberalism was guilty of confusing historical processes with the will of God, losing the thrust of Paul's teachings about Jesus as the only means through which a sinful world could encounter God's love. As the 1920s progressed, many European theologians followed a path similar to Barth, offering a range of critiques of Western theology and the problems of liberal modernity. By the early 1930s, Barth, along with Rudolf Bultmann, Emil Brunner, and Paul Tillich, was identified with the term "neo-orthodoxy." As later generations of scholars noted, the term neo-orthodoxy is a bit of a misnomer. Theologians, including Barth, did not share the same literalist worldview of American conservatives such as Machen, and they conceded that traditions of liberal scholarship (such as biblical higher criticism) had their place. Yet they distrusted the progressive optimism that characterized the liberalism of the social gospel. For Barth especially, what was needed was a return to a tradition of theology associated with the Protestant Reformation. While Barth's brand of neo-orthodoxy was not embraced by all the theologians associated with the neo-orthodox label, they shared a common wariness that modernity, on its own, could offer the world a better future.

For all of Barth's influence in Europe during the 1920s, his impact in North America would be felt more readily in the 1930s. Barth addressed a postwar European context characterized by economic and political instability, and it wasn't until the Great Depression hit America by the early 1930s that Barth and other European theologians began to attract a more sustained following in the United States. At the same time, the tradition of American neo-orthodoxy, or crisis theology as it was more often called in the United States, tended to have a much greater affinity for the social gospel, and indeed many of the first-generation American crisis theologians had strong commitments not only to social justice, but to leftist politics. No one embodied this tradition more than H. Richard Niebuhr's older brother, Reinhold.

In many ways, the parallels between Reinhold Niebuhr and Walter Rauschenbusch are striking. Like Rauschenbusch, Niebuhr was born into a German-American family, with his father serving as pastor of an Evangelical and Reformed synod German-immigrant congregation in the Midwest. Like Rauschenbusch, Niebuhr also spent several years as a parish minister before turning to seminary teaching, serving as pastor of a working-class congregation in Detroit. Yet far more than Rauschenbusch, Niebuhr threw himself into various political causes that he continued after his appointment to the faculty of Union Theological Seminary in New York in 1928. Throughout the 1920s and into the 1930s, he was a frequent speaker at colleges, political rallies, Christian socialist organizations, and ecumenical assemblies, speaking on behalf of various causes that dealt with religion's relationship to politics. In the 1920s, Niebuhr was drawn to socialism and, like a number of other social gospel clergy in the 1920s, pacifism. Even as Niebuhr ultimately turned against many aspects of his earlier liberalism, he continued to argue the case for a Christian social engagement that initially mandated the ending of the capitalist system.

In 1932 Niebuhr published his first major book, *Moral Man and Immoral Society*. At the time that this book appeared, Niebuhr was a committed socialist who that same year ran unsuccessfully for Congress in New York City on the Socialist Party ticket. Yet fundamental to Niebuhr's outlook was the sense that human existence was characterized not by an ability to overcome sin, but by the tragic consequences of sin upon human collectives. Although aspects of the earlier social gospel tradition also stressed this theme (in particular, Rauschenbusch's final book, *A Theology for the Social Gospel*), Niebuhr's vision of the future contained no hopeful reference to a coming kingdom of God, but a sense that humanity was bound in a web of tragedy that could never be fully overcome through efforts of social reform. With a theological bent that was reminiscent to many of Augustine, Niebuhr looked with suspicion on individuals who spoke too confidently of perfecting society, instead speaking in a language that saw America caught in a paradox between the need to believe in the ideals of human goodness and the possibility of creating a just world, with the tragic dimensions of human sinfulness that made the goal of a just world impossible. As he noted in the conclusion of *Moral Man*:

> In the task of that redemption the most effective agents will be men who have substituted some new illusions for the abandoned ones. The most important of these illusions is that the collective life of mankind can achieve perfect justice. It is a very valuable illusion for the moment; for justice cannot be approximated if the hope of its perfect realization does not generate a sublime madness in the soul.[8]

In the years following the publication of *Moral Man*, Niebuhr became increasingly radical. In 1935 his book *An Interpretation of Christian Ethics* (originally given as a series of lectures at Walter Rauschenbusch's old seminary in Rochester) spoke increasingly a Marxist language of class struggle, and signaled Niebuhr's break with other liberals over pacifism. Yet by the end of the decade, as Europe moved closer toward World War II, Niebuhr's understanding of Christian realism led him to call for American intervention against Adolf Hitler's Germany. By the end of World War II, he was by far the most prominent American church leader whose opinions on the relationship between Christianity and politics were sought out not only by church leaders and academics, but by politicians, business executives, and the news media as well. Later in the 1950s, as many churches experienced an unprecedented level of renewal, Niebuhr would emerge as a harsh critic of what he saw as the theological shallowness of a new religious revival taking place in America.

PROTESTANT RADICALISM

For all the ways that Niebuhr captivated many of his contemporaries and would perhaps emerge as the most important Christian intellectual since Jonathan Edwards, he was only one of many church leaders competing for the hearts and minds of many Americans during the 1930s. As the Great Depression worsened, numerous leaders within Catholicism and Protestantism offered their own solutions to the nation's troubled times. Yet, for all the forcefulness of personalities such as Reinhold Niebuhr, Dorothy Day, and (from the opposite end of the political spectrum) Charles Coughlin, they could not mask the fact that the nation's churches were in decline. In the aftermath of World War I, both Catholic and Protestant churches suffered membership losses, and although forms of popular religion remained strong in this period (as the career of Aimee Semple McPherson and Bruce Barton's bestselling book signify), there was a growing sense that churches could not speak to the perceived narcissism of the 1920s or the social-economic instability of the 1930s. Within American Protestantism, membership decline was in part a consequence of the denominational fracturing caused by the fundamentalist separations in the aftermath of the Scopes Trial. However, it was also a consequence of a growing antagonism between those who, like Niebuhr, built upon the ashes of the earlier social gospel and those in the churches who wondered what had happened to the "old-time religion" of their youth.

In some ways, the growing conflict between those who longed for this image of the past, with the political upheaval caused by the Great Depression, can be seen in the career of one of Reinhold Niebuhr's colleagues at Union Theological Seminary, Harry F. Ward. Born in London in 1873 to a working-class Methodist family, Ward immigrated to the United States as a teenager to pursue his education (eventually receiving a master's degree from Harvard). Although he had an extensive career as a Methodist minister in Chicago (including several years as pastor of churches in Chicago's notorious stockyards district), Ward's real passion was social activism. In 1907 he was one of the principal founders of the Methodist Federation for Social Service (MFSS), a caucus created by reform-minded ministers for the purpose of influencing northern Methodism to adapt measures in sympathy with the wider agenda of the social gospel. Ward was the primary author of what became the first denominational social creed, passed by the Methodist Episcopal Church in 1908, and adopted in modified form by the Federal Council of Churches at the end of that year. In the 1910s Ward kept up his activism as a part-time professor at Boston University and as leader of the MFSS. During World War I, he was an outspoken advocate for the rights of conscientious objectors (he would be a cofounder of the American Civil Liberties Union [ACLU] in 1919), and in the war's aftermath he was a strong defender of labor union rights.

In 1918 Ward was appointed to Union Theological Seminary as professor of social ethics where he taught until his retirement in 1941. In many ways Niebuhr's path as an activist was paved by Protestant radicals such as Ward. In the 1920s and 1930s, scores of Protestant leaders participated in a wide range of organizations, including the Fellowship of Christian Socialists, the League for Industrial Democracy, the Fellowship of Reconciliation, and the ACLU. Many of these organizations were committed to building political alliances with secular political groups and, increasingly, grew more radical in their calls for social reform and, in some cases, the end of capitalism.

Niebuhr became increasingly disillusioned with the ways in which Ward and other liberals clung dogmatically to an uncritical view of Marxist doctrines of class structure. This became more apparent as Ward by the early 1930s became associated with a cadre of religious and secular radicals who saw the state-controlled economy of the Soviet Union as a sign of the kingdom of God on earth. While Niebuhr held onto aspects of Marxism through the 1930s, he increasingly viewed Ward as an extremist and a dangerous example of liberalism's myopic tendencies.

The diverse perspectives taken by the heirs of the social gospel reveal a divided opinion not only on social-economic questions, but as the 1930s pressed on, the Christian's stance toward war. At the culmination of World War I, many influential Protestant ministers, such as Fosdick, served as chaplains in Western Europe under the auspices of the YMCA. The direct exposure to the conditions of combat drove many of these chaplains to embrace pacifism. During the 1920s, YMCA director Sherwood Eddy conducted a number of tours that exposed American church leaders first-hand to the military and economic carnage of the war. Within the context of liberal Protestant periodicals such as *The Christian Century* (in which Reinhold Niebuhr was a frequent contributor), a strong current of pacifism emerged in countless articles and editorials. In 1928 when the United States signed the international Kellogg-Briand Pact outlawing war, the measure was overwhelmingly supported by the clergy of the nation's more liberal denominations.

Yet as the Great Depression worsened, some clergy, including Harry Ward, spoke against pacifism, embracing a Marxist language of social revolution. In 1932 the Methodist Episcopal Church, the largest of the "mainline" churches in the country, revised its social creed that reflected this Marxist language of class struggle. Led by Ward and his close associate, Winifred Chappell (a Methodist deaconess), the MFSS engaged in an all-out propaganda war against capitalism, noting that its goal was "to abolish the profit system and to develop the classless society based upon the obligation of mutual service."[9]

Many laypeople did not draw theological or political distinctions between the likes of Fosdick, Niebuhr, and Ward, seeing these leaders as part of a dangerous spirit of radicalism that was infecting the citadels of institutional Protestantism. By the mid-1930s, newspaper mogul William Randolph Hearst funded and promoted a number of national "businessmen's caucuses" that focused on exposing and rooting out dangerous radicals from churches. These caucuses attacked radicals such as Ward, as well as prominent liberal ministers including Fosdick and Ernest Fremont Tittle, the senior minister of the First Methodist Church in Evanston, Illinois. Tittle's case is instructive for understanding how a genre of social gospel liberalism survived institutionally in American Protestantism during the interwar period. Tittle was one of the most outspoken figures in American Methodism on issues supporting antimilitarism, democratic socialism, and racial justice (he was one of a small number of northern white clergy to oppose the merger in the 1930s between the northern and southern branches of Methodism because the merger was predicated on maintaining a racially segregated structure). However, he was a loyal pastor who, like Fosdick, appealed to a professional (and often politically conservative) white middle-class base within his church. In 1933, when Tittle was being hounded by Hearst newspapers and attacked by a number of politically conservative groups in the Chicago area, members of his church drafted a "free pulpit" resolution. The document reflected a unique affirmation of pulpit freedom and illustrates how one of the major congregations in the country viewed Christianity's relationship to national affairs.

> We hold it particularly important in this day that the church should stand apart from all appeals to passion, prejudice, and partisanship, and that our nation should have in the Christian church a clear, strong voice rising above all divisions, speaking in the name of God for justice, mutual understanding, and good will.[10]

While this document was written within a specific context, the wording reflects a long-standing Protestant desire to speak with a united voice to the conscience of the nation. Specifically, this document's vision spoke on behalf of a liberal Christianity modeled after the virtues preached by Harry Emerson Fosdick in 1922, stressing tolerance, acceptance of opposing viewpoints, and the adaptability of the Christian message to the conditions of the modern world.

In the end, conservative attacks against liberal clergy such as Tittle did not drive these ministers from their churches. It did, however, underscore the fact that there was a great deal of resistance to what these liberals were preaching in many corners of the nation, as attendance in many Protestant churches continued to decline. In many ways, it wouldn't be until America entered World War II in 1941 that these "ecumenical" Protestant churches experienced what would be seen by some as a renewed golden age.

EVANGELICAL VERSUS LIBERAL
Who Really Won?

Questions raised by the classic social gospel of Walter Rauschenbusch were still valid in 1941: to what extent were American congregations able and willing to live out the mantle of being politically activist churches? In 1942 a Yale sociologist, Liston Pope, published an influential study entitled *Millhands and Preachers*. An analysis of labor unrest in a small North Carolina mill town during the late 1920s, Pope's account reflected how churches, regardless of their theological orientation, preferred to avoid political confrontations with the predominant power structures. Pope's conclusion seemed to point out that regardless of a church's theological orientation, Christianity was ineffective in transforming the powerful with the power of its ideals.[11]

The point is not that liberalism or the social gospel did not or has not had a formative influence on various movements of social transformation (a topic of central importance in the next chapter) or that Protestant leaders in the interwar period could not point to moments of institutional triumph. But the 1920s and 1930s underscores a reality that haunts many churches in the early twenty-first century, mainly, to what extent are congregations willing or able to advocate for specific political and economic models?

One perspective on the theological upheaval between the world wars is that it represented a vindication of the intellectual tradition of liberal pluralism championed by historians such as Winthrop Hudson. Representatives of the liberal heritage such as Fosdick, Niebuhr, and Tittle kept alive aspects of an earlier legacy of social gospel liberalism. Yet few theologians in the 1920s and 1930s were as intellectually rigorous, or incisive in their critique of modernity, than J. Gresham Machen. In his own way, Machen was a product of a waning era of Protestant cultural privilege, and many historians have noted Machen's social conservatism (especially on matters of race). Yet the issues that Machen raised concerning the role of doctrine, the defining marks of the Christian life, and the relationship between Christianity and culture represented arguments that conservatives would level against religious and secular liberals into the twenty-first century. Machen provided a blueprint that would be used effectively by future generations of American evangelicals from different theological perspectives, churches, and regions of the country. Mainly, Machen believed that the inevitable consequence of liberal modernity upon Christianity would be the killing off of Christianity.

Ironically, this was one of the issues raised by the journalist H. L. Mencken in an obituary written on Machen in 1937. Mencken's reputation in the 1920s was partly shaped as a critic of religion, in particular, of fundamentalism. In the aftermath of the Scopes Trial, he led a band-wagon of journalistic vitriol against religious conservatives that helped garner public opinion in favor of modernist sentiments. Yet in looking back on Machen's life, Mencken found much to commend. In his final years, Machen left the Presbyterian Church and Princeton Seminary to serve as the principal founder of the Orthodox Presbyterian Church and Westminster Theological Seminary in Philadelphia. Mencken was unequivocal in his assessment: in the final analysis when one looked at the struggle between the so-called fundamentalists and modernists, Machen was right and liberals such as Fosdick were wrong.

> It is my belief . . . that the body of doctrine known as Modernism is completely incompatible, not only with anything rationally describable as Christianity, but also with anything deserving to pass as religion in general. Religion, if it is to retain any genuine significance, can never be reduced to a series of sweet attitudes, possible to anyone not actually in jail for felony. It is, on the contrary, a corpus of powerful and profound convictions, many of them not open to logical analysis. Its inherent improbabilities are not sources of weakness to it, but of strength. It is potent in a man in proportion as he is willing to reject all overt evidences, and accept its fundamental postulates, however unprovable they may be by secular means, as massive and incontrovertible facts.[12]

Christian liberalism went through a period of adjustment and realignment between the world wars, but it largely ignored the assertions raised by H. L. Mencken.

Fosdick himself recognized by the time he wrote his autobiography in the 1950s that a new generation of Americans must confront a religious landscape far different from his youth. On one hand, he looked back at the years between the world wars as a chastened liberal. "All of us liberals, whose ideas of God and man were inevitably influenced by the slants and biases of the optimistic era before the wars, have been compelled . . . to welcome new insights, revise old judgments and acknowledge deplorable omissions in our understanding of the gospel."[13] By the same token, he remained confident that liberal Christianity was going to be chiefly responsible for opening up new theological vistas in the second half of the twentieth century.

In some ways, Christian liberals such as Fosdick embodied the later twentieth-century ideal of religious pluralism, with Christianity seeking to find ways to redefine its own identity within an increasingly diverse religious landscape. On the other hand, Machen represented fidelity to a classic sixteenth-century Reformation vision that stressed sound doctrine as being indispensable to the Christian's witness. As the twentieth century progressed, there has been an ongoing struggle between these two visions of Christianity, as faith communities struggled over what to believe and how to relate their beliefs to the contours of a rapidly changing America.

Yet the coming of World War II seemed to delay for a time a conflict over these competing visions within American Christianity. Suddenly, it seemed to appear that Christianity's fortunes in the nation had turned around and faith once again was to be at the center of a national ethos. A central issue for American Christianity in the 1940s and 1950s was not so much the specifics of what one believed, just as long as one believed in something.

« 13 »

CIVIL RELIGION, POPULAR RELIGION, AND
THE RENEWAL OF SOCIAL CHRISTIANITY

In the aftermath of the theological fragmentation of the 1920s and 1930s, World War II helped bring a renewed sense of unified mission to many American churches. Largely focusing on issues related to building a just and sustainable world order in the aftermath of World War II, the Protestant ecumenical movement reached its high-water mark when the Federal Council of Churches (FCC) and several smaller ecumenical organizations merged to form the National Council of Churches (NCC) in 1950. The spirit of internationalism embodied by the FCC and NCC played a significant role in the establishment of the World Council of Churches (WCC) that held its opening General Assembly in Amsterdam in 1948. Although organizations such as the NCC and WCC would still be associated in the American public's mind with a leftist political agenda, the leadership of these organizations shared with other Americans after World War II a desire to show how the Christian faith offered the most viable deterrent to the spread of international communism.

Some Protestant leaders who began their careers in the 1920s and 1930s as part of the radical end of the social gospel emerged at mid-century as the major spokespersons for American ecumenism. No person embodied this zeitgeist more than Reinhold Niebuhr. Although Niebuhr leaned heavily toward Marxism in the mid-1930s, by the end of World War II he represented a centrist political-economic ideology combined with a commitment to anticommunism. His association with high-level politicians such as President Dwight Eisenhower's future Secretary of State John Foster Dulles reflected the ways that many Protestants saw themselves at the center of American political and cultural power. The years during and after World War II represented the apex of what historians have called "the Protestant establishment." In the mid-twentieth century, Protestant institutions enjoyed renewed national status in terms of how its leaders seemed to embody an earlier Puritan ethos to serve as significant intellectual *and* moral voices for the larger society. Once again, Reinhold Niebuhr was paradigmatic of this Protestant model. In a 1958 television interview, journalist Mike Wallace lauded Niebuhr by quoting one of Niebuhr's colleagues. "No man has had as much influence as a preacher in this generation; no preacher has had as much influence outside the church."[1] The intellectual and cultural muscle of the liberal Protestant establishment went hand in hand with an emerging sociological understanding of what became known as "mainline Protestantism." As we will see, the term mainline Protestantism not only refers to the more liberal churches, but also to how these churches associated themselves with the cultural center of the country.

For all of Niebuhr's stature as a Protestant intellectual, however, it is debatable that his was the dominant popular religious voice of the mid-twentieth century (and as one of his biographers pointed out, Niebuhr's theology was hardly designed for preaching to the masses). Yet Niebuhr's status in the secular world was in part an expression of what many popular commentators during the 1950s saw as the nation's enthusiastic "return to religion." The end of World War II brought new levels of prosperity to the nation, as well as significant demographic changes that created the conditions for what many termed a "religious revival," on par, some believed, with earlier periods of great awakenings. Additionally, the emergence of yet another mass innovation, television, was embraced by some in a fashion analogous to what the printing press was in the sixteenth century and what the camp meeting had been in the early nineteenth century. As the sociologist Peter Berger observed in the early 1960s, the mid-twentieth century was a time during which the "religion business" was booming.[2] Yet Berger, Niebuhr, and other critics of popular religion questioned if what passed for a renewal of Christianity was truly a biblical and prophetic faith. Amid all of the various religious crosscurrents of that era, an unexpected voice emerged from the Deep South who sparked the most transformative social revolution of the twentieth century.

MAINLINE PROTESTANTISM AS
THE PROTESTANT ESTABLISHMENT

In March 1948 Reinhold Niebuhr was featured on the cover of a popular newsweekly, *Time* magazine. The fact that a Protestant intellectual like Niebuhr could garner the attention of *Time* was indicative of what many church leaders perceived to be a new era for American Protestantism in the aftermath of World War II—one in which prominent theologians such as Niebuhr would speak not only to the churches, but to the larger American public as well.

The term mainline Protestant, when applied to mid-twentieth-century America, reflects the continuation of the long-held notion that Protestant leaders such as Reinhold Niebuhr would speak to a wide range of political, civic, and economic power elites in the nation. As we have seen, this view of "the Protestantism establishment" was a character-istic of the social gospel era before World War I, and in the 1940s and 1950s, there were indications that many Protestant leaders had reinvigo-rated earlier institutional ties to important secular leaders—particularly leaders in government. Mainline denominations not only continued to build up earlier Protestant dreams of ecumenical unity and (increas-ingly) political internationalism, but took for granted that the voices of its prominent leaders would be heard and heeded by the nation's political and economic elite.

The 1920s and 1930s left Protestant churches battered by theologi-cal divisions and ideological battles. Yet with American entry into World War II, it appeared that the liberal denominations and churches that spearheaded the ecumenical movement earlier in the century were recov-ering their voice. From the early 1940s through the early 1960s, atten-dance in just about every Christian church in America rose exponentially. For many of the liberal churches that had been battered by dissent during the interwar years, the aftermath of World War II represented a new (and what many scholars saw as final) period during which several Protestant denominations were positioned at the cultural center of the country.

These mid-twentieth-century mainline churches were overwhelm-ingly white and middle class, and one of the key factors that character-ized them was that they often promoted a shared cultural identity. While Presbyterians and Methodists in the early nineteenth century fought back and forth on questions of free grace versus predestination, by the 1950s these theological differences between those churches would have been secondary for most churchgoers. The decision of whether one attended the First Presbyterian or First Methodist church in a particular city or town would have had as much to do with preferred homiletic style of a preacher, sanctuary design, quality of the Sunday school, and personal affinity with other congregants, as opposed to concrete differences in theology.

Another dimension to mainline Protestantism was the fact that many denominations and ecumenical organizations were building large headquarters and offices within the country's major metropolitan areas such as New York and Washington, D.C. These organizations often acted as lobbyists in their desire to bring their demands to the attention of politicians and the larger public. In the 1940s and 1950s, mainline Protestant activism was increasingly seen through the expanded bureaucracies within many of these churches.

This perspective was at odds with many of the churches and denominations that had been part of the so-called fundamentalist exodus of the 1920s and 1930s. During the early twentieth century, a few conservatives could concede the important role of ecumenical Protestantism embodied by groups such as the FCC. By the 1920s, however, the FCC was seen by disparate streams of evangelicalism as capitulating to the wider culture, focusing exclusively on matters of social engineering and misguided political schemes, as opposed to the business of saving souls. From 1942 to 1943 a cross section of evangelical Protestants responded by forming the National Association of Evangelicals (NAE). Embodying what one historian called "a cooperative clearing house for conservative Protestants,"[3] the NAE represented a diverse range of traditions including groups associated with the fundamentalist wars of the 1920s (Baptists and Presbyterians), as well as representatives from a wide range of holiness, pentecostal, and various other conservative churches.

The NAE served as a significant repository for numerous evangelical initiatives that by the end of World War II were not only designed to counter more liberal denominations, but also to sponsor a range of shared initiatives such as young people's organizations, including Youth for Christ, foreign missions programs, and the sponsorship of schools, seminaries, and publishing enterprises that could counter the slant of the liberal ecumenical churches. For all the ways that later historians saw the 1940s and 1950s as a time of ecumenical Protestantism's cultural triumph, seeds were being planting in these years by many conservative churches that would lead to a fuller awakening of a conservative public voice by the 1970s and 1980s.

While it is easy to see the 1940s and 1950s as a period of recovery for the mainline Protestant churches, the growth of the liberal denominations did not always keep pace with the growth rate of the country nor match the growth of more conservative denominations in terms of membership percentages and per capita giving. Yet various Protestant streams and their Catholic neighbors were caught up in many of the ideological currents of the era that reinforced the relationship between Christianity and the nation's purpose. World War II and the Cold War provided a common connection for many of the nation's Christian communities.

CHRISTIANITY AND WORLD WAR II

At the beginning of World War II in 1939, America's churches were divided on the question of participation in the European conflict. Yet with the Japanese attack on Pearl Harbor in December 1941, this situation rapidly changed. While some church leaders remained committed to pacifism, the overall tenor of most churches was to support the war effort. Part of what characterized ecumenical Protestantism's pronouncements during the war was the absence of the jingoism and triumphalism that characterized Protestantism at the climax of World War I. By the same token, many Protestant churches gravitated to the goal that victory over the Axis Powers would create unique opportunities both for interchurch cooperation and the creation of a just international political order. Typical of mainline Protestantism's stance during the war and its aftermath was that of one of the era's most prominent leaders, G. Bromley Oxnam.

Born in southern California in 1891, Oxnam entered the Methodist ministry in 1914, and with a commitment to the social gospel began a successful ministry as pastor of the Church of All Nations in Los Angeles. After serving as president of DePauw University in Greencastle, Indiana, Oxnam was elected a bishop in 1936 and over the next two decades became one of the most visible Protestant leaders in America. Although the Methodist Church had a high pacifist sentiment before the war, Oxnam embodied the mainstream of ecumenical Protestant thought that sought to mobilize church resources both to win the war and prepare for the realities of the postwar world. In addition to serving as the overseer of Methodist military chaplains during the war, he also spearheaded an effort by the Methodist Church called a "Crusade for a New World Order" that looked toward the creation of a sustainable world peace in the war's aftermath. This effort within the Methodist Church was paralleled by other Protestant efforts, especially within the FCC.

Through the work of its Commission on a Just and Durable Peace during the war, the FCC recommended a number of reform measures as a means of fostering church unity and a peaceful world. The membership on this committee read like a who's who of major Protestant leaders of the mid-twentieth century and included Reinhold Niebuhr; his colleague at Union Seminary, Henry Pitney Van Dusen; a prominent African American clergyman and president of Morehouse College, Benjamin Mays; and John Foster Dulles. Among the proposals embraced by the Commission were calls for human rights and freedom for indigenous peoples (in what would become known as the "third world"), the abuses of capitalism upon global economic development, and, most especially, the imperative for some sort of world government organization. Although ecumenical efforts to garner support for political reform during the war did not attract mass approval, ecumenical leaders did succeed in raising public support for American participation in what became the United Nations.

As president of the FCC (and later president of the WCC), Oxnam embodied the perceived cultural dominance of the ecumenical mainline Protestant establishment, whose influence extended to the highest reaches of government (reflected by the ways that prominent church leaders such as Oxnam regularly met with American Presidents and regularly appeared before the national news media during the 1940s and 1950s). For many evangelical Protestants, the efforts of the FCC and later the NCC were increasingly seen not only as suspect on a missional level, but also reflected the beliefs of some evangelicals that the so-called ecumenical churches were a sign of the end times (appealing to the Book of Revelation, some evangelical leaders of that era associated groups like the FCC and the WCC as part of an international conspiracy that they associated with the coming of the antichrist). The dispensationalist hold that was so strong for many evangelicals in the early twentieth century showed no sign of abating and continued to forge a bridge that united many disparate individuals and evangelical organizations together in common causes.

However, a generation after the fundamentalist-modernist controversy, few mainline and evangelical leaders showed a desire to engage in protracted battles with one another. Even before the end of the war, demographic signs pointed toward changes that would be beneficial to the nation's religious future. Allied victory in World War II was equally the product of American industrial production as it was battlefield success. American factories were churning out a constant supply of munitions essential to the war effort, and by 1944 the industrial output of America far outdistanced any other nation in the world. Unemployment practically disappeared, and most significantly birth rates toward the end of the war began to rise, setting the stage for what many Americans would see as a postwar religious boom.

POPULAR CHRISTIANITY AND THE RISE OF THE SUBURBS

In 1893 historian Frederick Jackson Turner viewed American history largely as a search for land.[4] His "frontier thesis" examined the nation's historical quest for property and how American uniqueness as a modern nation was defined by the ability to adapt socially and economically to the settlement of these western lands (often at the expense of Native Americans). Turner was able to see the close of the frontier as the end of an epic in American history. His ghost continues to influence various interpretations of American history, and many Americans after World War II kept Turner's spirit alive by unearthing a new frontier to discover: the suburb.

Suburbs have long been a feature of American life. However, developments in American culture from the end of World War II through the early 1960s would lead to a an iconic vision of suburbia. Although Americans faced political and economic uncertainty at the end of World War II, many Americans found themselves with unique social and economic opportunities to pursue the "American Dream." The GI Bill provided unprecedented government assistance to veterans to pursue a college education as well as financial benefits after graduation. While women occupied vital roles during the war as factory workers, they abandoned these jobs to make room for returning veterans. Marriage rates rose steadily, and most significantly so did birth rates, which created the generation frequently called "the baby boomers."

The difference between the creation of post–World War II suburbs with previous iterations of this model was both the scale of suburban growth and the class demographics that accompanied that growth. In the nineteenth and the early twentieth centuries, the suburbs (a term not commonly used until the twentieth century) were made up mostly of wealthy enclaves that lived in close proximity to urban areas. Often, these communities were carved out of specific neighborhoods adjacent to major cities near where these wealthy elites worked. With the progression of the twentieth century, and accelerating after World War II, suburbs increasingly were designed for middle-class Americans who could afford relatively inexpensive parcels of land that over time extended further out from the center city. The classic embodiment of the modern suburb emerged after the war in Levittown, Long Island. Featuring houses that were built on "tracks" that stressed uniform design, these houses were designed to be affordable and functional. The reality of the modern suburb is that it never could have developed without the aid of the automobile, which gave Americans the ability to live a considerable distance from their places of employment (and increasingly by the 1950s the development of an elaborate interstate highway system that gave Americans an unprecedented mobility to explore and move to new areas of the country, in particular, the West Coast and the Southwest).

As more suburban communities sprouted throughout the nation, new churches soon followed them. By the early 1950s, attendance in most American churches jumped considerably, and as the decade moved on, not only were new churches being built at record pace, but many existing congregations engaged in massive building programs, constructing Christian education wings and designing new (and larger) sanctuaries to accommodate the throngs of new attendees. Suburban growth would have far-reaching consequences on American society and religion. On one hand, the popular cultural images of the postwar era embodied by popular 1950s television programs such as *Leave It to Beaver* and *Father Knows Best*, celebrated the suburban image of the nuclear family and the "traditional" gender roles of the stay-at-home mother, the breadwinning father, and well-adjusted children. On the other hand, the suburbs were the perfect staging area for the growth of mainline Protestant churches, as these areas were mostly made up of white middle-class, economically mobile people whose churches by and large reflected their own values.

The paradox of suburban religion is that many people in the pews of these churches often reflected predominant (and conservative) political and social values of the time in ways that clashed with the pronouncements coming from their church's respective denominational bodies. Yet in its own way, the development of mid-twentieth-century suburban Christianity continued to show how the old-time gospel could be repackaged in new ways.

CHRISTIANITY CONFRONTS COMMUNISM

Although secular periodicals such as *Time* featured Protestant leaders such as Niebuhr on their covers, these same periodicals looked with suspicion at the political aspirations of mainline Protestantism. In the 1920s and 1930s, magazines such as *Time* and *Newsweek* echoed the fears of many Americans who worried that the radicalism of clergy such as

Harry F. Ward and (initially) Reinhold Niebuhr showed how churches were being infiltrated by communist sympathizers. As the euphoria over Allied victory in World War II gave way to the anticommunist hysteria of the Cold War, many media outlets renewed their battle against the dangers posed to America by communism and religion. In the late 1940s and early 1950s, the House Un-American Activities Committee, chaired by Harold Velde, and a Senate investigative committee chaired by Joseph McCarthy engaged in highly publicized hearings that targeted a cross section of Americans from government, entertainment, business, and religion for alleged Communist Party connections. For all the ways that many Americans after World War II proclaimed a "return to religion," old accusations that Protestant denominations were being infiltrated by communist sympathizers received new momentum. In the early 1950s, *Reader's Digest* was one of several periodicals to run features on the ways certain denominations were controlled by "pink" church leaders who were sympathetic to communism.

One of the culminating events of this anticommunist hysteria came in 1953 when G. Bromley Oxnam testified before the House Un-American Activities Committee. Oxnam's politics were hardly radical, yet he was caught up in accusations that he was a communist sympathizer—accusations that befell many religious leaders of that time. Oxnam demanded a hearing before the committee, and over several days of televised hearings, he castigated its members for its use of slander, innuendo, and blatant lies. "It is at once ungentlemanly and un-American to abuse the privilege of immunity by broadcasting a falsehood from the House of Representatives. There is no Congressional immunity from the Biblical injunction, 'Thou shalt not bear false witness.'"[5]

Although Oxnam's appearance was a momentary vindication for many leaders of mainline Protestantism, it did not put an end to accusations that the nation's Protestant leaders were well outside the American political mainstream, naïve liberals at best and dangerous radicals at worst. With the election of Dwight Eisenhower as president in 1952, a new impetus was given to the relationship between American democracy and Christianity. In 1954 Congress added the words "under God" to the Pledge of Allegiance, and in 1956 the motto of the United States was changed to "In God We Trust." These measures were wholeheartedly supported by the leaders of the ecumenical establishment. The same year that Congress took measures to solidify America's connection to God, the Second General Assembly of the WCC met in Evanston, Illinois (with many of the sessions held at First Methodist Church, the former congregation of one of the main proponents of the social gospel after World War I, Ernest Fremont Tittle). The theme of this assembly was "Jesus Christ, Hope of the World," and a special hymn celebrating that theme was penned by another one of the major leaders of ecumenical Protestantism after the war, Georgia Harkness (1891–1974).

In the middle of the twentieth century, Harkness was one of the few women who succeeded in garnering the attention of the predominantly male world of academic theologians. While an undergraduate at Cornell University, she initially signed a pledge to enter foreign missionary service, but after years of soul searching, she ended up receiving a Ph.D. from Boston University, where she studied with one of the premier liberal theologians of the first half of the twentieth century, Edgar S. Brightman. Brightman was one of the chief proponents of a tradition of liberalism known as personalism. Derived largely from the work of Borden Parker Bowne, a Boston University philosophy professor, personalism was a tradition that stressed that human personhood was the ultimate means by which one could understand God's being. Highly optimistic in its assessment of human capability, many personalists, including Harkness, became involved in a variety of social justice causes, including movements for racial justice and women's rights. In 1939 Harkness became a professor of theology at Garrett Biblical Institute and later on moved to the Pacific School of Religion. Harkness is often recognized as the first woman to hold a faculty chair of theology at an American seminary. In 1956 the Methodist Church finally removed its prohibitions to women entering the ordained ministry. Much of that church's decision to ordain women was due to Harkness' activism.

Like many mainline liberals of that time, Harkness strongly supported both the international ecumenical movement and a desire to strengthen Christian conviction at home. This can be noted in a verse for the hymn she wrote for the Evanston WCC assembly.

> Hope of the world, thou Christ of great compassion,
> Speak to our fearful hearts by conflict rent.
> Save us, thy people, from consuming passion,
> Who by our own false hopes and aims are spent.[6]

Harkness embodied a tension within mainline Protestantism of that era. She strove for a vision of ecumenical Christianity that was open to an emerging array of non-Western voices while also clinging to the suppositions of an earlier era of Protestant hegemony. In one of her major works,

Understanding the Christian Faith, which was published in 1948, she asserted the belief she shared with other liberals of the time that one of the nation's principal foundations was to promote biblical literacy in America, including in public schools. With her staunch support for racial equality and women's rights, Harkness reflected how far proponents of the social gospel had come since the era of the original social gospel. Yet she embodied the classic belief of social gospel liberalism that equated Christianity with a democratic society. "Whatever the political system, there can be no real democracy except that which is founded on the conviction that all human beings, of whatever race, or color, or class, or sex, are of supreme worth in God's sight and ought therefore to be treated as persons. . . . Not until this principle is extended to include the persons of all nations in the family of God, great nations and small, white and colored, victor and vanquished, shall we have an international order founded on the ideal of justice for all."[7]

Harkness was one of the most eloquent spokespersons within the prophetic stream of mid-twentieth-century liberal theology. Yet her calls for reform also reflected the fact that increasingly ecumenical Protestant leaders were backing down from the radicalism of a previous generation, preferring instead to affirm models for justice that avoided the endorsement of specific political and economic models. For all the ways that the ecumenical movement attempted to sway public opinion, by and large mainline Protestants were not looking to become activists, but seeking a message that would help them make sense of and prosper in postwar America.

THE CONTOURS OF 1950S POPULAR CHRISTIANITY

In the nineteenth century, revivalism was often associated with calls for personal conversion to flee from the wrath to come. But in the post–World War II years, what became associated with religious revivalism was geared more and more to middle-class Americans who were fleeing the nation's cities for an expanding network of suburbs. One Protestant leader who epitomized part of the 1950s ethos was Norman Vincent Peale. Peale was the product of a Midwestern Methodist upbringing. He was educated at two venerable Methodist institutions, Ohio Wesleyan University and Boston University School of Theology. Yet when Peale graduated from Boston University, he noted that his education was "too philosophical" and not helpful in his desire to be an effective pastor. While Peale started his ministry as a Methodist minister, by the 1930s he began a ministry at New York City's Marble Collegiate Church (originally founded as a

Dutch Reformed Church) that would last until his retirement in the early 1980s. On one hand, Peale's theology was fundamentally liberal, yet had much in common with earlier iterations of New Thought as opposed to the social gospel of figures such as Harry Emerson Fosdick. Peale's theology was intentionally apolitical, although he strongly affirmed a staunch anticommunism (as well as a backing of Republican political leaders). His theology was rooted in many of the self-help traditions of American Protestantism associated with Russell Conwell from the late nineteenth century, stressing how humans could harness the power of faith to build a better life.

Peale's arrival as a national figure was marked in 1952 with the publication of his bestseller *The Power of Positive Thinking*. In ways that echoed Bruce Barton's *The Man Nobody Knows*, Peale's fundamental message was to emphasize how faith could serve as a remedy for personal anxiety and lead to prosperity and happiness. Through the power of positive thinking (and prayer), "you do not need to be defeated by anything."[8] For Peale and other practitioners of "therapeutic Christianity," the primary theological message was not about needing God's forgiveness for human sins. Rather, it was about receiving affirmation from God that we are good people capable of doing great things for ourselves and for others. While many Protestant leaders castigated Peale's theology for its shallow messages (and its lack of intellectual rigor), it struck a note among many white suburbanites who saw in his message a spiritual tonic for the anxieties of the Cold War. Through his weekly sermons at Marble Collegiate, radio broadcasts, appearances on television, and a wide range of publications such as Peale's devotional magazine, *Guideposts*, Peale reached millions with his message that religion meant personal comfort and the power to overcome life's obstacles.

Although Peale's theology did tie into earlier models of New Thought, there was nothing "exotic" or sectarian about it. It fit a paradigm of an era that was fearful of the specter of international communism and was seeking an affirmation that life was good even amid the social-political uncertainties of the time. It wasn't that Christianity would make people millionaires (although that could happen), but it would provide a spiritual foundation that could lead to finding success in the world. Like earlier preachers in America, Peale gave ample illustrations in his sermons, usually centered upon people that he had counseled who had turned their lives around to find success. One of his most embellished publications was a 1954 edited book entitled *Faith Made Them Champions*, in which Peale includes testimonials to positive thinking from a range of sports figures and media celebrities ranging from Babe Ruth to Roy Rogers.

Many later sociologists of American religion have stressed that growing religious movements rely on a distinctive otherworldliness to secure converts. However, Peale's theology was hardly otherworldly and his formula for success would be duplicated effectively by evangelical and liberal ministers since the 1950s. For all of Peale's success, the one person who perhaps surpassed him as a spokesperson for therapeutic Christianity was Fulton Sheen. On the surface, Sheen was an unlikely candidate for this role. A Roman Catholic, Sheen was educated in a doctrinal tradition of Thomist theology. Since the early 1930s, Sheen had hosted a radio program, *The Catholic Hour*, and later was one of the first religious figures in the mid-twentieth century to see the benefits of television, reaching a wide audience with a long-running program with the pastoral title *Life is Worth Living.*

For much of the 1950s and into the 1960s, Sheen's broadcasts achieved a level of popularity that appealed to Catholics, Protestants, and agnostics alike. Consecrated as a bishop in 1951, Sheen appeared on television resplendent in his episcopal garb, yet speaking in a calm and at times humorous fashion about the obstacles and challenges of living a faithful life (Sheen's usual prop was a simple chalkboard that he used to illustrate his main points). For all his popular appeal, he largely recast a traditional Catholic moral theology (rooted in Thomas Aquinas) through a message that sought to show the centrality of Christianity to one's life. What he offered many Americans was not the Christianity of the social gospel, or the zealotry associated with Father Charles Coughlin decades earlier, but a faith that tied one's religious identity comfortably with one's responsibilities as an American. Given the fact that Protestant suspicion toward Catholics remained strong in the 1950s, Sheen reached a Protestant audience who otherwise would have wanted nothing to do with any form of Catholicism.

Peale and Sheen were classic representatives of a postwar tradition of therapeutic theology that was developing deep-seated roots throughout American Christianity. For all their differences in backgrounds and faith heritages, they provided a prototype of 1950s religion that, although apolitical, leaned strongly to a conservative and anticommunist worldview. Most significantly, however, Peale and Sheen tapped into a deeply rooted American tradition that Christianity could cure the deepest psychological wounds of the individual.

For all the ways that many religious commentators of the 1950s looked disdainfully at the commercialized gospel of Peale and Sheen, it signaled a wider concern among Catholics and Protestants that clergy needed to be up to speed with developments in modern psychology. In many theological seminaries, greater emphasis was placed on disciplines of pastoral care, particularly pastoral counseling. America still had its pulpiteers in the postwar era, but new studies were stressing that clergy had to be multitasking professionals, or what H. Richard Niebuhr called "pastoral directors."[9] Though American Protestants had gone through periods during which they had relied on a variety of clergy models, the second half of the twentieth century would be led by men who needed to be skilled professionals who could use their talents in a number of different ways—as preachers, teachers, therapists, and, in many large churches, CEOs.

Niebuhr's assessment reflects that ordained ministry was still defined largely as a male-dominated enterprise. However, there were signs of change. In 1956 both the Methodist and Presbyterian churches, the two largest mainline churches in the country, approved the full ordination of women. Although this did not lead to a floodgate of women into the ranks of ordained ministry, it anticipated future discussion and, at points, conflict that would occur among Protestant and Catholic women in decades to come, not only over the participation of women in the church, but over the nature of the church itself.

Even amid the confident posture taken by many churches during the 1950s, there were voices hinting at the fact that the future of religion, like the future of America itself, was quite uncertain. Perhaps no book accentuates this anxiety more than Paul Tillich's *The Courage to Be*. In some ways, one would be hard pressed to understand the success of Tillich's book. Tillich was part of the network of German crisis theologians to emerge to prominence after World War I. Like his colleague Karl Barth, he was disillusioned with theological liberalism. Yet Tillich's writing displayed a high regard for aspects of Western culture, even as he embraced, like other German scholars of his era, a form of existentialism that raised many critical questions toward the institutions of modern culture. After leaving Germany in 1934, Tillich ended up teaching at Union Theological Seminary in New York. Over time his theological writings garnered a great deal of attention in North America among a cross section of scholars.

The Courage to Be was hardly a self-help book in the theological tradition of Peale or Sheen, but it did reflect in its own way an uneasiness that some Americans had with the perceived sterility of 1950s America.

At a time during which popular preachers such as Peale seemed to relate liberal idealism to a euphemistic sense that because one has faith, one would find success, Tillich's answer seemed rooted in a desire of humanity to find meaning amid a backdrop of sterility and emptiness. In a fashion that echoed the Christian existentialism of Søren Kierkegaard from the nineteenth century, Tillich stressed that "the courage to be is rooted in the God who appeared when God has disappeared in the anxiety of doubt."[10] On one hand, Tillich can be seen as supporting an argument that notes the indispensable nature of religion to life in the modern world. Yet he also prefigures the realities of how, within a generation of the book's publication, Americans would not only question if religion could offer a shared meaning but also if religion still had anything of value to say.

BILLY GRAHAM AND THE RISE OF NEO-EVANGELICALISM

While many Americans sought solace with the likes of Peale or Sheen or even the existentialism of Paul Tillich, the figure who most epitomized the popular religious revival of the 1950s came from the ranks of the vanquished evangelicals from the previous generation: Billy Graham. Graham can be seen as an anomaly among many evangelicals of that time in that he reached a massive audience outside the subcultures of evangelical America. Yet Graham's success was indicative not only of the grassroots appeal of his theological conservatism, but also the largely apolitical tone of his message, which was similar to Peale's and Sheen's in that it strongly affirmed the need for Christianity to confront the challenge of communism.

Born in 1918, Graham emerged as a major revivalist by the end of the 1940s. By the end of the 1950s, his crusades, sponsored by a wide-ranging coalition of evangelical *and* mainline churches, attracted thousands of participants (and were seen by millions more on television). Although he projected a warm-sided nature in his delivery, Graham's preaching style sprung from a deeply rooted tradition of revivalism, generally steeped in a piety most often associated with the free-grace evangelicalism of the Second Great Awakening. Although his crusades featured an altar call to accept Christ or else face the consequences of eternal damnation, in the tradition of Dwight Moody, Graham stressed an "open-tent" view toward Christians of varying church backgrounds and contexts.

One of the most overlooked aspects about Graham is that he was one of the first southerners in the twentieth century to take a conservative Protestant theology to the entire nation—including many within the citadels of the liberal-Protestant establishment. Graham came out of a Southern Baptist background, a tradition heavily influenced by many currents of popular theology such as dispensationalism. However, Graham's preaching avoided speculation on the Rapture and stuck to the theme that part of the process of conversion was helping sinners find God. While some liberals such as Reinhold Niebuhr viewed Graham as a charlatan, Graham's eloquence, charisma, and patriotic tone struck a responsive note for the ways that many in America, Catholic and Protestant alike, associated Christianity's values with American patriotism. Beginning with Harry Truman and extending through the rest of the twentieth century, Graham was invited to the White House by numerous presidents who sought his spiritual counsel. Eventually, he provided invocations for several presidential inaugurals and held "prayer breakfasts" that served as occasions for national political leaders to affirm a shared faith unity.

Yet Billy Graham's success was only part of the story of larger changes within many evangelical traditions at the end of World War II. In 1948 Carl Henry, a Baptist minister, published *The Uneasy Conscience of Modern Fundamentalism*. While initially ignored by many liberals, Henry's book was an indication that what many liberals called "fundamentalism" was not a singular entity. Henry's own educational background was eclectic. Though he received his bachelor's degree from Wheaton College in Illinois, an institution that came to epitomize many of the virtues and values of twentieth-century fundamentalism (and where Billy Graham attended college), he received his doctorate from the liberal Boston University School of Theology. Henry's premise was that many evangelicals had become intellectually lazy and bogged down in incessant arguing over particular doctrines at the expense of witnessing to the gospel. Although Henry came out of a premillennialist background, he challenged evangelicals to use their faith not to renounce the world, but transform it. While affirming key historical fundamentalist concerns for doctrinal integrity, Henry was dismayed by what he saw as fundamentalism's inability to offer a distinctively Christian voice to what he perceived as the secular drift of America.

Henry's career showed that he was willing to put his faith into action. While serving as a professor at Northern Baptist Theological Seminary in Chicago, Henry sought out ways to promote a wider evangelical intellectual engagement with modernity (and with theological liberalism), while seeking to convince other evangelicals that they represented a tradition that could serve as an antidote for a drifting secular society. Along with Harold Ockenga, the pastor of Boston's historic Park Street Church (where

Charles Finney held many antislavery rallies before the Civil War), Henry was associated with what became known as neo-evangelicalism. Ockenga and Henry were always firmly rooted in the precepts of preserving the so-called fundamentals of faith (reflected by the fact that both played a role in the 1942 founding of the NAE) while also taking seriously an engagement with the world's major social ills (although avoiding the politicized liberalism of the social gospel). In 1949 both men were instrumental in the founding of Fuller Theological Seminary in Pasadena, California. While rooted doctrinally in classical conservative themes, Fuller came to embody a wide range of evangelical theological crosscurrents that impacted emerging incarnations of evangelical theology later in the twentieth century. In 1956 Henry and Billy Graham were principal founders of the monthly magazine *Christianity Today*. Modeled after the liberal *Christian Century*, *Christianity Today* soon found a wider circulation than its liberal competitor.

Efforts by conservative intellectuals such as Henry did not signal a thawing in the chasm between liberals and conservatives, nor did it necessarily reflect that Henry's voice spoke on behalf of a united conservative front. While Billy Graham and Carl Henry represented one side of conservative evangelicalism, a variety of figures emerged during the 1950s, embodying earlier currents of dispensationalism. Institutions such as the Evangelical Theological Seminary of Dallas (later Dallas Theological Seminary) sought to define an academic legacy of Christian theology rooted in both Common Sense Realism and premillennialist dispensationalism. At the same time, events of the late 1940s gave new meaning to various proponents of apocalyptic theology. The founding of the state of Israel in 1948 represented a decisive moment for many evangelicals, who saw in the establishment of a Jewish homeland the fulfillment of biblical prophecy. Although many evangelicals matched liberals in their calls to patriotism during the 1950s, the heightened tensions of the Cold War were one more indication that planet earth was involved in a cosmic countdown. For some premillennialists, the specter of a nuclear war between the United States and the Soviet Union was part of that design. As one premillennialist noted, "Wars and disasters may come and go; atom bombs may pose their threat of universal annihilation. . . . But these things are recognized as part of the great design of the God of Israel."[11] Although many mainline Protestant leaders fiercely attacked this pessimism, other observers of the mainline wondered if these churches were any more effective in their mission to transform the world.

FIGHTING AGAINST SUBURBAN CAPTIVITY

While Billy Graham came out of a distinctive subculture of twentieth-century evangelicalism, there is no doubt that part of his broader appeal within the American mainstream was that he took an irenic posture toward many churches, including mainline Protestants and (eventually) Roman Catholics. Although he preached the old-time gospel, there was a point when the disparate traditions of that era, whether Billy Graham's revivalism, Norman Vincent Peale's liberal take on New Thought themes, or Fulton Sheen's therapeutic Thomism, merged into one. For all the ways that these three popular figures had specific theological ends in mind, they appealed to a shared ethos that life in America has meaning and purpose, even against the backdrop of the Cold War. In other words, their message was one of taking comfort in the world as it was as opposed to a full-scale critique of what was wrong with the American Dream.

In 1955 Will Herberg, a former labor organizer and a professor at Drew University wrote a surprise bestseller, *Protestant, Catholic, Jew*. For later commentators, the book was seen as evidence that American religion had created a homogenous type of civic faith (or what became known by the 1960s as the "Judeo-Christian heritage"). Yet Herberg's analysis spoke a truth that would become a basis for many subsequent critiques of American religion. In the attempt of the three major strands of religious faith in America to assimilate, over time the distinctive aspects of these traditions had been absorbed into a kind of religion that was mostly defined around fidelity to cultural ideals that had little to do with biblical faith. "In this kind of religion it is not man who serves God, but God who is mobilized and made to serve man and his purposes—whether these purposes be economic prosperity, free enterprise, social reform, democracy, happiness, security, or 'peace of mind.'"[12] For Herberg and many critics of the time, religion had no place for repentance or sin, but merely became an outlet for Americans to affirm a national ideology. Religion "is something that reassures him about the essential rightness of everything American, his nation, his culture, and himself. . . ."[13]

Variations on the themes presented by Herberg were echoed by numerous other commentators, including Gibson Winter in *The Suburban Captivity of the Churches*, published in 1961, and Canadian Pierre Berton in *The Comfortable Pew*, published in 1965. For commentators such as Winter, the suburbs were analogous to a cancer in that it was an unnatural social grouping of persons not bound together by any other trait except for a common desire for anonymity and to escape the problems of neighboring cities. Like other scholars of religion, Winter believed that for all of Christianity's successes in growing suburban communities, the suburbs were taking resources away from the nation's cities. While the suburbs provided fertile ground for much vibrant church growth, they also signaled the death knell for many urban churches.

One aspect that Winter reflected upon in his analysis was that "suburban flight" was accompanied by its own manifestations of racism. Few whites who left the cities for the suburbs returned to the once "big-steeple" churches they left behind because these churches now resided within predominantly poor, black neighborhoods. Many of these once venerable "First Churches" moved out to white suburbs or sold their property to predominantly black and ethnic congregations. By the time that Berton's book appeared in 1965, the charge that mainline churches mostly saw suburban religion as a form of isolation from the nation and the world's problems seemed to be corroborated by larger national and global events. However, as many Americans perhaps saw suburban Christianity as an escape, it could not shelter the white middle-class from a powerful social movement that emanated from many black churches in the South.

AN ALTERNATIVE RELIGIOUS AWAKENING
Martin Luther King Jr. and the Civil Rights Movement

In 1955 an African American woman named Rosa Parks refused to give up her seat to a white man on a city bus in Montgomery, Alabama. This act of defiance set the stage for the Civil Rights movement of the 1950s and 1960s that became in many ways the most prophetic religious movement of social change in American history. For much of American history, the story of race has always served as a vivid portrait of the nation's division—one to which the nation's churches contributed. In the social gospel era, white theologians generally ignored issues of racial justice or struggled to come to grips with the ramifications of race. While separated by a generation, Walter Rauschenbusch and Reinhold Niebuhr tended to see the question similarly, mainly as a Southern problem that defied easy analysis. In the 1920s and 1930s, a few white clergy became more outspoken on issues of racism. However, they represented a minority within their denominations. In 1939, when the largest of the mainline churches, the Methodist Church, was formed primarily out of the northern and southern branches of Methodism that had separated over the slavery debate in the 1840s, the new church created a segregated African American jurisdiction that intentionally kept African Americans out of the mainstream of church life. Few Methodist liberals stood up to the enactment of this legalized segregation.

Yet by the 1940s, there existed in both the North and South a variety of ecumenical and denominational women's organizations that were deeply committed to issues of women's rights and racial equality. With a history that often went back to late nineteenth-century home missions, these women began to challenge the suppositions of institutional racism in church and society. Another conduit for change was the establishment prior to World War II of a number of "experimental communities" in the South that were mainly focused on racial justice and economic equality (in some ways this reflected the spirit of earlier nineteenth-century utopian communities such as Brook Farm). With roots that go back to the Great Depression, many of these communities during World War II were made up of religious conscientious objectors who were committed to the teachings of Mohandas Gandhi and the discipline of nonviolence. Throughout the 1950s, many of these communities offered classes and seminars in nonviolent direct action. One of the beneficiaries of this legacy was Rosa Parks, who, just prior to her arrest in 1955, trained in the tactics of nonviolence at Tennessee's Highlander Folk School, which was founded in the 1930s by a graduate of Union Theological Seminary, Myles Horton.

The success of the Civil Rights movement owed much to a wide range of individuals and organizations that initially were able to build alliances across ideological lines (and most importantly, play key roles in raising funds for the movement). But the heart and soul of the movement rested within a network of black churches from the South, centered upon the charismatic leadership of Martin Luther King Jr. King's life leading up to 1955 represented an eclectic range of influences. He was born in Atlanta, Georgia, in 1929. His father was a prominent (and conservative) Baptist minister in the National Baptist Convention (NBC), the largest African American denomination in the United States. Expressing a post–Civil War tradition within many African American churches, the NBC and other emerging black churches and denominations stressed the idea of raising up "the talented tenth," that is, the belief that churches must offer education and training to the top percentage of men and women who would later become the major civic and intellectual leaders for these communities. Many historically African American colleges in the South were established upon this principle, and at the age of 15, King headed to Morehouse College, one of the most prestigious African American liberal arts colleges in America.

For all the theological differences he had with his father, King's call to ministry led him to embrace this legacy of African American Christianity. Within many black church traditions, the ordained minister was not simply expected to be a fiery preacher, but a pastor, counselor, civic leader, and, in many instances, a political broker who could represent the interests of his church and the wider black community within the context of the dominant white power structure. In the North, a few prominent black ministers, most notably Adam Clayton Powell, found success beyond their pulpits: in Powell's case, through being elected and serving as a long-time member of the House of Representatives from Harlem in New York City.

While steeped in the rich heritage of the black church, King's formative education came in the North where he studied at Crozer Theological Seminary and Boston University, receiving a Ph.D. from the latter institution in the spring of 1955. King's education exposed him to many of the classic tenets of the social gospel and its legacy, and he developed a special appreciation for the writings of both Rauschenbusch and Niebuhr. In many respects, King's educational trajectory did not necessarily suggest that he would end up the prophet of the Civil Rights movement. While he was clearly drawn to the legacy of social Christianity associated with Rauschenbusch and Niebuhr, his study at Boston University was primarily in the philosophy of religion. King was heavily influenced by the theology of personalism, and under the tutelage of Edgar Brightman (also mentor to Georgia Harkness) and L. Harold DeWolf, King developed a strong belief that individuals had the capacity to change history. Part of that conviction was predicated on the power of nonviolence.

While King's intellectual development owed a great deal to the world of liberal Protestantism, his social context was squarely rooted in an African American church experience that arose from the Deep South. When King left Boston in 1955 to become pastor of the Dexter Avenue Baptist Church in Montgomery, Alabama, he initially harbored no desire to be a movement leader and possessed no clear sense of how to enact a mass movement of nonviolent resistance. "I had merely an intellectual understanding and appreciation of the position, with no firm determination to organize it in a socially effective situation."[14] Yet early in his public career, King reflected a long-standing liberal-Protestant fascination with Gandhi, who had been well known in America since the 1920s. Gandhi's example served King well when he found himself in December 1955 placed in the position as president of the Montgomery Improvement Association that pressed the Montgomery city council for an end to segregation in public transportation. Through a direct-action campaign against the city's bus company, in which thousands of African Americans refused to ride city buses, the nation's media spotlight was turned on Montgomery for much of 1956. In November, the Supreme Court ruled that segregation in public transportation was unconstitutional, marking the triumph of the Montgomery campaign for the integration of public transportation and establishing King as the preeminent voice of the Civil Rights movement in America.

King's emergence as a Civil Rights leader occurred one year after the U.S. Supreme Court in *Brown v. Topeka Board of Education* ruled that public school segregation was unconstitutional. His subsequent leadership, particularly his blending of Thoreau, Gandhi, theological liberalism, and the moral voice of the black church, helped shape the contours of the Civil Rights movement until King's assassination in 1968. The purpose of nonviolence was to expose the nation to injustice and to bring out the best motives of the oppressor, embodied by how the power of God's love could bring the oppressor to an awareness of one's participation in an unjust system of segregation.

King's success owed much to his intelligence and charisma as well as to the way that he brought a distinctive tradition of African American Christianity to the nation. The culmination of the first half of King's public career occurred in August 1963 during the March on Washington. In many ways, the events of August 28, 1963, represented one of the high-water marks of religion in American history. Addressing a group of approximately 250,000, including many leaders and representatives from the nation's major religious bodies, King gave expression to a religious vision that was both transcendent yet particular to the American context. The "I Have a Dream" speech embodied a host of American religious traditions. On one hand, its idiom reflected the cadences and rhythms of antebellum slave religion—its meter one of repetition, call, and response. Yet King spoke in an inclusive voice that defined the "American Dream" not in terms of the 1950s quest for prosperity, but in a prophetic mandate for justice for all Americans.

Two years later, in 1965, King led a voting rights march from Selma to Montgomery, Alabama, an event that preceded the signing into law of an historic voting rights act that summer. King's address at Montgomery used a similar cadence for the need to transform America, with a decidedly liberal philosophical bent that "the arch of the moral universe is long but it bends toward justice."[15] Yet even as King became a symbol of a modern-day prophet who united many of the nation's religious leaders and groups, America's mainline churches were growing increasingly fragmented.

GOLDEN AGE OR LAST GASP?

Following a succession of previous commentators on American religion, Winthrop Hudson saw Protestantism as central to shaping the contours of American democracy. "The separation of church and state has the additional virtue of guaranteeing the freedom of a church to be a church, to determine its own life, and to appeal to a 'higher law' than the statutory enactments of the state."[16] Yet the intellectually rigorous theological discussion that Hudson envisioned was often missing from various discussions about religion's place in American culture.

By the end of the twentieth century, scholars would use a number of interpretive lenses for making sense of religion in the 1940s and 1950s. However, a common thread that runs through many interpretations is the integral connection between the religious revival of the era with the emerging political realities of the Cold War. In this regard, religion's role has been seen as fostering an ideology predicated upon anticommunism whereby Christianity, in its mainline, evangelical, and Catholic iterations, did not challenge the dominant culture (as Hudson hoped it would), but bestowed a blessing upon it.

One popular perspective on the subsequent development of American Christianity is that the social, political, and cultural realities of the 1960s destroyed an illusion of American uniqueness in its politics, culture, and religion. The 1960s did cause a major theological reassessment among a variety of Protestant and Catholic communities. Yet a closer examination of the decades leading up to the social upheavals of the 1960s can easily suggest that mainline Protestantism was already in a sort of twilight era. In addition to the obvious chasm in churches on the issues of race, the critiques of American religion offered by figures such as Will Herberg and Gibson Winter challenged the assumption that Christianity was making any transformative inroads among the nation's powerbrokers (despite the posturing of leaders within organizations such as the NCC). In this era of mainline Protestantism's heyday (membership peaked by the early 1960s), one could argue that it wasn't the establishment figures such as Reinhold Niebuhr who most gripped the nation, but conservatives such as Billy Graham and self-help media figures such as Norman Vincent Peale and Fulton Sheen.

There is no doubt that the Civil Rights movement not only revealed the extent to which Americans were divided over questions of race, but how religious differences played in those divisions. From the 1940s through the 1960s, several mainline denominations and leaders regularly made pronouncements condemning the lynching of African Americans while often providing a large measure of personnel and financial support for King's nonviolent campaigns. Such support from evangelical churches and their leaders was minimal. For all of Billy Graham's openness toward Christians of all theological persuasions, he initially viewed King as a potentially dangerous radical who preached leftist politics rather than Christianity. It wasn't until the late 1960s that a new generation of evangelical leaders would view King as a prophetic figure who spoke to the consciences of their traditions.

Winthrop Hudson's perspective on religious liberty represents one of the most salient themes for understanding Christianity's role in American history. However, the consequences of that tradition at mid-twentieth century pointed Americans as much to the legacy of Graham, Peale, and Sheen as it did to the legacy of Reinhold Niebuhr and Martin Luther King Jr. Even as Hudson's vision of the "great tradition" largely affirmed the legacy of Christianity represented by Niebuhr and King, he embodied perhaps one of the last major historical voices to write with the assurance that this legacy would continue to dominate the religious terrain for years to come. When the 1960s hit, it still appeared for many figures in mainline Protestantism that the future promised further possibilities for growth and expansion (both in terms of ecumenical programming and congregational development on a grassroots level). Not only would those visions be under assault by the end of the 1960s, but many voices coming out of the so-called mainline began to signal a lament for what they now believed was a fading tradition.

PART V
The Restructuring of American Christianity, 1965–2009

At the conclusion of his magnum opus, *A Religious History of the American People*, written during the political and cultural tumult of the late 1960s, Sydney Ahlstrom sought to sum up over four hundred years of religion in American history by noting that the nation found itself wrestling with the ramifications of a post-Puritan era. Ahlstrom acknowledged an idea that has become fundamental to interpretations of American religion ever since, mainly how the decline of a Puritan ethos gave way to a vision of religious pluralism. Yet Ahlstrom's announcing of a post-Puritan America in the early 1970s was one of marked ambivalence, as he remained unclear about where America would be headed without this central religious narrative to guide it. "The idea of America as a Chosen Nation and a beacon to the world was expiring. . . . Yet unmistakably at the heart of the prevailing anxiety was the need for reexamining fundamental conceptions of religion, ethics, and nationhood."[1]

Ahlstrom had his hand on the pulse of how religion in twentieth-century America was pushing the country into unexplored terrain. As America approached the end of the century, it found itself a nation characterized by wide religious diversity. Yet, while the second half of the twentieth century revealed itself as a time of societal shifts to the point that it caused many public intellectuals to herald the demise of religion, Christianity in a variety of new iterations punctuated American life even during a time when a handful of theologians announced "the death of God." The public rhetoric surrounding the role of religion, and Christianity in particular, since the time of Sydney Ahlstrom has been largely defined by one of crisis and fear of the impending collapse of long-standing American religious institutions. By the 1980s some intellectuals posited that Americans were living at a time in which all grand intellectual narratives, including those offered by Christianity, no longer had any meaning. This fragmentation of knowledge that some have referred to as "postmodernity" came to symbolize for some theologians a collapse of all the signposts of belief that had brought cohesiveness and unity to Christianity in the West for hundreds of years.

And yet the irony is that in the decades since Ahlstrom's book first appeared, the heartbeat of Puritanism continued to pound, albeit in ways different from that of colonial New England. As certain academic segments of Christianity moved in the direction of what would become known as liberation theology, popular iterations of Christianity sought a return to the perceived glory of an earlier time when America was seen as a chosen land and when Christianity (in certain Protestant forms) dominated the nation. Yet even as many segments of American Christianity looked to the past for validation of their mission, new iterations of Christianity have emerged in recent decades that raise many questions of where Christianity might lead Americans in the twenty-first century. One way to look at these changes is to see the dawning of a new era of religious pluralism in America in which older traditions of mainline Protestants were but one component. Another interpretation, however, is to see events of the past half-century as a final twilight of perceived mainline Protestant hegemony not only characterized by a greater mixture of religious traditions in America, but where emerging iterations of evangelicalism represent the new heirs of Puritanism.

≪ 14 ≫

THE PARAMETERS OF PLURALISM

In October 1960, a prominent Methodist minister named Harold Bosley published an article in *Christian Century* magazine voicing concern about the prospect of electing a Roman Catholic as President of the United States. While expressing admiration for Senator John Kennedy, Bosley worried that a Kennedy presidency would not safeguard an American tradition of religious liberty. ". . . when Rome accepts the plain fact that any and all other religions have the same right to live and propagate themselves as she seeks for herself—then and only then can we afford to relax our vigilance on the walls we have been guarding for 400 years."[1] What is remarkable about this article is that it was not written by a conservative evangelical, but by one of the most respected liberal leaders of mainline Protestantism. In 1950 Bosley succeeded Ernest Fremont Tittle as senior minister of the First Methodist Church in Evanston, Illinois. Like Tittle, Bosley was an outspoken supporter of social justice and a prominent leader within mainline Protestantism. In 1954 his Evanston congregation hosted many of the sessions for the Second General Assembly of the World Council of Churches. For all of Bosley's progressivism as a religious leader, he harkened back to an earlier nineteenth-century ideology that questioned whether one could simultaneously be a Catholic and a truly loyal American. In his own way, Bosley reflected a more civil style of the Protestant vitriol that in 1928 had been used to target Alfred Smith, the first Roman Catholic presidential candidate from a major political party.

Bosley's remarks reflected the last gasp of a sentiment among several mainline Protestant leaders of the mid-twentieth century who were not simply arguing a case for religious liberty, but reflected a taken-for-granted assumption that they represented churches that would speak for the majority of Americans. Yet by the mid-1970s, Bosley's reflections read as echoes from a distant era. Not only did America see the election of John F. Kennedy as the nation's first Roman Catholic president, but subsequent events of the 1960s witnessed an unprecedented level of social, political, and cultural change that divided and fragmented the nation's religious communities. Protestants and Catholics alike found themselves split over issues related to civil rights, America's participation in the Vietnam War, and what to make of the larger societal crosscurrents associated with the so-called "counterculture" of the decade that early 1970s demographers noted were driving a young generation of baby boomers away from many long-standing American institutions, including its churches. By the end of the 1960s, the nation's mainline churches were witnessing a precipitous drop in membership. The United Methodist Church, the second largest Protestant church in the country (and the largest of the mainline churches) fell from eleven million members in the early 1960s to under ten million members by the mid-1970s. The Episcopal Church, with a membership of around 3.5 million in the mid-1960s, lost almost a million members in ten years, and a similar downward demographic held for the United Church of Christ (a denomination whose legacy in New England Congregationalism stretched back to the days of the Puritans). Some commentators questioned these data, noting that denominations had often inflated membership rolls and that the drop-off represented an effort of these churches to cull their rolls. At the same time, many Protestant commentators began to grow increasingly worried about what appeared to be a major reemergence of evangelical Christianity into the American social and political arena. As denominational data pointed to a precipitous drop in members among the more liberal denominations, churches with deeply engrained evangelical traditions, such as the Seventh-day Adventist, Church of the Nazarene, and the Southern Baptist Convention, were growing at a steady clip.

In 1972 Dean Kelley, a researcher under the auspices of the National Council of Churches (NCC), published one of the most discussed books of the 1970s among mainline Protestant leaders: *Why Conservative Churches Are Growing*. Kelley's book was a straightforward effort to wrestle not only with the successes of conservative evangelical churches, but also the apparent inability of the more liberal mainline churches to keep pace. For Kelley, the question of evangelical success revolved around their ability to proclaim an unambiguous theological message that preserved traditional doctrinal teachings. Kelley lauded the efforts of the Protestant ecumenical movement to forge a basis for Christian unity among various churches. However, he conceded that liberal-ecumenical movements, at their core, required their member churches to find common ground, sometimes at the expense of core doctrines. "Such ecumenical endeavors may be conducive to brotherhood, peace, justice, freedom, and compassion, but they are not conducive to conserving or increasing the social strength of the religious groups involved or—more important—the efficacy of the ultimate meanings which they bear."[2]

In the decades following its publication, Kelley's work served as a model for a host of writings by scholars and so-called "church growth" experts that sought to find ways for churches to reclaim a sense of theological vitality while also becoming "culturally relevant" to the needs of emerging generations of youth who increasingly were turning away from the faith of their parents. In the final quarter of the twentieth century, Americans became cognizant of what appeared to be new forms of Christianity embodied by a growing number of nondenominational megachurches. Increasingly, theologians spoke of American Christianity as passing through a phase that many called "postmodernism," and some predicted that Christianity, especially in its mainline forms, was in its final twilight. Many scholars spotlight the 1960s as a time when the social, cultural, and theological fabric of mainline religion completely unraveled, settling the context for late twentieth-century musings about the future of religion in America. Yet while the 1960s might have reflected endings, it also signaled the ways that Christianity, as it had been able to do in the past, was striking out in new directions.

JOHN COURTNEY MURRAY AND THE VATICAN II REFORM

Since the time of Sydney Ahlstrom, historians have commented on how the 1960s brought about a noticeable erosion of an earlier sense of mainline Protestant hegemony upon American culture. There is no doubt that numerous social-cultural events of the 1960s had a deep impact upon America's religious future, and two of the biggest factors affecting religion are ones that can easily be overlooked.

First, the 1962 and 1963 U.S. Supreme Court decisions of *Engel v. Vitale* and *Abingdon v. Schempp* struck down statutes upholding prayer and Bible reading in the nation's public schools. Since the early days of American public school education, Protestant leaders took for granted that these schools would serve as conduits to instill a Christian/Protestant worldview upon the nation's youth (a fact that drew the ire of many American Catholics). Yet as the nation's courts, and increasingly federal and state legislatures, made clear by the end of the 1960s, public education in America was to be decidedly secular and strove to avoid entanglement in First Amendment issues regarding the separation of church and state. Debates over the role of religion in public schools and within American civic life would continue over the next several decades as increasingly local municipalities debated an array of issues ranging from public displays of Christmas trees and nativity crèches to the extent to which the federal government could fund religiously sponsored social service programs.

The second major event that ultimately impacted the role of Protestantism was brought about by a change in decades-old immigration policy. In 1965 President Lyndon Johnson signed legislation that removed the nation's strict quotas on foreign immigration (quotas that initially had been enacted in the early 1920s). In the aftermath of this new legislation, waves of new immigrants from Africa, Latin America, and Asia came to the United States. These new immigrants not only brought to the nation a significant influx of people who practiced a range of non-Christian religions, but also immigrants with their own unique interpretations of Christianity. Increasingly, the growing religious diversity of the country, including a broad diversity among the nation's Christians, stoked fresh conversations among churches on questions of ecumenical and interfaith dialogue. Many of the most radical questions being raised on these themes came from global changes in the Catholic Church, changes that further signaled that the liberal-Protestant worldview of Harold Bosley was passing away.

One of the first stirrings of a new direction came from a Trappist monk who had converted to Catholicism as a young man: Thomas Merton. Born in 1915, Merton's life showed patterns reminiscent of Dorothy Day and Augustine in terms of his sexual promiscuity and how his faith and vocational quest ultimately led him to Catholicism and the decision to join a Trappist monastery in Kentucky. His 1949 autobiography, *The Seven Storey Mountain*, spoke to a generation of Catholics and non-Catholics who were seeking to find spiritual meaning in the aftermath of World War II and who felt a degree of ambivalence toward the growing social-cultural tensions of the Cold War era. In the years after the publication of his autobiography, Merton promoted his beliefs through an array of writings and, in the final years of his life, international travels that brought him in touch with many representatives of other world religions. Despite the antagonism he sometimes generated among his monastic superiors, Merton's writings made connections between Catholic mysticism with both the early-church desert fathers and themes that drew upon the insights of Zen Buddhism. His sudden death in 1968 (caused by accidental electrocution) came while he was attending an interfaith conference in Thailand.

Merton's popularity among Catholics and Protestants was a clear sign that earlier theological and cultural animosities between these two faith families were starting to thaw. While Merton's legacy would remain strong in America because of his writings on spirituality and mysticism, John Courtney Murray (1904–1967) represented a distinctive tradition of Catholic social teaching that would culminate in the worldwide Second Vatican Council of the Roman Catholic Church. Murray began his career as a Jesuit priest whose primary concern was the preservation of traditional Catholic teachings. By the 1950s, however, Murray's writings reflected a repeated emphasis that the Catholic Church needed to acknowledge religious freedom as a fundamental right of all citizens. Earlier Catholic social teachings often tended to ignore the value of Protestant social teachings (and even John Ryan, an individual who did acknowledge the importance of some representatives of the social gospel within his thought, tended to stress Catholic doctrine as the basis for the Church's social teachings). Murray angered many Catholics by noting that the task of building a just society was not simply consigned to the historical and theological truths within the Catholic tradition.

Murray's crowning achievement was writing a statement of religious liberty that became the American Catholic Church's central contribution to the Second Vatican Council. Held between 1962 and 1965, Vatican II introduced unprecedented reforms to Catholic liturgy (in particular, allowing the Mass to be read in the vernacular as opposed to the centuries-old tradition of Latin), while also allowing Catholics a degree of leeway to engage secular modernism. One of the major outcomes of Vatican II was how it allowed, and to a point encouraged, the Catholic Church to engage in ecumenical and interfaith dialogue. For Murray, the issue of religious freedom was not simply predicated on earlier traditions of Catholic natural law theory (as we saw earlier through the example of Thomas Aquinas), but was a foundation to any society, regardless of whether one was religious or not. "Christian freedom, as the gift of the Holy Spirit, is not exclusively the property of the members of the visible Church, any more than the action of the Spirit is confined within the boundaries of the visible Church."[3]

The newfound freedoms of American Catholics had mixed results. On one hand, many Catholics relished the liberal freedoms of Vatican II to take their ministries into the secular realm (one example being the fact that many female religious orders abandoned traditional habits in dress). On the other hand, some Catholics lamented the loss of tradition (such as the abandonment of the Latin mass), the perceived radicalism of many Catholic social activists, and the declining significance of earlier ethnic models of Catholic parish communities.

Part of the changes of Vatican II in the 1960s and 1970s reflected wider patterns of change that affected many of the nation's churches. While some Catholic leaders worried about the ways their tradition appeared to be embracing the modern world, both Catholics and Protestants were wrestling with the consequences of what one scholar called religious "restructuring,"[4] whereby the nation's older churches were challenged to rethink their mission and, in many cases, come to grips with an unprecedented array of theological voices within these traditions.

THE DECENTERING OF THE MAINLINE AND
THE COMING OF LIBERATION THEOLOGY

During the 1960s, reform-minded Catholics and ecumenically oriented Protestants increasingly found common cause not only in terms of a growing spirit of cooperation, but also a shared passion for civil rights advocacy in the early part of the decade and united in protests against the Vietnam War toward the end of the decade. Yet these political upheavals, combined with emerging debates about the youth counterculture of that time, were also causing fractures within numerous Protestant and Catholic churches. In 1964 President Lyndon Johnson won a landslide reelection, in part running on a platform that promised an unprecedented number of social and economic reforms modeled after Franklin Roosevelt's New Deal (what Johnson referred to as "the Great Society") and a pledge to limit American involvement in Vietnam. President Kennedy had sent American military personnel into Vietnam as early as 1961, and Johnson soon after his 1964 election took further measures to escalate American involvement in the war. By 1968 America had 500,000 ground forces in Vietnam and public opinion, once favorable toward American military intervention, had turned against the war.

At the same time that American churches debated issues such as the nation's involvement in Vietnam, the global ecumenical movement took a decisive turn against America's involvement in the war, growing increasingly critical of American foreign policies in general. For years, the Protestant ecumenical movement had been dominated by churches and church leaders from the West, especially from Northern Europe and the United States. By the 1960s, however, the tone of the ecumenical movement expressed a greater plurality of voices from churches in the southern hemisphere, especially from developing nations in South America, Africa, and Asia. Increasingly, these church leaders leveled criticisms at American political-economic policies, and in 1966 a Church and Society conference of the World Council of Churches, held in Geneva, Switzerland, condemned American military involvement in Vietnam and justified the use of violence by Christian communities fighting for liberation against Western imperialism.

This rhetoric was too radical for many American churches leaders. Paul Ramsey, an ethicist at Princeton Theological Seminary, wrote a scathing critique of the Geneva Conference and raised questions about the extent to which ecumenical assemblies could speak with authority to grassroots constituencies.[5] By the end of the 1960s, the majority of mainline Protestant churches adopted statements calling for American withdrawal from Vietnam even though many congregants in these churches supported the war. However, the spirit of anticolonialism that characterized aspects of the World Council of Churches' social agenda had its corollaries within America. The assassination of Martin Luther King Jr. in April 1968 brought despair to many Americans, but also brought to light a growing disillusionment of many African Americans with the perceived gradualism of King's nonviolent tactics. In the years leading up to his death, many young African Americans were drawn to the teachings of Malcolm X, seeing within his example not only a model of black political and economic liberation, but a wider lens to engage white racism both in America and globally.

Malcolm X was born Malcolm Little in 1925. His early life was characterized by the breakup of his family and an early life victimized by racism. While serving a jail sentence for armed robbery, Malcolm came under the influence of a small sectarian movement called the Nation of Islam. Under the leadership of Elijah Muhammad, the Nation of Islam embodied an unorthodox form of Islam that stressed a revised creation story (in which blacks were the chosen people and whites were devils) and a belief in black separatism. For all the ways that the Nation of Islam would garner attention for its militant stance against whites, the group embodied a distinctive historical tradition of African American nationalism that stretched back to such nineteenth-century religious leaders as the African Methodist Episcopal Church leader, Bishop Henry McNeal Turner (who called upon African Americans to return to Africa). After Malcolm's conversion to the Nation of Islam, he became the movement's most eloquent spokesperson, drawing headlines for his impassioned and often vitriolic sermons aimed at the sins of white America toward African Americans. Before his assassination in 1965, he broke from the Nation of Islam, became an orthodox Muslim (where he disavowed his earlier stance that white people were devils), and increasingly sought ways to build an international coalition of activists committed to the promotion of human rights for people of color.

While Malcolm X became more inclusive in the final years of his life, he never abandoned a sense that African Americans were part of a wider web of injustice that stemmed from larger Western practices of colonialism, imperialism, and racism. He also drew attention to the fact that while the nonviolent tactics of Martin Luther King Jr. were admirable, they were not enough to achieve the economic and political liberation of black people. In the years after his death, Malcolm X's ideals found their way into a variety of social movements, including emerging movements in American theology. In the spring of 1969, James Forman, a prominent leader of the Civil Rights movement, interrupted a service at Riverside Church in New York City with a "Black Manifesto," demanding that reparations be paid to African Americans for the past abuses of slavery and the ongoing abuses of racism. That same spring, African American seminarians at Colgate Rochester Divinity School (the same institution where Walter Rauschenbusch once taught) staged a lockout protesting the absence of black faculty and the lack of attention in the curriculum to the historical and theological currents of black theology. This evolving spirit of black nationalism had one of its chief spokespersons in American Christianity through the writings of James Cone.

Born in rural Arkansas in 1938, Cone remarked that his childhood exposed him to the unique theologies and rhythms of the black church experience. "I encountered the presence of the divine Spirit, and my soul was moved and filled with an aspiration for freedom."[6] Like Martin Luther King Jr. before him, Cone's education was largely in the North; he received a Ph.D. from Northwestern University in 1963. After teaching at Philander Smith College in Arkansas and Adrian College in Michigan, Cone moved to Union Theological Seminary in 1970 already established in what became known as black liberation theology. Cone's first two books, *Black Theology and Black Power* and *A Black Theology of*

Liberation, established many of the significant contours that characterized much of his subsequent work. Although in many ways indebted to
an earlier tradition of European crisis theology (in particular, the work
of Karl Barth and Paul Tillich), Cone's writing shows his strong indebtedness to Malcolm X. While African American leaders such as Martin
Luther King Jr. called for Christians to uncover the prophetic meaning of
Christianity in ways that lifted up a commitment to racial justice, Cone
called for a complete overhaul of Christian tradition that challenged his
readers to see African American suffering as paradigmatic of the gospel message of liberation. Cone castigated Christian theological traditions for ignoring the fact that the central tenet of Jesus' ministry was
his solidarity with those who experienced the brunt of suffering, and in
the context of America, this meant people of color. "There is no truth
in Jesus Christ independent of the oppressed of the land—their history
and culture," Cone asserted in his 1975 book *God of the Oppressed*, and
"in America, the oppressed are the people of color—black, yellow, red,
and brown. Indeed it can be said that to know Jesus is to know him as
revealed in the struggle of the oppressed for freedom."[7] For Cone and for
successive movements of liberation theology that emerged in the 1970s
and 1980s the challenge of theology was to move beyond grand metanarratives in discussions of Christian theology and to focus on the experience of the suffering and oppressed. This meant that theology, in order to
be valid, needed to speak to the experiences of American racism. As he
noted succinctly, "any interpretation of the gospel . . . that fails to see Jesus
as the Liberator of the oppressed is heretical."[8]

The theme of particularity, whereby theology focused upon the suffering and oppression of specific groups, became a dominant pattern in
formal theological studies in the aftermath of the 1960s. With important parallels to emerging movements of third-world liberation theologians such as Gustavo Gutiérrez in Latin America and C. S. Song in Asia,
American theologians in the 1970s and 1980s reflected a desire to explore
new theological directions from a liberationist perspective. In addition to a
burgeoning movement of black liberation theology spearheaded by James
Cone, the late 1960s brought the first stirring of what became known as
feminist theology.

Although the growth of feminist theology had much in common with
the larger national campaign for women's liberation in the 1960s, and the
failed movement in the 1970s and the early 1980s to pass an equal rights
amendment to the U.S. Constitution, many pioneering feminists picked

up on themes that had been used by women's rights activists since the nineteenth century. The most radical of the early feminist theologians was Mary Daly. While raised Roman Catholic, Daly's writings reflected a tradition of radical feminism that had much in common with the late nineteenth-century women's rights activist Matilda Joslyn Gage.

Along with Elizabeth Cady Stanton and Susan B. Anthony, Gage was one of the major leaders of the women's suffrage movement who also wrote extensively on the relationship between feminism and religion. In the mid-1890s, Gage was a contributor to Stanton's ambitious publication *The Woman's Bible,* an attempt by several prominent feminists to weed out of the Bible all its patriarch elements (very much like Jefferson's efforts in the early nineteenth century, it reduced the Bible to parts of the Old Testament and sections of the synoptic gospels). Yet Gage went further than Stanton's analysis when in 1893 she published *Women, Church and State,* a classic of late nineteenth-century radical feminism. Gage argued that the earliest human civilizations were based upon matriarchies that stressed social equality and wrote about how women's spiritual natures had flourished before the arrival of patriarchy. According to Gage, the values of male-dominated patriarchy (epitomized by Christianity) had hopelessly bonded the world within oppressive social structures that subjugated the voices and authority of women. Writing less than a century later, Mary Daly echoed these themes in a number of books such as *Beyond God the Father, Gyn/Ecology,* and *Pure Lust* that directly questioned whether Christianity as a religion could be redeemed.

A more mainstream type of religious feminism was advocated by another Roman Catholic, Rosemary R. Ruether. Ruether came of age as a scholar while a professor at Howard University in Washington, D.C. during the 1960s and her early work reflected her passions for civil rights and uncovering the history of Christian anti-Semitism. Like Daly, Ruether called to question the ways that male-dominated political, economic, and theological systems had corrupted the natural order of religion. Unlike Daly, however, Ruether called for the retrieval of an authentic Christianity through the elevation of women's experiences, while also reflecting on ways that Christianity could address a wide range of social-political issues. "The critical principle of feminist theology is the promotion of the full humanity of women. Whatever denies, diminishes, or distorts the full humanity of women is, therefore, appraised as not redemptive. Theologically speaking, whatever diminishes or denies the full humanity of women must be presumed not to reflect the divine or an authentic relation to the divine, or to reflect the authentic nature of things, or to be the message or work of an authentic redeemer or a community of redemption."[9]

Ruether's work was indebted to earlier models of social Christianity, reflecting a broad concern for political and economic justice—especially predicated on models of democratic socialism. As she noted in one of her most well-known books, *Sexism and God-Talk,* the goal of Christian feminism was to lead to a just society for women *and* men. "We seek a society that affirms the values of democratic participation, of the equal value of all persons as the basis for their civil equality and their equal access to the educational and work opportunities of the society. But more, we seek a democratic socialist society that dismantles sexist and class hierarchies, that restores ownership and management of work to the base communities of workers themselves, who then create networks of economic and political relationships."[10]

By the time Ruether published these words in 1983, an emerging generation of African American women critiqued first-generation white feminist theologians for their lack of engagement with the experiences of African American women. With a movement dubbed "womanist" (a term associated with the novelist Alice Walker), theologians such as Katie Canon and Jacquelyn Grant offered critiques of both traditional feminism (in particular, the work of Mary Daly) as well as the work of James Cone that spoke mostly of the experience of African American men.

While liberation theologians such as Cone and Ruether garnered a great deal of attention in theological seminaries, their work created suspicion among many mainline church leaders and embodied proof for some of how the church was moving further to the left on a number of social-political issues. At the same time, various tenets of liberation theology challenged many segments of American Christianity to reexamine their understanding of inclusivity. That is, was the goal of inclusiveness merely to allow others access to the church, or was it primarily about changing the ways of conceiving of the church?

Starting with the Presbyterian and Methodist churches in the mid-1950s and culminating with the acceptance of women's ordination in the Lutheran and Episcopal Churches, by the mid-1970s, mainline Protestant denominations (as well as Reform Judaism) had formally approved the ordination of women. Yet as more women entered theological seminaries in the 1970s and 1980s, questions arose about the extent to which women were truly welcome as clergy on an equal basis with men. In churches with a call system (that is, hired by the local church), women were often denied opportunities, while in churches under the appointment system (overseen by bishops), women often found it difficult to advance beyond entry-level congregations. As many mainline Protestant churches and liberal Catholics debated these issues over inclusiveness, several evangelical churches were devising strategies that led some people to believe that these once-disgraced evangelicals were in fact becoming the new American religious mainline.

EVANGELICAL PUBLIC RESURGENCE

Even at a time in the mid-twentieth century when many evangelical Christians focused their activities within a range of subcultures, they were hardly a minority presence in American Christianity. While liberal mainline denominations were growing in the 1950s, conservative denominations kept pace and often surpassed the growth of their mainline competitors. The successful use of mass media by evangelicals such as Billy Graham was duplicated by a wide range of conservative Christians who represented a cross section of theological currents historically associated with American evangelicalism. Additionally, many evangelical figures, such as Graham, developed strong followings among grassroots constituencies within the more liberal churches, much to the consternation of many mainline leaders. While the 1960s brought a sense of fragmentation to the mission of many mainline churches, for many evangelicals the social turmoil of the 1960s appeared to be a vindication of sorts for their missional direction.

The story of the Southern Baptist Convention (SBC) in the latter half of the twentieth century is indicative of that story. For much of its history, the SBC was seen by many northern churches (including northern Baptists) as a backwoods denomination that was isolated from the major theological battles that had beleaguered northern churches in the late nineteenth and early twentieth centuries. On one hand, the SBC's congregational polity allowed it a degree of flexibility in creating new churches that, at least until the early 1980s when the denomination moved to embrace a more stringent theological fundamentalism, forged a level of theological freedom of the local church from denominational control. By the same token, historically, liberalism never had the same impact upon the SBC as it did among northern Baptists, as much of the theology within the SBC was a mixture of earlier evangelical movements that carried forth variations of General and (mostly) Particular Baptist beliefs. Most importantly, however, by the mid-twentieth century, Southern Baptist churches were being established outside of the South. By the end of century, SBC congregations existed as far north as the state of Alaska.

The Southern Baptist Convention was a classic example of what Dean Kelley first pointed out in 1972, mainly, that strong commitment to certain doctrinal beliefs does matter—at least in terms of church growth. Even though the SBC passed the Methodist Church in the mid-1960s (the United Methodist Church in 1968) as the largest Protestant denomination in the country, this process of rapid growth had started several years earlier. As mainline churches struggled and cut back their commitments to foreign missions in the 1920s and 1930s, conservative churches such as the SBC poured money into missions, succeeding in building a range of successful missions in Africa and Asia. While mainly ecumenical denominations such as the Methodists, Presbyterians, Lutherans, and Congregational churches went through a series of mergers extending from the 1930s through the early 1980s, these efforts could not stave off the fact that the exclusive theology practiced by churches such as the SBC was effective in terms of numbers. In 1958 the membership of the SBC was approximately 9.2 million; by 1975 it was 12.7 million.[11]

Yet the evangelical resurgence of the 1960s and 1970s went beyond a discernable growth within traditionally conservative churches such as the Southern Baptist Convention. It was also accompanied by an emergence of what many commentators saw as a new phenomenon of the 1970s and 1980s, the nondenominational megachurch. In many ways, the prototype for this new paradigm of Christianity was the Willowcreek Community Church located in South Barrington, Illinois, a suburb of Chicago. The story of Willowcreek and its founding pastor, Bill Hybels, reflects upon an important aspect that has characterized much of the history of American evangelicalism: an ability to adapt its message to the culture that it simultaneously critiqued. As a young pastor in the early 1970s, Hybels was concerned about the disillusionment and alienation of many of his fellow baby boomers from several churches. Unapologetic in his insistence that he was trying to build a model of ministry for a target suburban audience, Hybels constructed a distinctive type of church at Willowcreek that did away with traditional worship styles and reshaped worship around the use of contemporary media—including popular music, drama, and sermons that were designed to be short but clear statements of how Christianity was essential to one's life in the contemporary world. By the end of the 1980s, Willowcreek was one of the nation's largest churches, and its success became the pattern for future iterations of American megachurches within both evangelical *and* mainline denominations (and Hybels' Willowcreek Association later developed a substantial following among both conservative *and* mainline church leaders).

Critics of the Willowcreek model castigated Hybels for his lack of prophetic acumen and for promoting an understanding of Christianity that elevated a corporate model of organizational success at the expense of theological integrity (in some ways this is reminiscent of the tradition of self-help Christianity associated with nineteenth-century figures such as Russell Conwell). Yet Hybels has consistently returned to the theme that Willowcreek is taking the timeless truths of the gospel and repackaging them in a way that connects to the suburbanites who are searching for meaning and who, by and large, were alienated from earlier historical iterations of Christianity. Behind all the media trappings of Willowcreek was nothing more than the old-time religion. Hybels emphasized that Willowcreek was not simply a place to follow a set tradition, but where followers could *experience* something that connected them to the world of the early church, where "the New Testament is happening right here in the town of Barrington, Illinois, and collectively we know that what Christ-followers for centuries have dreamed of we are getting to see up close and personal. . . ."[12]

In his own way, Hybels fits a unique late twentieth-century model of an old style of revivalism. From the evangelistic crusades of George Whitefield, the camp meetings of the Second Great Awakening, and even from liberal ministers like Henry Ward Beecher and Norman Vincent Peale, the free-market aspects of American religion have often necessitated innovation. While there is no doubt that many megachurch pastors who followed in Hybels' wake could be castigated for developing a model of Christianity that was predicated on preserving a vision of theological and cultural homogeneity, it is also true that the model of the megachurch provided inspiration for a disparate range of American Christians to engage in innovative missions by the latter decades of the twentieth century. One of them was an African American United Church of Christ minister Jeremiah Wright, who would build one of the largest megachurches in the country—the predominantly African American–based Trinity United Church of Christ in Chicago. Among those who would become a member of Trinity was the first African American president of the United States, Barack Obama.

EVANGELICAL POLITICAL ACTIVISM

Part of the success of these conservative churches in the 1970s and 1980s was not simply a sense of commitment to traditional theological beliefs, but also a growing convergence around a shared identity about America's social, cultural, and political future. While many liberal Catholics and Protestants wrestled over issues pertaining to Vietnam and the Watergate political scandal that forced the resignation of President Richard Nixon, other American Christians saw within the social-political crises of the time a clarion call for public action. Nowhere was this more acute than the political activism among a cross section of Protestant evangelicals who, in many ways, represented the vanquished churches and denominations stemming from the fundamentalist-modernist controversy of the 1920s. While many religious and secular liberals would see the public renewal of what became known as "the Religious Right" as a sudden emergence, it in fact represented how long-latent tendencies in American evangelicalism came to the surface.

Part of what characterized emerging networks of evangelicalism during the mid-twentieth century was the way that disparate streams within the movement began to coalesce theologically, organizationally, and politically. During the 1950s preachers such as Billy Graham combined both messages of Christian conversion with a desire to warn Americans about the dangers of communism. Although differences between pre- and postmillennialism still kept many streams of evangelicalism separate, the 1970s and 1980s witnessed a shared consensus among several evangelicals on social and political questions.

Later commentators on the "reemergence" of American evangelicalism in the 1970s and 1980s would note its conservative political tendencies. However, it is important to note that subsections of evangelicals also sought to align themselves with more liberal/progressive political causes. In the late 1960s and early 1970s, many younger evangelicals expressed a desire to connect traditional views of Christian doctrine with a call for evangelicals to support movements of civil rights and anti-Vietnam protests, leading to the establishment of the caucus Evangelicals for Social Action in 1973. This movement of progressive evangelicalism, associated with persons such as Ron Sider and Jim Wallis (the latter the editor of the influential periodical *Sojourners*), supported the 1972 presidential campaign of George McGovern. McGovern, whose father was a minister in the conservative Wesleyan Methodist Church, was drawn to the progressive liberalism of the social gospel while a graduate student at Northwestern

University (where he encountered the liberal preaching of Ernest Fremont Tittle at First Methodist Church in Evanston, Illinois).

Although McGovern's courtship of evangelical support was largely unsuccessful, the 1976 campaign of former governor of Georgia Jimmy Carter was a different story. Carter's political progressivism often took a back seat to the fact that he ran as a "born-again" Christian who not only spoke frequently about his Christian beliefs but backed them up through long-standing involvement in the local Baptist church of his hometown of Plains, Georgia. When *Newsweek* magazine claimed 1976 as the "Year of the Evangelical," Carter garnered a significant share of evangelical support in the South and in the "heartland" states of the nation, making him the first southerner to be elected president of the United States since post–Civil War Reconstruction. While Carter continued to reflect his strong Christian convictions during his presidency, economic and foreign policy crises, as well as Carter's own progressive politics, worked against him. By the end of the decade, evangelicals had found a new "born-again" champion in former California governor Ronald Reagan.

In the aftermath of President Jimmy Carter's presidential election, Jerry Falwell, a conservative Baptist minister in Lynchburg, Virginia, launched an organization called the Moral Majority in 1979. Falwell had built a successful ministry that for years was largely apolitical (although he vehemently opposed the direct-action campaigns of Martin Luther King Jr. in the 1950s and 1960s) and predicated on a dispensationalist brand of fundamentalist theology. Yet his sudden rise to national prominence reflected the fact that by the mid-1970s a cross section of evangelical Christians felt empowered to step into the public realm in a new way. On one hand, the Moral Majority was deeply troubled not just by the perceived godlessness of the counterculture of the late 1960s and early 1970s, but by a series of Supreme Court decisions, beginning with the school prayer cases of the early 1960s and culminating in the *Roe v. Wade* decision of 1973 that legalized abortion. Many late twentieth-century evangelicals saw the *Roe* decision as the decisive event that led to the galvanization of conservative Christianity into an organized political movement. Scholars have noted, however, that throughout the 1970s, many conservative churches, including the Southern Baptist Convention, said little about abortion in their policy statements, tending to see abortion primarily as a Catholic issue. Yet by the end of the decade, a pattern started to emerge whereby many conservative evangelicals such as Falwell, who previously had little interest in political engagement, were now stressing how American promiscuity embodied by two issues—legalized abortion and (increasingly) gay and lesbian rights—was indicative of how America had lost is moral compass. Conservatives such as Falwell talked about not only the need to challenge the social forces in America that were breaking down the traditional nuclear family, but also the mandate to stave off liberal political interests that were weakening America's moral resolve to stand firm in its battle against communism, as epitomized by the military threat of the Soviet Union.

What made the Moral Majority unique was not simply the way that it drew an array of fundamentalists such Falwell into its fold, but how it attracted an eclectic coalition of religious conservatives that included fundamentalists, pentecostals, conservative mainline Protestants, *and* Roman Catholics. Although Reagan himself never showed Carter's proclivity for involvement within a Christian fellowship (he had been raised in the Disciples of Christ and, by most accounts, was a nominal member of that tradition), his announcement during the 1980 presidential campaign that he too was "born again" had the desired effect. In 1980 Reagan scored a resounding victory over Carter, and the support he received from what became known in the 1980s as the "Religious Right" was critical to that success.

While the Moral Majority suffered a decline in organizational support during the 1980s, its initial success helped serve as a template for later efforts to bring together conservative Christianity and conservative politics. Activists who identified themselves with the agenda of the Moral Majority included Phyllis Schlafly, a Roman Catholic attorney who became one of the principal opponents of the ratification of a proposed equal rights amendment to the U.S. Constitution, and a pentecostal-leaning Southern Baptist minister named Pat Robertson.

By the mid-1970s, Robertson had built a media empire that revolved around his powerful Christian Broadcasting Network. Whatever theological differences may have divided them, Robertson and Falwell supported a shared vision of America as both militarily superior (to stave off the threat of communism) and, in the tradition of the Puritans, people who shared a covenant with God. Both also reflected a fixation among many evangelicals in their support of the state of Israel, seeing American defense of that nation as both a political *and* biblical necessity (as was discussed in the previous chapter, the establishment of the modern state of Israel in 1948 was seen by many dispensationalists as part of Bible prophesy that foreshadowed the end of the world). In the eyes of religious and secular liberals few distinctions were made about the theological mixing within the Moral Majority, and preceding Ronald Reagan's presidential reelection campaign in 1984, bumper stickers appeared declaring "*The Moral Majority is Neither.*"

What many Americans missed, however, was the way that this movement, despite its gradual decline in the 1980s, embodied its own form of religious pluralism. With its ability to build common cause among Christians that traditionally had been enemies (Protestant-Catholic, fundamentalist-pentecostal), the Moral Majority provided a taste of what was to come by century's end. Fidelity to conservative politics and "family values" rhetoric (often manifested in efforts to stave off laws that promoted the civil rights of gays and lesbians) served as an effective catchall for building deeply rooted coalitions that would follow in the wake of Jerry Falwell's Moral Majority.

SHIPS IN OPPOSITE DIRECTIONS?

Even as membership within the ecumenical-mainline churches continued to fall off in the 1970s and 1980s, mainline leaders did not stand idly by. United Methodist bishop and president of the NCC James Armstrong was paradigmatic of the mainline Protestant stance of the time. As a church leader, Armstrong's ministry was devoted to propagating the legacy of the social gospel. While still a local church minister, he had advocated against the Vietnam War, and upon his elections as a bishop and president of the NCC, Armstrong engaged multiple constituencies with the hope that the ecumenical churches could provide a prophetic social witness in the church, the nation, and the world. In an address to a group of United Methodist clergy in 1972, Armstrong accentuated the tradition of mainline theology that had been embodied by generations of Protestant leaders since the time of Walter Rauschenbusch. "The public servant needs to understand the fundamental claims of Christian love on his vocation," he asserted. "To the Christian, love and justice are one and the same. . . . Love and justice as demonstrated on the cross, righteousness as defined in the prophetic tradition, give the public servant his reason for being. His devotion to informed and unselfish love, his consistent determination to weave it into the laws and structures of society, validate his 'election' both theologically and politically."[13]

From the end of the 1960s until the end of the 1980s, this tradition of "public church" liberalism still had its major figures in American society. In addition to Armstrong, perhaps the most well-known embodiment of this tradition was William Sloane Coffin. Originally gaining fame as Chaplain of Yale University in the 1960s, in 1977 Coffin became senior pastor of the church that perhaps most epitomized the legacy of the liberal mainline, the Riverside Church, New York. In the context of the pulpit that represented the culmination of Harry Emerson Fosdick's career, Coffin continued to embody this legacy both in his preaching and social activism.

Yet Armstrong and Coffin in many ways represented a disappearing reality in the American religious landscape. Mainline churches in this period were not only dealing with dwindling resources of persons and money, but a continued inability to inculcate their values within mainstream America. Specifically, the theological and political currents expressed by groups such as the Moral Majority were not just coming from persons within the subcultures of evangelicalism. They were being expressed by many rank-and-file members within mainline churches. In the early 1980s, the NCC drew the ire from many conservatives for allegedly funding initiatives that supported leftist political regimes in Latin America and Africa. The situation continued to grow more tense in subsequent years as conservative caucus groups within several mainline churches protested against the doctrinal laxity of their denominations and their traditions' uncritical embrace of numerous currents of political secularism (often targeting various traditions of liberation theology). Often complaints of the perceived left-leaning denominations were met by calls from conservatives to withhold monies to denominational boards and agencies (as J. Gresham Machen had argued conservatives should have done back in the 1920s).

By the end of the 1980s, however, there were signs that the influence of the Religious Right was waning. Pat Robertson's attempt to win the Republican presidential nomination in 1988 went down in defeat, and a Democratic religious and social progressive (and a former associate of Martin Luther King Jr.), the Reverend Jesse Jackson, garnered as much support for his bid for the White House as did Robertson. Additionally, the election of George H. W. Bush, an Episcopalian who had little personal interest in cultivating a "born-again" religious rhetoric as had been the case with his two presidential predecessors, seemed to confirm that this period of religious conservative activism was winding down. However, the 1988 presidential campaign revealed another side to this alleged evangelical decline.

Bush's opponent in the 1988 presidential election was Michael Dukakis, Massachusetts' governor and a figure who embodied many of the political values associated with a long line of Democratic presidential candidates going back to Franklin Roosevelt in the 1930s. However, Dukakis' campaign was plagued by what one scholar dubbed "fatal composure," manifested in an inability to stave off accusations from the Bush campaign not only that Dukakis was too liberal, but that his worldview lacked the moral foundation that one received from a strong Christian background (an irony, given that Dukakis was the first Greek Orthodox candidate to run for president in American history). Garry Wills observed that Michael Dukakis was "the first truly modernist candidate in our politics" because of his affirmation both of a specific style of secular politics and his trust in human rationality and reason.[14] What is clear is that George Bush's campaign understood far better than Dukakis' that people's *perception* of religiosity in the public square matters. In the years after the election of George H. W. Bush, political conservatives would grow in their sophistication in how they addressed a range of political concerns, while often succeeding in framing the future of the nation along clear-cut political, theological, and cultural lines.

In many ways, Pat Robertson, more so than Jerry Falwell, represented the maturing of this perspective of an evangelical public theology. Part of what made the emergence of the Religious Right so effective was that it represented a coming together of traditions within evangelical theology that historically had been at odds. While Robertson, like Falwell, at times expressed himself in an idiom of premillennialism, his emergence by the end of the 1980s reflected what has been called a "Dominion theology," whereby belief in the end times was absorbed into a postmillennial belief not only in the exclusive role of America as a God-fearing people, but in the ways in which the Bible served as a basis for ordering the nation's democratic traditions. Even as the late twentieth century would continue to witness the popularity of earlier models of theological dispensationalism that spoke of the imperative to get Christians ready for heaven, many dispensationalists were drawn to a belief that one's salvation was connected to a need to promote a conservative political vision on earth.

In some ways, the Religious Right sought to claim the mantle of a chosen people that was reminiscent of the Puritan's earlier "City upon a Hill." And yet, by the end of the twentieth century, this politically conservative movement found itself challenged by ongoing and emergent realities of American Christianity—including by some within their own evangelical heritage.

≪ 15 ≫

Retraditioning—Again

In 2002 an evangelical minister named Rick Warren published a best-selling book, *The Purpose Driven Life*. As pastor of the Saddleback Community Church, a nondenominational megachurch in Lake Forest, California, Warren touched a nerve among many middle-class Americans that went beyond the confines of his theological tradition. On one hand, *The Purpose Driven Life* reflected an affinity with numerous late twentieth-century self-help (or twelve-step) movements, not to mention a connection to the historical currents of therapeutic Christianity. However, at the core of Warren's book was a straightforward fidelity to deeply rooted traditions of American evangelicalism, stressing that the central importance of one's life was to have a personal relationship with God through Jesus Christ—and leading others to have that same relationship. "Imagine the joy of greeting people in heaven whom you helped get there. The eternal salvation of a single soul is more important than anything else you will ever achieve in life. Only people are going to last forever."[1] Warren came out of a Southern Baptist background where he was deeply influenced by the ministry of W. A. Criswell, a prominent minister at the center of the fundamentalist takeover of the Southern Baptist Convention that occurred in the early 1980s. While Warren had a historical connection to fundamentalism, his wide-ranging popularity revealed how the face of evangelicalism, and American Christianity, was continuing to evolve.

The example of Rick Warren reflects upon how American Christianity stood in continuity with its past, even as it confronted new challenges as it entered the twenty-first century. For many theologians, the late twentieth century was a time when American Christianity was facing head on the throes of what was being termed "postmodernity," whereby earlier patterns of Christian belief and practice were coming to an end. One example of postmodernity was highlighted in 1990 by Stanley Hauerwas and William Willimon in one of the most talked about theological books of the decade, *Resident Aliens*. Seeing much of mainline Christianity's efforts of the past several decades as a "saccharine residue of theism in demise," the authors saw an end to a Christendom era and called for churches to embrace models of Christianity predicated on examples from the early church.[2]

Yet for all of the attention placed upon theologies of postmodernity, it could easily be said that the end of the twentieth century and the beginning of the twenty-first century represent the continuation of an ongoing reality—throughout American history, Christianity has always been changing, and it will continue to change. The coming of the twenty-first century reflected the continuation of patterns that seemed to confirm the arguments of scholars in the 1960s and 1970s that Christianity was facing a twilight era in the West. Mainline church attendance continued to fall off, and institutional citadels of power within the mainline, such as the NCC, as well as churches within the liberal Protestant denominations, not only struggled with declining members but also with shrinking financial resources. Roman Catholics not only were faced with the need to close or merge once-large urban parishes, but also were rocked by a worldwide pedophilia scandal among its clergy. Evangelicalism flourished in a new way, but in the first decade of the twenty-first century religious and secular commentators raised the question of whether evangelicalism would continue to play a dominant role in America's future or if it would implode. In the backdrop of this era was the emerging theme of Christianity's impact as a global faith, with an explosion of indigenous church growth in Latin America, Africa, and Asia that has made the global South the new center of the Christian world.

Yet for all the pessimism expressed about Christianity's future (and about religion in general), indications existed that Christianity in America would still play a significant role in twenty-first century American society. Sociologist Diana Butler Bass refers to the early twenty-first century as a time of "retraditioning," whereby people of faith are adapting to new cultural and contextual realities of an age characterized by an explosion of technologies, especially in telecommunication.[3] The terrorist attacks on the World Trade Center and the Pentagon on September 11, 2001, revealed both the sentiment of religious feeling in the nation and showed that the alleged religious consensus of a "Judeo-Christian" heritage spoken of by many Americans back in the 1950s was far more complex and confusing. Perhaps the major issue to consider at the close of the first decade of the twenty-first century is not whether Christianity will survive. Rather, the issue will be—as it has always been historically—where it is going.

EVANGELICALS ASCENDING—AGAIN

Ronald Reagan's presidency from 1981 to 1989 marked a visible public phase for American evangelicalism. Despite the fact that Reagan by his own admission was not an active churchgoer, his strong anticommunist stance and his conservative social and economic policies captured the political ethos of the 1980s. While earlier evangelicals such as Billy Graham strove to maintain a semblance of neutrality on political questions, the evangelical awakening of the 1970s and 1980s carried not only a strident sense of America's providential place in God's design, but an imperative to engage directly in political activism to achieve that vision.

For all the attention that Jerry Falwell garnered in the early 1980s, his star was quickly eclipsed by other Protestant evangelical leaders who acknowledged him as an important symbol of the Christian Right's emerging status, yet developed strategies that showed greater organizational sophistication and sounder long-range tactics. Perhaps the most influential figure to emerge out of the Religious Right in the late twentieth century was Ralph Reed. Born in 1961, Reed was involved in conservative politics at a young age and, in addition to earning a Ph.D. in history at Emory University in 1989, he emerged as the major strategist for a fledgling organization that arose out of the ashes of Pat Robertson's failed presidential campaign in 1988: the Christian Coalition. In the early 1980s, Jerry Falwell had succeeded by crafting an organizational model that galvanized a wide cross section of conservative Christian support. Reed not only built upon this model, but in many ways perfected the strategy. Although Pat Robertson was more the public face of the Christian Coalition, Reed served as the master strategist. While Reed shared Falwell's desire to elect Christian conservatives (or those sympathetic to a Christian conservative agenda) into national office, Reed placed equal value on electing conservatives on a grassroots level. By the mid-1990s, Reed's strategy appeared to be paying off, as increasingly conservative Christians not only won high-profile elections on a state and national level, but in local elections as well.

Reed's language reflected what was coming to be known in the 1990s as the "culture wars," in which Reed and other religious conservatives saw America as divided into two camps: those who affirmed a religious (Christian) vision of America predicated on what were perceived to be traditional American values, and those who stressed a pluralist, and what was often seen as a secular, vision of the future. Reed left no doubt that he spoke on behalf of many Americans who shared a consensus for the former. "Religious conservatives do not claim to have all the answers, but we do think we have identified many of the problems: illegitimacy, family breakup, cultural decay, crime, violence, and a poverty of spirit afflicting our land."[4] Yet while Reed joined other conservatives in castigating the problems with modern liberalism, he invoked many aspects of liberal Christianity's heritage as a justification for the public advocacy of the Christian Coalition. Central in this regard for Reed was the important role that he placed on the legacy of social Christianity, citing such figures as Walter Rauschenbusch, Reinhold Niebuhr, and, most especially, Martin Luther King Jr. as indispensable models for conservative Christian activism. Although somewhat vague in his understanding in his interpretation of the social gospel (for example, he identifies the theologically conservative William Jennings Bryan with this tradition), part of what Reed saw in earlier models of social Christianity was how these movements combined appeals to the moral conscience of the public, with the desire to advocate for political change. The full power of conservative evangelical political action was realized in the presidential elections of 2000 and 2004 when George W. Bush, a born-again Christian and the eldest son of George H. W. Bush, was elected and reelected as president.

Not all evangelicals welcomed these developments. Throughout the 1990s, a wing of progressive evangelicals such as Tony Campolo chided evangelicals for abandoning their rich heritage of social reform associated with the antebellum nineteenth century. This progressive wing of evangelicals also drew attention to the fact that the political agenda of the Christian Coalition appeared to equate the will of God with the Republican Party. "God is neither a Republican nor a Democrat" became a common message from Campolo, Jim Wallis, and other influential progressive evangelicals who increasingly found common cause with many liberal mainline leaders on several political issues.

At the same time, numerous public opinion polls conducted in the early twenty-first century continued to suggest that there was a correlation between one's theology and one's politics. In particular, data suggested a strong connection between political and theological conservatism. What these evangelical debates over politics missed, however, was that the face of American evangelicalism, always a diverse cacophony, was becoming even more difficult to categorize. In many ways, this diversity had much to do with the ongoing success of pentecostalism.

By the end of the twentieth century, pentecostalism had emerged as the fastest-growing movement of Christianity in the world. Part of what makes it difficult to track this movement is that pentecostal beliefs have become woven into the fabric of hundreds of religious movements worldwide, manifested in more traditional churches and denominations as well as in countless emerging forms of Christianity. In America, pentecostalism has spread through immigration, as has been the case with religious patterns in the past. Many practitioners of churches identified with pentecostalism come from historically marginalized groups and, in the tradition of William Seymour, the movement has found a home in numerous "storefront" churches in many urban areas of the country. Additionally, there were signs that pentecostal churches were pushing more into the fabric of the American middle class. While larger pentecostal churches such as the Assemblies of God embraced a more formal denominational structure (and to an extent, a decreased emphasis on the type of spiritual ecstasy so important to Seymour), several of its churches also moved toward a greater embrace of what was becoming commonly known as the prosperity gospel. While William Seymour's eschatological vision was of an inclusive fellowship, many iterations of late twentieth-century pentecostalism saw Christianity as a religious movement that promised its adherents personal happiness and wealth in life.

Yet the fires of pentecostal faith have also carried into a wide range of churches that blanket a broad national demographic. This pattern has been especially noticeable among many Hispanic immigrants. Consistent with demographic patterns in Central and South America, many Hispanic Americans have abandoned Catholicism for some form of pentecostalism—or have integrated pentecostal themes within their understanding of Catholicism.

CATHOLICISM AND PENTECOSTALISM
A Blended Religious Frontier?

Despite constant harassment from a Protestant culture that has often sought to marginalize its influence, the Roman Catholic Church has remained the single most dominant religious body in terms of membership and, as some would argue, in terms of that church's cultural influence. By the early twenty-first century, American Catholic membership stood at approximately sixty million, or almost a quarter of the American population. Historically, American Catholicism has found ways to adapt itself to changing cultural realities while also struggling with how to define the theological uniqueness of the Catholic experience. Like other Americans, Catholics have had to negotiate many of the paradoxes of defining the meaning of being a Catholic while also discerning how far to embrace aspects of a dominant Protestant culture. On one hand, the reforms of Vatican II reflected how many Catholics stood at the cultural center of the country, and surveys have shown how Catholic attitudes on social issues such as abortion and sexual orientation accentuate beliefs in line with a more liberal, progressive orientation. One striking example of this moderation can be seen in 1984 by New York governor Mario Cuomo's support for abortion rights. Cuomo built a strong reputation as a progressive reformer on both economic and social issues. Yet Cuomo was also a Catholic and drew the ire of many conservatives when he came out publically in support of preserving a woman's right to choose whether or not to have an abortion. Although Cuomo's views were staunchly condemned by numerous Catholic leaders (including Cuomo's own bishop in New York), the fact that Cuomo and the eventual Democratic Party candidate for vice president in 1984, Geraldine Ferraro, another Roman Catholic, continued to advocate for legalized abortion rights showed that American Catholics, at least as individuals, were not following the teachings of their church.

On another level, however, the years after Vatican II saw a succession of popes and cardinals who stressed fidelity to traditional Catholic teachings, and many of these conservative positions found a hearing among American Catholics. In addition to affirming age-old teachings of papal infallibility, the Church has sought to move global Catholicism further away from the reforms of Vatican II. By the early twenty-first century, little evidence suggests that the Catholic hierarchy will yield to pressure advanced by many American Catholics who have called for an end to clerical celibacy and that the church hierarchy open up debate over the question of the ordination of women. By the end of the twentieth century, American Catholic bishops were largely dominated by conservatives who made it clear that they were not interested in any sort of discussions on issues that they believed had already been settled through the Holy See of Rome. In 1996, Cardinal Joseph Bernardin, one of the major American Catholic leaders within the tradition of Vatican II, sought to open a dialogue between liberal and conservative Catholics through what he called the Common Ground Initiative. Bernardin's effort to create a public conversation over issues that divided American Catholics, such as abortion, gay and lesbian rights, and women's ordination, drew a rebuke from several conservative Catholic cardinals and bishops. The head of the Boston archdiocese, Cardinal Bernard Law, noted tersely that "dissent from revealed truth or authoritative teaching of the church" was not something up for dialogue, in effect asserting that these matters of church tradition were not and would never be open for debate.[5]

By 2002, however, public revelations of sexual misconduct and pedophilia rocked many Catholic dioceses and drew anger from many American Catholics who feared that their church was out of touch with the realities of contemporary life. The clergy sexual misconduct scandal revealed that many high-ranking Catholic leaders knew about the abuses of priests and failed to act (one of whom was Cardinal Law, who resigned in 2003 from his position as head of the Boston archdiocese).

However by the early twenty-first century, American Catholics were not only struggling like Protestant churches with a declining membership (reflecting in a decline of priests, nuns, and the closing of many historic parishes), but the defection of many Catholics to pentecostal churches, a reality that was especially evident among recent immigrants from Latin America. Since the sixteenth and seventeenth centuries, Hispanic Catholic communities have been firmly rooted in what is now the southwestern United States, and by the end of the twentieth century these communities were a foundation for continued Hispanic immigrant Catholic growth. Demographic studies have suggested that Americans of Hispanic origin might very well reflect the majority of Americans by the late twenty-first century, and the arrival of Hispanics in recent decades from Mexico and other parts of Latin America has had a profound impact on the nation's religious demographics. On one hand, the vast majority of Hispanic immigrants were raised in strongly Catholic nations, and on the surface, these Catholic loyalties have been transferred to the United States. Yet many of these recent immigrants have also turned to various forms of pentecostalism, a movement that not only continues to flourish in the United States, but also reflects a series of traditions that have been growing exponentially in Latin America for several decades.

What is fascinating, however, is while the Catholic Church has sought to stave off the influence of pentecostalism, many Catholics find within pentecostalism a natural meeting place to combine themes of a deep-seated tradition of Catholic spirituality and pentecostal ecstasy. In the late twentieth century, one scholar who drew attention to the wide-ranging appeal of pentecostalism was Harvard professor Harvey Cox. In the mid-1960s, Cox had been trying to make sense of how theological traditions would survive a growing age of secularization in the West. In 1965 his best-selling work, *The Secular City*, not only saw the collapse of institutional religious meaning, but raised the question of how religion would survive a secular age. By the early 1990s, Cox had revised his judgment noting that pentecostalism forced him to rethink whether it was secularism that was on the verge of extinction in America. The growth of pentecostalism reflects not only the power and appeal of religious ecstasy, but very much like Catholicism, it is a movement that relies heavily on premodern views of religious experience, as opposed to many Protestant traditions that stress the centrality of written traditions centered upon various interpretations of the Bible.

Part of Catholicism's greatest success in America was the means by which it allowed disparate groups of Americans to experience the divine, while also preserving aspects of one's own cultural tradition (and the late twentieth-century growth of Hispanic Catholicism reflects a unique iteration of earlier nineteenth-century models of the ethnic parish). For all the contemporary crises in the Catholic Church, the tradition has continued to speak to perhaps the widest range of Americans—even as it has been attacked historically by a dominant Protestant culture for the perception that its values lie outside an alleged cultural mainstream. For several Americans, Catholicism speaks to many who yearn for experiencing the mystery of the sacred through ancient tradition *and* popular practices. At the end of the twentieth century, some Americans noted that it wasn't only the Catholic Church that had a monopoly on these ancient traditions.

ORTHODOXY
A Third Christian Option?

Historically, the break between the Roman Catholic Church and the Eastern Orthodox churches occurred in 1054. In reality, however, historical patterns caused a separation between these two historical wings of Christianity much earlier. While part of the division revolved around which ecclesiastical head would have ultimate authority over the Church (the Bishop of Rome of the West or the Ecumenical Patriarch of Constantinople of the East), important theological and liturgical differences emerged as well. Eastern Orthodoxy developed a more nuanced doctrine of the church's sacraments (although by the early twenty-first century, most Eastern Orthodox communions affirmed the Roman Catholic tradition of seven sacraments) as well as different perspectives on historical doctrines such as Christology, the Trinity, salvation, and, most especially by the seventh and eighth centuries, the role of iconography in the Christian life. Yet perhaps the biggest difference between the two was that although Catholicism found itself historically in competition with other forms of Christianity (mostly Protestants), the majority of Orthodox churches remained heavily tied to national and ethnic identities. Consequently, for much of American history, Orthodox churches in America have existed mostly as small ethnic enclaves representing a range of faith communities coming from Eastern Europe.

For most of American history, churches associated with the historical traditions of Eastern Orthodox Christianity have been a tiny minority in the country. The earliest Russian Orthodox churches were located in Alaska (dating back to when the future state of Alaska was owned by Russia), and a small number of Greek Orthodox churches in Florida and Louisiana that date from the eighteenth and nineteenth centuries. In the late nineteenth century, a handful of Greek Orthodox churches were established in the Upper Midwest (Minnesota), finding a hostile reception from both their Protestant and Catholic neighbors. In the early twentieth century, there were only about 50,000 adherents to Eastern Orthodoxy in the United States (mostly coming from Greek and Russian Orthodoxy). Throughout the twentieth century, Orthodox churches and traditions grew slowly, representing national Orthodox communions that included Greek, Russian, Serbian, Romanian, Armenian, Coptic, and Ethiopian.

Much of Orthodoxy's growth, comparable to the Catholic Church, has been related to immigration (and even more so than the history of Catholicism, many Orthodox immigrants were refugees from political persecution, especially from communist-bloc countries in Eastern Europe). Although American Orthodox churches comparable to the Roman Catholic Church often defined their communities around ethnic parishes, the Catholic tradition of parish missions, a model of evangelism so vital to the spread of the Catholic Church in the nineteenth and early twentieth centuries, was missing from Eastern Orthodox communities. Additionally, Orthodox communities suffered increasing fragmentation along lines of ethnicity and over questions of ecclesiastical control and supervision. By the early twenty-first century, debates existed as to the exact number of Orthodox adherents in the United States, with a high estimate at six million and a low estimate of only 1.2 million.

Part of the discrepancy in membership data is that many Orthodox parishes define their membership rolls upon the size of one's family (assuming that because the parents were raised in a particular parish, so would their children). Yet second and third generation immigrants from traditionally Eastern Orthodox countries have confronted a drift away from the earlier traditions that formed their parents and grandparents— a reality that has characterized many immigrant churches throughout American history.

Even as membership has apparently leveled off by the early twenty-first century, there have been tentative signs that some Orthodox churches are drawing converts from outside of ethnic enclaves. Certain Orthodox churches have shown a willingness to embrace members from outside of a specific ethnic group, and the liturgical power of many Orthodox communions has appealed to what some scholars have seen as the desire of Americans to embrace premodern expressions of Christianity. While Scripture is not abandoned, it is channeled through the experiential, holding up for adherents a deeply mystical genre of faith. One of the most interesting questions of the twenty-first century will be to see how the churches associated with Eastern Orthodoxy will respond to the American context. Will these churches remain largely sectarian, or will they, like other American churches before them, extend their mission beyond ethnic enclaves?

CHRISTIANITY AND POSTMODERNISM

In the twilight of the twentieth century, mainline denominations still advocated for a number of social justice initiatives associated with earlier movements of liberal Progressivism (such as the official policy statements coming from mainline Protestant churches and the Roman Catholic Church in the 1970s and 1980s on the imperative of nuclear disarmament). However, a growing number of theologians questioned if Christianity could survive in America while carrying on this earlier model of public theology associated with mid-twentieth-century figures such as Reinhold Niebuhr. The belief that mainline Protestantism could no longer speak to core American social, political, and cultural values was seen by some as part of the general malaise of postmodernity.

While numerous theologians used the term "postmodernity" to define the religious context of the late twentieth century, often they were unclear about what they meant by the term. Generally, postmodernism is a term that defines the larger eclipse of grand historical and intellectual narratives for understanding ultimate reality. In particular, postmodernism was seen by many as abandoning faith in a modernist-rationalist worldview to shape meaning. In the realm of Christianity, the term is often used to designate the collapse of an earlier taken-for-granted intellectual worldview centered upon clearly delineated historical and theological standards of universal truth. Further, the fall of the Soviet Union in 1991 reflected a degree of disillusionment with earlier models of theology predicated on Marxist theory and the championing of democratic socialism—and signaled a reaction by some theologians not to abandon the essential truth claims of the gospel. As theology at the end of the twentieth century continued to look to questions of the particular, as it dealt with a range of traditions associated with black, feminist, womanist, and gay and lesbian theologies, several theologians emerged who critiqued how the universality of the gospel message was being lost amid the increasing fragmentation of postmodern America.

Theologically, postmodernism often became associated with a wide range of thinkers who often had little in common other than a belief that an era of Christian history had come to an end. Postmodern theologians often were united on a couple of central suppositions. First, they emphasized what they perceived to be the collapse of larger metanarratives that had served as the intellectual foundations of truth in previous historical periods. Studies by a range of scholars pointed increasingly to the ways that modern Americans were largely listless and had come to distrust in traditional faith narratives to guide the lives of individuals and communities. Several scholarly and popular works in the late twentieth century noted what appeared to be the lack of religious and moral certainty among the baby boom generation on matters of faith. In 1985, Robert Bellah and a team of researchers published *Habits in the Heart,* a book that reported on how many baby boomers appeared to be guided by an erosion of meaningful traditions to guide them in their moral and spiritual discernment. In one of his more famous illustrations, Bellah talked about a young woman named Sheila whose individualistic and uncritical appropriation of different fragments of religion he referred to as "Sheilaisms."[6] In terms of religion, this often meant an individualistic application of tradition that had little to do with fidelity to the values of a faith community, but merely one's personal fulfillment.

Part of what Bellah's research pointed toward was an increasing emphasis among young generations to speak vaguely about the importance of a spiritual worldview while also showing a lack of trust in the power of religious traditions to form and shape meaning. In many ways, the mantra of the late twentieth century "I'm spiritual, not religious" was a theme picked up by many postmodern theologians who saw in this type of rhetoric the utter failure of an earlier Christian worldview to shape a new generation of believers.

Second, postmodernist theologians tended to stress that the late twentieth century was witnessing the rapid disintegration of a "Christendom" worldview, a belief that Christian institutions could no longer rely on the support of a "Christianized" culture to support the dominant cultural, usually Protestant, worldview of the church. Indicative of these themes was the influence of Stanley Hauerwas. An ethicist at Notre Dame and later Duke Divinity School, Hauerwas challenged the "Christ the Transformer of Culture" suppositions of 1950s Protestant spokespersons such as Reinhold and H. Richard Niebuhr. Hauerwas believed that liberal-Protestant public theology was no longer in a position to speak to the conscience of the larger society. Amid the complete failure of Christendom to transform the world to its point of view, what was needed were churches that committed themselves to a strict reinterpretation of theology to draw a clear distinction between the church and the secular society. With a theology that often reflected upon themes coming out of Catholic natural law theology, Hauerwas embodied a tradition of ethics that defined its mission not by earlier Protestant attempts to convert the world to its point of view, but by how Christians might bear witness to the possibilities of a just world through the faithful witness of the church.

While people gravitated to the sectarian leanings of theologians such as Hauerwas, many denominations still struggled with how best to accommodate these postliberal perspectives into their missions—and whether or not it was possible to let go of earlier historical iterations of the mainline. A book that reflected the struggles of many Protestant leaders over the perceived decline of the mainline was Loren Mead's *The Once and Future Church* (1991). Mead discussed how American Christianity was finding itself at the end of a "Christendom Paradigm" and how religious leaders in the twenty-first century must face the challenge of constructing new models of Christianity for a changing world. Part of Mead's analysis was to point out what he saw as the long-standing disconnect between denominational leaders (and clergy in general) with rank-and-file membership. "A new church is being born. *It may not be the church we expect or want.* The church of the future may not include our favorite liturgy or hymn, our central theological principle, or even our denomination!"[7] Behind Mead's assertions and a subsequent spate of books on church growth and church renewal that followed in the 1990s was his belief that churches needed to become more improvisational in their leadership, especially focusing on the needs of local congregations to develop missions that reflected one's unique context of ministry. As opposed to a Christendom age that often saw ministry through the channeling of resources through denominational boards and ecumenical agencies, the church of the future would encounter a mission field where ministry would begin at the church's front door.

Part of what connected many disparate commentators on postmodernity, whether from theologians or church leaders, was a sense that religion in America was encountering unchartered waters. Often there was a tendency to see previous historical benchmarks as irrelevant to the new social realities facing American Christianity. Yet as mainline church leaders lamented the perceived loss of their public voice, many evangelicals such as Rick Warren were garnering mass attention from diverse cross sections of the American public. In the mid-twentieth century, it was mainline Protestant leaders such as Reinhold Niebuhr that were featured on the covers of the nation's major secular periodicals. By the early twenty-first century, evangelicals such as Rick Warren had replaced figures like Niebuhr with that distinction. These changes raise a question at the beginning of the twenty-first century: are mainline-church fortunes a consequence of postmodernity or a sign of Christianity's adaptation to new historical circumstances?

FINDING GOD IN AMERICA
Christianity in the Early Twenty-First Century

While some church leaders saw the dawn of the twenty-first century as the end of modernity, some commentators and intellectuals sought to remind Americans not to abandon the legacy of modernity, especially its emphasis on universal standards of reason. By the early twenty-first century, scholars (and atheists) such as Richard Dawkins and Christopher Hitchens published a range of books that not only challenged the validity of religious belief, but saw religion as the basis for many of the world's historical problems. Hitchens' *God Is Not Great* saw continued fidelity to religion to be blamed for just about every problem in human history (including the genocidal regimes of Hitler and Stalin). Yet even as survey data in the early twenty-first century point to a rise in the number of Americans who claim no formal religious beliefs, popular indicators still point to the public's interest on matters of religion and aspects of Christian tradition.

In the early twenty-first century, popular scholars and church leaders such as Marcus Borg and John Shelby Spong were attempting to recast more traditional understandings of Christianity in ways that were decidedly modern. Borg and Spong attracted a following based on the ways that they sought to mine the sources of Christian tradition without succumbing to a faith predicated on an uncritical supernaturalism. An Episcopal clergyman and longtime bishop of the diocese of Newark, New Jersey, Spong gained attention, and at times controversy, for his insistence that the future of Christianity lay in the ability of its followers to separate the faith from its moorings in outdated traditions and doctrines. Part of Spong's agenda was to challenge various factions of evangelical Christianity on questions of theology and politics. Frequently castigating conservative suppositions on issues such as homosexuality, abortion, and a literal interpretation of biblical miracles, Spong was adamant that the Christian church of the twenty-first century needed a more realistic and prophetic assessment of Christianity. "I want to provide our world with a new way to look at and to enter the essence of this faith," he noted in 1996. "I do not believe that the Christian life can be so narrowly defined that those who probe and question traditional conclusions are to be judged, by the narrow-minded believers of yesterday's popular Christian assumptions, to be non-Christians or even heretics."[8] By the early 2000s, Spong and other Christians associated with various liberal movements increasingly were identified under the label of "Progressive Christianity." This category, embodied by numerous organizations such as the Network of Spiritual Progressives, reflected an interfaith coalition of religious leaders committed to causes such as abortion and gay, lesbian, bisexual, and transgendered (GLBT) rights as well as a wide range of progressive political policies.

By the same token, many members of mainline denominations reacted strongly against the activism of figures such as Bishop Spong and the majority of mainline churches were represented by caucus groups that viewed part of their mission to bring their churches in line with traditional "biblically based" theological values and doctrines. In part, these groups represented a continuation of conservative agitation that had existed in many mainline churches since the early twentieth century. However, by the end of the twentieth century many of these conservative caucuses showed their effectiveness in both membership recruitment and in becoming an influential voice within the citadels of the mainline. In 1993 an ecumenical women's conference was held in Minneapolis, Minnesota, under the theme of "Reimagining." This clergywomen's gathering featured many prominent feminist theologians who explored alternative images for God (stressing the tradition of divine wisdom, or Sophia, as a metaphor to explore the nature of God). Vitriol erupted almost immediately as several mainline church leaders condemned the gathering as nothing more than a pagan ritual that undermined the foundations of historical Christianity. In large measure, these debates continually circled back to divisions over GLBT rights within mainline churches.

Until the 1970s, most mainline churches had little to say about issues of sexual orientation. However, with a growing movement of gay and lesbian rights emerging by the end of the 1960s (as well as agitation by groups such as the Christian Coalition), churches began to pay more attention to the issue. Increasingly, many mainline churches such as the United Methodist Church and the Presbyterian Church consistently affirmed policies that placed restrictions on openly gay individuals being ordained. One response to this issue was the formation in the late 1960s of the Metropolitan Community Church (a church founded by an openly gay former pentecostal preacher, Troy Perry), a fellowship that defines its ministry primarily along the lines of its outreach and advocacy to GLBT persons. By the beginning of the twenty-first century, mainline Protestant debates over questions of sexual orientation represented one of the most divisive issues for churches, and it remains to be seen if this issue will represent a further fragmentation of the mainline as the century progresses.

Even with tension over questions of human sexuality dominating the agenda of many Protestant and Catholic churches, new forms of Christianity were gaining popularity. Yet another response to the new century went by the name "Emergent Church." Rather than being an organized denominational movement, the Emergent Church represented a disparate range of movements often made up of persons on the perimeters of mainline and evangelical Christianity who sought to find meaning and vitality within a range of Christian traditions. At the center of this movement was an evangelical minister, Brian McLaren. On one hand, McLaren represented a genre of progressive evangelicalism in the tradition of Jim Wallis and Tony Campolo. Not only did McLaren show a remarkably irenic posture toward theological liberalism, he also displayed a desire to combine various elements of Christian tradition—including drawing on the distinctive liturgical practices coming from Catholicism and Orthodoxy.

While the emergence of megachurches often reflected a disillusionment with earlier forms of Christian tradition (and, in a sense, the desire to break away from more traditional forms of Christianity), the Emergent Church movement reflected a desire to experiment with earlier traditions, in particular, the desire of these communities to "re-create" the feel of the early church (most notably traditions of "house" churches). Part of the appeal of the Emergent Church movement is that it ties into a strong emphasis on lay leadership—and in many ways a desire to forsake formal clergy leadership altogether (in a sense reminiscent of leadership patterns that occurred in previous historical great awakenings).

As has been a pattern throughout American history, the religious landscape of the early twenty-first century is not dominated by one particular model. The ongoing popularity of the megachurches and the Emergent Church movement reflect two unique expressions of what Christianity might resemble in the future. Yet American Christianity in the early twenty-first century is still epitomized by a diffuse mix of congregations representing a wide range of theological perspectives, social locations, ethnic-cultural identities, and worship practices. By the second decade of the twenty-first century, the size and diversity of American Christianity was easily overlooked amid continued efforts by religious leaders and scholars to discern contemporary patterns and predict future trends.

« Epilogue »

Seeing the Future through the Past

In January 2009 Barack Obama was inaugurated as the first African American president of the United States. While growing up indifferent to religion, Obama came to embrace a specific heritage of African American Christianity and understood well the importance of a faith-based (loosely Christian) civil-religious language to achieve political and electoral success. At Obama's inauguration, the invocation was offered by Rick Warren. In keeping with previous traditions at presidential inaugurals, Warren evoked a highly Christocentric prayer (embodied by the fact that he concluded his invocation with the Lord's Prayer). Yet he reflected upon a larger history of American Christianity that stressed God's blessings upon America while also lifting up the prophetic mandate that America stood under divine judgment. If one listens carefully, one can hear in Warren's words the faint echoes of John Winthrop's address on the *Arbella* from 1630:

> Help us, oh God, to remember that we are Americans. United not by race or religion or by blood, but by our commitment to freedom and justice for all. When we focus on ourselves, when we fight each other, when we forget You, forgive us.
>
> When we presume that our greatness and our prosperity is ours alone, forgive us. When we fail to treat our fellow human beings and all the earth with the respect that they deserve, forgive us. And as we face these difficult days ahead, may we have a new birth of clarity in our aims, responsibility in our actions, humility in our approaches and civility in our attitudes—even when we differ.[1]

The image of Barack Obama joining hands with Rick Warren serves as an appropriate image to conclude this study. The connection between Obama and Warren, while perhaps offering hope that Christians from differing theological contexts may find common ground over the next century, also suggests that the future of American Christianity, as has been the case in the past, is filled with unknowns. During Obama's 2008 presidential campaign, he frequently spoke of the connection between his political commitments to an activist tradition of Christianity most often associated with Reinhold Niebuhr. Also, Obama's minister in Chicago was Jeremiah Wright, pastor of a large African American megachurch that embraced a legacy of progressive Christianity with deep roots in the liberalism of the social gospel and in the historical legacy of the black church.

During the summer of 2008, Obama was criticized for his association with Wright after one of Wright's sermons went viral on the Internet. Over several weeks, Americans were exposed to sound bites of Wright uttering the angry refrain, "God damn America!" at the end of his sermon. Faced with mounting political pressure, Obama severed his connection to Wright. While this decision perhaps was necessary in order for him to build the coalition that ultimately led to his victory in the presidential election of 2008, the episode underscored the failure of many Americans to comprehend a theology that spoke in a way that challenged the sacred connection between religion and the nation's purpose. "When it comes to treating the citizens of African descent fairly, America failed. She put them in chains. The government put them on slave quarters. Put them on auction blocks. Put them in cotton fields. Put them in inferior schools." As Wright continued to provide a litany of abuses of white Americans against people of color, he came to a crescendo as he reflected upon the historical and contemporary problems of race in America. "The government gives [African Americans] the drugs, builds bigger prisons, passes a three strike law and then wants us to sing God Bless America. Naw, naw, naw. Not God Bless America. God Damn America! That's in the Bible. For killing innocent people. God Damn America for treating us citizens as less than human. God Damn America as long as she tries to act like she is God and she is Supreme."[2]

Amid the reactions that followed the surfacing of Wright's sermon, a few media pundits critiqued Wright as a left-leaning "reverse racist" who was influenced by the leftist ideology of figures such as James Cone. While Cone's legacy could be heard in that sermon, there are other influences present as well. You can hear in Wright's words the prophetic critique of much of the tradition of the twentieth-century social gospel with its reliance on the themes of the fiery Old Testament prophets. You can hear the cadence of numerous representatives of nineteenth-century evangelicalism, which believed that God's righteousness could only manifest itself if the nation wiped away social evils such as slavery. And most especially, you can hear within Wright's words the heart and soul of two centuries of the black church experience in America, including the voices of countless slave preachers such as Nat Turner, as well as numerous African American leaders such as Richard Allen and Frederick Douglass who found their faith an indispensable resource to fight for justice in a society fragmented and torn by racial injustice.

The Wright incident underscores a clear insight about the context of the early twenty-first century and of American history, in general. As historian Stephen Prothero has noted, for all the ways that Americans love to be religious, it is a nation that is not well informed about religion, particularly when it comes to its own religious heritage.[3] The terrorist attacks on New York City and Washington, D.C. on September 11, 2001, underscored the best and worst aspects of American religion, and Christianity in particular. On one hand, many of the nation's churches were speaking of the need for religious toleration and seeking to provide a prophetic and pastoral witness to their Muslim neighbors. Yet other Christian voices used the occasion to speak of the terrorist attacks either as a form of divine judgment upon the nation, or as a rallying cry to a superficial patriotism that stoked memories of Americans as a chosen people whose mission was nothing short of redeeming the world. Yet instead of framing these post-9/11 reactions along the lines of "good" versus "bad" religion, I believe it is more helpful for us to see these reactions as examples of how devout and pious persons are often selective about how they understand and interpret their traditions—in terms of both what they tell and what they leave out.

I believe that one reason future historians will continue to turn to Sydney Ahlstrom—and many of the historians discussed in this volume—is because Ahlstrom not only framed a compelling interpretation of the past, but (willingly or unwillingly) projected his own anxieties and hopes for how religion, particularly American Christianity, would continue to impact the future. In concluding this work, I am not trying to predict the future (Ahlstrom, among others, was insistent that no good historian should do so), but provide a sense of how this narrative might be of value to someone who reads this book in the distant future. The summation that follows represents my belief that many of the themes that I have discussed in this book will still be present—even as the institutional realities faced by faith communities will continue to change and evolve.

First, if one takes seriously the resiliency and adaptability of the Puritan intellectual heritage in American history, then one must not dismiss the possibility that this ideal will continue to adapt to the cultural realities of the twentieth-first century. Sydney Ahlstrom recognized in the early 1970s that America was in the twilight of its fidelity to a Protestant Puritan narrative dominating the nation's religious terrain, and many historians since Ahlstrom's day have noted ways in which the country's religious makeup has moved away from this central historical narrative. Yet, for better or worse, the appeal of that tradition has been slow to disappear in American history; the contours of that earlier Puritan tradition are alive and well and evident within the fabric of early twenty-first-century American life. Since the 1970s, scholars of American religion have justifiably critiqued this Puritan narrative, and have often been adamant in wishing that it would die out. However, there are still plenty of signs in the twenty-first century that this ideal isn't quite dead yet. The theological ideals of a divine covenant, America as a chosen people, and the imperative to use Christianity to perfect the world have not disappeared from the American landscape.

Beyond the connection of Puritanism to what can be dubious ideologies of American exceptionalism, it is also important that the echoes of this legacy have been heard not simply in the rhetoric of conservative Christian groups like the Christian Coalition, but also through the witness of what could be called "Progressive Christianity." For all their differences in historical and social contexts, figures such as Ralph Waldo Emerson, Frances Willard, Walter Rauschenbusch, Reinhold Niebuhr, Georgia Harkness, and Martin Luther King Jr. believed that there were inherent truths within Christianity that called upon Americans to envision how the resources of that legacy could lead to a just world. The achievement of that vision would occur not simply through individual morality, but by calling upon persons to use the resources of Christianity to envision a better society—personally *and* communally. As we have seen, that quest has engaged a variety of Christian movements since the time of the Puritans and it would be premature to see this theme disappearing from American history any time soon—even as the demographics of American religion and society will continue to evolve and change.

Additionally, while this book does reflect the historian's concern to find a representative range of voices and perspectives, Christianity at its best and worst has largely been about the faith of people whose beliefs and practices may or may not be in synch with what "formal" religious bodies teach the faithful. There is no denying that much of the history of American Christianity has been a series of popular movements that have sought to supplant more dominant movements of religion. Yet part of what the history of popular religion reveals is how new and emerging religious movements have the ability to reinvigorate earlier faith traditions. The history of dispensationalism is especially instructive in this regard. Since its inception in the mid-nineteenth century, dispensationalist models of the end times have repeatedly been ridiculed by secular and religious leaders as bordering on the ridiculous—schemes that would certainly die out over time. Yet, the tradition lives on, and for scholars to ignore it is to overlook part of what has become one of America's enduring folk theologies. A recent example of this phenomenon is the hugely popular *Left Behind* book series by Tim LaHaye and Jerry Jenkins. In addition to selling millions of copies, the books were made into a series of feature films depicting events chronicling the Rapture and its aftermath.

Despite late twentieth-century discussions about postmodernity that often stressed the collapse of grand historical narratives to forge a common bond of unity, the story of American Christianity has been set against the backdrop of an increasingly complex modern world—one predicated on the wisdom of reason, science, and technology that has been ongoing since at least the nineteenth century. Yet even as significant numbers of Christians have sought to accommodate their faith to various iterations of a modern worldview, the way in which Christianity has offered its followers a unique doorway to experience the miraculous and the supernatural and to give order and meaning to one's life has been a consistent theme throughout American history. While the early twenty-first century is an era of remarkable religious pluralism, that pluralism has as much to do with various popular iterations of Christianity as it does with the rise of non-Christian religions.

Focusing on these pluralistic dimensions reminds us that American Christianity has been as much a sign of people's prejudices as it has been a symbol of transformation. Just as a mainline Protestant leader such as Harold Bosley in 1960 expressed earlier nineteenth-century Protestant reservations about electing a Roman Catholic president, many evangelical Christians found it hard to take seriously the presidential candidacy of former Massachusetts governor Mitt Romney in 2008. This rejection centered not so much on Romney's politics but on the fact that he was a

Mormon (although at the time of this writing, Romney appears to have overcome many of those religious objections during his 2012 presidential campaign). Such prejudices may or may not disappear in the future, and the question arises: do these prejudices reflect the flaws of religion, as secularists like Hitchens and Richard Dawkins assert, or are they simply the flaws of our own worst selves? Historically, Christianity has certainly used the name of God in ways that have led to violence and prejudice. Yet Christianity in its various institutional and popular forms has also produced persons and movements that have served Americans prophetically, in exposing injustice in our society and providing a healing balm for those injustices.

Finally, one of the realities that the future reader must take into consideration is that history shows the remarkable adaptability of Christianity, even amid repeated prognostications that its best days are behind it. At the time of this book's publication, great fears existed among a variety of church leaders in the United States that Christianity would cease to be relevant in the twenty-first century. Perhaps the central question of the future will not be whether Christianity will continue to play a role in America. The question might likely be, as it has been throughout American history, how one chooses to interpret the benefit of that legacy. If one rereads the pages of this book, one does not read a "happily-ever-after" story about how Christianity realized the kingdom of God or the New Jerusalem coming to America. Rather, one encounters a very messy, and very human, story of how diverse groups of people of faith have struggled over how the tenets of Christianity apply not just to their personal beliefs and religious practices, but upon their politics, cultural worldviews, and identity as Americans.

There is no doubt that religious scholars do need to pay attention to questions of religious growth and decline. However, throughout this narrative, my perspective has been to see the growth of Christianity in America as more than a simple story of winners or losers (that is, which churches won out in the marketplace). Rather, one is compelled to see the history of American Christianity as an ongoing process of adaptation and readjustment that is not confined to one era of history, but represents an ongoing process. Does this mean that liberal-mainline churches will still exist a hundred years from now? I believe that history supports the verdict that components of those traditions will still be speaking to Americans. Yet if the past is a guide, it might be difficult to say in what forms those future voices might take.

For all the ways that the early twenty-first century represents a time of challenge for American Christianity, it could be said that there has never been an era in American history when religion wasn't changing and readapting itself to a context that was not, in Jon Butler's words, "awash in a sea of faith." The accounts in this book—of new theologies, new sects, schisms, and, most especially, of engaging and reshaping Christian tradition—represent a sample of how Christianity has helped shape the ideas, character, biases, culture, politics, and faith of Americans.

In large part, the histories of American Christianity that this book has sought to describe reflect upon a movement that has been amazingly innovative in the face of changing historical circumstances. Yet the reader must always remember that these are innovations set against the backdrop of repeatedly trying to renew and revitalize an old, old story.

NOTES

INTRODUCTION

1   For a development of this argument surrounding American religious pluralism that examines the late twentieth-century growth of traditions outside of Christianity, see Diana Eck, *A New Religious America: How a "Christian Country" Has Become the World's Most Religiously Diverse Nation* (San Francisco: Harper & Row, 2001).

2   For membership data, see Roger Finke and Rodney Stark's *The Churching of America 1776–1990: Winners and Losers in Our Religious Economy* (New Brunswick, N.J.: Rutgers University Press, 1992) and Edwin Scott Gaustad and Philip L. Barlow, *New Historical Atlas of Religion in America* (New York: Oxford University Press, 2000). Unless otherwise indicated, statistical data on churches/denominations are drawn from Gaustad and Barlow.

3   See "American Piety in the 21st Century: New Insights to the Depth and Complexity of Religion in the US" (Waco, Tex.: Baylor Institute for Studies of Religion, 2006), http://www.baylor.edu/content/services/document.php/33304.pdf (accessed January 20, 2012).

4   R. Laurence Moore, *Religious Outsiders and the Making of Americans* (New York: Oxford University Press, 1986).

5   See, e.g., the essays in Thomas A. Tweed, ed., *Retelling U.S. Religious History* (Berkeley: University of California Press, 1997); David D. Hall, ed., *Lived Religion in America: Toward a History of Practice* (Princeton: Princeton University Press, 1997); and Philip Goff and Paul Harvey, eds., *Themes in Religion and American Culture* (Chapel Hill: University of North Carolina Press, 2004).

6   A complete listing of sources for this section can be found in the book's bibliography.

7   Jon Butler, *Awash in a Sea of Faith: Christianizing the American People* (Cambridge, Mass.: Harvard University Press, 1990), 4.

8   See Moore's discussion in *Religious Outsiders*, 3–21.

PART I

1   Robert Baird, *Religion in America* (1844; repr., New York: Arno Press, 1969), 7.
2   Baird, *Religion in America*, 288.
3   Philip Schaff, *America: A Sketch of Its Political, Social and Religious Character* (1855; repr., Cambridge, Mass.: Harvard University Press, 1961), xxii.

Chapter 1

1   Quoted in Amanda Porterfield, ed., *American Religious History* (Oxford: Blackwell, 2002), 173.
2   See H. Richard Niebuhr, *Christ and Culture* (New York: Harper, 1951).
3   Perry Miller, *The New England Mind: The Seventeenth Century* (Cambridge, Mass.: Harvard University Press, 1954), 285.
4   See Edmund S. Morgan, *The Puritan Dilemma: The Story of John Winthrop*, 2nd ed. (New York: Pearson Longman, 2006).
5   Morgan, *The Puritan Dilemma*, 186.
6   Quoted in Susan Hill Lindley, *"You Have Stept Out of Your Place": A History of Women and Religion in America* (Louisville: Westminster John Knox, 1996), 5.
7   Quoted in Morgan, *The Puritan Dilemma*, 161.
8   Quoted in Perry Miller, *Errand into the Wilderness* (Cambridge, Mass.: Belknap, 1956), 43.
9   Quoted in Edwin S. Gaustad, *Liberty of Conscience: Roger Williams in America* (Grand Rapids: Eerdmans, 1991), 42.
10   Quoted in Perry Miller, *Roger Williams: His Contribution to the American Tradition* (Indianapolis: Bobbs-Merrill, 1953), 151–52.

Chapter 2

1   Cotton Mather, "Theopolis Americana: An Essay on the Golden Street of the Holy City," Digital Commons @ University of Nebraska, Lincoln, http://digitalcommons .unl.edu/cgi/viewcontent.cgi?article=1029&context=etas (accessed October 30, 2011).
2   Kenneth Silverman, *The Life and Times of Cotton Mather* (New York: Harper & Row, 1984), 425.
3   Quoted in David D. Hall, ed., *Puritans in the New World: A Critical Anthology* (Princeton: Princeton University Press, 2004), 347.
4   Quoted in Edwin S. Gaustad and Mark A. Noll, eds., *A Documentary History of Religion in America to 1877* (2 vols.; 3rd ed.; Grand Rapids: Eerdmans, 2003), 1:99.
5   Quoted in Gaustad, *Liberty of Conscience*, 29.
6   Quoted in Hall, *Puritans in the New World*, 320–21. Emphasis in original.
7   Quoted in Albert J. Raboteau, *Slave Religion: The "Invisible Institution" in the Antebellum South* (Oxford: Oxford University Press, 1978), 102.
8   Quoted in Raboteau, *Slave Religion*, 101. Emphasis in original.
9   Quoted in Silverman, *The Life and Times of Cotton Mather*, 404–5.
10   Quoted in Silverman, *The Life and Times of Cotton Mather*, 417. Emphases in original.

Chapter 3

1   Quoted in Edwin Scott Gaustad, *The Great Awakening in New England* (Chicago: Quadrangle Books, 1957), 18.

2   Quoted in Gaustad and Noll, *A Documentary History of Religion in America to 1877*, 1:165.
3   Jonathan Edwards, *A Treatise Concerning Religious Affections in Three Parts*, ed. John E. Smith (New Haven: Yale University Press, 1959), 114.
4   Quoted in Gaustad and Noll, *A Documentary History of Religion in America to 1877*, 1:170.
5   Quoted in Gaustad, *Great Awakening in New England*, 95.
6   Charles Chauncy, "Divine and Glorious View," http://www.tentmaker.org/articles/divineglory.htm (accessed June 8, 2012).
7   Quoted in William Hutchison, *Errand to the World: American Protestant Thought and Foreign Missions* (Chicago: University of Chicago Press, 1987), 30.
8   Quoted in Lindley, *"You Have Stept Out of Your Place,"* 45–46.
9   Quoted in Mark A. Noll, *The Rise of Evangelicalism: The Age of Edwards, Whitefield and the Wesleys* (Downers Grove, Ill.: IVP Academic, 2003), 175–76. Emphasis in original.

CHAPTER 4

1   Quoted in George M. Marsden, *Jonathan Edwards: A Life* (New Haven: Yale University Press, 2003), 467–68. Emphasis in original.
2   Quoted in Mark A. Noll, *America's God: From Jonathan Edwards to Abraham Lincoln* (New York: Oxford University Press, 2002), 273–74.
3   Ruth H. Bloch, "Religion and Ideological Change in the American Revolution," in *Religion & American Politics: From the Colonial Period to the 1980s*, ed. Mark A. Noll (New York: Oxford University Press, 1990), 49.
4   Quoted in Noll, *America's God*, 80–81.
5   Quoted in Paul Boyer, *When Time Shall Be No More: Prophecy Belief in Modern American Culture* (Cambridge, Mass.: Belknap, 1992), 72.
6   Quoted in Jon Butler, Grant Wacker, and Randall Balmer, *Religion in American Life: A Short History* (New York: Oxford University Press, 2003), 146.
7   Quoted in Gaustad and Noll, *A Documentary History of Religion in America to 1877*, 1:221. Emphasis in original.
8   Quoted in Gaustad and Noll, *A Documentary History of Religion in America to 1877*, 1:228.
9   Butler, *Awash in a Sea of Faith*, 188.
10   See Finke and Stark, *The Churching of America*, 15–16.
11   See Edwin S. Gaustad, *Faith of the Founders: Religion and the New Nation, 1776–1826*, 2nd ed. (Waco, Tex.: Baylor University Press, 2004), 161.
12   Quoted in Gaustad and Noll, *A Documentary History of Religion in America to 1877*, 1:229–31. Emphasis in original.
13   Quoted in Gaustad and Noll, *A Documentary History of Religion in America to 1877*, 1:231. Emphasis in original.
14   Quoted in Gaustad, *Faith of the Founders*, 144–45.
15   Nathan Hatch, *The Democratization of American Christianity* (New Haven: Yale University Press, 1989).
16   Quoted in William G. McLoughlin, *Revivals, Awakening, and Reform* (Chicago: University of Chicago Press, 1978), 65.

17 Quoted in Gaustad and Noll, *A Documentary History of Religion in America to 1877*, 1:238.
18 Quoted in Gaustad and Noll, *A Documentary History of Religion in America to 1877*, 1:240. Emphasis in original.
19 See, e.g., John Eidsmoe, *Christianity and the Constitution: The Faith of Our Founding Fathers* (Grand Rapids: Baker, 1987). Eidsmoe's arguments on the Christian moorings of the American government have gained great popularity among the so-called "Religious Right," a topic discussed in chapters 14 and 15 of this book.
20 See Isaac Kramnick and R. Laurence Moore, *The Godless Constitution: The Case Against Religious Correctness* (New York: W. W. Norton, 1996).
21 Quoted in Gaustad, *Faith of the Founders*, 105.
22 Quoted in Winthrop Hudson, *The Great Tradition of the American Churches* (New York: Harper & Row, 1953), 63–64.
23 See Butler, *Awash in a Sea of Faith*, 225ff.

PART II

1 Leonard Woolsey Bacon, *A History of American Christianity* (New York: Christian Literature, 1897), 399.
2 Bacon, *A History of American Christianity*, 405.

CHAPTER 5

1 Jesse Lee, *A Short History of the Methodists* (1810; repr., Rutland: Academy Books, 1974), v.
2 Nathan O. Hatch, "The Puzzle of American Methodism," *Church History* 63 (June 1994): 178.
3 *The Journal and Letters of Francis Asbury* (London: Epworth, 1958), 3:322.
4 Lee, *A Short History of the Methodists*, 361–62.
5 See Hatch, *Democratization of American Christianity*, 17–46.
6 *The Journal and Letters of Francis Asbury*, 3:326.
7 See Finke and Stark, *Churching of America*, 54–108; Hatch, "Puzzle of American Methodism"; and David Hempton, *Methodism: Empire of the Spirit* (New Haven: Yale University Press, 2005), 212, 216.
8 Quoted in John Wigger, *Taking Heaven By Storm: Methodism and the Rise of Popular Christianity in America* (New York: Oxford University Press, 1998), 150. Emphasis in original.
9 Quoted in Russell Richey, *Early American Methodism* (Bloomington: Indiana University Press, 1991), 89.
10 Quoted in Frederick Norwood, ed., *Sourcebook of American Methodism* (Nashville: Abingdon Press, 1982), 143.
11 See S. D. McConnell, *History of the American Episcopal Church* (London: A. R. Mowbray, 1916), 335–36.

CHAPTER 6

1 See Stephen J. Stein, *The Shaker Experience in America* (New Haven: Yale University Press, 1992), 89.

2   Bacon, *A History of American Christianity*, 335.

3   See Jan Shipps, *Mormonism: The Story of a New Religious Tradition* (Urbana: University of Illinois Press, 1985).

4   Butler, *Awash in a Sea of Faith*, 242.

5   Luther Gerlach and Virginia Hine, *People, Power, Change: Movements of Social Transformation* (Indianapolis: Bobbs-Merrill, 1970).

6   Quoted in Hatch, *Democratization of American Christianity*, 159.

7   See Ronald Numbers and Jonathan Butler, *The Disappointed: Millerism and Millenarianism in the Nineteenth Century* (Bloomington: Indiana University Press, 1987), 198ff.

8   Gaustad and Noll, *A Documentary History of Religion in America to 1877*, 1:261.

9   Ralph Waldo Emerson, "Divinity School Address," http://www.emersoncentral .com/divaddr.htm (accessed June 1, 2012).

10 Henry David Thoreau, *Selections from Thoreau* (London: Macmillan, 1895), 24.

11 See, e.g., George Hicks, *Experimental Americans: Celo and Utopian Communities in the Twentieth Century* (Urbana: University of Illinois Press, 2001).

CHAPTER 7

1   Jay Dolan, *In Search of an American Catholicism: A History of Religion and Culture in Tension* (New York: Oxford University Press, 2002), 3.

2   Thomas O'Gorman, *A History of the Roman Catholic Church in the United States* (New York: The Christian Literature, 1895), 506.

3   Estimates of the Roman Catholic Church's membership vary tremendously. See, for example, the discussion on Catholic growth in Finke and Stark, *The Churching of America*, 110–15. Finke and Stark's data fall in the range of growth reported by many Catholic scholars in the late nineteenth century. See, e.g., O'Gorman, *A History of the Roman Catholic Church*, 495–96; and John Gilmary Shea, *History of the Catholic Church* (Ann Arbor: University of Michigan Library, 1886), http://books.google .com/books/about/History_of_the_Catholic_Church_in_the_Un.html?id=YUw _AAAAMAAJ (accessed June 1, 2012).

4   Moore, *Religious Outsiders*, 56.

5   Quoted in John R. G. Hassard, *Life of the Most Reverend John Hughes, First Archbishop of New York* (New York: D. Appleton, 1866), 389.

6   Patrick Carey, *Orestes Brownson: American Religious Weathervane* (Grand Rapids: Eerdmans, 2004).

7   Quoted in Gaustad and Noll, *A Documentary History of Religion in America to 1877*, 1:444.

8   Quoted in Gilbert J. Garraghan, *The Jesuits in the Middle United States* (1938; repr., Chicago: Loyola University Press, 1983), 58–59.

9   Quoted in Garraghan, *The Jesuits*, 59.

10 Quoted in Gaustad and Noll, *A Documentary History of Religion in America to 1877*, 1;276

11 Quoted in Gaustad and Noll, *A Documentary History of Religion in America to 1877*, 1:534.

12 Quoted in Albert J. Raboteau, *Canaan Land: A Religious History of African Americans* (Oxford: Oxford University Press, 2001), 40. Emphasis in original.

CHAPTER 8

1   Quoted in Gaustad and Noll, *A Documentary History of Religion in America to 1877*, 1:521–22.
2   Quoted in Harry S. Stout, *Upon the Altar of the Nation: A Moral History of the Civil War* (New York: Viking, 2006), 54.
3   Bacon, *A History of American Christianity*, 349.
4   E. Brooks Holifield, *Theology in America* (New Haven: Yale University Press, 2003), 367.
5   Quoted in William G. McLoughlin, *Revivals, Awakening, and Reform* (Chicago: University of Chicago Press, 1978), 129.
6   Quoted in Finke and Stark, *The Churching of America*, 256.
7   Quoted in Harold E. Raser, *Phoebe Palmer: Her Life and Thought* (Lewiston, N.Y.: Edwin Mellen, 1987), 47. Emphasis in original.
8   Quoted in Jean Miller Schmidt, *Grace Sufficient: A History of Women in American Methodism* (Nashville: Abingdon, 1999), 137.
9   Raser, *Phoebe Palmer*, 153–54.
10 Raser, *Phoebe Palmer*, 96.
11 Raser, *Phoebe Palmer*, 77.
12 Quoted in Noll, *America's God*, 421.
13 Quoted in Allen C. Guelzo, "Charles Hodge's Antislavery Moment," in *Charles Hodge Revisited*, ed. John W. Stewart and James H. Moorhead (Grand Rapids: Eerdmans, 2002), 311.
14 Quoted in Gaustad and Noll, *A Documentary History of Religion in America to 1877*, 1:531.
15 Raboteau, *Canaan Land*, 45.
16 Quoted in Lindley, *"You Have Stept Out of Your Place,"* 112.
17 Quoted in Scott C. Williamson, *The Narrative Life: The Moral and Religious Thought of Frederick Douglass* (Macon, Ga.: Mercer University Press, 2002), 94.
18 Williamson, *The Narrative Life*, 96.
19 Williamson, *The Narrative Life*, 153–55.
20 Quoted in Noll, *America's God*, 432.
21 Quoted in Gaustad and Noll, *A Documentary History of Religion in America to 1877*, 1:575.
22 Baird, *Religion in America*, 3rd rev. ed. (New York: Harper & Brothers, 1856), 686.
23 Bacon, *A History of American Christianity*, 415–16.
24 Bacon, *A History of American Christianity*, 417.
25 Quoted in James Washington, ed., *A Testament of Hope: The Essential Writings of Martin Luther King, Jr.* (San Francisco: Harper, 1985), 219.

PART III

1   H. Richard Niebuhr, *The Social Sources of Denominationalism* (New York: Henry Holt, 1929), 21.
2   Niebuhr, *The Social Sources*, 25.
3   Niebuhr, *The Social Sources*, 284.

CHAPTER 9

1 See Finke and Stark, *The Churching of America*, 109–44.
2 Josiah Strong, *Our Country: Its Possible Future and Its Present Crisis*, rev. ed. (New York: Baker & Taylor, 1891), 77.
3 Strong, *Our Country*, 79–80.
4 William R. Hutchison, *The Modernist Impulse in American Protestantism* (Cambridge, Mass.: Harvard University Press, 1976), 48–58.
5 See Debby Applegate, *The Most Famous Man in America: The Biography of Henry Ward Beecher* (New York: Three Leaves Press, 2006).
6 See Paul Harris, "The Social Dimensions of Foreign Missions: Emma Rauschenbusch Clough and Social Gospel Ideology," in *Gender and the Social Gospel*, ed. Wendy J. Deichmann Edwards and Carolyn DeSwarte Gifford (Urbana: University of Illinois Press, 2003), 87–100.
7 Quoted in Gillian Gill, *Mary Baker Eddy* (Reading, Mass.: Perseus Books, 1998), 221.
8 Strong, *Our Country*, 264.
9 See Robert Handy, *A Christian America: Protestant Hopes and Historical Realities*, 2nd ed. (New York: Oxford University Press, 1984).

CHAPTER 10

1 Quoted in Charles Howard Hopkins, *The Rise of the Social Gospel in American Protestantism* (New Haven: Yale University Press, 1940), 3.
2 See Sidney Mead, *The Lively Experiment: The Shaping of Christianity in America* (New York: Harper & Row, 1963).
3 Quoted in S. Gaustad and Mark A. Noll, eds., *A Documentary History of Religion in America Since 1877* (2 vols.; 3rd ed.; Grand Rapids: Eerdmans, 2003), 2:243.
4 For a discussion of this concept, see Kendal P. Mobley, *Helen Barrett Montgomery: The Global Mission of Domestic Feminism* (Waco, Tex.: Baylor University Press, 2009).
5 Quoted in Christopher H. Evans, *Social Gospel Liberalism and the Ministry of Ernest Fremont Tittle: A Theology for the Middle Class* (Lewiston, N.Y.: Edwin Mellen, 1996), 22.
6 Quoted in Robert Handy, ed., *The Social Gospel in America* (New York: Oxford University Press, 1966), 48.
7 William Stead, *If Christ Came to Chicago!* (Chicago: Laird & Lee, 1894), 445.
8 See Peter J. Frederick, *Knights of the Golden Rule: The Intellectual as Christian Social Reformer in the 1890s* (Lexington: University of Kentucky Press, 1976), 166.
9 Walter Rauschenbusch, *Christianity and the Social Crisis* (New York: Macmillan, 1907), 420–21.
10 Walter Rauschenbusch, *Christianizing the Social Order* (1912; repr., Waco, Tex.: Baylor University Press, 2010), 323.
11 Quoted in Gary Dorrien, *Social Ethics in the Making: Interpreting an American Tradition* (Malden, Mass.: Wiley-Blackwell, 2011), 166.
12 Quoted in Gaustad and Noll, *A Documentary History of Religion in America since 1877*, 2:122.
13 Two of the most prominent hymns to come out of that era were Gladden's "O Master, Let Me Walk with Thee," and North's "Where Cross the Crowded Ways of Life."
14 Martin Luther King Jr., *Stride Toward Freedom* (New York: Harper & Row, 1958), 91.

CHAPTER 11

1   Quoted in Robert A. Schneider, "Voice of Many Waters: Church Federation in the Twentieth Century," in *Between the Times: The Travail of the Protestant Establishment in America, 1900–1960*, ed. William R. Hutchison (Cambridge: Cambridge University Press, 1989), 95.
2   I. M. Haldeman, *The Second Coming of Christ: Both Pre-Millennial and Imminent* (New York: Charles Cook, 1906), 10.
3   Haldeman, *The Second Coming of Christ*, 241.
4   Haldeman, *The Second Coming of Christ*, 12.
5   Quoted in Hutchison, *Errand to the World*, 141.
6   Niebuhr, *The Social Sources*, 11.
7   H. Richard Niebuhr, *The Kingdom of God in America* (New York: Harper & Row, 1937), 193.
8   J. J. Reeve, "My Personal Experience with the Higher Criticism," http://user.xmission .com/~fidelis/volume1/chapter19/reeve.php (accessed October 2, 2011).

PART IV

1   Hudson, *The Great Tradition of the American Churches*, 262.

CHAPTER 12

1   Paul Bock, *In Search of a Responsible World Society: The Social Teachings of the World Council of Churches* (Philadelphia: Westminster, 1974), 32–33.
2   Edwin S. Gaustad, "The Pulpit and the Pews," in *Between the Times: The Travail of the Protestant Establishment, 1900–1960*, ed. William R. Hutchison (Cambridge: Cambridge University Press, 1989), 23–26.
3   Harry Emerson Fosdick, *The Living of These Days* (New York: Harper & Brothers, 1956), 94.
4   Harry Emerson Fosdick, "Shall the Fundamentalists Win?" http://historymatters .gmu.edu/d/5070/ (accessed April 30, 2012).
5   J. Gresham Machen, *Christianity and Liberalism* (New York: Macmillan, 1923), 160.
6   See Mobley, *Helen Barrett Montgomery*.
7   Robert Moats Miller, *American Protestantism and Social Issues, 1919–1939* (Chapel Hill: University of North Carolina Press, 1958), 26.
8   Reinhold Niebuhr, *Moral Man and Immoral Society* (New York: Charles Scribner's Sons, 1932), 277.
9   Quoted in Evans, *Social Gospel Liberalism*, 223.
10 Quoted in Evans, *Social Gospel Liberalism*, 195.
11 Liston Pope, *Millhands and Preachers: A Study of Gastonia* (New Haven: Yale University Press, 1942).
12 H. L. Mencken, "Dr. Fundamentalist: H. L Mencken's Obituary for Machen," in the *Baltimore Evening Sun* (January 18, 1937).
13 Fosdick, *The Living of These Days*, 265.

CHAPTER 13

1   Mike Wallace interview of Reinhold Niebuhr (1958), the Henry Ransom Center, University of Texas, http://www.hrc.utexas.edu/multimedia/video/2008/wallace/niebuhr_reinhold.html (accessed February 1, 2012).

2   See Peter Berger, *The Noise of Solemn Assemblies: Christian Commitment and the Religious Establishment in America* (Garden City, N.Y.: Doubleday, 1961).

3   Joel A. Carpenter, *Revive Us Again: The Reawakening of American Fundamentalism* (New York: Oxford University Press, 1997), 141.

4   Frederick Jackson Turner, "The Frontier in American History" (essay originally published in 1893).

5   G. Bromley Oxnam, *I Protest* (New York: Harper & Brothers, 1954), 27.

6   *The United Methodist Hymnal* (Nashville: United Methodist Publishing House, 1989), 178.

7   Georgia Harkness, *Understanding the Christian Faith* (Nashville: Abingdon, 1947), 98.

8   See Carol V. R. George, *God's Salesman: Norman Vincent Peale & the Power of Positive Thinking* (New York: Oxford University Press, 1993), 138.

9   See H. Richard Niebuhr, *The Purpose of the Church and Its Ministry* (New York: Harper & Row, 1956); and Joseph C. Hough Jr. and John B. Cobb Jr., *Christian Identity and Theological Education* (Chico, Calif.: Scholars Press, 1985), 14–15.

10   Paul Tillich, *The Courage to Be* (New Haven: Yale University Press, 1952), 190.

11   Quoted in Paul Boyer, *When Time Shall Be No More: Prophecy Belief in Modern American Culture*, 126.

12   Will Herberg, *Protestant, Catholic, Jew* (Garden City, N.Y.: Doubleday, 1955), 268.

13   Herberg, *Protestant, Catholic, Jew*, 269.

14   King, *Stride Toward Freedom*, 101.

15   Quoted in Washington, *A Testament of Hope*, 230.

16   Hudson, *The Great Tradition of the American Churches*, 262.

PART V

1   Sydney Ahlstrom, *A Religious History of the American People* (1972; repr., Garden City, N.Y.: Doubleday, 1975), 2:465.

CHAPTER 14

1   Harold A. Bosley, "A Catholic President: Con," *The Christian Century*, October 26, 1960, 1247.

2   Dean Kelley, *Why Conservative Churches Are Growing*, rev. ed. (San Francisco: Harper & Row, 1977), 175. Membership data in this chapter is taken from this source.

3   Quoted in J. Leon Hooper, ed., *Bridging the Sacred and the Secular: Selected Writings of John Courtney Murray, S.J.* (Washington, D.C.: Georgetown University Press, 1994), 189.

4   See Robert Wuthnow, *The Restructuring of American Religion: Society and Faith since World War II* (Princeton: Princeton University Press, 1988).

5   See Paul Ramsey, *Who Speaks for the Churches?* (Nashville: Abingdon, 1967).

6   James Cone, *God of the Oppressed* (Minneapolis: Seabury Press, 1975), 1.

7   Cone, *God of the Oppressed*, 33–34.

8   Cone, *God of the Oppressed*, 37.
9   Rosemary R. Ruether, *Sexism and God-Talk: Toward a Feminist Theology* (Boston: Beacon Press, 1983), 18–19.
10 Ruether, *Sexism and God-Talk*, 232.
11 Kelley, *Why Conservative Churches Are Growing*, 22.
12 Bill Hybels, *Axiom: Powerful Leadership Proverbs* (Grand Rapids: Zondervan, 2008), 62.
13 A. James Armstrong, *The Public Servant and the Pastor* (Nashville: Tidings, 1972), 23–24.
14 Garry Wills, *Under God: Religion and American Politics* (New York: Simon & Schuster, 1990), 93.

CHAPTER 15

1   Rick Warren, *The Purpose Driven Life* (Grand Rapids: Zondervan, 2002), 295.
2   Stanley Hauerwas and William Willimon, *Resident Aliens* (Nashville: Abingdon, 1990), 120–21.
3   Diana Butler Bass, *The Practicing Congregation* (Herndon, Va.: Alban, 2004).
4   Ralph Reed, *Active Faith: How Christians Are Changing the Soul of American Politics* (New York: Free Press, 1996), 25.
5   See Peter Steinfels, *A People Adrift: The Crisis of the Roman Catholic Church in America* (New York: Simon & Schuster, 2003), 24.
6   See Robert Bellah et al., *Habits of the Heart: Individualism and Commitment in American Life* (New York: Harper & Row, 1985).
7   Loren Mead, *The Once and Future Church* (Herndon, Va.: Alban, 1991), 87. Emphasis in original.
8   John Shelby Spong, *Liberating the Gospel: Reading the Bible with Jewish Eyes* (San Francisco: Harper, 1996), 328.

EPILOGUE

1   Rick Warren, "Inaugural Prayer," http://blog.christianitytoday.com/ctpolitics/2009/01/rick_warrens_in.html (accessed March 1, 2012).
2   Quoted in Tamelyn N. Tucker-Worgs, *The Black Megachurch: Theology, Gender, and the Politics of Public Engagement* (Waco, Tex.: Baylor University Press, 2011), 187.
3   Stephen Prothero, *Religious Literacy* (San Francisco: Harper, 2007).

SELECT BIBLIOGRAPHY

This bibliography is both an acknowledgment of sources that were consulted in the writing of this text and an effort to provide a resource that will be useful for future students and scholars. This book hopes to contribute toward an ongoing conversation on the nature of American religious historiography, with particular focus on the study of American Christianity. An indispensable guide to beginning an overview on the history of scholarship on American religion is Philip Goff, ed., *The Blackwell Companion to Religion in America* (Malden, Mass.: Wiley-Blackwell, 2010). Each chapter in this reference volume provides an overview of changing historical themes in the study of American religious history with a significant focus on movements, concepts, and churches discussed in this book. This resource will serve future researchers and students well in identifying predominant trends and sources. Two other indispensable sources are Edwin S. Gaustad and Mark A. Noll, eds., *A Documentary History of Religion in America Since 1877* (2 vols., 3rd ed.; Grand Rapids: Eerdmans, 2003) and Edwin Gaustad and Philip Barlow, *New Historical Atlas of Religion in America* (New York: Oxford University Press, 2000). Michael Glazier and Thomas Shelly, eds., *The Encyclopedia of American Catholicism* (Collegeville, Minn.: Liturgical Press, 1997) and Hans Hillerbrand, ed., *The Encyclopedia of Protestantism* (4 vols.; New York: Rutledge, 2003) are reference works that contain numerous articles dealing with topics central to this narrative.

I. THE HISTORIOGRAPHIES OF AMERICAN CHRISTIANITY

By the early twenty-first century, American religious historiography has moved in a variety of directions, examining themes related to religious pluralism, racial, ethnic, and gender diversity, and the relationship between religion and geographical location. By the same token, major studies on American religion have found it impossible to ignore the significance of Christianity, especially Protestantism, toward developing an understanding of religion's role in American history. In summarizing these developments in historiography, one gets a sense of how the discipline has changed while also seeing the need to continue to understand the importance of Christianity in America.

1. NINETEENTH CENTURY

Much of the legacy of American religious historical writings was set by two mid-nineteenth century texts, Robert Baird's *Religion in America* (originally published in 1844; revised in 1856) and Philip Schaff's *America: A Sketch of Its Political, Social, and Religious Character* (originally published in 1855). Both of these books reflect upon themes that had characterized earlier nineteenth-century denominational chronicles that saw the history of American Christianity not only as a Protestant story, but one of God's providence leading these churches.

This theme held through the late nineteenth century, although one sees within subsequent histories a stress on the ecumenical character of American Protestantism—reflecting the hope that the major Protestant churches would find a means to unite, missionally and institutionally. Yet the late nineteenth century was especially important as a time when the discipline of church history (and historical studies in general) was becoming more established as a distinctive academic pursuit. One of the first major critical studies of American Christianity after the Civil War was Daniel Dorchester's *Christianity in the United States from the First Settlement Down to the Present Time* (New York: Phillips & Hunt, 1888). This text served as a useful model for many late nineteenth-century and early twentieth-century historical interpretations of Protestant successes. Dorchester's book helped shape the contours of an influential book series edited by Philip Schaff: The American Church History Series. This influential series featured a range of titles on numerous American churches and denominations, and it was as part of this series that Leonard Woolsey Bacon's *A History of American Christianity* (New York: Christian Literature, 1897) was originally published. As noted in this book, Bacon's work remained a popular textbook on American religion into the 1920s.

The late nineteenth century was also a time when many American Catholics sought to interpret how their tradition fit into the rubric of Protestant-dominated America. A blueprint for many future accounts of American Catholicism was provided by John Gilmary Shea's *History of the Catholic Church in the United States* (New York: John G. Shea, 1892). Shea provided a workmanlike narrative into the development of the Catholic Church in America, focusing largely on the institutional successes of that church (and with a significant treatment of nineteenth-century Catholic leaders such as Bishop John Hughes). One of the most significant texts on American Catholicism of that time was a book included in Schaff's Church History Series: Thomas O'Gorman, *A History of the Roman Catholic Church in the United States* (New York: The Christian Literature, 1895). Although O'Gorman clearly wanted to reflect upon the distinctive role of the Catholic Church in America, his perspective reflected how Catholicism fit into an assimilationist worldview whereby Catholicism would be seen in a non-threatening manner by a Protestant reader.

2. Twentieth Century

While still centered upon American Protestantism, historians by the 1930s expanded their analysis of how religion contributed to shaping the intellectual contours of the nation. Embodied primarily by traditions that had moved in the direction of theological liberalism, these historians were undergirded in a belief that the nation's religious heritage was intellectually rigorous and culturally vibrant. The central book in this historical turn was William Warren Sweet's *The Story of Religion in America* (New York: Harper & Brothers, 1939), which influenced historical scholarship for several generations. Successive works that reflect upon how American Protestantism helped shape the intellectual contours of America include Winthrop Hudson's *The Great Tradition of the American Churches* (New York: Harper & Row, 1953) and Sidney Mead's *The Lively Experiment: The Shaping of Christianity in America* (New York: Harper & Row, 1963).

As noted in this book's introduction, all American religious historians owe a debt to Sydney Ahlstrom's *A Religious History of the American People* (New Haven: Yale University Press, 1972). Although Ahlstrom had his blind spots (in particular, the absence of attention to the role of women and his lack of engagement with certain iterations of evangelical theology, particularly pentecostalism), few survey texts have matched his comprehensive scope. While accounts of Protestantism dominate his narrative, he helped model for many late twentieth-century historians the need to move beyond telling a story of mainline Protestantism to examining multiple movements and religious traditions. Important textbooks that built upon Ahlstrom's foundations include Catherine Albanese's highly influential *America: Religion and Religions* (Belmont, Calif.: Wadsworth, 1981) and Martin E. Marty's *Pilgrims in Their Own Land* (New York: Penguin, 1984). Albanese's book has been reprinted in subsequent editions and is still in wide demand as a textbook. Marty's three-volume *Modern American Religion* (Chicago: University of Chicago Press, 1986–1996) was a major undertaking that contributed to an engagement with American religious pluralism, focusing on the period from the late nineteenth to the mid-twentieth centuries.

3. Historiography in the Late Twentieth and Early Twenty-First Centuries

A major and still emerging theme in the writing of American religious history has been to shift away from narratives that focus primarily on the centrality of American Protestantism. A major work in terms of this scholarship is Thomas A. Tweed, ed., *Retelling U.S. Religious History* (Berkeley: University of California Press, 1997).

Yet a spate of survey scholarship on American religion since Ahlstrom makes clear that a full understanding of American religion needs not only to take seriously the role of Protestantism, but more specifically, the impact of American evangelicalism. In this regard, the work of Mark Noll is especially significant. See Noll, *A History of Christianity in the United States and Canada* (Grand Rapids: Eerdmans, 1992) and *The Old Religion in the New World: The History of North American Christianity* (Grand Rapids: Eerdmans, 2001). These books provide a helpful reference for understanding how American religious developments compare to wider developments of Christianity in North America, with particular attention to the religious history of Canada. For additional useful survey texts, see Edwin Gaustad and Leigh Schmidt, *The Religious History of America*, rev. ed. (San Francisco: Harper & Row, 2002); Jon Butler, Grant Wacker, and Randall Balmer, *Religion in America Life: A Short History* (New York: Oxford University Press, 2003); and Winthrop Hudson and John Corrigan, *Religion in America*, 7th ed. (Upper Saddle River, N.J.: Pearson/Prentice Hall, 2004). For an important overview in terms of new historical directions into the study of American Christianity, see Catherine A. Brekus and W. Clark Gilpin, *American Christianities: A History of Dominance & Diversity* (Chapel Hill: University of North Carolina Press, 2011). Many of the contours opened up in the excellent essays in this volume follow paths uncovered by many late twentieth-century historians who have focused on racial-ethnic diversity and the role of women in American religion. The question of how best to understand American religious pluralism remains hotly debated. Two distinctive and contrasting perspectives on this issue come from Diana Eck, *A New Religious America* (San Francisco: Harper & Row, 2001) and William R. Hutchison, *Religious Pluralism in America: The Contentious History of a Founding Ideal* (New Haven: Yale University Press, 2003).

Studies on the role of women in American religion owe a great debt to the three-volume anthology edited by Rosemary S. Keller and Rosemary R. Ruether entitled *Women in American Religion* (originally published in three volumes by Harper & Row from 1981 to 1983). Many of the writings in this three-volume anthology were republished in Keller and Ruether, eds., *In Our Own Voices: Four Centuries of American Women's Religious Writing* (San Francisco: Harper, 1996). One of the most significant survey texts is Susan Hill Lindley, *"You Have Stept Out of Your Place": A History of Women and Religion in America* (Louisville: Westminster John Knox, 1996). Lindley's work serves as a useful orientation to previous and subsequent scholarship on the role of women within a variety of religious traditions, once again, mostly dominated by Protestant women. For an excellent overview on emerging directions on the study of women in American religion, see Catherine A. Brekus, ed., *The Religious History of American Women: Reimagining the Past* (Chapel Hill: University of North Carolina Press, 2007). Brekus' introductory chapter in this work, "Searching for Women in Narratives of American Religious History," is important for an overview of how historians have discussed women's voices in their narratives.

An emerging theme in historical scholarship has been to examine the regional proclivities within American religion. See the nine-volume series by Mark Silk and Andrew Walsh, eds., *The Religion by Region Series* (Blue Ridge Summit, Pa.: AltaMira Press, 2004–2007).

II. THEMATIC ORIENTATIONS IN THE HISTORY OF CHRISTIANITY

As I noted in the introduction, I believe it is possible to discern at least three major thematic orientations that have persistently characterized the historical study of American Christianity since the early twentieth century.

Although many of the above survey studies fit into these categories, the following is a selection of works specifically on American Christianity that fit into the three historical orientations outlined in the introduction:

1. AMERICAN CHRISTIANITY AS INTELLECTUAL TRADITION

Since the time of Robert Baird's *Religion in the United States of America* in 1844, the idea that understanding American Christianity as a series of intellectual traditions, mostly emanating from New England Puritanism, represents a persistent theme in the writing of American religious history. In the context of the twentieth century, this tradition of historical writing was central to how many historians argued how the theological worldview of the Puritans was indispensable toward understanding the philosophical and political development of America. Central to this direction in historical writing was the work of Perry Miller. See Miller's *The New England Mind* (in two volumes, originally published in 1935 and 1939) and *Errand into the Wilderness* (Cambridge, Mass.: Belknap, 1956). Miller's work reflects the long-standing association of American religion not just with Protestantism, but the distinctive heritage of Protestant theology that emerged from New England Calvinism.

Most recently this path of inquiry has served as the basis for two masterful studies into the history of American theology: Mark Noll, *America's God: From Jonathan Edwards to Abraham Lincoln* (New York: Oxford University Press, 2002) and E. Brooks Holifield, *Theology in America: Christian Thought from the Age of the Puritans to the Civil War* (New Haven: Yale University Press, 2003). Both Noll and Holifield are typical of earlier generations of historians in identifying the uniqueness of American Christianity primarily with the Reformed theological tradition (most associated with a legacy of New England Calvinism), showing how these traditions helped shape a larger tradition of American theology that extended through the Civil War.

2. AMERICAN CHRISTIANITY AS SECTARIAN PHENOMENON

As noted in the introduction of this book, the perspective that sees Christian history more through its sectarian quality owes a debt to Ernst Troeltsch. See, in particular, *The Social Teaching of the Christian Churches* (1911; repr., Louisville: Westminster John Knox, 1992.). It was Troeltsch's perspective on the nature of Christian sectarianism that informed H. Richard Niebuhr's *The Social Sources of Denominationalism* (New York: Henry Holt, 1929). Although Niebuhr's assessment on historical development was not dominant for much of the twentieth century, numerous historians toward the end of the century picked up on variations of his arguments, especially in terms of examining what R. Laurence Moore termed "religious outsiders." See Moore, *Religious Outsiders and the Making of Americans* (New York: Oxford University Press, 1986). For a nuanced perspective on the theme of religious outsiders, see William R. Hutchison, *Religious Pluralism in America* (New Haven: Yale University Press, 2003).

One of the most important topics in the study of American Christianity is represented by various iterations of African American Christianity (or what is often called the black church tradition). One of the most comprehensive treatments of African American Christianity is C. Eric Lincoln and Lawrence H. Mamiya, *The Black Church in the African American Experience* (Durham, N.C.: Duke University Press, 1990). A short treatment of African American Christianity is Albert J. Raboteau, *Canaan Land: A Religious History of African Americans* (New York: Oxford University Press, 2001).

3. AMERICAN CHRISTIANITY AS POPULAR RELIGION

Closely related to the theme of sectarianism, many scholars since the 1980s have focused greater attention on the contributions of American evangelicalism, reflecting much study on the most successful religious movement of the early nineteenth century: Methodism. Perhaps the most significant historian who focused upon popular iterations of evangelicalism was Nathan O. Hatch. See his *The Democratization of American Christianity* (New Haven: Yale University Press, 1989) and "The Puzzle of American Methodism," *Church History* 63 (June 1994): 175–89. This latter piece not only summarizes predominant trends in American religious historiography, but also makes a strong argument that Methodism as a popular religious movement challenges earlier assumptions on the dominance in America of Calvinist-oriented traditions.

For textbooks that focus on different orientations to popular religion in America, see Peter Williams, *Popular Religion in America* (1980; repr., Urbana: University of Illinois Press, 1989), and Roger Finke and Rodney Stark's *The Churching of America, 1776–1990: Winners and Losers in our Religious Economy* (New Brunswick, N.J.: Rutgers University Press, 1992). Finke and Stark challenge earlier views that the history of American religion was primarily one of a movement toward more liberal theological perspectives, focusing instead on how Christianity's success historically has been its ability to provide followers a sense of the otherworldly.

R. Laurence Moore's *Touchdown Jesus: The Mixing of Sacred and Secular in American History* (Louisville, Ky.: Westminster John Knox, 2003) provides an engaging look at the often-permeable lines between sacred symbols and American popular culture.

III. TOPICS IN AMERICAN CHRISTIANITY

The following section represents a small sample of important works that lift up various topics discussed in this book.

1. COLONIAL PERIOD (CHAPS. 1 AND 2)

Studies on colonial America, particularly New England, dominate the scholarship of American Christianity. See, e.g., many of the works of Perry Miller (previously listed), as well as Edmund S. Morgan's short biography of the Massachusetts Bay Colony's first governor, John Winthrop, *The Puritan Dilemma: The Story of John Winthrop*, 2nd ed. (New York: Pearson Longman, 2006). A useful update into the insights of scholars such as Miller and Morgan can be found in Harry Stout, *The New England Soul: Preaching and Religious Culture in Colonial New England* (New York: Oxford University Press, 1986). David D. Hall, ed., *Puritans in the New World: A Critical Anthology* (Princeton: Princeton University Press, 2004) provides a needed perspective on the role of Puritan community life, especially looking at the role of women and families. On the role of women in the context of colonial New England, see Laurel T. Ulrich, *Good Wives* (New York: Alfred Knopf, 1982). In terms of understanding the importance of Cotton Mather to an evolving New England theological ethos, see Robert Middlekauff, *The Mathers: Three Generations of Puritan Intellectuals, 1596–1728* (New York: Oxford University Press, 1971), and Kenneth Silverman, *The Life and Times of Cotton Mather* (New York: Harper & Row, 1984).

For a helpful understanding of the impact of Roger Williams, see Edwin S. Gaustad, *Liberty of Conscience: Roger Williams in America* (Grand Rapids: Eerdmans, 1991). A useful overview into the theological roots of the early Baptists is Winthrop Hudson's "Who Were the Baptists?" *The Baptist Quarterly* 16 (July 1956): 303–12. On the rise of Baptists in seventeenth-century America, see Edwin Gaustad, ed., *Baptist Piety: The Last Will and Testimony of Obadiah Holmes* (Valley Forge, Pa.: Judson Press, 1994). On the origins of Methodism, see Richard Heitzenrater, *Wesley and the People Called Methodists* (Nashville: Abingdon, 1995).

Recent historians have looked increasingly to developments in the southern colonies for a contrast to the type of Puritan ethos that predominated in New England. See Jon Butler, *Awash in a Sea of Faith: Christianizing the American People* (Cambridge, Mass.: Harvard University Press, 1990). Butler's book is significant not only for his attention to the colonial South, but for his wider discussion on the role of Christianity as popular religion in the early republic.

2. Great Awakening (chap. 3)

Mark A. Noll, David W. Bebbington, and George A. Rawlyk's edited volume *Evangelicalism: Comparative Studies of Popular Protestantism in North America, the British Isles, and Beyond, 1700–1990* (New York: Oxford University Press, 1994) and Noll's *The Rise of Evangelicalism: The Age of Edwards, Whitefield and the Wesleys* (Downers Grove, Ill.: IVP Academic, 2003) provide excellent overviews into the transatlantic connections that gave rise to what became known as the Great Awakening in America and to the rise of the most important new religious movement of the eighteenth century: Methodism. The central figure in connecting both movements was the revivalist George Whitefield. On Whitefield's life, see Harry S. Stout, *The Divine Dramatist: George Whitefield and the Rise of Modern Evangelicalism* (Grand Rapids: Eerdmans, 1991) and Jerome Dean Mahaffey, *The Accidental Revolutionary: George Whitefield & the Creation of America* (Waco, Tex.: Baylor University Press, 2011).

Works on Jonathan Edwards are in abundance. For a useful overview and a helpful list of biographical resources on Edwards, see George Marsden's *Jonathan Edwards* (New Haven: Yale University Press, 2003). For a classic description and definition of the concept of "Great Awakening," see Edwin Gaustad, *The Great Awakening in New England* (Chicago: Quadrangle Books, 1957) and William McLoughlin, *Revivals, Awakenings, and Reform* (Chicago: University of Chicago Press, 1978). Some scholars have seen the concept of Great Awakening more as a form of historical redaction that obscures the actual events of that era. See, in particular, Jon Butler, "Enthusiasm Described and Decried: The Great Awakening as Interpretive Fiction," *Journal of American History* 69 (September 1982): 305–25. On Gilbert Tennent and the story of eighteenth-century revivalism outside New England, see Milton Coalter Jr.'s *Gilbert Tennett, Son of Thunder: A Case Study of Continental Pietism's Impact on the First Great Awakening in the Middle Colonies* (Westport, Conn.: Greenwood Press, 1986).

382 « Histories of American Christianity

3. American Revolution (Chap. 4)

The issue of how religion influenced the American Revolution and the subsequent republican ideology of American independence represent a persistent theme in the writing of American religious history. A useful overview can be found in Mark A. Noll, Nathan O. Hatch, and George M. Marsden, *The Search for Christian America, expanded ed.* (Colorado Springs: Crossway Books, 1989) and Ruth H. Bloch's chapter on "Religion and Ideological Change in the American Revolution," in Mark A. Noll's *Religion & American Politics: From the Colonial Period to the 1980s* (New York: Oxford University Press, 1990), 44–61. Mark Noll's *America's God* and E. Brooks Holifield's *Theology in America* provide two of the most detailed studies of eighteenth-century American theology. In particular, Noll points to many sources that deal with the relationship between themes in Christian theology (especially associated with traditions of New England Calvinism) and the republican ideology of the nation's founding. One of the most straightforward explanations surrounding the disestablishment clause of the U.S. Constitution can be found in Isaac Kramnick and R. Laurence Moore, *The Godless Constitution: The Case Against Religious Correctness* (New York: W. W. Norton, 1996) and Edwin S. Gaustad, *Faith of the Founders: Religion and the New Nation, 1776–1826,* 2nd ed. (Waco, Tex.: Baylor University Press, 2004).

The period of the American Revolution also witnessed the stirrings of the type of evangelical Christianity that would become dominant in the war's aftermath. See Rhys Isaac, *The Transformation of Colonial Virginia: 1740–1790* (Chapel Hill: University of North Carolina Press, 1982).

4. Second Great Awakening and Protestant Responses (Chaps. 5 and 6)

Many scholars of the Second Great Awakening look to Whitney Cross, *The Burned-Over District* (originally published in 1950) as an important early study that focuses upon the spread of revivalism in upstate New York in the early nineteenth century. Recent historians, however, are in debt to Nathan O. Hatch's *The Democratization of American Christianity.* Hatch's work is significant in that he both widens the category of popular religion in terms of the traditions he examines (including disparate traditions such as Methodists, Mormons, and African American slave churches, among others) and also shifts the story of the Second Great Awakening to the American South. Also important for understanding the spread of evangelical revivalism in the aftermath of the American Revolution are

Robert Wiebe's *The Opening of American Society: From the Adoption of the Constitution to the Eve of Disunion* (New York: Alfred Knopf, 1984) and R. Laurence Moore's *Selling God: American Religion in the Marketplace of Culture* (New York: Oxford University Press, 1995).

The major focus in recent studies on the Second Great Awakening has revolved around the success of American Methodism as an institutional and popular movement. One of the earliest primary sources on the rise of Methodism was written by the Methodist circuit rider Jesse Lee in *A Short History of the Methodists* (originally published in 1810). Significant studies dealing with the Methodist presence in the early nineteenth century include Russell Richey's *Early American Methodism* (Bloomington: Indiana University Press, 1990), Cynthia Lyerly's *Methodism and the Southern Mind* (New York: Oxford University Press, 1998), John Wigger's *Taking Heaven by Storm* (New York: Oxford University Press, 1998), and Wigger's *Francis Asbury: American Saint* (New York: Oxford University Press, 2009). The southern character of American evangelicalism is discussed in Christina Leigh Heyrman, *Southern Cross: The Beginnings of the Bible Belt* (Chapel Hill: University of North Carolina Press, 1997). In terms of understanding the political commitments of American evangelicals in the early nineteenth century, see Richard Carwardine, *Evangelicals and Politics in Antebellum America* (New Haven: Yale University Press, 1993).

Perhaps the most significant book for understanding the legacy of evangelical social action is Timothy Smith, *Revivalism and Social Reform* (New York: Abingdon, 1957). Smith's work has been picked up by numerous historians, showing not only the concern of antebellum evangelicalism to engage in social reform, but also how these currents influenced later movements of social Christianity in America. See Donald Dayton, *Discovering an Evangelical Heritage* (New York: Harper & Row, 1976) and Randall Balmer, *Mine Eyes Have Seen the Glory* (New York: Oxford University Press, 1989). On the role of women revivalists in this period, see Catherine A. Brekus, *Strangers and Pilgrims: Female Preaching in America* (Chapel Hill: University of North Carolina Press, 1998) and Leonard I. Sweet, *The Minister's Wife* (Philadelphia: Temple University Press, 1981).

Not all American churches were swept up in the revivalist ethos of the early nineteenth century. For an understanding of the theological developments within American Unitarianism and Transcendentalism, see Gary Dorrien, *The Making of American Theological Liberalism: Imagining Progressive Religion, 1805–1900* (Louisville: Westminster John Knox, 2001) and Dean Grodzins' *American Heretic: Theodore Parker and*

Transcendentalism (Chapel Hill: University of North Carolina Press, 2004). For a perspective on developments within the Episcopal Church before the Civil War, see S. D. McConnell, *History of the American Episcopal Church* (London: A. R. Mowbray, 1916) as well as Holifield, *Theology in America:* (New Haven: Yale University Press, 2003).

5. PRE–CIVIL WAR SECTARIANISM (CHAP. 6)

Millennial and apocalyptic themes are vital in the development of American Christianity. For an excellent overview into the important role apocalyptic theology has played in American history, see Paul Boyer, *When Time Shall Be No More: Prophecy Belief in Modern American Culture* (Cambridge, Mass.: Belknap, 1992).

On the Shaker presence, see Stephen J. Stein, *The Shaker Experience in America: A History of the United Society of Believers* (New Haven: Yale University Press, 1992). Ronald L. Numbers and Jonathan M. Butler's, *The Disappointed: Millerism and Millenarianism in the Nineteenth Century* (Bloomington: Indiana University Press, 1987) represents a definitive work on one of the most important, and understudied, popular religious movements in American history.

Studies on Mormonism abound. An excellent starting point is Jon Butler's chapter "Toward a Spiritual Hothouse" in *Awash in a Sea of Faith*. For an excellent overview of early Mormon history, see Jan Shipps, *Mormonism: The Story of a New Religious Tradition* (Urbana: University of Illinois Press, 1985) and Richard Bushman, *Joseph Smith: Rough Stone Rolling* (New York: Alfred Knopf, 2005). On the Oneida community, see Pierrepont B. Noyes' memoir, *My Father's House: An Oneida Boyhood* (New York: Farror & Rhinehart, 1937).

6. AMERICAN CATHOLICISM (CHAP. 7)

The nineteenth and twentieth century produced many "mission narratives" that highlight the struggles of Catholic priests to spread the gospel in America. For example, see Gilbert J. Garraghan's *The Jesuits in the Middle United States* (1938; repr., Chicago: Loyola University Press, 1983). On John Hughes, see John R. G. Hassard, *Life of the Most Reverend John Hughes: First Archbishop of New York* (New York: D. Appleton, 1866). While partially hagiographical, these sources give the reader the sense of hostility faced by many Catholics in the mid-nineteenth century. Central to presenting a view of Catholicism that was in line with an assimilationist perspective was the work of John Tracy Ellis. See his *American Catholicism* (Chicago: University of Chicago Press, 1956).

Historiography on American Catholicism has blossomed since the 1960s. See Philip Gleason, *Keeping the Faith: American Catholicism, Past and Present* (South Bend, Ind.: University of Notre Dame Press, 1987) and the many works of Jay P. Dolan. See, in particular, Dolan's *The American Catholic Experience: A History from Colonial Times to the Present* (Garden City, N.Y.: Doubleday, 1985), and *In Search of an American Catholicism: A History of Religion and Culture in Tension* (New York: Oxford University Press, 2002). On the significance of Orestes Brownson, see Patrick Carey, *Orestes Brownson: American Religious Weathervane* (Grand Rapids: Eerdmans, 2004).

The relationship between American Catholicism and popular religion has become a significant field of scholarship. Central to this movement has been the work of Robert Orsi. See *The Madonna of 115th Street: Faith and Community in Italian Harlem* (New Haven: Yale University Press, 1985). On issues of Protestant responses to Catholicism in the first half of the nineteenth century and the shaping of anti-Catholicism in American popular culture, see Jenny Franchot, *Roads to Rome: The Antebellum Protestant Encounter with Catholicism* (Berkeley: University of California Press, 1994).

7. AFRICAN AMERICAN CHRISTIANITY AND CIVIL WAR (CHAPS. 7 AND 8)

Historians of antebellum religion owe a debt to Albert Raboteau, author of *Slave Religion: The "Invisible Institution" in the Antebellum South* (New York: Oxford University Press, 1978). Raboteau's book represents a definitive study on developments into African American Christianity in the South, from the eighteenth century through the early nineteenth century. For additional studies, see Eugene Genovese, *Roll, Jordan, Roll: Religion That the Slaves Made* (New York: Random House, 1972), Donald Mathews, *Religion in the Old South* (Chicago: University of Chicago Press, 1977), and Lawrence Levine, *Black Culture and Black Consciousness* (New York: Oxford, 1978). On the influence of Frederick Douglass, see John C. Williamson, *The Narrative Life: The Moral and Religious Thought of Frederick Douglass* (Macon, Ga.: Mercer University Press, 2002). On the role of Christianity in the Civil War, see Ernest Lee Tuveson, *Redeemer Nation: The Idea of America's Millennial Role* (Chicago: University of Chicago Press, 1968), Harry Stout, *Upon the Altar of the Nation: A Moral History of the Civil War* (New York: Viking, 2006), and Drew Gilpin Faust, *This Republic of Suffering: Death and the American Civil War* (New York: Alfred Knopf, 2008). On the relationship between Christianity and Abraham Lincoln, see Allen C. Guelzo, *Abraham Lincoln: Redeemer President* (Grand Rapids: Eerdmans, 2003).

8. MID- AND LATE NINETEENTH-CENTURY
TRANSITIONS (CHAPS. 8 AND 9)

The postmillennial trajectory of American evangelicalism was embodied by the careers of Charles Finney and Phoebe Palmer. On Finney, see Charles E. Hambrick-Stow, *Charles G. Finney and the Spirit of American Evangelicalism* (Grand Rapids: Eerdmans, 1996). Although her formative influence was before the Civil War, the legacy of Phoebe Palmer was vital to later theological developments in the nineteenth and twentieth centuries. See Harold Raser, *Phoebe Palmer: Her Life and Thought* (Lewiston, N.Y.: Edwin Mellen Press, 1987). On the career of Antoinette Brown, see Elizabeth Cazden, *Antoinette Brown Blackwell: A Biography* (Old Westbury, N.Y.: Feminist Press at CUNY, 1993).

Studies on American Christianity from the late nineteenth to the early twentieth centuries have focused upon wider theological developments in American Protestantism. Martin E. Marty's *Righteous Empire: The Protestant Experience in America* (New York: Dial, 1970) postulated the argument of a "two-part" split between conservatives and liberals, while Robert T. Handy's *A Christian America: Protestant Hopes and Historical Realities,* 2nd ed. (New York: Oxford University Press, 1984) represents a definitive study on the changing cultural and theological realities facing American Protestants. On the ascendency of theological modernism (liberalism), see especially William R. Hutchison, *The Modernist Impulse in American Protestantism* (Cambridge, Mass.: Harvard University Press, 1976) and Christopher H. Evans, *Liberalism without Illusions* (Waco, Tex.: Baylor University Press, 2010). An important nuance to this era is offered by Grant Wacker in "The Holy Spirit and the Spirit of the Age in American Protestantism, 1880–1910," published in *The Journal of American History* 72 (1985): 45–62. For a study that captures well the theological complexities of Horace Bushnell, see Robert Bruce Mullin, *The Puritan as Yankee* (Grand Rapids: Eerdmans, 2002). On Dwight Moody, see James F. Findlay Jr., *Dwight L. Moody: American Revivalist* (Chicago: University of Chicago Press, 1969). A fascinating account into the theological shifts of that era is recounted in Gaius Glenn Atkins, *Religion in Our Times* (New York: Round Table Press, 1932).

William Hutchison's *Errand to the World: American Protestant Thought and Foreign Missions* (Chicago: University of Chicago Press,

1987) represented a significant work in relating the wider history of American Protestantism to developments in Protestant foreign mission at that time. For expanded treatments on this topic, see Dana L. Robert, *American Women in Mission* (Macon, Ga.: Mercer University Press, 1996) and *"Occupy Until I Come": A. T. Pierson and the Evangelization of the World* (Grand Rapids: Eerdmans, 2003).

On developments within Christian Science and comparisons with New Thought movements, see Gillian Gill, *Mary Baker Eddy* (Reading, Mass.: Perseus Books, 1998), and on the role of the Protestant minister in the late nineteenth century, see E. Brooks Holifield's *God's Ambassadors: A History of the Christian Clergy in America* (Grand Rapids: Eerdmans, 2007) and Debby Applegate, *The Most Famous Man in America: The Biography of Henry Ward Beecher* (New York: Three Leaves Press, 2006).

Before the Civil War, Methodist and Baptist traditions most embodied the theological and historical ethos of African American Christianity. By the end of the nineteenth century, numerous black Baptist denominations emerged as powerful regional religious and cultural forces in the South. For an important perspective on this transition, and for an excellent perspective on the rise of late nineteenth-century women's organizations, see Evelyn Brooks Higginbotham, *Righteous Discontent: The Women's Movement in the Black Baptist Church, 1880–1920* (Cambridge, Mass.: Harvard University Press, 1993).

9. The Rise of Social Christianity (chap. 10)

Students wishing to understand the changes in American religion from the late nineteenth century to the early twentieth century will benefit from Martin Marty's *Modern American Religion: The Irony of It All, 1893–1919* (Chicago: University of Chicago Press, 1986). As the first volume in a three-part series, this book reflects upon the changing social, theological, and interreligious patterns that impacted subsequent events in American religion. For an overview on scholarship on the social gospel movement in America, see Ralph E. Luker's "Interpreting the Social Gospel: Reflections on Two Generations of Historiography," in *Perspectives on the Social Gospel*, Christopher H. Evans, ed. (Lewiston, N.Y.: Edwin Mellen, 1999). Luker summarizes the extensive scholarship surrounding this movement. Some of the noteworthy titles in his summary include Charles Howard Hopkins, *The Rise of the Social Gospel in America* (New Haven: Yale University Press, 1940); Ronald C. White Jr. and C. Howard Hopkins, *The Social Gospel: Religion and Reform in Changing America* (Philadelphia:

Temple University Press, 1976); and Luker, *The Social Gospel in Black and White* (Chapel Hill: University of North Carolina Press, 1991). For a thorough discussion of the theological developments behind the social gospel, see Gary J. Dorrien, *Soul in Society: the Making and Renewal of Social Christianity* (Minneapolis: Fortress, 1995) and *The Making of American Theological Liberalism: Idealism, Realism, and Modernity* (Louisville: Westminster John Knox, 2003).

On the role of women in the social gospel tradition, see Wendy J. Deichmann Edwards and Carolyn De Swarte Gifford, eds., *Gender and the Social Gospel* (Urbana: University of Illinois Press, 2003) and Christopher H. Evans, ed., *The Social Gospel Today* (Louisville: Westminster John Knox, 2001). Gifford also provides an insightful look into the life of Frances Willard through her one-volume edition of Willard's journal. See Gifford, ed., *Writing Out My Heart: The Journal of Frances Willard* (Urbana: University of Illinois Press, 1995). For an overview of how important social gospel leaders related their theology to models of political socialism, see Henry May, *Protestant Churches and Industrial America* (New York: Harper, 1949), Peter Frederick, *Knights of the Golden Rule: The Intellectual as Christian Social Reformer in the 1890s* (Lexington: University of Kentucky Press, 1976), and Jacob Dorn, "The Social Gospel and Socialism: A Comparison of the Thought of Francis Greenwood Peabody, Washington Gladden, and Walter Rauschenbusch," *Church History* 62 (March 1993). On the significance of Walter Rauschenbusch, see Winthrop Hudson, ed., *Walter Rauschenbusch: Selected Writings* (New York: Paulist Press, 1984) and Evans, *The Kingdom Is Always but Coming: A Life of Walter Rauschenbusch* (Grand Rapids: Eerdmans, 2004).

10. FUNDAMENTALISM AND PENTECOSTALISM (CHAP. 11)

The topic of Protestant fundamentalism represents a major path for historians since the 1970s. Ernest Sandeen's *The Roots of Fundamentalism* (Chicago: University of Chicago Press, 1970) represents a significant effort to define fundamentalism and a benchmark for later scholarship. However, George Marsden's *Fundamentalism and American Culture*, 2nd ed. (New York: Oxford University Press, 2006) presents a definitive view of fundamentalism and contrasts this movement with other forms of evangelicalism (such as pentecostalism). Another useful work for students, in terms of defining fundamentalism in an interreligious global context, is Scott Appleby and Martin Marty's *The Power and the Glory* (Boston: Beacon Press, 1992). On the relationship between fundamentalism and cultural views of women, see Betty Deberg, *Ungodly Women: Gender and the First Wave of American Fundamentalism* (Minneapolis: Fortress, 1991) and Margaret Lamberts Bendroth, *Fundamentalism and Gender* (New York: Yale University Press, 1993).

While studies on pentecostalism abound, two works stand out. Part I of Harvey Cox, *Fire from Heaven: The Rise of Pentecostal Spirituality and the Reshaping of Religion in the 21st Century* (Cambridge: Da Capo Press, 1995) discusses the origins of pentecostalism, focusing especially on the life of William Seymour. Grant Wacker's *Heaven Below: Early Pentecostals and American Culture* (Cambridge, Mass.: Harvard University Press, 2001) represents a significant study on pentecostalism's historical impact, accentuating how this movement is perhaps the most predominant American religious movement of the twentieth century.

Protestant debates over theology ultimately raised questions about the church's mission, especially regarding the nature and purpose of foreign mission. On this debate, see Hutchison, *Errand to the World: American Protestant Thought and Foreign Missions* (Chicago: University of Chicago Press, 1987) and Ernest William Hocking et al., *Re-thinking Missions: A Laymen's Inquiry after One Hundred Years* (New York: Harper & Brothers, 1932). The Hocking study captures the liberal-modernist critique of Protestant foreign mission that ultimately carried the day within twentieth-century mainline churches.

11. CHRISTIANITY BETWEEN THE WORLD WARS (CHAP. 12)

The traditional view that the social gospel "died" after World War I has been debunked by several scholars. See, for example, Paul Carter, *Decline and Revival of the Social Gospel* (Ithaca: Cornell University Press, 1954); Robert Moats Miller, *American Protestantism and Social Issues, 1919–1939* (Chapel Hill: University of North Carolina Press, 1958); Donald Meyer, *The Protestant Search for Political Realism* (Berkeley: University of California Press, 1960); and William McGuire King, "The Emergence of Social Gospel Radicalism: The Methodist Case," *Church History* 50 (December 1981): 436–49. On Harry F. Ward, see David Nelson Duke, *In the Trenches with Jesus and Marx: Harry F. Ward and the Struggle for Social Justice* (Tuscaloosa: University of Alabama Press, 2003). On Ernest Fremont Tittle, see Christopher H. Evans, *Social Gospel Liberalism and the Ministry of Ernest Fremont Tittle* (Lewiston, N.Y.: Edwin Mellen, 1996). On Reinhold Niebuhr, see Richard Fox, *Reinhold Niebuhr: A Biography* (San Francisco: Harper, 1985). The important role of John Ryan to a legacy of Catholic social teaching is discussed in Harlan Beckley, *Passion for Justice: Retrieving the Legacies of Walter Rauschenbusch, John Ryan, and Reinhold Niebuhr* (Louisville: Westminster John Knox, 1992). Significant trajectories in twentieth-century Protestant and Catholic social teachings are discussed in Garry Dorrien, *Social Ethics in the Making* (Malden, Mass.: Wiley-Blackwell, 2008).

Developments within American evangelicalism during this critical period are chronicled by Joel A. Carpenter in *Revive Us Again: The Reawakening of American Fundamentalism* (New York: Oxford University Press, 1997) and Gary Dorrien in *The Remaking of Evangelical Theology* (Louisville: Westminster John Knox, 1998). On Aimee Semple McPherson, see Edith L. Blumhofer's *Aimee Semple McPherson: Everybody's Sister* (Grand Rapids: Eerdmans, 1993). Kendal Mobley's *Helen Barrett Montgomery: The Global Mission of Domestic Feminism* (Waco, Tex.: Baylor University Press, 2008) provides a significant account into the life and ministry of this important twentieth-century Baptist leader.

12. Christianity at Midcentury (Chap. 13)

A general theme of historians since Robert Handy's *A Christian America: Protestant Hopes and Historical Realities*, 2nd ed. (New York: Oxford University Press, 1984) has been the eclipse of an earlier taken-for-granted Protestant hegemony. See, e.g., Robert Wuthnow, *The Restructuring of American Religion* (Princeton: Princeton University Press, 1988); David Lotz, ed., *Altered Landscapes: Christianity in America, 1935–1985* (Grand Rapids: Eerdmans, 1989); William R. Hutchison, ed., *Between the Times: The Travail of the Protestant Establishment in America, 1900–1960* (Cambridge: Cambridge University Press, 1989); and Amanda Porterfield, *The Transformation of American Religion* (New York: Oxford University Press, 2001). On G. Bromley Oxnam, see Robert Moats Miller, *G. Bromley Oxnam: Paladin of Liberal Protestantism* (Nashville: Abingdon, 1990), and on Georgia Harkness, see Rosemary Skinner Keller, *Georgia Harkness: For Such a Time as This* (Nashville: Abingdon, 1992). For a nuanced reinterpretation of earlier arguments surrounding the decline of mainline Protestantism, see Robert Wuthnow and John Evans, *The Quiet Hand of God* (Berkeley: University of California Press, 2002) and David A. Hollinger, "After Cloven Tongues of Fire: Ecumenical Protestantism and the Modern American Encounter with Diversity," *The Journal of American History* (June 2011): 21–48.

For an overview of post–World War II American Christianity, see James Hudnut-Beumler, *Looking for God in the Suburbs: The Religion of the*

American Dream and Its Critics (New Brunswick, N.J.: Rutgers University Press, 1994) and Robert S. Ellwood, *The Fifties Spiritual Marketplace: American Religion in a Decade of Conflict* (New Brunswick, N.J.: Rutgers University Press, 1997). On the significance of Norman Vincent Peale and the so-called prosperity gospel, see Carol V. R. George, *God's Salesman: Norman Vincent Peale & the Power of Positive Thinking* (New York: Oxford University Press, 1994).

13. LATE TWENTIETH-CENTURY DEVELOPMENTS (CHAP. 14)

On the life and thought of John Courtney Murray, see J. Leon Hooper, ed., *Bridging the Sacred and the Secular: Selected Writings of John Courtney Murray, S. J.* (Washington, D.C.: Georgetown University Press, 1994). On Martin Luther King Jr. and Malcolm X, see James H. Cone, *Martin & Malcolm & America: A Dream or a Nightmare* (Maryknoll: Orbis, 1991). For an interesting perspective on the relationship between Christianity and mid-twentieth-century social movements, see James Tracy, *Direct Action: Radical Pacifism from the Union Eight to the Chicago Seven* (Chicago: University of Chicago Press, 1996).

Numerous studies have been written dealing with the resurgence of conservative Christianity since the mid-1970s. See Dean M. Kelley, *Why Conservative Churches Are Growing*, rev. ed. (San Francisco: Harper & Row, 1977). On the efforts of George McGovern to court evangelical support, see Mark Alexander Lempke, "A Caucus of Prophets: George McGovern's 1972 Campaign and the Crucible of Protestant Politics" (Ph.D. dissertation, University of Buffalo, 2011). For various interpretive angles on evangelicalism and politics in the late twentieth century, see Garry Wills, *Under God: Religion and American Politics* (New York: Simon & Schuster, 1990); Robert Jewett, *Mission and Menace: Four Centuries of American Religious Zeal* (Minneapolis: Fortress, 2008); and Randall Balmer, *The Making of Evangelicalism: From Revivalism to Politics and Beyond* (Waco, Tex.: Baylor University Press, 2010). On the theological shifts within the Southern Baptist Convention, see Nancy T. Ammerman, *Baptist Battles* (New Brunswick, N.J.: Rutgers University Press, 1990).

14. CHRISTIANITY POST-9/11 (CHAP. 15/EPILOGUE)

For an overview of Eastern Orthodoxy in America, see Alexei D. Krindatch's "Orthodox (Eastern Christian) Churches in the United States at the Beginning of a New Millennium: Questions of Nature, Identity, and Mission," *Journal for the Scientific Study of Religion* 41, no. 3 (2002): 533–63.

The impact of evangelicalism on American politics represents an ongoing theme into the twenty-first century. See Ralph Reed, *Active Faith: How Christians Are Changing the Soul of American Politics* (New York: The Free Press, 1996) and Justin Watson, *The Christian Coalition: Dreams of Restoration, Demands for Recognition* (New York: St. Martin's, 1997). For a critique of these conservative movements, see Balmer, *The Making of Evangelicalism*. On African American megachurches, see Tamelyn N. Tucker-Worgs, *The Black Megachurch: Theology, Gender, and the Politics of Public Engagement* (Waco, Tex.: Baylor University Press, 2011). For an assessment of American Catholicism in the early twenty-first century, see Peter Steinfels' *A People Adrift* (New York: Simon & Schuster, 2003) and Timothy Matovina's *Latino Catholicism: Transformation in America's Largest Church* (Princeton: Princeton University Press, 2011). Important resources on changing late twentieth-century and early twenty-first century religious demographics include Robert Wuthnow, *Christianity in the Twenty-First Century: Reflections on the Challenges Ahead* (New York: Oxford University Press, 1993); Wade Clark Roof, *A Generation of Seekers* (San Francisco: Harper, 1993); Diana Butler Bass, *The Practicing Congregation* (Herndon, Va.: Alban, 2004); Mark Chaves, *Congregations in America* (Cambridge, Mass.: Harvard University Press, 2004); Nancy T. Ammerman, *Pillars of Faith: American Congregations and Their Partners* (Berkeley: University of California Press, 2005); and Robert D. Putnam and David E. Campbell, *American Grace: How Religion Divides and Unites Us* (New York: Simon & Schuster, 2010).

Index of Names

Williams, Roger, 34–35, 37–42, 47–48, 56, 76, 80, 97, 100, 102, 104, 204; books on, 380
Wills, Garry, 338
Wilson, Woodrow, 236, 272, 279
Winter, Gibson, 310–11, 315

Winthrop, John, 21–22, 32–34, 37–38, 40–42, 44, 112, 355; books on, 380
Wright, Jeremiah, 332, 356–57

Young, Brigham, 139

Zinzendorf, Nicholas von, 59–60

SUBJECT INDEX

abolitionism, 58, 94, 148, 171, 173, 177, 184–90, 211; *see also* slavery
Adventists, 13, 143–44, 150, 250–51, 254; Seventh-day Adventists, 143–44, 150, 251, 320; *see also* Millerites
African American Christianity, 4, 53, 57–58, 80–82, 84–85, 94–95, 118, 132, 155, 166–72, 173, 185–90, 192, 228, 238–39, 259–63, 270, 273, 275–76, 289, 298, 302–3, 311–14, 316, 325–27, 329, 332, 349, 355–57, 379, 382, 385, 387, 392; the black church, 155, 166, 168–72, 238, 311–14, 326, 356–57, 379, 385, 387, 392; ordination of African Americans, 169–70
African Methodist Episcopal Church (AME), 166–71, 238, 261, 326
American Civil War, 108–9, 124, 128, 155, 170–75, 179, 183–85, 188–94, 196–97, 199–200, 205, 210–11, 213–15, 220, 222–23, 227–28, 248–50, 253, 257, 259, 264, 306, 312, 374, 378, 384–87; Reconstruction, 207, 334
American Home Missionary Society (AHMS), 130, 200
American Revolution, 2, 31, 52, 54, 65–66, 68, 74, 76, 81–82, 85, 87–90, 92–99, 101, 103–4, 106, 111–15, 117–18, 120, 125–26, 130, 133–34, 154, 156, 166, 168, 174, 190, 215; books on, 382

Anabaptists, 23, 27, 37, 39, 48, 51–52, 59, 95, 132, 250; Amish, 52; Mennonites, 52, 59, 97, 132
Andover Theological Seminary, 140, 145, 178
Anglicanism, 27, 29–33, 35, 37, 41, 44–45, 49–50, 52–54, 58, 60–63, 68–70, 73, 75–76, 78, 82–83, 95–98, 100, 111–12, 114, 118, 126–27, 129–30, 145, 203, 232, 252; Church of England, 29–32, 44–45, 50, 60, 83, 95–96, 114, 121, 126, 203; Protestant Episcopal Church, 100, 126–27, 130, 161, 169, 182, 184, 210, 219, 227, 232, 240, 263, 320, 329, 337, 352, 384
Arminianism, 27–28, 30, 54, 61, 63, 69, 76, 79, 82, 113, 120, 175–77, 182, 210, 249, 263
Asia, 108, 200, 215, 263, 322, 325, 327, 331, 340
Azusa Street revivals, 261–63; *see also* pentecostalism; revivalism

Baptists, 27, 29, 32, 61, 108, 119–20, 124–25, 127–28, 130, 142, 146, 167–68, 174, 176–77, 182, 184, 187–88, 204, 215–16, 223–25, 227, 245–46, 253, 255, 258, 263–64, 266, 270, 274, 276, 308, 312–13, 320, 330–31, 334–35, 339, 380, 387, 390–91; in colonial America, 39, 49, 54, 62–63, 70, 76,